Central
Scotland

LAND - WILDLIFE - PEOPLE

Editors
General - L Corbett   N J Dix
Naturalist - D M Bryant   D S McLusky
Historical - B J Elliott   N L Tranter

Forth Naturalist and Historian

Published by The Forth Naturalist and Historian, Stirling University, 1993. F N & H is a University/Central Regional Council collaboration and an approved charity. Honorary Editor/Secretary L. Corbett.

Sponsors

The BP Companies of Grangemouth
Scottish Natural Heritage
United Glass of Alloa

Contributors

University of Stirling:
M.V. Bell, P. Bilsborough, D.M. Bryant, B.J. Elliott, I.C. Grieve, S.J. Harrison, C.J. Henty, I.G.C. Hutchison, O. Lassiere, D.S.McLusky, S.F. Newton, J. Proctor, I. Thomson, N.L. Tranter.

British Geological Survey, Edinburgh:
M.A.E. Browne, J.R. Mendum, S.K. Monro.

Scottish Natural Heritage, Stirling:
C. Crawford, J. Gallacher, J. Evans.

Wallace High School, Stirling:
J. Haddow.

Cumbria College of Art and Design, Carlisle:
G. Thomson.

Acknowledgements

All tables, figures, photographs are by the authors unless otherwise stated. In addition to the sponsors, and to those mentioned in the text, tables, figures and photographs, we are grateful for assistance in various ways to the University of Stirling and Central Regional Council and to many others including - P. Brown, L. Taylor, W. Jamieson and S. Craig of the University of Stirling; staff of the Education Advisory Service and R. Blair of Central Regional Council: C. Will, indexer and the Stirling Field and Archaeological Society.

For additional help with illustrations, thanks also to - J. Hume, Historic Scotland; R. McCutcheon; R.H. Campbell; R. McOwan; M. Dobson; M. Trubridge; Scottish Agricultural Museum; Dunning Parish Historical Society.

Finally, and not least, the forbearance of the wives of L. Corbett and M. Dickie.

British Library Cataloguing in Publication Data
Central Scotland - Land, Wildlife, People.
1. Corbett, L. et al
914-1312
ISBN 1-898008-00-0

Design consultant:
G. Thomson

Cover illustrations:
Blackcock, A. Mitchell
Grangemouth, B.P. (Rae Studios)
Stirling Castle, K. Mackay
Sundew, insectivorous plant, J. Proctor
Highland cattle at Stirling medieval market, L. Corbett.

Production preparation and editorial assistance :
M. Dickie, Central Region Education Department

Set in 9 on 10 point Bookman and Palatino italic.
Printed and bound by The Charlesworth Group, Huddersfield

Contents

Introduction
Sir Kenneth Alexander   I

Central Region (Scotland) map   II

Foreword   VI

Preface   VII

The Ochils and Hillfoots   VIII

Geology -
M.A.E. Browne, J.R. Mendum, S.K. Monro   1

Climate -
S.J. Harrison   18

Soils -
I.C. Grieve   32

Vegetation and Flora -
J. Proctor   43

Birds -
D.M. Bryant, M.V. Bell, C.J. Henty, S.F. Newton   57

Mammals -
J. Haddow   76

Butterflies and Moths -
G. Thomson   86

Aquatic Life: Lochs, Rivers, Estuary -
D.S. McLusky, O. Lassiere   90

Conservation -
C. Crawford, J. Gallacher, J. Evans   107

Maps of parts of the area in the 1890s   121

Agriculture -
B.J. Elliott   125

Industry and Services -
B.J. Elliott   141

Population: Growth, Location, Structure -
N.L. Tranter   160

Parliamentary Politics -
I.G.C. Hutchison   177

Sport and Physical Recreation -
I. Thomson, P. Bilsborough   193

Index   212

Foreword

The BP Companies in Grangemouth, BP Oil, BP Chemicals and BP Exploration, are pleased to sponsor this *Central Scotland*, a new survey of the land, wildlife, industry and people of the area.

We recognise our influence as a major industry on the region's economic well being, and on the environment where we aim to be industry leaders in environmental practices and standards

E.L. Ferguson, Works General Manager, BP Chemicals Ltd., Grangemouth.

Preface

This book is for all those who wish to learn something of the natural and human history of the area presently comprising Central Region, extending from Balmaha on Loch Lomond in the west to Blackness on the Forth estuary in the east, and from Tyndrum in the north to Slammannan in the south.

It provides a current overview of an area which is historically and geographically at the heart of Scotland. It begins with a survey of the geology - the ancient framework of the rocks moulded by successive ice ages and weathered to form the scenery (**land**) that we see today. Then follow chapters on climate and soils which have been so important in shaping the habitats of the region. The richness of the flora and the diversity of aquatic and terrestrial animal life within this variety of habitats is described in chapters on vegetation, aquatic life, butterflies and moths, birds and mammals. These give an authoritative, extensive, and up to date record of the **wildlife** of central Scotland.

Man appeared on this scene some 7000 years ago. Since then he has changed the environment in many ways. The book records the more recent history (**people**) of agriculture, mining, manufacturing and trade in the area, the effect these have had on the growth and location of population, developments in opportunities for sport and recreation, and aspects of the region's recent political history.

The book is a successor, but for a wider area, to the survey *The Stirling Region* produced in 1974 by the University of Stirling. Over 20 years many things have changed. In 1974 the University was only a few years old and Regional and District Authorities were but embryonic beings. Since then the University has come of age, and the local Authorities are bracing themselves for reorganisation. From this perspective, the book looks forward into the 21st century.

We hope the book will stimulate the reader to learn more about the land, wildlife and people of 'Scotland's heartland'. For residents and visitors, students and researchers, it aims to be a valuable record of life in the 90s and a source of information on how and why central Scotland looks as it does today.

Looking east along the Ochils and Hillfoots. The unique characteristic of the Ochils lies in the contrast between the north's rolling braes and smooth grassy ridges, and the south, where in consequence of the Ochil Geological Fault, the hills drop steeply some 600 metres to the plain of the Forth. The result is a spectacular precipitous south face some 20 kilometres long behind the Hillfoot towns and villages. The downthrows of the fault bring the harder Lower Devonian volcanic rocks to the north into juxtaposition with the softer Carboniferous sedimentary sequence to the south.

Geology

M.A.E. Browne, J.R. Mendum and S.K. Monro

"The science of Geology is concerned with the study of the Earth, its origin, structure, composition and history, and the nature of the processes which give rise to its present state. From the Earth we obtain our material needs of water, food and minerals, and to it we return our waste products. Consequently, geology assumes particular importance because it impinges directly on our material well-being" (Monro and Hull 1987).

Within this central region many of the differing rock types that make up Scotland as a whole come to the surface, from the very old rocks of the Highlands to the yet unconsolidated sediments currently being deposited in the Forth estuary. A view of its geology is a snap shot of the geology of Scotland as a whole, and the relationships with other aspects of natural history are also typical of those of much of Scotland. The majority of geological terms used in the following account are defined in *Chambers Earth Sciences Dictionary* (Walker 1991) and are not qualified here.

LANDSCAPE AND GEOLOGY

The landscape of central Scotland normally reflects the weathering characteristics of the bedrock, being upstanding where underlain by harder, generally igneous and metamorphic, rocks and low-lying where consisting of softer rocks such as mudstones and some sandstones. Large faults (the Highland Boundary, Campsie and Ochil faults) contribute linear scarp features to the landscape where they bring hard rocks against soft. The main river catchment is that of the Forth, but the drainage of the Breadalbane area is to the Tay-Earn catchment, and the Campsies to Loch Lomond.

The northeast-trending Highland Line forms both a topographical and a cultural divide between lowland and highland Scotland. The Line is the surface manifestation of the Highland Boundary Fault, which separates the older, mostly Precambrian (> 570 m yrs) rocks to the northwest from the generally softer, younger, Palaeozoic (< 570 m yrs) rocks to the southeast **(Figure 1)**. In this area the Line stretches from Balmaha on Loch Lomond, through Aberfoyle to west Glen Artney. North of the Highland Line the mountainous terrain reflects the underlying ancient, hard, metamorphic rocks, resistant to weathering, but much affected by glaciation during the ice ages. Peaks over 900 m OD include Ben Lomond. Large lochs are present in some of the glaciated U-shaped valleys. South of the Highland Line is a blend of gently sloping, heavily cultivated,

partly industrialised lowland and surrounding hilly ground (< 600 m OD). The occurrence of isolated crags of igneous rocks such as at Stirling Castle is a characteristic feature of the scenery not only of this area but also the rest of the Midland Valley of Scotland. The hills, such as the Gargunnocks and Ochils, are formed predominantly of volcanic rocks.

BEDROCK GEOLOGY - North of the Highland Boundary Fault

Highland Boundary Fault/Highland Border Complex

The Highland Boundary Fault is a near-vertical major fault which has been active over a long period of geological time. It affects the structure of the adjacent rocks and has strongly influenced the trend of dykes, near vertical, sheet-like bodies of igneous rock, intruded subsequently and cutting across the pre-existing rock types. The Devonian rocks immediately south of the Highland Boundary Fault are tilted up to near vertical, partly as a result of the drag effects against the fault, and partly as a result of later major folding **(Figure 2)**.

Immediately northwest of the Highland Boundary Fault is a series of discontinuous fault-bounded lenses, characterised by a distinctive assemblage of rock types. Though not present everywhere, the lenses are up to 1.2 km wide near Balmaha and northwest of Callander. This assemblage of rock types, termed the Highland Border Complex, consists mainly of igneous, metamorphic and sedimentary rocks of oceanic rather than continental origin, and it includes serpentinite, hornblende-schist, metamorphosed basaltic lavas, chert, black shales, conglomerates and limestone, overlain by sandy to gritty greywackes. The rocks range in age from late Cambrian (c. 500 m yrs) to early Ordovician (c. 450 m yrs). Their overall steep orientation and subsequent fault movements make it difficult to assess the original relationships between the lenses within the complex. The rocks are interpreted as slivers of material ranging from oceanic to shallow marine in origin, which became attached to the Highland block as a result of major lateral fault movements during the late Ordovician or Silurian (440 to 410 m yrs). During such movements the rocks were deformed and metamorphosed causing the growth of new minerals and, in the finer- grained rocks, notably mudstones, the formation of a slaty cleavage.

North of Balmaha two belts of serpentinite are exposed. The southern belt on the southwest flank of Conic Hill consists of highly altered fragmental serpentinite, probably formed by submarine erosion of ultrabasic rocks. The northern belt on Arrochymore Point consists of jasper, and foliated, partly silicified

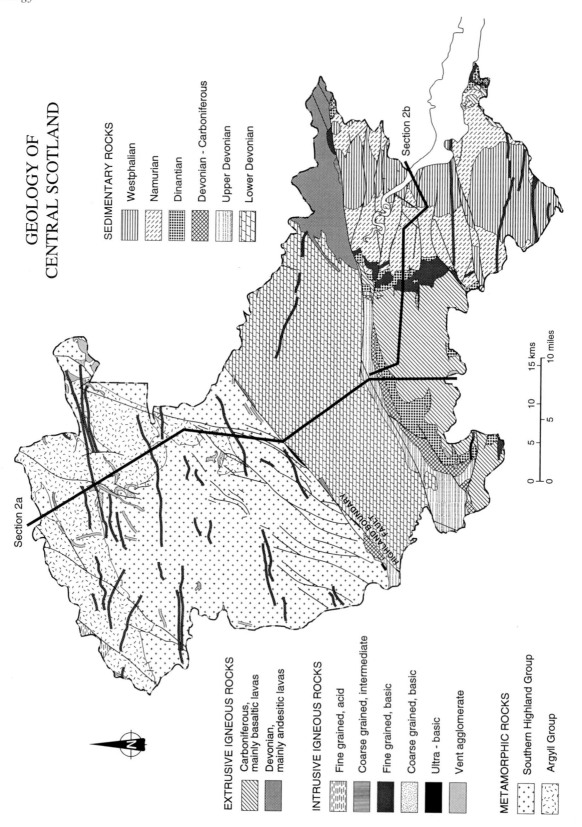

Figure 1 Geological Map of Central Scotland

serpentinite. Faulted down between the two serpentinite belts are cleaved gritty to sandy greywackes which are metamorphosed and partly inverted. The greywackes are unconformably overlain by unmetamorphosed and gently dipping early Carboniferous (c. 360 m yrs) purple-grey to pink sandstones and concretionary limestones. Many of the Highland Border Complex rock types are best exposed on Inchcailloch and Creinch islands in Loch Lomond.

Northwest of Callander are sparse exposures of a sequence of limestones and black shales within which the Leny Limestone forms a prominent unit. In the Leny Quarry this limestone has yielded abundant trilobites and brachiopods. These fossils are of lower Middle Cambrian age and are the oldest fossils found in the Highland Border Complex.

At Upper Dounans, 1.5 km northeast of Aberfoyle, a conglomerate with an altered serpentinite matrix and containing pebbles mainly of metamorphic rocks, occurs in a 10 m-wide strip adjacent to downfaulted Lower Devonian conglomerates. A similar rock type is found in the Keltie Water, and on Inchcailloch and Inchmurrin in Loch Lomond. In the Lime Craig quarry by Aberfoyle and for some 250 m southwest of the quarry steeply dipping limestone is seen to be unconformably overlain by Lower Devonian conglomerate. This is the Dounans Limestone which has yielded fossils, including trilobites, brachiopods and ostracods of Lower Arenig age (Lower Ordovician - c. 480 m yrs). Cleaved gritty and sandy greywackes, seen close to the Leny, Aberfoyle, Keltie Water and Loch Lomond exposures are thought to be of Caradoc age (Upper Ordovician - c. 450 - 440 m yrs).

Dalradian Supergroup

Northwest of the Highland Boundary Fault and the Highland Border Complex metamorphic rocks are the dominant rock type. They form part of the Precambrian Dalradian Supergroup, a sequence of metamorphosed sedimentary and subsidiary volcanic rocks. These rocks were originally deposited over 600 m yrs ago in the sea, offshore from the margin of a large continent, which at that time lay some distance to the northwest. This continent included, at that time, parts of North America, Greenland and the northwest Highlands. A large ocean, the Iapetus Ocean, lay southeast of the area, separating it from southern Britain which was part of another distant and geologically unrelated ancient continent. The Dalradian rocks were subsequently intensely folded and metamorphosed. The consequent increase in temperature and pressure resulted in the crystallisation of new minerals (eg garnet, hornblende) and the formation of schists, strongly foliated, micaceous, metamorphic rocks, and more rarely gneisses, metamorphic rocks with characteristic colour and mineral banding.

The Dalradian rocks can be divided into four main groups. From oldest to youngest these are the Grampian, Appin, Argyll and Southern Highland groups.

The older two groups represent original shallow marine shelf deposits, whereas the Argyll Group rocks were deposited in fault bounded basins at the edge of the continental shelf. The Southern Highland Group rocks were deposited mainly as turbidites, probably in deep water submarine fans some distance offshore from the continental shelf.

The two older groups are only sparsely represented in this area. They are exposed only to the northwest of Tyndrum, where they are folded into large-scale early recumbent folds. The **Grampian Group** rocks are dominantly metamorphosed sandstones (psammites), whereas the **Appin Group** rocks are quartzites, metamorphosed graphitic mudstones (pelites), siltstones (semipelites) and marbles.

The younger **Argyll Group** rocks are more widespread, notably in Breadalbane, where they form the higher hills, and from Killin southwards to Loch Lubnaig. They consist of graphitic schists, quartzites, calcareous semipelites (originally limy silts), marbles and metamorphosed volcanic rocks, mainly tuffs originally. Some greywackes occur towards the top of this group in the Ben Lui Schists.

Argyll Group metamorphosed sedimentary rocks in the Auchtertyre - Ben Challum area, and on Beinn Heasgarnich contain mineralisation, mainly pyrite (FeS_2), but with significant chalcopyrite $(CuFeS_2)$ and sphalerite (ZnS) confined to certain sedimentary layers. Although the mineralisation occurs over a strike length of 9 km, it is not currently economic. The graphitic schists and calcareous semipelitic schists that extend southwest from Beinn Heasgarnich were deposited originally as anoxic carbonaceous muds, marls and calcareous silts in a restricted marine basin starved of oxygen in the water. These rocks were later metamorphosed and structurally modified. It is at the black graphitic schist boundary with the younger calcareous schist that bedded barite $(BaSO_4)$ mineralisation is extensively developed farther eastnortheast at Foss and Duntanlich, north of Aberfeldy. The graphitic and calcareous schists are succeeded by garnetiferous mica schists (formerly silty greywackes) in much of Glen Lochay and the high ground above Glen Ogle. As the beds are regionally inverted, the older beds form the higher ground and the younger beds the valley floors. Hence the youngest Argyll Group rocks, crystalline limestones, are found around Killin, Lochearnhead and Glen Ogle. Later folding has modified their simple inverted pattern, and in Glen Lochay the limestones and younger Southern Highland Group rocks occur within the core of a fold.

The **Southern Highland Group** rocks are dominantly greywackes with some slate and 'Green Bed' units. 'Green Beds' are greywackes with a substantial volcanic component, probably deposited originally as volcanic detritus, either air-fall tuff or reworked material from earlier eruptions. They now contain abundant chlorite and epidote, both green minerals; hence the name. The 'Green Beds' form a useful marker zone and are best seen above Loch Chon and around the southeast end of Loch Katrine.

In their northern area of outcrop, Southern Highland Group rocks are metamorphosed to quartz-mica schists and in Glen Dochart garnet is common in both the schists and the amphibolites (basaltic sills intruded into the sedimentary sequence and subsequently metamorphosed). As the Highland Boundary Fault is approached the degree of metamorphism and structural modification decreases gradually and the originally sandy, silty and gritty nature of the rocks becomes more apparent. In the sandy greywackes cleavage has not developed as a fine parallel alignment of micas, as in the slates, but is manifest as a series of spaced chlorite and mica concentrations. This spaced cleavage, initially at about 1 cm spacing in the south, becomes progressively more attenuated to the northwest as the metamorphic grade and structural complexity increase. Secondary deformations also form spaced cleavages and the subsequent folding gives rise to structurally very complex patterns. Good examples are seen just north of Stronachlachar by Loch Katrine.

Within the Southern Highland Group a prominent zone of slates up to 2 km wide trends near parallel to the Highland Boundary Fault. These have been worked for roofing slates and extensive quarries can be found 2.5 km northwest of Aberfoyle, west of the Duke's Pass.

Intrusive igneous rocks

In the Dalradian rocks is a series of dark, sheetlike bodies. These are basalt, dolerite and gabbro sills which were intruded soon after deposition of the sedimentary rocks and were affected by the subsequent structural and metamorphic events. Their massive and resistant nature has meant that in places they still retain vestiges of their original igneous features, although they are typically metamorphosed to amphibolites. Good examples are seen in Kirkton Glen and in the Ledcharrie Burn valley north towards Glen Dochart. These rocks are concentrated around the Loch Tay Limestone unit at the top of the Argyll Group. An ovoid serpentinite body (c. 500 m by 300 m) crops out by Corriecharmaig in Glen Lochay.

Intrusive igneous rocks which post date the deformation and metamorphism vary from small bodies of diorite and breccia to felsite sheets and dykes of lamprophyre and microdiorite. They range in age from Silurian to Devonian (430 to 390 m yrs). The diorite bodies are outlying, small representatives, of the Arrochar and Garabal Hill complexes farther west. Their major occurrences lie immediately north of Inversnaid and on the watershed between Glen Gyle and Loch Lomond, where they are known as the Doune Farm Complex. The Doune Farm Complex consists of seven separate diorite bodies with associated breccia, appinite, and granodiorite. In the Inversnaid body a marginal breccia, formed by the explosive action of gas ahead of the diorite intrusion, passes inwards to a fine-grained diorite and thence to a central, medium-grained, pyroxene-mica-diorite.

Lamprophyre and microdiorite dykes and sills are common adjacent to the diorite intrusions. Lamprophyres are ultramafic rocks which vary from the typical potash feldspar-hornblende, to plagioclase feldspar-hornblende-bearing types. They commonly weather to a pink-brown crust and a good example is seen 1 km southsoutheast of Rowardennan. This dyke is displaced 2.6 km by a northeast-trending fault east of Rowardennan. Microdiorites are igneous rocks consisting of plagioclase feldspar and hornblende with biotite and minor quartz. They form sills and east- to eastnortheast-trending dykes up to 5 m thick, notably on Stob a'Choin. Like the lamprophyres they cross-cut the diorite intrusions and breccias.

Grey to salmon pink felsite and andesite occur as thin dykes and sills, generally less than 2 m thick, in the area. Good examples of plagioclase-bearing porphyritic felsite dykes are found in the burn section below Inversnaid Lodge.

The prominent late Carboniferous (c. 295 m yrs ago), east-west-trending quartz-dolerite dykes which can be traced right across the region average some 12 m in width. They commonly occur in pairs spaced at 4 km to 8 km intervals. They weather to a rusty brown soil and commonly lie in linear gullies. The Rowardennan dyke has been traced for over 100 km from west of Loch Long to east of Auchterarder.

Structure

Within the Dalradian rocks of the region the outcrop patterns of both the 'Green Beds' and the Aberfoyle Slates can be used to define the main early structure of the Southern Highlands, the Tay Nappe. This structure dominates the overall structural pattern seen at the current level of exposure (**Figure 2**). Near Aberfoyle the adjacent gritty and sandy greywackes can be shown to become younger away from the central slate belt. The slates and greywackes form a downfold or synform, but instead of the youngest beds forming the hinge zone as in the normal situation (a syncline), here the oldest beds form the hinge zone and the beds become younger downwards. This inverted anticline, here termed the Aberfoyle Anticline (see cross-section, **Figure 2**) forms part of the downbent nose of the large Tay Nappe structure.

Dalradian rocks have been strongly deformed and metamorphosed during mountain building events in both the late Precambrian (c. 600 m yrs ago) and the early Palaeozoic (c. 500 to 440 m yrs ago). These events resulted in the formation of Caledonian mountains, more akin to the Alps and Himalayas than to the present Scottish Highlands. Such orogenesis, or mountain building, was caused by plate tectonic movements of crustal blocks, giving rise to crustal thickening and compression of the thick Dalradian sedimentary pile. The earlier deformation phase gave rise to the large recumbent overfolds or nappes such as

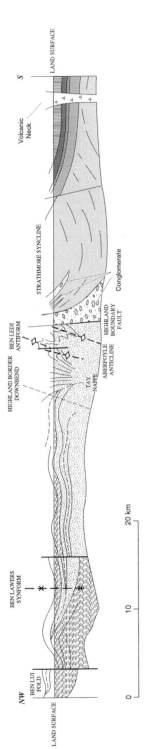

Figure 2a. Cross - section through the Highland Border and Strathmore syncline

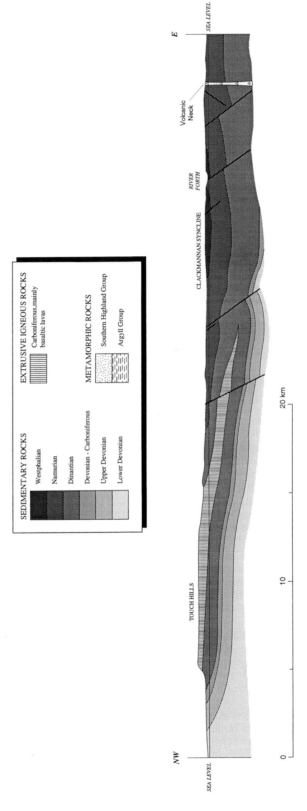

Figure 2b. Cross - sections through Clackmannan syncline

Figure 2. Geological cross - sections of Central Scotland

the Tay Nappe, as noted above. The result of this deformation is that the overall sequence became overturned in parts, so that the older rocks structurally overlie the younger rocks. The subsequent deformation has complicated the structural pattern and in individual rock exposures it is very difficult to decipher the early structures. However, the overall disposition of the major rock units does confirm the regional inversion and in Glen Ogle, Kirkton Glen and on the north side of Glen Dochart, limestones of the upper part of the older Argyll Group clearly overlie the greywackes and 'Green Beds' of the younger Southern Highland Group. The beds are not generally steeply dipping except in a zone some 7-10 km wide adjacent to the Highland Boundary Fault where they dip between 70° southeast and vertical. The areas of generally shallow and steep dips in the Dalradian are known respectively as the 'Flat Belt' and 'Steep Belt'. They are separated by a near horizontal monoformal or 'knee bend' fold axis termed the Downbend, which trends eastnortheast, near parallel to the Highland Boundary Fault. Across the Downbend the regional 'Flat Belt' turns down towards the southeast, as though draped over a deeper crustal basement step. This structure formed late in the overall Caledonian structural history of the area, probably associated with uplift of the orogenic belt.

Uplift is associated with the intrusion of the diorite bodies and related suites of minor intrusions. They are coeval with a period of major faulting, which not only saw reactivation and large-scale movements occurring on the Highland Boundary Fault, but also saw the formation of the northeast-trending faults which are prominent in the Southern Highlands. These faults show sinistral or left lateral movement, combined with downthrow generally to the northwest.

The Tyndrum Fault is one such example of this suite of late sinistral faults. It also has associated lead-zinc mineralisation of probable Permo-Carboniferous age, which was worked mainly from adits west of the village. The waste tips are prominent on the hillside southwest of Tyndrum. Farther southwest up the Cononish valley a quartz vein trending parallel to the Tyndrum Fault, formerly with a minor working for copper at Eas Anie, has recently been shown to contain significant reserves of gold by Ennex International plc. This mineralisation is thought to relate to Devonian granite intrusion.

Exhumation of the deeper levels of the Caledonian Mountain Belt by uplift and rapid erosion occurred under semi-arid tropical conditions during the late Silurian and early Devonian as mountains were reduced to near peneplained relics of their former selves. On the resulting land surface Lower Devonian river deposits were laid down. A further period of gentle folding, faulting and tilting occurred during the Middle Devonian. Upper Devonian to Lower Carboniferous sandstones were deposited subsequently over at least part of the Highland area; they are now preserved in down faulted blocks as, for example, to the northwest of the Highland Boundary Fault near Balmaha on Loch

Lomond. These fault movements, which reversed the earlier movement sense, probably occurred in early Permian times (c. 290 m yrs ago). Just prior to this faulting in the late Carboniferous (c. 295 m yrs) the suite of quartz-dolerite dykes was emplaced.

BEDROCK GEOLOGY - South of the Highland Boundary Fault

The rocks seen in the region, south of the Highland Boundary Fault, are either sedimentary or igneous in origin and were formed between 410 and 290 million yrs ago. The map (**Figure 1**) shows the distribution of these rocks according to age. The succession may also be divided into Formations and Groups according to their lithological characteristics and these subdivisions are shown in stratigraphical order in the vertical section (**Figure 3**).

Rocks of Devonian age

Rocks of Devonian age (410-360 million years ago), occur in the central part of the region from Callander south to the northern margin of the Campsies and east to include the Ochil Hills. The sedimentary sequences are generally terrestrial in origin but there are thick volcanic successions such as those forming the Ochil Hills. During Devonian times central Scotland occupied a global position south of the equator, having 'drifted' northwards from the southern polar latitudes which it occupied in Precambrian times. The climate was semi-arid and large volumes of detritus, from the Caledonian mountains to the north were moved in large river systems, into a subsiding basin which formed in response to general north/south crustal extension. The sedimentary rocks formed by these processes are mostly sandstones, with conglomerates and mudstones. The grain size of these rocks reflects the energy of the system in which the sediments were deposited. The conglomerates represent deposition in a high energy alluvial fan environment or as flood and channel deposits of a river system, the sandstones were mostly laid down in river channels and the mudstones in a low energy environment, either in lakes or floodplains.

The oldest rocks are the early Devonian **Ochil Volcanic Formation** of the Ochil Hills which form part of the **Arbuthnott Group**. They comprise over 2000 m of basaltic and andesitic lavas with interbedded debris-flow conglomerates. They crop out on the prominent scarp formed by the Ochil Fault near Stirling. This fault has a maximum vertical downthrow to the south of about 1100 m and brings the harder Lower Devonian volcanic rocks to the north into juxtaposition with the softer Carboniferous sedimentary sequence to the south. This fault is thought to have been active through much of Carboniferous time. Arbuthnott Group lavas and associated conglomerates interbedded with finer grained sedimentary rocks also crop out on the southern downthrow side of the Highland Boundary Fault. Here,

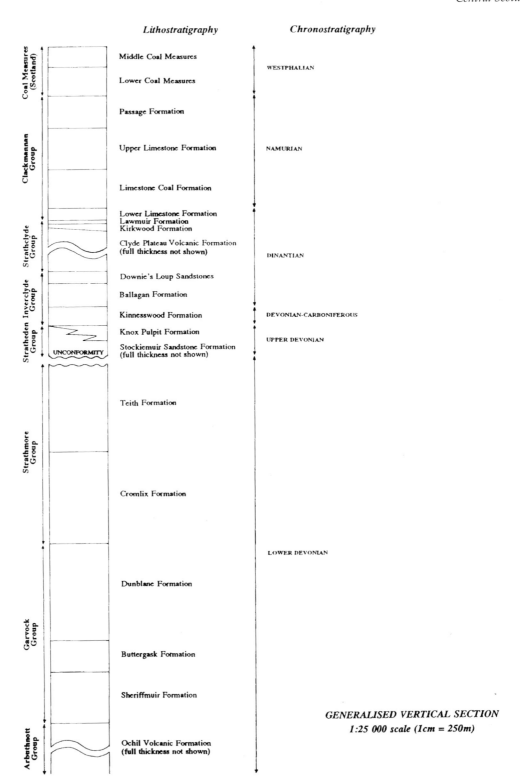

Figure 3   Generalised vertical section of strata, central Scotland

in the Menteith Hills, around Callander and on Conic Hill and Gualann, northeast of Balmaha, vertical beds of conglomerate and sandstone form very prominent linear ridges, running near parallel to the Highland Boundary Fault.

The **Garvock Group** are sedimentary rocks comprising a lower, 430 m-thick, **Sheriffmuir Formation**, and an upper, 820 m-thick, **Dunblane Formation**. These consist largely of brown or grey, cross-bedded, fluvial sandstones. An intervening **Buttergask Formation** consists of 270 m of thinly-bedded, purplish-brown or grey fine-grained sandstones, siltstones and mudstones deposited in an ephemeral lake environment.

The **Strathmore Group** represents a continuation of the pattern of fluvial and lacustrine sedimentation. The lower, **Cromlix Formation** is a lacustrine silty mudstone sequence about 760 m thick followed by some 810 m of fluvial sandstones of the **Teith Formation**. Towards the Highland Boundary Fault, around Callander, the sedimentary rocks are predominantly sandy, but at Uamh Bheag, north-east of Callander, the sandstones are overlain by conglomerates containing clasts of both metamorphic and volcanic rocks. These are alluvial fan deposits emerging from the fault scarp of the Highland Boundary Fault.

The Upper Devonian **Stratheden Group**, locally up to 1000 m thick, was laid down unconformably on an eroded surface of folded older rocks. There is no evidence of any rocks of Middle Devonian age and so the unconformity represents a considerable interval of time and of the tectonic uplift of the Lower Devonian basin. The rocks continue the pattern of sedimentation established in the Lower Devonian with deposition of fluvial sandstones and conglomerates forming the **Stockiemuir Sandstone Formation** which is over 300 m thick. These sedimentary rocks tend to become finer-grained upwards indicating that the topography was becoming more subdued with a decrease in the volume of detritus being supplied from the Highlands.

Towards the top of the Devonian succession widespread aeolian sandstones, (c. 130m thick) become interbedded with the fluvial deposits. These rocks of the **Knox Pulpit Formation**, indicate that Scotland, though still south of the equator, had 'drifted' into a desert belt broadly similar to the present day Kalahari desert.

The sedimentary rocks of the Devonian period contain few fossils. Preservation is potentially better in lower energy lakes than in the higher energy rivers, and it is in the lake environments that fossils, most notably fish, may rarely be found (Wolf's Hole Quarry, Bridge of Allan). The paucity of fossil evidence makes definition of the junction between rocks of Devonian and Carboniferous age uncertain.

Rocks of Carboniferous age

The rocks of Carboniferous age represent deposition over a period of time from 360 to 290 million years ago. The earliest strata record a transition from the terrestrial environments of the Devonian to the marine or coastal environments which prevailed during most of the Carboniferous period.

At the base of the **Inverclyde Group** is the **Kinnesswood Formation**, about 150 m thick, which may be partly Devonian in age. It consists mainly of sandstones with nodules of carbonate. These rocks, called cornstones are formed by rapid evaporation pulling salts into the soil layer where they precipitate to form the carbonate nodules.

These are followed by coastal lagoonal sediments of the **Ballagan Formation** which consist mainly of mudstone with thin beds of muddy limestone, ferroan dolomite (cementstones) and nodular gypsum/anhydrite (sabkha evaporites). These beds, up to 200 m thick, record the continuing environmental change from the arid terrestrial environments of Devonian age to the tropical coastal marine environments of later Carboniferous times.

The **Downie's Loup Sandstones** are calcareous fluvial rocks about 100 m thick. They are associated with conglomerates containing cementstone clasts and algal bodies. Uplift of part of the early Carboniferous basin may have provided the source of the sediments.

The oldest rocks in the **Strathclyde Group** are the **Clyde Plateau Volcanic Formation**; a large pile of lavas, up to 1000 m thick, which extends throughout much of central Scotland. The lavas are mostly basalts and would have been erupted from large, low-profile volcanoes or from fissures. Pyroclastic tuffs, the product of volcanic ash falls, also occur within the sequence. The locations of the volcanoes are now represented by necks and pipes infilled by vent agglomerate and basalt intrusions.

The **Kirkwood Formation** consists of strata made up of reworked volcanic detritus immediately overlying the lavas of the Clyde Plateau Volcanic Formation. The formation is about 30 m to 60m thick.

During the remaining part of Carboniferous time, central Scotland may be envisaged as a small part of an extensive low-relief continental margin with a pattern of sedimentation comprising a series of depositional cycles. The cycle may be repeated many times in each formation although it may not be complete: with one or more rock types not represented. A single ideal cycle is given in the table below.

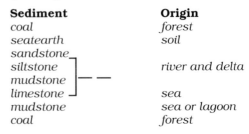

Sediment	Origin
coal	*forest*
seatearth	*soil*
sandstone	
siltstone	*river and delta*
mudstone	
limestone	*sea*
mudstone	*sea or lagoon*
coal	*forest*

Coal seams are formed by the compaction and lithification of thick deposits of peat by burial under reducing conditions. Coal may occur as a single seam or as leaves separated by 'dirt' partings. In some instances, sideritic (iron carbonate) ironstone layers may have developed interleaved with the coal. These are known as blackband ironstones and were formerly mined as iron ore. **Seatearth** consists of mudstone, siltstone or hard sandstone, penetrated by roots. It is a fossil soil. High alumina seatearths or fireclays have refractory qualities and have been worked locally for the manufacture of firebricks, etc. **Sandstone** is the dominant rock type in most cycles, typically forming half or more of the succession. The characteristics of the sandstone vary greatly, from coarse- to fine-grained, from porous to cemented, from massive to bedded, and of variable colour though mostly light grey. Deposition may have occurred in river channels, deltas or shallow seas. **Siltstone** is a bedded deposit of very fine-grained sandy and silty sediment, which may contain plant fragments but few other fossils. Deposition may have occurred in a deltaic environment where the siltstone normally passes downwards into mudstone or in a river environment where the siltstone commonly passes down into sandstone. **Mudstone** is consolidated clay and may contain fossil shells. It formed in a variety of quiet-water environments such as lakes, lagoons or embayments of the sea. Sideritic ironstone nodules are commonly present in the mudstones and these may coalesce to form beds of clayband ironstone. **Limestone** is formed from the consolidated debris of calcareous marine or freshwater shelly fossils and limy mud. Such beds are uncommon in the local sequence and rarely exceed 2.5 m in thickness but their characteristic lithology and fauna make them useful for correlation between different areas.

The sedimentary cycles of deposition are normally about 5 to 10 m thick, but can be over 30 m. Variations in the thickness of cycles and in the extent to which different rock types occur, give a characteristic pattern of cycles to each of the formations into which the Carboniferous sequence is divided. The repetition of cycles is, in part, controlled by the migrarion of deltas and river channels in a generally subsiding basin as well as changes in world sea-levels and by regional earth movements. The rate of compaction of soft sediments is also a factor.

The **Lawmuir Formation**, up to 30m thick at the top of the Strathclyde Group, consists of mudstones, siltstones, sandstones and rare thin limestone beds. The succession is a transitional one between terrestrial and marine conditions and represents the first elements of a marine transgression onto a major land area, in part, formed by rocks of the Clyde Plateau Volcanic Formation.

At the base of the **Clackmannan Group** is the **Lower Limestone Formation**. It is over 100m thick and consists of sandstones, siltstones, mudstones and several fossiliferous marine limestones. These sedimentary rocks were deposited in a shallow sea which was regularly silted up as deltas built out seaward. Coal seams are thin and insignificant.

The **Limestone Coal Formation** is at least 500 m thick in the Alloa area but is thinner farther west. It consists predominantly of sandstones, siltstones, mudstones and many coals deposited in cyclic sequence on broad alluvial plains at the terrestrial end of an extending delta. Marine strata form only a minor part of the formation.

The **Upper Limestone Formation** consists of sandstones, siltstones and mudstones with up to seven thin limestones; the marine phase of delta migration. Not all of the limestones are present throughout the area. There are a few coals but only the Upper and Lower Hirst seams and the Quarry Coal are known to have been worked. The Upper Hirst Coal is currently mined at the Longannet Mine Complex, Fife but working panels are located beneath the Alloa area. The formation is up to 600 m thick.

The **Passage Formation** is about 270 m thick and consists predominantly of sandstones with subordinate poorly bedded siltstones and mudstones (including fireclays), several thin impure limestones and calcareous mudstones with fossils, and some thin coals. These rocks represent a return to terrestrial, fluvial conditions with only very occasional incursions of the sea. Seams of fireclay are present near the base and top of the Passage Formation, but only the Lower Fireclays have been worked extensively for, amongst other uses, refractory bricks. During the deposition of this formation uplift of the area may have occurred leading to breaks in the sedimentation such that the base of the formation is locally marked by an unconformity.

The **Scottish Coal Measures** are represented by two, generally non-marine, sequences. The **Lower Coal Measures** consist of thick sandstones, siltstones, mudstones and seatearth with coals, deposited on broad alluvial plains at the landward end of a delta. The maximum thickness of the sequence is about 240 m. The Lower Coal Measures underlie most of the eastern part of the region including Alloa, Airth and Kincardine. At least nine coals in the Lower Coal Measures have been worked and some locally exceed 1m in thickness.

The full thickness of the **Middle Coal Measures** is not present in this area. Only the lowest 170 m remain, the rest having been removed by erosion since Carboniferous times. The succession is generally similar to the Lower Coal Measures and includes numerous coals, most of which are less than 1 m thick. The base is marked by the Queenslie Marine Band which is a persistent bed of mudstone containing characteristic marine fossils.

Intrusive Igneous rocks of Carboniferous and Permian ages

The majority of these intrusions are composed of dolerite, and occur as both dykes and sills. They form dark, hard, generally medium-grained crystalline rocks. Two main types of dolerite are found, namely: olivine-dolerite, which formed at various times during the

Carboniferous; and quartz-dolerite, which was intruded in the late Carboniferous (c.295 m yrs). Large outcrops of the quartz-dolerite form the Midland Valley Sill, which crops out prominently around Stirling and farther to the south.

Structure, south of the Highland Boundary Fault

The region is dominated by two major synclinal structures forming broad downfolds. The **Strathmore Syncline** trends northeast to southwest immediately to the southeast of the Highland Boundary Fault. It is markedly asymmetrical with a vertical northwestern limb adjacent to the Highland Boundary Fault. Movement on this fault contributed to the present geometry of the fold. The **Clackmannan Syncline** is a broad downfold with an axial trace trending north/ south through a position close to Alloa. Rocks of Carboniferous age are folded by this gentle structure, the axis of which corresponds to the original centre of subsidence of the Upper Carboniferous sedimentary basin.

Faulting is common, with vertical displacements ranging from less than 1 m to more than 200 m, although the Ochil Fault has a much greater displacement. The major faults are aligned roughly east-west or northwest-southeast. Displacement on the faults took place relatively soon after the strata were deposited and, although many fractures were probably reactivated subsequently, there is only one record of undoubted movement in historical times (the 1736, Dollar Earthquake).

An indication of the general structure in the region is given in cross section on Figure 2. The oldest rocks crop out in the west, and as the axis of the Clackmannan Syncline roughly coincides with a north-south line through Alloa, the younger rocks are found in the central and eastern parts of the region. The overall pattern of folding and faulting reflects the extensional origin of the Midland Valley, but minor sideways slip in a dextral, right lateral, direction took place on some faults.

Post-Permian geological history

From the Permian onwards, Scotland remained as a positive landmass, with sedimentation confined to the fringes. The landmass continued to drift northwards through regions corresponding to the present day Sahara and into the temperate belt. Evidence of the changing environment caused by this northward drift is contained in rocks formed in the post-Permian period. Unfortunately Triassic, Jurassic and Cretaceous age sedimentary rocks are unknown anywhere in central Scotland. There is no evidence therefore of the major sedimentary and tectonic events which led to the development of the hydrocarbon-rich North Sea rocks during this time. However, a veneer of Cretaceous age sedimentary rocks may have been deposited on the present onshore area.

The igneous activity associated with the break-up of the continental mass and the opening of the Atlantic in Tertiary times is not represented in the area. However, the basic topographic configuration of the Forth valley may have been fashioned by prolonged erosion during this period. The ultimate consequences of the northward shift in latitude are the ice ages that occurred in the last 2 million years during the Quaternary Era.

QUATERNARY GEOLOGY

The Quaternary Era was a time of extensive glaciations. However, there is little reliable evidence of the older glacial (and interglacial) events that have affected central Scotland. Indeed, most of the accessible Quaternary deposits and features in the area are less than 30 000 yrs old (late-Devensian and Flandrian age). Geological history during Quaternary glacial periods is described in time 'slices' called stades and interstades. These represent colder and warmer climatic episodes within a glaciation. A simplified map showing the surface distribution of Quaternary deposits forms **Figure 4**.

Pre Dimlington Stade (>27 000 yrs ago)

In Central and Strathclyde Regions, there are pockets of sand and gravel (**Cadder Formation**) and beds of glacial till (**Baillieston Till Formation**) that pre-date the Main late-Devensian glaciation of 27 000 yrs ago. These deposits are found in so-called 'buried channels'. These elongate, deep hollows in the bedrock surface are probably not ancient river valleys graded to sea-levels (much) lower than present. Rather, their form is probably that of closed basins, the shape suggesting that they are likely to be glacially related scours. Major bedrock depressions (level below present sea-level) exist under the rivers Forth (200 m), Devon (90 m) and Carron (90 m). Since few of the deposits infilling these depressions have yielded fossils, it is not known how much older than late-Devensian age they may be. In the Kelvin valley, just south of the Stirling area, the age of the sediments is known because they contain bones of the woolly rhinoceros dated at about 27500 yrs old. These sand and gravel deposits were possibly formed in delta or braided river environments formed adjacent to the ice mass. However, thick sand and gravel deposits that were encountered in mine workings under the Forth estuary during the 19th century are likely to have formed below the ice; these have been compared with tunnel valley fills such as those in East Anglia.

Dimlington Stade (c.27 000 - 13 500 yrs ago)

The Main late-Devensian ice sheet of the Dimlington Stade eroded the landscape producing

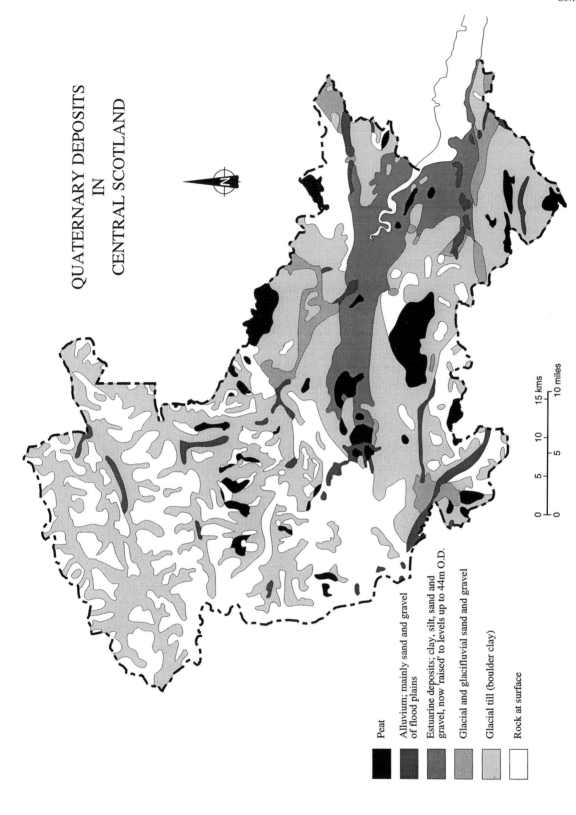

QUATERNARY DEPOSITS
IN
CENTRAL SCOTLAND

Peat

Alluvium; mainly sand and gravel of flood plains

Estuarine deposits; clay, silt, sand and gravel, now 'raised' to levels up to 44m O.D.

Glacial and glacifluvial sand and gravel

Glacial till (boulder clay)

Rock at surface

Figure 4   Generalised surface distribution of Quaternary deposits, central Scotland

striated bedrock surfaces, rôche montonées and crag and tail features. Both the promontory on which Stirling Castle is sited and Abbey Craig are examples of the latter landform. Erosion by the ice removed pre-existing glacial and interglacial sediments (except in the bedrock depressions) and may also have contributed to major changes in the pattern of the pre-glacial (Tertiary) river-system in central Scotland. The ice deposited substantial spreads of glacial till (**Wilderness Till Formation**) at its base, which it commonly sculpted into streamlined ovoid mounds called drumlins. The National Monument at Bannockburn is located on one such feature.

In the area of the Forth valley, the 1 to 2 km-thick Main late-Devensian ice sheet probably extended 30 or 40 km beyond the coast of east Fife as far as the Marr Bank. As a result of the global low sea-level at the time, most of the North Sea was exposed as land and the former sea bed was subjected to freeze-thaw processes. All of the west coast of Scotland was covered by the advancing ice. After the Main late-Devensian ice sheet began to retreat about 16000 yrs ago, substantial volumes of glacifluvial sand and gravel (**Broomhouse Formation**) were deposited by the meltwaters. These ice contact deposits often have characteristic landforms such as mounds, eskers (ridges) and terraces with kettle-holes. Such deposits and features are common in the Falkirk area and in the Teith valley around Doune. The Polmont esker is a classic of its kind, but like many ice contact features in the Stirling area, has been mutilated by sand and gravel extraction and urban growth.

When a thick ice-sheet forms, it imposes a heavy load on the earth's surface. The crust responds by warping downwards, the amount of downwarp being greatest at the centre of accumulation and diminishing to zero a short distance beyond the edge of the ice-sheet, where uplift (forebulge) may occur. Unloading by melting of the ice is accompanied by crustal uplift (isostatic recovery) in the area of previous depression. The return of water to the oceans from melting land-based ice reverses the effect of world sea-level lowering that occurs during an ice age when water is extracted from the sea to form the ice. The interplay of the local isostatic recovery with world sea-level changes has caused fluctuations in relative sea-level in the Forth area. These are marked by raised beach features and by raised marine deposits. The changing coastline of the Stirling area in latest late-Devensian (<16 000-10 000 yrs ago) and Flandrian times (10 000 yrs ago to present) may be appraised using these two lines of evidence. There is still debate, however, about the precise relationship between them (and associated glacifluvial sand and gravel terraces) and the location of the retreating ice-front at certain times.

During deglaciation, local relative sea-level was high in central Scotland and it is not uncommon to find raised marine sediments at about 40 to 45 m above OD. In eastern areas, the decaying glaciers retreated westwards towards the Highlands and by about 13 000 yrs ago, the sea had invaded the valleys of the Tay, Earn, Eden and Forth reaching both Crieff and Aberfoyle. The characteristic marine sediment associated with the deglaciation of the Scottish east coast is a red clay that is finely colour laminated in shades of pink and grey. These clays contain macro- and micro-fossils which indicate the local climate was Arctic (**Errol Beds**). In the Forth valley retreat of the glacier may have slowed around Rosyth and then in the Kincardine Bridge area. A large delta and terrace complex composed largely of sand was formed where glacial meltwaters discharged from the Carron/Bonny valley into the sea at Falkirk. The retreat also appears to have halted at Stirling where the valley is constricted by the Castle Rock etc. On the basis of the presence of unfossiliferous clay at altitudes up to 43 m OD east of Stirling, it has been suggested that the nearby glacial sand and gravel deposits around Cambusbarron formed in an ice-contact, marine, morainic delta when the sea stood at about this altitude. That the Stirling ice-front position is an important glacier-retreat feature is apparently confirmed west of Stirling, where marine deposits are only known to 34 m OD. On the Scottish west coast the ice was also retreating to the Highlands and the sea occupied both the lower Clyde valley and Loch Lomond. Marine and estuarine processes deposited sparsely fossiliferous, highly laminated clay and silt (**Paisley Formation**).

The most conspicuous of the former coastlines associated with deglaciation in the Forth is the Main Perth Shoreline, tenuously dated to around 13 500 yrs ago. This shoreline may have formed during a period of improved climate, when isostatic recovery of the land and eustatic sea-level rise were temporarily in balance. The **Loanhead** and **Kinneil Kerse formations** of the Grangemouth area probably date from about this time. The Main Perth Shoreline has not been recognised west of Alloa but there is a lower and younger shoreline present in Stirling. The distribution of former ('raised') estuarine deposits in **Figure 5** broadly depicts the shape of the local coastline just after deglaciation.

Windermere Interstade (13 500 - 11 000 yrs ago)

Late-Devensian seabed sediments that are characteristic of the fully deglaciated sea lochs of the Forth and Loch Lomond area are usually rather massive-looking silty clays (**Linwood Formation**) which commonly contain many marine fossils. The fauna indicate that the climate was warmer than that before 13 500 yrs ago. Drop-stones in the sediments were probably derived from the melting of rafts of winter shore-ice rather than calved icebergs. The **Abbotsgrange Formation** in the Grangemouth area, by exception, consists of well-layered pro-delta sediments. Raised beaches, mainly composed of sand and gravel (**Killearn Formation**), provide evidence that during the Windermere Interstade local relative sea-level fell from c. 40m above OD to present, or below,

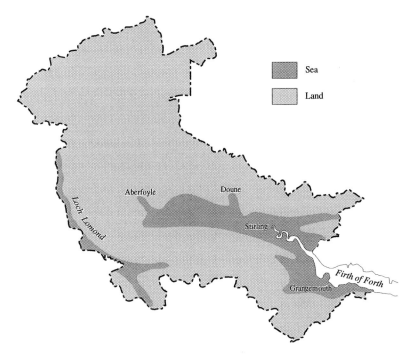

Figure 5. Coastline about 13 000 years ago

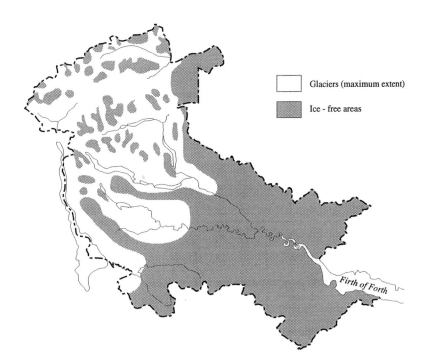

Figure 6. Glaciers of Central Scotland during the Loch Lomond Stade (11 000 to 10 000 years ago)

before glaciers reappeared in central Scotland during the Loch Lomond Stade. During the Interstade the local landscape was largely devoid of trees and generally tundra-like.

Loch Lomond Stade (11 000 - 10 000 yrs ago)

The Loch Lomond Stade ice accumulated on Rannoch Moor and in the high corries of the southwest Highlands and advanced into lowland areas to reach Callander, Lake of Menteith and Drymen **(Figure 6)**. Beyond the ice margins there is evidence of frozen ground including frost wedge casts and materials moved by freeze-thaw action. In the Highlands, the extent of the Loch Lomond Stade ice-sheet is often indicated by widespread tracts of hummocky moraine ('morainic drift') especially in the valleys north of the Trossachs. In section, most of the mounds are formed of glacial till with a clayey, sandy matrix containing many stones and boulders (**Gartocharn Till Formation**). Sand and gravel deposits showing classical ice meltout kame and kettle landforms were formed (depressions created where buried ice has melted) and are well-displayed in the Cononish valley northwest of Crianlarich.

In Loch Lomond, glacimarine sediments (**Balloch Formation**) were laid down that contain an arctic fauna. When glacier-ice advanced southwards through Loch Lomond, it 'bulldozed' the marine sediments and other pre-existing deposits, such as the Main late-Devensian till, and formed terminal moraines at Drymen and also at Alexandria in the Leven valley. The glacier also dammed a lake in the Strathblane area that is associated with the terminal moraine at Drymen. The moraine is mainly composed of deltaic sand and gravel (**Drumbeg Formation**) but passes eastward into seasonally-laminated (varved) lake-bottom clay and silt (**Blane Water Formation**). Similarly glaciers in the Forth and Teith valleys bulldozed pre-existing deposits. In the Forth valley, the conspicuous terminal moraine stretches northeast from near Gartmore to Arnprior and north to the Lake of Menteith. In the Teith valley the terminal moraine is present at Gart just to the southeast of Callander. In this area at Torrie Farm, organic silts of Windermere Interstade age have been found beneath the re-advance till.

During the Loch Lomond Stade local relative sea-level in the Forth valley is known to have fallen well below that of the present day. In the Grangemouth area, where the Main Lateglacial Shoreline is widely developed at about OD, it is generally agreed that the level of the sea may have fallen to around 10 m below OD but some scientists have suggested much lower levels of exposure and erosion of valleys in pre-existing deposits. There is evidence of freeze-thaw induced consolidation of 'soft' marine clay on the Main Lateglacial Shoreline's beach platform at 9 m below OD. The shore platform is normally covered by the 'buried gravel layer' (**Bothkennar Gravel Formation**) which is usually only about a metre thick. A glaciated shore platform of a comparable age has also been recognised in the southern part of Loch Lomond. The extent of both these beach platforms and the scale of the cliffline, especially west of Stirling, has been ascribed to enhanced marine erosion under the prevailing periglacial conditions, but shoreline inheritance may also have played a part. Whilst the ice-front remained at Menteith, there was a marked relative rise of the sea to the level of the resultant 'High Buried Beach' at about 12 m above OD. This rise drowned the outwash plain (sandur) in front of the glacier.

Flandrian Interstade (<10 000 yrs ago)

About 10 000 yrs ago, there was a major change in the climate that may have taken place in as little as a hundred years. This was associated with the disappearance of glacial ice from Scotland, the melting of which produced the kettlehole in which the Lake of Menteith is located. From arctic conditions, the climate improved such that at the postglacial optimum about 6500 yrs ago the local climate was warmer and wetter than at the present day.

The 'Main' and 'Low Buried Beaches' (at about 11 m and 8 m above OD near Menteith) in the Forth valley formed on the fall of relative sea-level due to continuing isostatic recovery after the retreat and decay of the Forth Glacier. On the exposed surfaces of the deposits of clay, silt and sand, peat was able to accumulate and thus form the well known **Sub-Carse Peat**. The basal peat on the 'Main Buried Beach' dates from about 9600 yrs ago and on the 'Low Buried Beach' from about 8800 yrs. In the Grangemouth area the deposits of the buried beaches have been assigned to the **Letham Formation** which contains an impoverished estuarine fauna.

When the main Flandrian marine transgression started about 8000 yrs ago, most of the Sub-Carse Peat was drowned except where coastal bogs continued to form in small areas such as at Larbert and Falkirk and in two larger areas, namely, at East and West Flanders Moss west of Stirling. Extensive fine-grained estuarine sediments of the carse clay were laid down (**Claret Formation**) in the estuary. These sediments contain a diverse boreal fauna including the remains of large whales. In the period between 8000 yrs ago and the acme of the Flandrian transgression, around 6500 yrs ago, the whole of the Forth valley-floor west of Stirling silted up. At the acme, local relative sea-level reached a maximum of about 16 m above OD in the Aberfoyle area. In the Edinburgh area, the equivalent relative sea-level was only at about 10 m above OD because of the slope on the fossilised estuarine surface caused by the isostatic tilting of the land. This tilting is in response to the continuing relief of the much more significant Main late-Devensian ice loading rather than that of the Loch Lomond Stade. The Main Flandrian Shoreline, with which these levels are associated, has been widely recognised in the Forth valley from east of

Grangemouth to Aberfoyle. When this shoreline formed about 6500 yrs ago, the sites of Falkirk, Stirling and Aberfoyle were coastal **(Figure 7)**. It took longer for the Grangemouth area to silt up and in consequence lower and younger Flandrian shorelines and raised mudflats are to be found there. About 4000 yrs ago a minor oscillation of sea-level caused some erosion to levels a few metres below OD, and a peat-rich bed forms the base of the succeeding **Grangemouth Formation** which consists of clay, silt and sand. These deposits include the contemporary intertidal and subtidal sediments. Evidence of man's prehistoric presence in the general area has been provided by the finding of a canoe in the Sub-Carse Peat at Perth. Contemporary creatures included wolf, bear, boar, reindeer, elk and wild cattle. Kitchen middens, 3 to 4 m deep, consisting of oyster shells are common west of Bo'ness at the foot of the prehistoric (5-6000 yrs old) shoreline cliff.

Carse clays have not been recognised in the Loch Lomond area. However, Loch Lomond may have briefly become a sea loch again immediately after the Loch Lomond Stade (more than 9500 yrs ago) and also about 7900 yrs ago. Between 6800 to 5500 yrs ago the sea certainly re-entered Loch Lomond and raised marine shorelines of Flandrian age have also been identified at 13, 12 and 9 m OD. These events and the associated generally muddy sediments (mainly of the

Buchanan and **Erskine** formations) represent brief intervals in the generally non-marine history of the loch since the end of the last ice age. The lacustrine sediments are generally muddy (**Kelvin** and **Kilmarnock** formations) but are sandy where deltas formed at river mouths (**Law** and **Endrick** formations).

As central Scotland is an area of significant overall postglacial fall in sea-level, the consequent incision of the drainage has produced scenically attractive river gorges such as those of the River Avon at Birkhill Fireclay Mine and the River Devon at Rumbling Bridge.

GEOLOGY RELATED TO LAND USE PLANNING AND DEVELOPMENT

The natural extension of looking at the geology of the region is to see the impact it makes on the local economy and on land use planning and development, in particular in the areas of mineral resource and ground condition.

Resources

Sand and gravel deposits are a valuable source of aggregate and are extracted locally. These occur mainly as morainic deposits in the Highlands and as

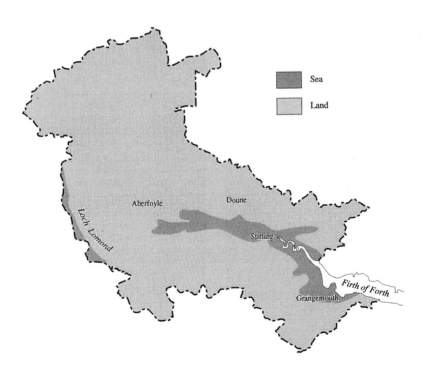

Figure 7   Coastline, central Scotland during mid Flandrian, about 6 500 years ago

glacifluvial deposits in the lowland areas. Large **peat** deposits are not particularly common but peat is cut commercially at Letham Moss. Bings of **colliery waste** have potential for use as bulk fill, for provision of mudstone for brick-making or for the recovery of their coal content. Many tips in the region have been landscaped and much of the material redistributed and used in land reclamation and in industrial redevelopment. Locally the fine-grained deposits of the Claret (carse clay) and Loanhead formations have been exploited for **brick and tile** manufacture.

In the past the main natural resource within central Scotland was **deep-mined coal** but prolonged extraction has depleted the reserves to such an extent that large-scale underground mining is now limited to extraction by British Coal from the Longannet Complex. **Opencast coal** has already been obtained from the Lower Coal Measures, and the Passage and Limestone Coal formations, and potential resources exist in parts of their outcrops. Opencast coal extraction can be an economic way of preparing unstable land underlain by shallow mineworkings for future development. **Hydrocarbons** have been prospected for with little success and interest is centred currently on **coal-bed methane**. There are noteworthy resources of **hardrock aggregate** in the area from the extensive outcrops of quartz-dolerite in the Stirling Sill. **Limestone** beds in the Lower and Upper Limestone formations have been mined locally, but are too thin to be regarded as a resource under present economic conditions. **Sandstone** is found throughout the local sedimentary sequence and some beds were formerly quarried for building stone. Sandstones of the Passage Formation have potential as a source of silica sand and recently small quantities have been quarried for building stone. There are considerable resources of **fireclay** in the Passage Formation and to a lesser extent in the lower part of the Lower Coal Measures which have been mined and worked opencast. Coal and **mudstones for brick** are extracted along with fireclay where they occur together, the combined exploitation being more viable economically. There may also be resources of mudstones for brick, particularly in the Upper Limestone Formation. **Metalliferous ores**, including lead and barytes, are present in Dalradian, Lower Devonian and Carboniferous rocks. Gold has been found in currently sub-economic concentrations near Tyndrum where zinc also occurs. Silver was once mined in the Ochil Hills.

Groundwater has not been a key resource in the region, but it is likely that its development, particularly in the Passage Formation, will take place as the cost of water increases. Potential future demand implies a valuable, under-utilised and renewable resource which must be husbanded for future users and protected from damage by pollution. To this end, the creation of landfill sites on and in the carse clay is taking advantage of the natural impermeable seal provided by this deposit to prevent the **migration of leachate** into the surface- and ground-waters. Thus local landfill practice reflects the change from the long-standing practice of dilution and dispersal of leachates to containment. **Geothermal power** may be available from deeply buried aquifers such as the aeolian sandstones of the Knox Pulpit Formation.

Ground conditions for development

In planning for land use, it is important to consider foundation conditions. Rock, till and sand and gravel generally provide good conditions below the top weathered zone. Engineering properties of rock vary markedly depending on the rock type. Potential foundation problems from **undermining at shallow depths** are possible anywhere within the outcrops of the Lower and Middle Coal Measures and the Limestone Coal Formation. Similar problems occur locally and to a lesser extent in areas underlain by the Passage Formation, and Upper and Lower Limestone formations.

Poor foundation conditions can be caused by superficial deposits such as peat, clay and silt, alluvial deposits on a valley floor, and landfill. All these deposits require careful site investigation. Foundation conditions may also be affected by **variably compressible** buried superficial deposits, in particular the Sub-Carse Peat, a deposit buried beneath the carse clay (Claret Formation). The stability of drift deposits on steep slopes may be affected by loading and excavation making them susceptible to **landslip** and **debris flow**. Similarly the stability of bedrock in cliffs and steep-sided excavations may depend on its resistance to weathering and the presence of joints, faults and smooth, inclined bedding planes. Movement on such planar features may give rise to **rockfalls** as well as landslip.

Faulting can produce zones of broken rock or can juxtapose rocks of greatly varying geotechnical competence. Faults in undermined areas commonly concentrate **mining subsidence** on the fault plane, so that one side subsides markedly whilst the other remains stable. Such strongly differential settlement can be highly destructive to buildings and other structures. Although small **earthquakes** do occur in the region, normally deep in the Earth's crust, there is no evidence that natural earthquakes have led to measurable movement along mapped geological faults in historical times. Nevertheless, it has been postulated that dislocations in the levels of former shorelines of early Flandrian age in the western part of the Forth valley, discovered after detailed altitude measurements, might be explained by postglacial movements on major faults caused by ice loading and unloading. Small magnitude earthquakes may be a significant factor in planning the location of sensitive developments like high-tech factories. In addition to natural earthquakes, **man-made events** may occur associated with coal extraction or the collapse of old mine workings. This is common in areas of active mining where the events occasionally cause alarm or even slight damage due to their very shallow depth.

Although most geohazards affecting Scotland are not likely to be on the scale represented by volcanic eruptions or major earthquakes with major loss of life, the financial burden caused by landslip, collapse of mineworkings etc. could be large. **Coastal erosion** and **flooding** may be enhanced by **rising sea-level** associated with the greenhouse effect thus threatening areas such as Grangemouth and its important petrochemicals industry. This low-lying town is sited partly on reclaimed tidal flats. The recognition of a **possible tsunami** sand deposit in the Sub-Carse Peat, formed in response to unusually high sea waves created by a submarine landslip in the North Sea, is perhaps also a warning to planners to think more globally about environmental hazards.

REFERENCES AND FURTHER READING

BROWNE, M.A.E. 1987. The physical geography and geology of the estuary and Firth of Forth, Scotland. *Proceedings of the Royal Society of Edinburgh* 93B, 235-44

BROWNE, M.A.E., GRAHAM, D.K. and GREGORY, D.M., 1984. Quaternary estuarine deposits in the Grangemouth area, Scotland. *Report of the British Geological Survey* 16, No.3

BROWNE, M.A.E., ROBINS, N.S., EVANS, R.B., MONRO, S.K. and ROBSON, P.G., 1987. The Upper Devonian and Carboniferous sandstones of the Midland Valley of Scotland. Investigation of the geothermal potential of the UK. *British Geological Survey Open-File Report.*

BROWNE, M.A.E. and McMILLAN, A.A., 1989. Quaternary Geology of the Clyde valley. *British Geological Survey Research Report* SA/89/1.

CAMERON, I.B. and STEPHENSON, D., 1985. The Midland Valley of Scotland. British Regional Geology. Third edition. HMSO

CRAIG, G.Y., Editor. 1991. Geology of Scotland. Third Edition. The Geological Society: London.

DINHAM, C.H. and HALDANE, D., 1932. The Economic Geology of the Stirling and Clackmannan Coalfield. Memoir of the Geological Survey of Great Britain.

EHLERS, J., et al, Editors. 1991. Glacial Deposits in Great Britain and Northern Ireland. A.A. Balkema : Rotterdam.

FRANCIS, E.H., FORSYTH, I.H., READ, W.A. and ARMSTRONG, M., 1970. The geology of the Stirling district. *Memoir of the Geological Survey of Great Britain.*

GOSTELOW, T.P. and BROWNE, M.A.E., 1981. Engineering geology of the Upper Forth Estuary. *Open-File Report of the Institute of Geological Sciences.*

HARTE, B., BOOTH, J.E., DEMPSTER, T.J., FETTES, D.J., MENDUM, J.R. and WATTS, D., 1984. Aspects of the post-depositional evolution of Dalradian and Highland Border Complex rocks in the Southern Highlands of Scotland. *Transactions of the Royal Society of Edinburgh: Earth Sciences*, 75, 151-163.

JARDINE, W.G. 1986. The geological and geomorphological setting of the estuary and Firth of Clyde. *Proceedings of the Royal Society of Edinburgh* 90B, 25-41

McMILLAN, A.A. and BROWNE, M.A.E., 1987. The use and abuse of thematic mining information maps. In CULSHAW, M.G., BELL, F.G., CRIPPS, J.C. and O'HARA, M. Editors. Planning and Engineering Geology. Geological Society Engineering Geology Special Publication No. 4. pp 237-245.

MONRO, S.K., CAMERON, I.B. and HALL, I.H.S., 1991. Geology for land use planning: Stirling. *British Geological Survey, Technical Report* WA/91/25.

MONRO S.K. and HULL J.H., 1987. Environmental Geology in Great Britain. In Geo-resources and Environment BGR : Hannover pp 107-124.

PATERSON, I.B., ARMSTRONG, M. and BROWNE, M.A.E., 1981. Quaternary estuarine deposits in the Tay-Earn area, Scotland. *Report of the Institute of Geological Sciences*, No.81/7.

PRICE, R.J., 1983. Scotland's environment during the last 30 000 years. Scottish Academic Press: Edinburgh.

READ, W.A., 1985. The interplay of sedimentation, volcanicity and tectonics in the Passage Group (Arnsbergian, E2 to Westphalian A) in the Midland Valley of Scotland. In ARTHURTON, R.S., GUTTERIDGE, P. and NOLAN, S.C. Editors. The role of tectonics in Devonian and Carboniferous sedimentation in the British Isles pp 143-152. Yorkshire Geological Society, Occasional Publication No.6.

READ, W.A., 1988. Controls on Silesian sedimentation in the Midland Valley of Scotland. In BESLY, B.M. and KELLING, G. Editors. Sedimentation in a synorogenic basin complex. The Upper Carboniferous of north-west Europe pp 222-241. Blackie.

ROSE, J., 1989. Stadial type sections in the British Quaternary. In ROSE, J. and *Aquatic Life* SCHLUCHTER Ch. Editors, Quaternary type sections: imagination or reality? pp 45-67. A A Balkema : Rotterdam.

SISSONS, J.B., 1974. The Quaternary in Scotland: a review. *Scottish Journal of Geology*, 10, 34-87

SISSONS, J.B., 1976. The Geomorphology of the British Isles: Scotland. Methuen: London.

STEDMAN, C., 1988. Namurian E1 tectonics and sedimentation in the Midland Valley of Scotland: rifting versus strike-slip influence. In Besley, B.M. and Kelling, G. Editors. Sedimentation in a synorogenic basin complex. The Upper Carboniferous of north-west Europe pp 242-254. Blackie.

SUTHERLAND, D.G., 1984. The Quaternary deposits and landforms of Scotland and the neighbouring shelves: a review. *Quaternary Science Reviews* 3, 157-254

WALKER, P.M.B., Editor, 1991. Chambers Earth Sciences Dictionary. Chambers, Edinburgh.

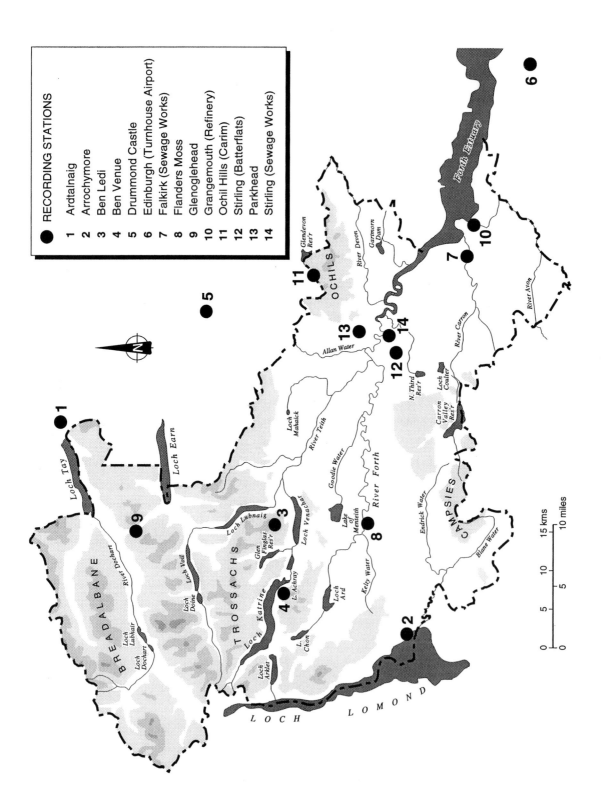

Figure 1 Locations of weather data sources, central Scotland

RECORDING STATIONS

1   Ardtalnaig
2   Arrochymore
3   Ben Ledi
4   Ben Venue
5   Drummond Castle
6   Edinburgh (Turnhouse Airport)
7   Falkirk (Sewage Works)
8   Flanders Moss
9   Glenoglehead
10 Grangemouth (Refinery)
11 Ochil Hills (Carim)
12 Stirling (Batterflats)
13 Parkhead
14 Stirling (Sewage Works)

Climate

S. J. Harrison

The Setting

The location of Scotland, in the middle latitudes, between the warmth of the tropics and the cold of the polar ice, and on the maritime western approaches to the largest continental land-mass on the Earth's surface, means that its climate is characterised by both temporal and spatial variability. Thus in many respects it is almost impossible to establish an average, or typical, climatic condition. The dominant airflow in these latitudes is from the west, imparting a moist and windy character to the climate, which is generally mild in winter and cool in summer. Easterly airstreams originating in continental Europe are less frequent but can be associated with spells of extreme summer heat or winter cold.

The interaction between Tropical and Polar air-masses along the Polar Front leads to the development of extra-tropical cyclones, or depressions, which track eastwards from the Atlantic and exert a dominant influence on the weather of the British Isles. These very active weather systems are not only associated with often the strongest winds but, more importantly, they have complex internal structures. The frontal discontinuities within them are marked by bands of cloud and associated precipitation, and rapid changes in, for example, temperature and wind direction, over timescales measured in hours or less. During the winter months most of Britain is affected by the passage of depressions and their associated fronts, but as global pressure systems drift polewards in the summer months depressions begin to follow a more northerly track. Thus while England and Wales can expect to experience extended spells of stable weather as high pressure extends north-eastwards from the Azores, Scotland can remain under the influence of depressions and experiences usually less settled summers.

The climatic picture in central Scotland is, therefore, one of a characteristic variability which is further complicated by the effects of a land surface extending from the coastal plain of the Forth Estuary to the Highlands in the west. The presence of the urban areas of Falkirk and Stirling, and the industrial complex around Grangemouth, add another layer of local influence on climate.

The dominant local influence is, however, that of topography which, in presenting such a variety of slope angles and aspects, can generate a complex array of local climates. There are very steep gradients of change in climate with increasing elevation above sea-level, which is most marked when comparing the sheltered glens and exposed hill slopes of the Highlands (Johnson 1985). Increasing altitude is accompanied by increases in wind speed, atmospheric humidity and cloudiness, and precipitation, together with decreases in incoming

Parkhead climatological station, Stirling University

solar radiation, and surface and air temperature. The altitudinal gradients of change in these climate variables is particularly steep in the Region, which contributes in no small way to a very obvious contrast between hill moorland and lowland arable farmland.

Given the very distinctive climatic variation across the Region it is a great pity that so little climatological observation has been undertaken since the excellent rainfall records which were collated by Colonel Stirling for the *Transactions of the Stirling Natural History and Archaeological Society* from the late 19th century onwards (Harrison 1980). Smith (1974), in his earlier survey of the climate of the Stirling area, made particular reference to the paucity of data and use had to be made of intermittent records, often of quite short duration. This problem is not peculiar to central Scotland but tends to be most acute in rural areas and on inhospitable higher ground. In Scotland as a whole only 3% of the climatological stations which send their data to the Met Office lie above the very modest elevation of 300m OD. To a large extent, the situation in Central Region has improved very little since 1974. Although the number of climatological stations has increased, many have short records which are of very limited value (**Table 1**).

Table 1   Climatological stations in Central Region reporting to the Monthly Weather Report of the Met Office   (C = current)

Station	Alt. (m)	Grid Ref.	Record
Aberfoyle	27	NN 530 004	1969 - 1975, 1985 - C
Arrochymore	30	NS 415 918	1972 - C
Balquhidder	136	NN 520 206	1983 - C
Callander	107	NN 634 080	1967 - 1981
Crianlarich	174	NN 367 284	1975
Earls Hill	335	NS 725 882	1963 - 1980
Falkirk (Sew.Wks)	3	NS 902 820	1967 - C
Grangemouth (Ref.)	2	NS 943 813	1971 - C
Killin	116	NN 546 348	1987 - 1989
Loch Venacher	84	NN 598 063	1982 - C
Mugdock Park	165	NS 546 780	1991 - C
Parkhead	35	NS 815 969	1971 - C
Stirling (B'flats)	38	NS 786 925	1918 - 1982
Stirling (Sew.Wks)	7	NS 808 935	1984 - C
Tyndrum	168	NN 359 283	1991 - C

Stirling (Batterflats), which has now closed, provided the most substantial record. The University of Stirling's station (Parkhead) has been operational since 1971 and more recent work by the Institute of Hydrology in the vicinity of Balquhidder has provided much needed observations for this area. In this current analysis considerable use has again been made of short-duration records which are considerably shorter than the 30 to 35 years adopted as standard by the Met Office for the calculation of climatological averages. However, the emphasis has been on establishing contrasts within the region for which it is reasonable to use the shorter records. Use has also been made of observations from sites immediately outwith the region but which nevertheless provide some indication of climatic conditions within particular settings, such as Ardtalnaig on the shores of Loch Tay (**Figure 1**).

Solar Radiation

Central Scotland's northerly location within the British Isles offers some advantages in terms of the duration of solar radiation, expressed in terms of 'hours of bright sunshine'. The longer summer days, in combination with an atmosphere which contains relatively little suspended dust and smoke, can lead to sunshine hours not dissimilar, if not superior on some occasions, to those recorded at coastal resorts in southern England. The story is, however, very different during the winter when daylength is relatively shorter. For much of the time the greater amount of cloud cover in Scotland brings about a marked reduction in the amount of direct solar radiation reaching the ground. This is particularly true in the higher parts of Scotland which, because of lower temperatures and more westerly location, tend to have a more persistent cloud cover. Land at 300m OD can receive on average 0.7 MJm^{-2} less solar radiation per day than the less cloudy lowlands (Harding 1979) but even here sunshine can be masked by fog (Jones et al 1979).

There is very little useful data on solar radiation in the region. The data that do exist are in the form of hours of bright sunshine, which are recorded using a Campbell-Stokes Sunshine Recorder. Daily averages have been derived for each month for Ardtalnaig, Arrochymore and Drummond Castle (**Figure 1**) for the period 1972 to 1990 using observations published in the Monthly Weather Report of the Met Office. Long-term averages were available from the Met Office for Stirling (Batterflats) and Drummond Castle. Averages (1972-1990) for Stirling (Sewage Works) were derived from the station's short 7-year record by making cross reference to longer records from Ardtalnaig, Arrochymore, Drummond Castle and Edinburgh Airport (Turnhouse). Local data were also compared with sunshine hours for Sandown on the south coast of the Isle of Wight.

The mean daily hours of bright sunshine in each month (**Table 2**) show very little local variation during the summer months, values falling between 5.4 and 6.0 hours in June, although there is a tendency for the more westerly, and more cloudy, location at Arrochymore to receive slightly less sunshine. The strongest differentiation within the Region occurs during the winter months when the solar elevation can be less than 10° above the horizon which means that local topography exerts a strong influence on the amount of solar radiation received. Deep glens and steeper north-facing slopes can be in shade for lengthy periods. Ardtalnaig, for example, is on a north-west facing slope and will often be shaded in the first half of the day while Stirling is in a more open location and receives almost double the amount of sunshine (**Table 2**). Differences in angle of slope of the ground surface, and in aspect, also have a marked effect on solar radiation received and in an area of such diverse topography there is considerable local variation in the solar heating of surfaces. For example, Bridge of Allan, with its south-facing aspect, contrasts in winter with the much cooler north-facing Gargunnock 9 km away across the Forth Valley which affects, for example, the duration of snow-lie at this time of year.

A comparison between Stirling (Sewage Works)

Table 2   **Average daily hours of bright sunshine** **(1971-1990 unless shown)**

	J	F	M	A	M	J	J	A	S	O	N	D	Yr
1	0.63	1.87	2.93	4.63	5.53	5.39	5.32	4.46	3.34	2.04	1.07	0.34	3.14
2	1.00	1.89	2.79	4.84	5.51	5.47	5.28	4.43	3.29	2.26	1.50	0.80	3.26
3	1.14	2.24	3.39	5.19	5.79	5.85	5.77	5.18	4.15	2.80	1.86	0.72	3.68
4	1.31	2.43	3.35	5.29	5.80	5.98	5.43	4.84	4.00	2.81	1.76	0.94	3.67
5	1.42	2.12	3.09	4.81	5.81	5.94	5.87	5.02	3.81	2.74	2.02	1.01	3.65
6	1.46	2.33	3.08	4.87	5.68	5.87	5.29	4.58	3.68	2.66	1.84	1.17	3.55
7	2.11	2.82	4.20	6.39	7.44	7.48	7.82	7.57	5.55	3.83	2.83	1.92	5.01
5/7	0.67	0.75	0.74	0.75	0.78	0.79	0.75	0.66	0.69	0.72	0.71	0.53	0.73

1 = Ardtalnaig   2 = Arrochymore   3 = Drummond Castle
4 = Drummond Castle (1951-1980) 5 = Stirling (Sewage Works)   6 = Stirling (Batterflats, 1951-1980)
7 = Sandown (Isle of Wight)

and Sandown (**Table 2**) illustrates the effect of a greater cloud cover at the former which results in ratios of sunshine hours which are less than 1.0 for every month despite the greater summer daylength in Scotland. The difference amounts to more than 1.5 hours per day between June and September. The effect of differences in daylength is seen in the pattern of ratio values, the most unfavourable (0.53) during December when days are shortest, and the most favourable (0.79) when days are longest in June.

Air Temperature

There is a large amount of variation in air temperature in central Scotland, most of which arises from the effects of topography. During the summer, sheltered valleys and glens can become exceptionally warm, especially if aspect is favourable and there is a degree of shelter from the wind. Areas such as the Forth lowlands, for example, experience some of the highest daytime temperatures in Scotland during the summer (Met Office 1989). In contrast, during the winter months the combined effects of shading and the drainage of cold air towards lower ground can make these same areas very cold, especially away from the ameliorating influence of coastal waters. The exposed hills offer a sharp contrast to the valleys below and are generally very much cooler during the summer but in autumn and winter they can lie above a layer of cold air which may develop over lower ground.

A 30-year record (1951-1980) for Stirling (Batterflats) provides a clear indication of the very variable nature of the thermal climate of the area. While the 30-year average of daytime maximum temperatures follows a relatively subdued annual cycle (**Figure 2**) reaching its lowest (5.6°C) in January and

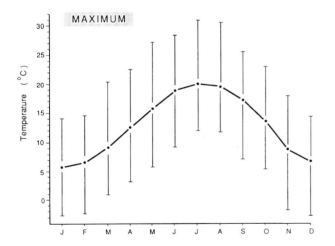

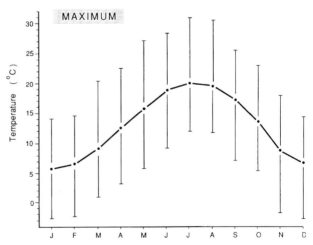

Figure 2   Average maximum and minimum air temperatures at Stirling (Batterflats) 1951-1980

highest (19.5°C) in July, and lagging one month behind the winter and summer solstices, the most noteworthy feature is the very large range of variation about the average. In winter, daytime temperatures over the period varied between -2.4°C and 13.8°C (range = 16.2°C), and in summer the extremes were 9.0°C to 30.4°C (range = 21.4°C). The lowest winter maxima tend to be associated with incursions of cold continental air from the east when pressure is high over Scandinavia, while the highest maxima usually occur in warm Tropical maritime air from the south or south-west. The highest summer maxima occur during spells of warm sunny anticyclonic weather while dull rainy spells tend to subdue daytime temperatures. The thirty-year average of nocturnal minimum temperature varies from -0.6°C in January to 10.0°C in July and also exhibits large variation about these values particularly during the winter months. Nocturnal temperature varied between -17.0°C and 11.0°C (range = 28.0°C) during the winter. Winter minima are usually lowest in cold easterly winds or on calm anticyclonic nights, while cloud and rain tend to keep temperatures well above freezing. The last spring frosts in the Forth valley usually occur before mid-May and the first autumn frosts tend to appear towards the end of October although early frosts in mid-September 1986 caused considerable damage to sensitive plants in the Forth valley.

The 20-year averages of air temperature for other stations provide some insight into the localised nature of temperature variation (**Table 3**). Over lower ground there is very little spatial variation in daytime maximum temperature and it is altitude which provides the principal variation. A comparison of records from the Ochil Hills (Carim Lodge) climatological station, at 332m OD on open moorland, and Parkhead, at 35m OD in the shelter of the north side of the Forth valley, has revealed large differences in daytime temperatures with a gradient of change between them of 9.8°C per 1000m rise (Harrison et al 1988), which is close to the 10.2°C per 1000m derived for the Balquhidder area

(Johnson 1985).

There is much more variation in minimum temperature, which is due to the greater sensitivity of night-time temperatures to local surface conditions, principal amongst which are topography and proximity to extraneous sources of heat such as expanses of open water and urban and industrial areas. The difference in minimum temperature between Parkhead and Ochil Hills stations is considerably less than that for maximum temperatures, and the mean gradient change between them is only 7.1°C per 1000m (Harrison et al 1988). This is to some extent a result of more stable thermal structures in the lower atmosphere as the underlying ground surface cools radiatively, but it is also attributable to the katabatic, or downslope, drainage of denser cooler air into lower-lying areas. This 'frost-hollow effect' is well developed in many parts of the Region. Aberfoyle, for example, experiences a very high incidence of frosts as a result of its location in a sheltered valley. An investigation carried out in the Forth valley during the cold winter of 1981-82 revealed a frost-hollow to the west of Stirling in which the valley floor was 5°C cooler than 100m higher up the valley sides (Harrison et al 1982). The greatest frequency of these valley inversions of temperature occurs between October and December when air reaching the Region can be relatively mild after its passage over a relatively warm sea. When this flows over radiatively cooled land surfaces there is a strong thermal contrast between air and surface which can create inversions of temperature. This is reflected in the seasonal incidence of air frosts at Ochil Hills (Carim) and Falkirk (**Table 4**) in which there is tendency for a greater frost frequency at the lower station in October.

The effect of elevation on air temperature results in a rapid decrease in the length of the growing season. The rate of decrease calculated for the Ochil Hills is 16.7 days for every 100m increase in elevation (Harrison et al 1988) which means, for example, that there is a reduction in the length of the growing season of seven weeks between the Forth Valley and the land above

Table 3   Average maximum and minimum air temperatures 1981 - 1990

		J	F	M	A	M	J	J	A	S	O	N	D
1	max	5.4	5.6	7.8	11.3	15.0	17.4	19.3	18.4	14.9	11.6	8.1	6.3
	min	0.5	0.3	1.6	2.6	5.6	8.4	10.5	10.0	7.7	5.7	2.9	1.2
2	max	6.4	6.6	9.1	11.5	14.8	17.2	19.8	19.0	16.2	12.8	9.1	7.1
	min	0.8	0.8	2.1	3.2	6.1	8.9	11.1	10.8	8.3	6.0	3.0	1.2
3	max	6.9	7.1	9.4	11.8	15.3	17.7	20.3	19.4	16.5	13.4	9.5	7.7
	min	1.4	1.3	3.0	4.1	7.0	9.8	11.8	11.5	9.1	6.8	3.7	2.2
4	max	3.7	3.6	5.8	8.8	12.3	14.6	16.8	16.1	13.0	9.9	6.5	4.9
	min	-1.6	-2.1	-0.7	0.3	3.2	5.9	8.1	7.9	6.0	3.7	0.7	-0.6
5	max	6.3	6.8	9.0	11.7	15.3	17.5	20.0	19.2	15.9	13.0	9.3	6.3
	min	0.3	0.2	1.6	3.0	5.7	8.5	10.8	10.2	7.9	5.2	2.5	0.8

1 = Ardtalnaig   4 = Ochil Hills (Carim)
2 = Falkirk (Sewage Works)   5 = Parkhead
3 = Grangemouth (Refinery)

Table 4   Average number of air frosts per month 1981 - 1990

	J	F	M	A	M	J	J	A	S	O	N	D
Ardtalnaig	11.3	11.8	7.8	5.3	0.6	0.0	0.0	0.0	0.3	1.6	3.5	7.4
Falkirk	10.5	9.9	6.5	4.3	0.5	0.1	0.0	0.0	0.1	2.0	6.5	10.2
Grangemouth	9.2	7.9	3.8	2.2	0.1	0.0	0.0	0.0	0.0	1.3	5.3	8.0
Ochil Hills	17.3	17.0	12.6	9.6	1.5	0.1	0.0	0.0	0.4	1.4	8.0	12.8

300m which encloses it.

The effect of open water on air temperature is more difficult to detect but the waters of the Forth Estuary act to reduce the range of diurnal temperature variation (Harrison 1987a). The possible influence of the larger lochs on air temperature is shown in the record for Ardtalnaig on the shores of Loch Tay which reveals a lower frequency of winter frosts than would perhaps be expected for a location at 130m OD (Smith 1974). Urban and industrial areas tend to increase night-time temperatures as heat-islands develop. The slightly higher minimum temperatures and reduced incidence of frost at Grangemouth would appear to indicate this, but it is difficult to separate the industrial influence from that of the nearby open waters of the estuary. Existing models of urban effects on minimum air temperatures (Oke 1990) suggest that the centre of Stirling could possibly be as much as 3.0°C warmer than the surrounding rural area on clear nights with light air movement. Measurements taken by students of Stirling University have shown that the centre is more likely to be between 0.5°C and 1.0°C warmer.

Soil Temperature

The temperature of the soil depends not only on solar heating and night cooling but also on the thermal properties of the particular soil. The considerable variation in topography in the region ensures that soil temperatures show very marked differentiation between, for example, warm south-facing and cold north-facing slopes, and between valley side and valley floor on calm and cold winter nights. In Scotland as a whole, mean annual soil temperatures at a depth of 0.3m decrease at an average rate of 0.6°C for every 100m increase in elevation (Gloyne 1971). There is considerable variation in soil within the Region (Grieve, this volume) from the lowland peat of Flanders Moss to the blanket peat and peaty podzols of the hills, and from the deep brown-earths of the lowlands to the skeletal soils of rocky highland slopes. The peats tend to be slow to warm but also slow to cool while temperatures in soils with a greater mineral content tend to change much more readily.

Daily fluctuations in soil temperature are greatest close to the ground surface and decrease very rapidly with depth so at 0.3m diurnal variation is generally less than 1.0°C. Variation at this depth is greater in sandy than in peaty soils. Soil temperatures at 0.3m are recorded at 09.00 GMT at some weather stations and provide an indication of seasonal changes in thermal conditions beneath the ground surface. Records for Stirling (Batterflats) and Parkhead (**Figure 3**) are indicative of typical fluctuations in a lowland brown-earth. The annual cycle of temperature reaches a minimum in January or February and a maximum in July or August, approximately six weeks after the winter and summer solstices respectively. There is considerable variation about these averages but winter freezing at this depth is exceptionally rare. However, during the harsh winter of 1981-82 soil temperatures in the Stirling area fell below freezing from mid-December to late January and shallow water-pipes remained frozen well into February in colder soils.

Airflow

As Scotland tends to be affected by Atlantic depressions for much of the year, average wind speeds tend to be higher on the whole than in England and Wales, and a westerly directional component is dominant. Easterly airflows, however, are not uncommon and can be particularly strong in the

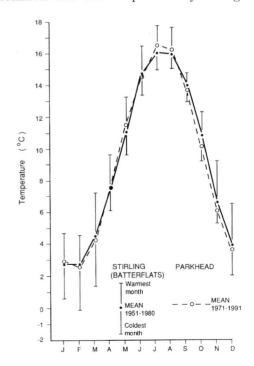

Figure 3   Average soil temperatures (0.3m) at Stirling (Batterflats) and Parkhead

Stirling area when high pressure becomes established over Scandinavia and the winds blow up the Forth valley from the North Sea. This tends to be most frequent during spring and early summer but during the winter such an east wind has been referred to evocatively as 'Siberian'. Average wind strength is greatest from November through to March when most, but certainly not all, gales tend to occur. The most memorable such gale was the 'Glasgow gale' of January 15th 1968 when westerly winds gusted over 45ms^{-1} and caused a great deal of structural damage. Since the mid-1980's there has been an increase in the number of winter storms, one of the most recent of which was the Burn's Day storm of January 1990 when maximum wind speeds exceeded 25 ms^{-1} over the Region (McCallum 1990).

In the absence of a continuous wind record, 09.00 GMT observations of wind force (Beaufort scale) and wind direction at Parkhead for the period 1982-1990 provide some indication of airflow character in the Forth valley. There is a well-marked diurnal variation in wind speed (Harrison 1987b) in which a minimum is reached immediately after sunrise and a maximum towards mid-afternoon, so observations at the fixed hour of 09.00 GMT will not only contain a large proportion of calms (21.7%) but will also not fully reflect the true nature of airflow. Parkhead is exposed to the south-east and very sheltered to the north which is reflected in the distribution of wind directions. However, the observations confirm that the most frequent wind direction is south-westerly, the direction from which most of the strongest winds tend to blow (**Figure 4**).

Local topography has marked effects on airflow not least of which is an increase in mean wind speed with altitude. This is a result of greater wind speeds at higher elevations in the free atmosphere combined with the vertical compression of airflow as it rises over the hills and a general reduction in topographic shelter on higher ground. It is not an uncommon experience for hill walkers to set off in gentle breeze in the glens only to find a gale blowing on the exposed hill tops. Spot observations made in the early afternoon on the southern slope of Dumyat by students of the University of Stirling have established that the effect of altitude on wind speed is highly variable (**Figure 5**). The long-term average difference in wind speed between 35m OD and 305 OD is 4.2 ms^{-1}, or a rate of increase of 1.6 ms^{-1} per 100m rise.

The orientation of relief features in relation to airflow exerts an important influence on both wind speed and direction. Winds which are blowing along valley axes can be laterally constricted and thereby strengthened. In Strathyre, for example, both northerly and southerly winds are strengthened, while Glen Dochart has a particular exposure to south-westerly gales and cold north-easterly winds. In Stirling the west-east orientation of the Forth valley leads to a dominance of winds from these directions. When airflow is at right-angles to valley axes the surrounding hills

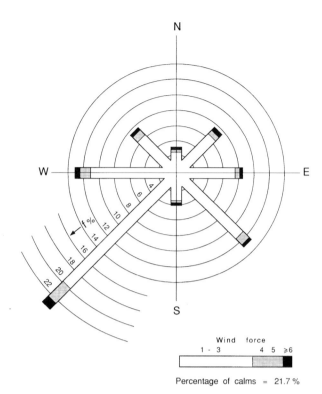

Wind force

| 1 - 3 | 4 | 5 | ≥6 |

Percentage of calms = 21.7 %

Figure 4   Frequency distribution of wind direction and force at 09.00GMT at Parkhead 1982-1990

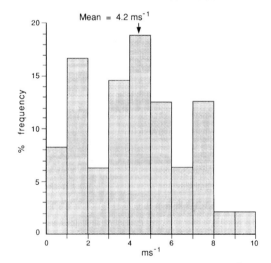

Figure 5   Differences in mean wind speed between 35m and 305m OD on Dumyat

can provide a degree of shelter from the wind. This is in evidence in the Hillfoots towns which are favourably sheltered from cold northerly winds. However, wind blowing off the hills in this way tends to be gusty in nature and violent eddies can cause localised structural damage.

Under certain atmospheric stability conditions

airflow across local hills may result in the development of a standing wave in the lower atmosphere, known as a 'lee-wave' (Fyfe 1953). While the downflow part of such waves can result in very localised gustiness on the valley floor, the corresponding upflow provides ideal soaring conditions for birds and can also lead to the formation of lee-wave clouds. These appear as parallel bands of cloud at right angles to the wind direction or, more frequently, as the distinctive lens-shaped cloud *Altocumulus lenticularis*.

The open Forth Estuary to the east experiences much stronger winds than the adjacent coastal plain especially when they are blowing on-shore. A wind record for the intertidal mudflats at Skinflats, for example, revealed much higher frequencies of gales (Harrison 1987b). A land-sea breeze system develops along the Forth coast, which is reinforced by thermal contrasts between cold hill and warm valley surfaces inland. On warm and calm days, from April through to October, an on-shore easterly sea-breeze may develop which sometimes reaches Stirling by mid-day. Its arrival is marked not only by a freshening of the wind but also by a distinct drop in temperature in the cooler North Sea air. The wind dies away during the late afternoon and may be replaced by a cool westerly breeze from inland, which is strengthened by the drainage of cooler denser air from the hills and valley

sides. This nocturnal breeze is less vigorous than the sea-breeze but is readily detected in, for example, changes in direction in smoke plumes from near-ground sources such as bonfires.

Humidity

The amount of water vapour present in the atmosphere can be expressed in terms of the partial pressure it exerts, known as vapour pressure, or more frequently as the ratio between vapour pressure and saturation vapour pressure, known as relative humidity. Although both change over the course of 24 hours, values are routinely derived from measurements of dry bulb and wet bulb temperature taken only at 09.00 GMT. Observations from Parkhead for the period 1987 to 1990 provide an indication of the typical seasonal variation of both vapour pressure and relative humidity (**Figure 6**). Vapour pressures are highest during the summer months when evaporation of surface water into the atmosphere is greatest. However, because there is an inverse relationship between air temperature and relative humidity, the latter is highest during the winter months when it can approach 100%, or saturation point.

Visibility through the lower atmosphere tends to be poorest at the extremes of relative humidity. The

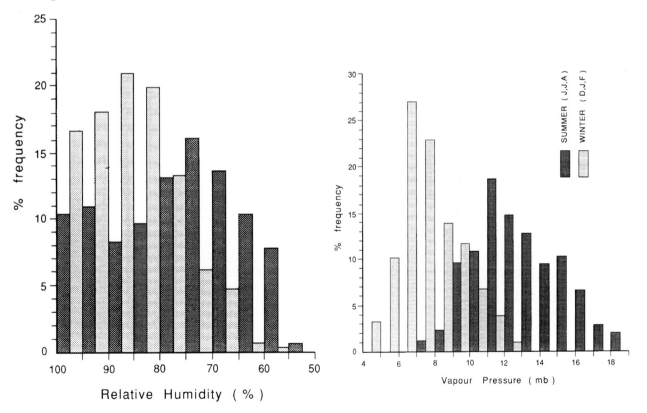

Figure 6 Frequency distribution of relative humidity and vapour pressure at 09.00GMT at Parkhead 1987-1990

controlling effect of the open sea on the Scottish climate means that relative humidities rarely fall to values low enough to be associated with dust hazes but as humidities approach 100% visibility is reduced in mist and fog . Fogs occur in four main forms, sea, ground, valley and hill fogs.

As warm air travels westwards across a cooler North Sea, particularly during the late spring and early summer, it picks up moisture and also becomes more stable. The result can be either low stratus cloud or ground-level sea fog known as 'haar' along the east coast of Scotland. Dixon (1939) referred to the Firth of Forth as being the foggiest sea area around the Scottish coast but sea fogs tend to have a very limited penetration landwards up the Forth Estuary. The greatest penetration tends to occur on an incoming tide (Harrison et al 1985) and the fog may also be driven inland by a sea breeze, but it rarely travels far beyond Alloa. Falkirk is thus more prone to this type of fog during the summer than Stirling (**Table 5**).

Table 5 Total number of fogs recorded at 09.00GMT at Parkhead and Falkirk 1981 - 1990

	winter (D,J,F)	spring (M,A,M)	summer (J,J,A)	autumn (S,O,N)
Falkirk (Sewage Works)	19	6	11	21
Parkhead	28	16	4	20

Ground fogs are a direct result of the rapid radiative cooling of moist ground surfaces on relatively calm cloudless nights. As the air from the surface cools upwards these fogs tend to start as shallow mists over wetter ground in the early evening. By sunrise a more substantial fog layer may have developed but this rarely exceeds a depth of 50 to 100m. The drainage of cold air into damp valley floors makes these areas particularly vulnerable to a derivative form referred to as valley fog. Viewed from the clear hills above, structures such as the Wallace Monument can stand above a mobile sea of white cloud. The risk of both ground and valley fogs is greatest during the longer winter nights when cooling is greatest and away from the warming influence of the open sea and deep water lochs, and extraneous sources of heat such as the Grangemouth industrial complex. There is a measureable increase in fog risk westwards from the coast, the combined winter and spring total number of fogs at 09.00GMT at Parkhead being almost double that at Falkirk (**Table 5**), but the Forth valley is not particularly prone to fog occurrence.

The association between fogs and particular weather patterns is expressed in local weather sayings (Harvey 1900) -

"*When the mist taks the hills* (Ochils)
Guid weather spills (rain is due)
When the mist taks the Howes (Hillfoots)
Guid weather grows" (stable, fine weather is due)

Thus valley fogs tend to be associated with calm anticyclonic weather patterns, but hill fog is linked to wet 'dreich' weather. Low stratus cloud can shroud hills down to very low elevations often as warm fronts approach from between south and south-west. For example - (ibid)

"*When the castle of Stirling gets a hat* (low cloud)
The carse of Cornton pays for that" (rain falls)

The cloud which often shrouds the hills is also a result of the cooling of the atmosphere as it is forced to rise from the lowlands. Observations made on Dumyat by students of Stirling University indicate that vapour pressure may decrease with elevation during the afternoon at an average rate of 0.3 mb per 100m rise, which is due to the greater amount of mixing of the air in the stronger hill winds. The over-riding control over relative humidity is, however, the sharp decrease in temperature as elevation increases. An increase in relative humidity frequently leads to a capping of cloud on the hills which means that average cloud cover in many parts of Scotland is much higher than, for example, southern England where topography is more subdued.

This cloudiness not only reduces visibility but the cloud water droplets may also be intercepted by ground and vegetation surfaces. Although the amounts intercepted are relatively insignificant but they have been associated with episodes of high deposited acidity (Davies et al 1984). The combination of dampness, low temperature and high wind speed can also lead to a real risk of hypothermia in the unwary hill walker. The most obvious association is, however, between cloudiness and the precipitation of water from the atmosphere in the form of rain or snow.

Precipitation

In the region, the precipitation of liquid water (rain and drizzle) from the atmosphere is derived mainly from eastwards moving Atlantic depressions and their associated frontal systems (cyclonic), but also occurs as a result of locally rapid vertical uplift of the atmosphere above warm surfaces (convectional) and hill slopes (orographic). Cyclonic rainfall is greatest in the west and decreases eastwards across Scotland, a gradient of change which is enhanced by the rainshadow effect of the Highlands and orographic rain in the hills themselves. The general pattern of rainfall is thus one in which there is a very large difference between the wetter high ground to the west, where annual rainfall totals exceed 2500mm, and the drier coast of the Forth Estuary which receives less than 900mm, a decrease of more than 1600mm over the relatively short distance of 70km. However, this is far from being a uniform gradient of change. The rate of decrease down the Forth valley is relatively gentle as is shown in a comparison between Flanders Moss (15m OD) and Falkirk (3m OD)

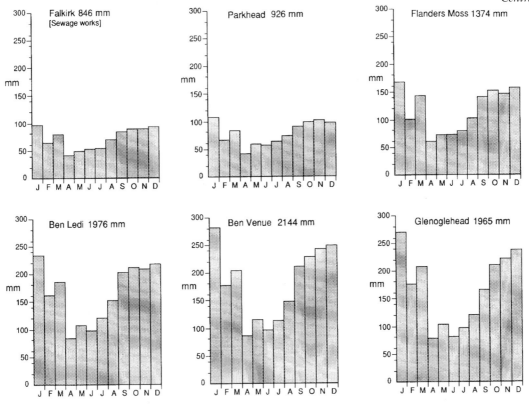

Figure 7   Average monthly rainfall 1971-1990

(**Figure 7**) annual rainfall decreasing by a little more than 500mm over 50km. In contrast, between Flanders Moss and Ben Venue (274m OD) there is a difference of 800mm over the short distance of 15km. Altitudinal gradients are very steep and are the dominant controlling factor in the spatial distri-bution of rainfall in the Region. A comparison between two raingauges in the Gargunnock Hills to the west of Stirling, only 3km apart but differing in altitude by 340m, has shown that the altitudinal gradient of increase in annual rainfall is of the order of 120mm for every 100m rise (Harrison 1986).

The year to year and month to month variation in rainfall, which is typical of a mid-latitude maritime climate, is shown in the monthly rainfall observations from Parkhead (**Figure 8**). Variation in each month's rainfall has been shown as the range between upper and lower quintiles and is clearly greatest during the winter months, and smallest between April and June. Monthly mean rainfalls throughout the Region (**Figure 7**) reveal a broadly consistent seasonal pattern with April to June being, on average, the driest months, and October to January the wettest. This pattern is principally driven by the greater duration and intensity of cyclonic rainfalls during the winter months but the marked increase from June through to September can also be attributed, in part, to summer rainstorms, some of which are accompanied by thunder. An analysis of references to exceptional rainstorms in the *Stirling*

Journal from 1870 to 1919 revealed a very clear maximum frequency during the summer months (Harrison 1980). However, thunderstorms are a relatively infrequent occurrence, there being usually less than 8 per year, in comparison to, for example, East Anglia where this figure exceeds 20.

A particular feature of the seasonal distribution of rainfall in Scotland is that the amplitude of variation between wettest and driest months increases westwards (Met Office 1989) (**Figure 7**). The ratio between average rainfalls in wettest and driest months increases from 2.4 at Falkirk, to 2.6 at Parkhead and 2.8 at Flanders Moss, while the ratios for the higher raingauges exceeds 3.0. Although part of this can be attributed to seasonal changes in altitudinal rainfall gradients, which are at their greatest in the wet winter months, it does mean than differences in rainfall between western and eastern parts of the region are greatest in winter and least in spring and early summer.

Substantial daily rainfalls in excess of 50mm are rare on lower ground but a 24hr fall of 68.3mm in November 1984 resulted in a catastrophic slope failure in Menstrie (Jenkins et al 1988). Rainfalls of this magnitude are more frequent on higher ground and McNaughton (1963) has estimated that in the higher western parts of central Scotland a daily fall of 63mm may be exceeded on average almost twice per year. Rowling (1989) has shown that during the 1980's there was a sharp increase in the frequency of heavy falls,

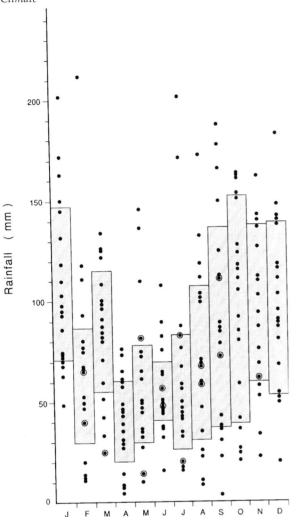

Figure 8   Rainfall dispersion diagram for Parkhead

which was reflected in the number of times local rivers overtopped their banks. At the other end of the scale, the number of days with rainfall in excess of 0.2mm and of 5.0mm at Parkhead reflects the pattern of average monthly rainfalls, but heavier falls of 25mm or more have occurred at all times of the year (**Figure 9**). The fact that 51.5% of days are, on average, rain-days (>0.2mm) emphasises the general wetness of the climate.

Between September and April, particularly on higher ground, some precipitation falls in the solid form of snow. The depth of snow accumulation, and the length of time that it lies on the ground surface, are both extremely variable and depend on thermal conditions in the atmosphere and at the ground surface, which are affected in turn by topography. Snow also may not remain where it falls but is liable to drift from exposed sites and accumulate in sheltered hollows, and in the lee of structures such as hedges and stands of trees.

Snow in the Region may fall in a cold arctic or polar *continental* airstream arriving from between south-east and north-east. Under such conditions, air and surface temperatures are usually well below 0ºC and the snow is relatively powdery, which leads to a problem of drifting. Snow also falls in cold arctic and polar *maritime* air arriving from between west and north. This wetter snow is more adhesive and less prone to drifting and, as ground surface temperatures tend to be somewhat higher than in an easterly wind, much of the snow may melt as it lands, particularly on lower ground. Snow from both west and east tends to fall in bands which sweep across the region and its accumulation can vary quite considerably over relatively short distances. For example, snow may lie in Stirling but not in Bridge of Allan only 4km away.

One of the strongest influences on both snow depth and duration of snow lie is altitude, through enhanced precipitation and lower temperatures, and there is a sharp increase in snow risk over small height increments. The result is a very marked contrast

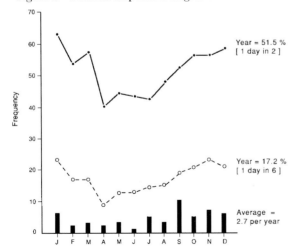

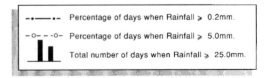

- –•– –•–   Percentage of days when Rainfall ≥ 0.2mm.
- –○– –○–   Percentage of days when Rainfall ≥ 5.0mm.
- Total number of days when Rainfall ≥ 25.0mm.

Figure 9   Frequencies of days when fixed rainfall thresholds were exceeded at Parkhead 1971 - 1990

between the snow-prone west of the Region and the Forth valley where snow is less frequent, and where a degree of protection from northerly winds is afforded by the Ochil Hills.

From the limited amount of snow data available it has been possible to estimate the number of days with snow lying at 09.00GMT during the winter months November to March using a statistical model developed for Scotland (Harrison 1992). Under continental easterly snow-bearing weather systems the coastal plain of the Forth Estuary may experience 15 to 20 days with snow lying, while in the hills to the west this increases to 85 days or more at 400m OD. In contrast, under milder westerly maritime conditions the coastal lowlands receive very little snow or may remain snow-free, while at 400m there will be 20 or more days with snow lying. Using the same model, Strathyre (135m OD) should have an average of 25 to 30 days with snow lying but the observed value for the site is only 19 (Dunsire 1971), a discrepancy which serves to illustrate the importance of exposure to snow-bearing winds. Although Strathyre is exposed to northerly winds it is sheltered from those from east or west.

Endpiece

The effects of topography and variation in the the type of ground surface, from the Forth Estuary to the Highlands, have been superimposed on a middle-latitude climatic setting in which the principal gradients of change lie along a west to east axis. The dominance of westerly over easterly winds, in terms of both frequency and strength, means that, although much of the region drains to the North Sea, its climate is a blend of both west and east coast characteristics. Travellers passing through this part of Scotland can expect to experience a rich tapestry of climatic conditions from the drier, milder and calmer estuarine lowlands to the generally wetter, cooler and windier hills to the west. In their travels they would also come across isolated pockets of contrasting warmth and shelter amongst the hills, and bleak exposure along the shores of the estuary. Indeed, such is the richness of the variety that neighbouring gardens are likely to experience subtly different climatic conditions.

The depressions which sweep in from the Atlantic ensure that the climate is characterised by a day to day variation in which long spells of consistently similar weather are relatively infrequent. Consecutive years are rarely similar in character and there is some evidence that in recent years there has been a subtle change in the climate of central Scotland. Annual rainfall has been increasing steadily to stand as much as 40% higher than during the drier years of the early 1970's, and winters have become slightly milder with less snow on the hills. Whether these are part of a longer-term climate change linked to global warming or whether they are merely a feature of the natural variation of climate remains an unanswered question.

ACKNOWLEDGMENTS

The 1951-1980 averages for Drummond Castle and Stirling (Batterflats) were supplied by the Met Office (Edinburgh) and all other data, with the exception of Parkhead and Ochil Hills (Carim), were extracted from the *Monthly Weather Report* of the Met Office (Bracknell). Professor Keith Smith's 1974 analysis of the climate of the Stirling area proved to be a very helpful and informative starting point, for which I am very grateful. Thanks must go to the very many groups and societies on whom I have inflicted my enthusiasm for the local weather over the years, and who have shared so freely of their own experiences. In this respect particular thanks go to the late Professor 'Chuck' Brown who was very much a fellow enthusiast.

REFERENCES AND FURTHER READING

DAVIES, T. D., ABRAHAMS, P. W., TRANTER, M., BLACKWOOD, I. L. 1984. Black acidic snow in the remote Scottish Highlands. *Nature* 312, 58-61

DIXON, F. E. 1939. Fog on the mainland and coasts of Scotland. *Met Office Professional Notes* No.88 (Vol.VI No.8)

DUNSIRE, A. 1971. Frequencies of snow depths and days with snow lying at stations in Scotland for periods ending winter 1970-71. *Climatological Memorandum* No.70. Met Office

FYFE, A. J. 1953. Lee waves of the Ochil Hills. *Weather* 7, 137-139

GLYONE, R. W. 1971. A note on the average annual mean of daily earth temperature in the United Kingdom. *Meteorological Magazine* 100, 1-6

HARDING, R. J. 1979. Radiation in the British uplands. *Journal of Applied Ecology* 16, 161-170

HARRISON, S. J. 1980. Rainfall in the Stirling area. *Forth Naturalist and Historian* 5, 23-34

HARRISON, S. J. 1986. Spatial and temporal variation in the precipitation-elevation relationship in the maritime uplands of Scotland. In: Erpicum, M. (Editor) *Proceedings of the International Conference on Topoclimatology and its Applications, Liege 1985.* University of Liege Press, 117-133

HARRISON, S. J. 1987a. Climatic conditions over the estuary and Firth of Forth, Scotland *Proceedings of the Royal Society of Edinburgh* 93B, 245-258

HARRISON, S. J. 1987b. Characteristics of airflow over estuaries with particular reference to the Forth Estuary, Scotland *Intertidal Microclimate Research Projects Reports* No.8 University of Stirling 59pp

HARRISON, S. J. 1992. Global warming and winter road maintenance *Highways and Transportation* 39, 45 - 50

HARRISON, S. J. and HARRISON, D. J. 1988. The effect of elevation on the climatically determined growing season in the Ochil Hills. *Scottish Geographical Magazine* 104, 108-115

HARRISON, S. J. and PHIZACKLEA, A. P. 1985. Tide and the climatology of fog occurrence in the Forth Estuary. *Scottish Geographical Magazine* 101, 28-36

HARRISON, S. J. and WALLACE, R. 1982. Frost in the Forth Valley, Scotland. *Journal of Meteorology (UK)* 7, 84-86

HARVEY, W. 1900. Rhymes, proverbs, and proverbial expressions of Stirling and district. *Transactions of the Stirling Natural History and Archaeological Society* 22, 10-11

JENKINS, A., ASHWORTH, P. J., FERGUSON, R. I., GRIEVE, I. C., ROWLING, P. and STOTT, T. A. 1988. Slope failures in the Ochil Hills, Scotland. *Earth Surface Processes and Landforms* 13, 69-76

JOHNSON, R. C. 1985. Mountain and glen contrasts at Balquhidder. *Journal of Meteorology (UK)* 10, 105-108

JONES, R. J. A., TINSLEY, J. and COURT, M. N. 1979. Mesoclimatic studies in the upper Dee basin, Aberdeenshire. *Meteorological Magazine* 108, 239-308

McCALLUM, E. 1990. The Burns Day storm 25 January 1990. *Weather* 45, 166-173

McNAUGHTON, D. 1963. Heavy falls of rain in short periods in the counties around Glasgow. *Memorandum No 1.* Glasgow Weather Centre 3pp

METEOROLOGICAL OFFICE. 1989. The Climate of Scotland: Some Facts and Figures HMSO London

OKE, T. R. Boundary Layer Climates (2nd edition). Routledge, London

ROWLING, P. 1989. Rainfall variation and some implications for flooding in the Allan catchment, Central Scotland. *Weather* 44, 146-154

SMITH, K. 1974. Climate and hydrology In: Timms, D. W. G. Editor. The Stirling Region. University of Stirling pp 47-65

Cumulus clouds forming over the hills to the south of Stirling   (S.J.Harrison)

Rippling effect in clouds over the University of Stirling caused by the Ochil Hills   (J. McArthur)

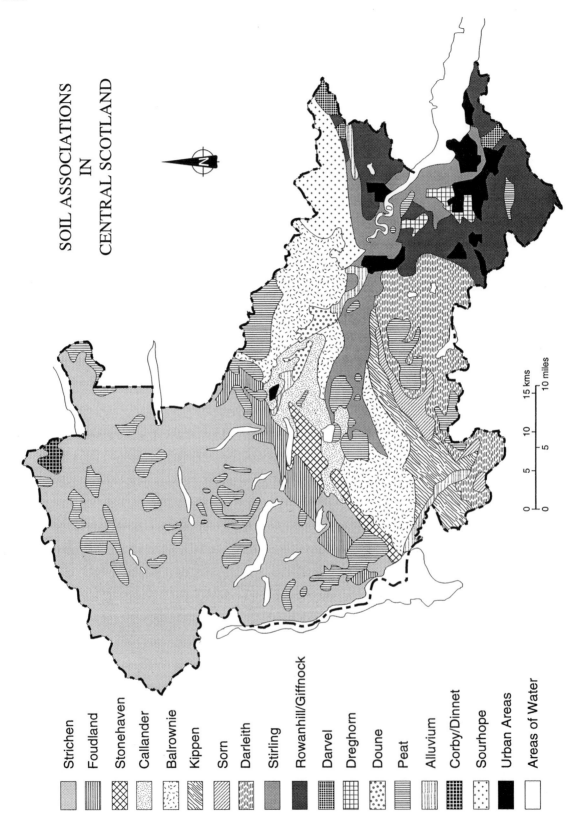

SOIL ASSOCIATIONS
IN
CENTRAL SCOTLAND

Strichen
Foudland
Stonehaven
Callander
Balrownie
Kippen
Sorn
Darleith
Stirling
Rowanhill/Giffnock
Darvel
Dreghorn
Doune
Peat
Alluvium
Corby/Dinnet
Sourhope
Urban Areas
Areas of Water

Figure 1 Distribution of major soil associations (Soil Survey)

Soils

I. C. Grieve

INTRODUCTION

Soils have been systematically surveyed by the Soil Survey of Scotland since 1947, with the aim of achieving an understanding of their distribution and characteristics. The main effort in the early years was devoted to surveying the arable areas of Scotland. Maps were published initially at a scale of 1:63360 (1 inch per mile) and later at 1:50000. Land use capability maps detailing the potential for agricultural land use were first published with the soil maps in the 1960's. A more recent review of the mapping programme led to the authorization of a 1:250000 mapping programme for the whole of Scotland in 1978. This used the existing maps of the Midland Valley and Southern Uplands and a new rapid survey of the previously unsurveyed areas in the Highlands. 1:250000 maps of soil and land capability for agriculture for the whole of Scotland were published in 1982.

The soil classification used by the Soil Survey of Scotland for the 1:250000 maps is based on field criteria, with only limited use of chemical characteristics determined by laboratory analysis. The classification includes five **divisions**, each of which is subdivided into **major soil groups**:

1 **Immature soils** have indistinct or weakly developed horizons. The only major group of agricultural significance is the group of **alluvial soils**, developed in recent river alluvium.
2 **Non-leached soils** have free lime (calcium carbonate) and a neutral or alkaline pH. No soils in this division are mapped in central Scotland.
3 **Leached soils** have uniformly coloured B horizons, no free lime and acid pH in the A and B horizons. Two major groups are mapped: **Podzols** are acid and have a surface organic horizon, a grey E horizon and a brighter coloured B horizon. The colours of the E and B horizons are the result of leaching of iron, aluminium and/or organic matter from the E to the B horizon. In the less acidic **brown earth** group, the surface organic matter is mixed in with the mineral soil by the action of earthworms, horizon boundaries are less distinct and the colour is more uniform.
4 **Gleys** form under waterlogged, anaerobic conditions. Iron is chemically reduced giving the soil a greyish colour, rather than the reddish brown of oxidised iron compounds. **Ground water gleys** develop where the ground water table is high and the intensity of gleying increases with depth. **Surface water gleys** form in areas of high rainfall and the intensity of gleying decreases with depth.
5 **Organic soils** form under waterlogged conditions, where the breakdown of plant material added to the soil is slowed and partially decomposed organic material accumulates to a thickness of greater than 50 cm. The division includes one major group, **peat**. Each major soil group is subdivided into more homogenous **subgroups** and soil **series**. A soil series includes all soil profiles with the same arrangement of horizons and developed from the same parent material (i.e. same type and age of rock or sediment). Soil series are usually named after the locality where first mapped.

The 1:250000 scale used for the national soil map is too small to show individual soil series, and the map makes use of a further classification unit, the soil **association**. An association is a grouping of soil series developed on one parent material type. The national soil map shows soil associations and map units within these. In the key the soil groups in each map unit are listed. For many areas a map unit is broadly equivalent to a soil series. Thus the 1:250000 map identifies the Stirling association, developed on estuarine and lacustrine silts and clays. The association includes map unit 488, noncalcareous gleys, which is mapped on the larger 1:63360 maps as the Stirling series.

DISTRIBUTION AND CHARACTERISTICS OF SOILS

Figure 1 shows the distribution of the major soil associations mapped within central Scotland by the Soil Survey. The percentage area occupied by each association in the region is shown in **Table 1**. Areas were measured by recording the number of times each unit occurred at the 1 km intersects of the National Grid. A similar method was used by the Soil Survey to estimate map unit areas for individual map sheets and for Scotland as a whole. Areas of map units on individual map sheets were quoted to the nearest 0.1%. Percentages for the smaller area of this region are probably reliable to within 0.2%.

The pattern of occurrence of soil associations

Table 1: Percentage by area of each soil association

Association	%	Association	%
Alluvium	2.1	Basin Peat	1.6
Blanket Peat	9.0	Balrownie	8.4
Callander	3.4	Carpow	1.0
Corby/Dinnet	0.5	Darleith	6.4
Darvel	1.1	Doune	1.0
Dreghorn	0.5	Foudland	3.1
Gleneagles	0.2	Kippen	3.6
Rowanhill	9.3	Sorn	1.3
Sourhope	2.2	Stirling	7.3
Stonehaven	1.3	Strichen	36.8

consists of geologically controlled southwest/northeast trending bands. North and west of the Highland Boundary Fault, the Strichen association is dominant with significant occurrences of Foudland and Peat soils. Tills derived from sandstones and acid metamorphic rocks occur as a band from southern Loch Lomond to Callander and are the parent material of the Stonehaven and Callander associations. Balrownie and Kippen association soils occur on sandstone tills to the south east of this. Volcanic rocks and tills of the Ochil and Gargunnock/Touch Hills are dominated by the Sourhope and Darleith associations respectively, with blanket peat on the higher ground. Till derived from Carboniferous rocks in the southeast of the Region are the parent material of the Rowanhill/Giffnock association. The Carse of Stirling cuts across this zonation from Flanders Moss in the west to Grangemouth in the east and is dominated by Stirling association soils over silts and clays. Alluvial soils also interrupt the pattern, with significant areas mapped along the flood plains of the Rivers Teith, Forth, Allan and Endrick Water.

Table 2 gives the percentage area (to the nearest 1%) of major soil groups within each association in central Scotland. In the discussion, reference will also be made to the map unit numbers shown on the 1:250000 Soil Survey maps. The principal soil groups included in each map unit are indicated in this discussion, but many map units, particularly in the upland areas, consist of more than one soil type, with variations related to topography. For fuller information the reader should consult the publications of the Soil Survey of Scotland.

The Carselands: Stirling and Basin Peat Soils

Raised beach silts and clays deposited in estuaries and lake beds when sea levels were relatively higher during the Glacial and Post-Glacial form the parent material of the Stirling association soils, which are found on 7.2% of this area of central Scotland. The association occurs as a well defined band coinciding with the Carselands of the Forth valley east of the Lake of Menteith. The Carse was previously covered by basin peats, the most extensive remnant of which is Flanders Moss. Reclamation of the peatlands has exposed gley soils (map unit 488; 86% of the association) and gleyed brown forest soils (unit 487, 14%). Climatic conditions range from warm and wet to warm and moderately dry, with annual precipitation decreasing from 1500 mm in the west of the Carse to 900 mm in the east.

Gleys: Grey silty clays forming infills to buried valleys and estuaries occur at altitudes of about 15 m OD and are the parent material of the noncalcareous gleys of the Stirling series. Topsoils are silt loams with moderate or weak blocky structure. When these soils are used for pasture, soil structures are better developed and the stability of aggregates is greater. Fungi, age-hardening (thixotropy) and organic compounds released from plant decay are all known to be important influences on stabilisation of the structural aggregates in grassland soils (Molope et al 1985, 1987). Under arable cultivation organic matter content of the soil is reduced and surface aggregates are more likely to break down when wet (slaking). The fine particles thus dispersed form a thin surface layer which can reduce aeration, permeability and seedling emergence. Subsoil textures are heavy silty clay loams and silty clays. Permeability is moderate when subsoils are drier than field capacity in the summer, but in the winter subsoil cracks close and permeability is poor. The land is therefore fairly difficult to manage for arable agriculture, as satisfactory seedbeds are difficult to obtain. Arable crops are restricted to cereals, with permanent pastures in the wetter western areas. Subsoil drainage is necessary and the gleys must also be managed carefully to avoid the formation of surface crusts.

Brown forest soils with gleying (unit 487)

Table 2:			Percentage by area of each soil group within associations with more than one soil group.					
Association	G	GBF	BF	PP	PG	P	SA	Pt
Balrownie	23	56	3	2	14	1	-	-
Callander	24	-	70	-	-	5	-	-
Darleith	16	7	48	20	5	-	-	-
Foudland	22	-	10	10	23	18	4	-
Kippen	21	-	43	7	24	5	-	-
Rowanhill	28	58	3	-	8	3	-	-
Sorn	44	37	9	-	9	-	-	-
Sourhope	-	-	61	39	-	-	-	-
Stirling	86	14	-	-	-	-	-	-
Stonehaven	-	-	27	9	-	64	-	-
Strichen	6	-	-	35	17	28	8	6

Key to soil groups

G:	gley	GBF:	brown forest soil with gleying	BF:	brown forest soil	PP:	peaty podzol
PG:	peaty gley	P:	podzol	SA:	sub-alpine podzol	Pt:	peat

occur on higher terraces at about 30 m OD, where the parent material is a reddish brown silty clay. These soils have some evidence of gleying, but are generally better drained than the gleys. Topsoils are mainly silt loams, but many of the drainage and structural problems noted above for the gleys also limit the agricultural use of the gleyed brown forest soils. Soils of this unit in the east are mainly used for cereals and ley grassland, with permanent pasture in the west.

Remnants of the original **basin peat** occur in Flanders Moss and the smaller Blairdrummond Moss. The peats are thick (1-5 m), and much of the land has been afforested with conifers. Flanders Moss is also important as a Site of Special Scientific Interest, as it represents a rare example of a large lowland raised bog.

The Carboniferous Lowlands and plateau: Rowanhill and associated soils

The parent material of the Rowanhill and Giffnock associations is drift derived from Carboniferous sandstones, shales and limestones. Tills with a clay loam texture dominate, although the texture is lighter (sandy clay loam) where the proportion of sandstone material is large. Climatic conditions are warm and moderately dry, with 900-1250 mm annual precipitation. The Rowanhill and Giffnock associations cover 9.3% of the area of central Scotland and soils are dominantly gleyed brown forest soils (58% of the association) or gleys (28%) on the clay loam tills.

Map units 444 and 445, mainly **gleyed brown forest soils** with subsidiary brown forest soils and gleys respectively, dominate the areas east of Alloa and around Falkirk. Undulating lowlands with till ridges and drumlins are the characteristic topographic features. Unit 444 has well structured sandy loam and loamy topsoils and permeable subsoils, and forms some of the best agricultural land in the area with few limitations for sustained arable cropping. Unit 445 has moderately structured loamy topsoils and subsoil drainage is poorer. Drainage is thus necessary for arable cultivation or intensive pasture, and careful management of pastures to prevent soil structure damage is necessary. **Noncalcareous gleys** (map unit 446) are developed from clay loam tills on more subdued topography than unit 445 and occupy 28% of the area of the association. Weakly or moderately structured loamy topsoils and very slowly permeable subsoils require drainage for productive use and rush infestation is a problem on pastures on undrained land. Most of the land is under grass and careful management is needed to prevent compaction damage by livestock trampling . **Brown forest soils** of the Darvel and Dreghorn associations have also been mapped in this area, on sand and gravel parent materials of fluvioglacial and raised beach origin respectively. The Darvel and Dreghorn associations each account for around 1% of the area of the region. These have moderately or well structured sandy loam topsoils and are fertile and well suited to arable cultivation, although the Darvel soil is readily leached of nutrients and can be stony especially where the parent material is gravelly.

The Gargunnock/Touch Hills: Darleith and Sorn soils

These hills rise sharply to the south of a line between Balfron and Stirling and are underlain by basaltic lavas of Carboniferous age. Climate is cool and wet with up to 1800 mm annual precipitation. The dominant soil association is the Darleith, covering 6.4% of the area of the region, while the Sorn association (1.3% of the region) occurs as a narrow band to the northwest of the hills.

Darleith soils have a parent material of drifts derived from basaltic rocks and **brown forest soils** (map units 147, 150 and 158) account for almost 50% of the area of the association. Topsoils are loamy and have well developed crumb and blocky structures. Rock outcrops often limit cultivation, but on undulating lowlands much of the land is cultivated. **Gleys** (unit 149; 19% of the area) occur on massive tills and these have weakly structured subsoils of low permeability. The soils are mainly under long-ley or permanent pasture, and require under-drainage for cultivation or intensive grassland use. At higher altitudes, **peaty podzols**, **peaty gleys** and **peats** (unit 154, 16%) occur under white bent grassland and heather moor. The surface peaty horizons of these soils are acid and often waterlogged. Grazing is of poor quality and possibilities for reclamation are limited. The highest parts of the plateau are dominated by blanket peat.

The parent materials of the Sorn association are clayey tills derived from Lower Carboniferous and Upper Old Red Sandstone sediments and lavas. Two soil groups dominate, **gleys** (unit 467; 44%) and **brown forest soils with gleying** (unit 466; 37%). Moderately and weakly structured loamy topsoils are subject to trampling by cattle (poaching damage) especially where the silt content is large. Clayey subsoils are slowly permeable and require efficient under-drainage to reduce waterlogging of the topsoil. Although these soils provide good moisture holding capacity in drier parts of eastern Scotland, they are of limited use for agriculture in the wetter areas of central Scotland.

The Ochil Hills: Sourhope soils

The Ochil Hills lie to the north of the Carse of Stirling, but only partly within the boundary of Central Region. Climate is cool and wet with up to 2000 mm annual precipitation. Underlying geology consists of lavas of Old Red Sandstone (ORS) age, principally basalts and andesites. Loamy and clay loam till derived from the lava is the parent material of the Sourhope association, which occurs on 2.2% of the area of the region.

Sourhope soils are dominantly **brown forest soils** (unit 472; 61% of the association) at lower altitudes on steeper slopes and **peaty podzols** (unit 476; 39%) at higher altitudes. The brown forest soils are freely drained and loamy in texture, but shallow and stony. Permanent pasture is the dominant land use on the steep slopes of the western Ochils. Peaty podzols on loamy drifts have a semi-natural vegetation of heather moor and *Nardus stricta* grassland and these soils are of limited value for grazing. Improvement by ploughing and reseeding is possible on less steep slopes. As in the Gargunnock Hills, the higher areas of the plateau have extensive blanket peat.

The Old Red Sandstone Lowlands: Balrownie soils

The Old Red Sandstone (ORS) lowlands are dominated by tills derived from sandstones of Lower and Upper ORS age, with localised occurrences of fluvioglacial sand and gravel in the upper Teith valley. Precipitation ranges from 1100-1500 mm, increasing on higher ground nearer the hills, and temperatures are warm. The Balrownie association occurs on Lower Old Red Sandstone tills and occupies 8.4% of the area of the region. These tills are bright reddish brown compact loams or clay loams with a moderate stone content, and the soils often show features of gleying.

A **brown forest soil with gleying** (map unit 41; 56% of the association) is the principal soil group mapped. Imperfect drainage minimises drought susceptibility, but structural breakdown and capping of fine seedbeds and susceptibility to poaching damage to grasslands are agricultural limitations. Other map units occurring as more than 10% of the area of the association are **gleys** (unit 42; 23% of the association) and **peaty gleys** (unit 46; 14%). The gleys are poorly drained and more subject to capping than the gleyed brown forest soils. They require comprehensive drainage schemes for improved pasture or arable use. The peaty gleys occur under moorland at altitudes of more than 250 m and require comprehensive drainage for reclamation and pasture improvement. Trace element problems can occur on both these soil types when improvements are carried out.

Kippen soils occur on Upper ORS sandstone tills (3.6% of the area). The till is sandier in texture (loam or sandy clay loam) and a **brown forest soil** (map unit 337; 43% of the association) is the most common group. This soil is generally well drained and occurs on undulating lowlands well suited to cultivation. **Peaty gleys** (unit 344; 24%) are mainly under rough grazing. **Gleys** on sandy clay loam tills (unit 338; 21%) have weakly structured, slowly permeable subsoils and require efficient under-drainage to prevent poaching damage if used as improved pasture.

A further 1% of the area has Doune association soils on fluvioglacial sands and gravels in the Teith valley. These are freely drained **brown forest soils** (unit 168) on gravels with sand lenses. Much of this map unit is used for permanent pasture or arable cultivation, but topsoils are often thin and stony.

The Highland border and Old Red Sandstone Uplands: Callander and Stonehaven soils

This zone lies immediately southeast of the Highland Boundary fault and includes both lowland areas and significant uplands such as the Menteith Hills. Climatic conditions vary with altitude from warm and wet to cool and wet, with annual precipitation in the range 1600 to 2200 mm. Soils belong to two associations, the Stonehaven and Callander, occupying 1.3 and 3.4% of central Scotland respectively.

The Stonehaven association is developed in colluvial drifts derived from lower ORS conglomerates and lavas. The parent material is stony and loamy or sandy in texture. Soils are dominated by **humus iron podzols** (unit 493; 64% of the association) on sandy drift. Humus iron podzols are strongly acid and their upper horizons are leached of both humus and iron. Atlantic heather moorland and acid grasslands form pastures of moderate grazing quality. On loamy drifts, **brown forest soils** (unit 490; 27%) occur. These form permanent pastures of good grazing quality. Much of the land is also afforested, mainly with conifers.

The Callander association has a greater areal extent than the Stonehaven, and is developed in generally heavier textured mixed drifts derived from rocks including acid schists and slates, acid sandstones, and intermediate and basic lavas. Parent materials thus vary in colour and texture. **Brown forest soils**, some with gleying, (unit 274; 70% of the association) occur on stony coarse-textured drift on undulating lowlands and foothills. The fine sandy texture of the topsoil increases the possibility of capping of seedbeds and most of the land is pasture. **Noncalcareous gleys** occur on compact, slowly permeable tills. Natural drainage is poor and these soils need comprehensive under-drainage for improved grass.

The Highlands: Strichen and Foudland soils

Within this large area soil patterns are extremely complex and the agricultural potential is least favourable. Relief is hilly or mountainous with intervening valleys and hummocky moraines on some valley floors, and the distribution of individual soil types is closely controlled by topography. Climate varies from warm and wet (1500 mm annual precipitation) on Loch Lomondside to cold and wet (2500 mm) in the mountain areas. Soils of the Strichen association occupy the greatest area, some 37% of central Scotland. Foudland soils occur as a narrow band north of the Fault, with a total area of 3.1%. Extensive areas of **hill peat** also occur and a small area of **humus iron podzols** of the Corby/Boyndie/Dinnet association developed in fluvioglacial sands has been mapped at the western end of Loch Tay.

The Foudland association is developed in a parent material of drifts derived from slates, phyllites and other weakly metamorphosed fine-grained rocks, mainly the Aberfoyle slates and slaty schists. The drifts are compact and contain a large proportion of silt and fine sand particles. Due to the complexity of the topography and the variability of the parent material, no one soil group dominates the association; rather the association consists of a range of soil units including gleys, peaty gleys, peaty podzols, humus-iron podzols and brown forest soils. **Brown forest soils** are limited in their areal occurrence, and restricted to sloping lower valley sides under a vegetation of broadleaved woodland or acid grasslands of good grazing potential. **Gleys** and **peaty gleys** (unit 241; 22% of the association) occur on hollows and lower slopes on compact loamy tills. These soils require efficient drainage schemes for maintenance of improved pastures; without improvements grazing quality is moderate. **Humus iron podzols** (within map units 243 and 250; a total of 31% of the association) occur on mid and upper non-rocky and moderately rocky slopes on colluvial drift. These give way to peaty podzols at higher altitudes and to peaty gleys on wetter sites. Much of this land is moderate or poor rough grazing or is afforested with conifers.

The Strichen association is developed in drifts derived from Dalradian schists and grits. These drifts are frequently colluvial and of sandy loam texture, but with considerable local variability. Soil patterns are related to topography and drift type. Much of the higher land is under blanket peat, peaty podzols or peaty gleys. Humus-iron podzols occur on steeper slopes and valley moraines, with noncalcareous gleys on gentler slopes. Brown forest soils are restricted to lowlands and lower valley slopes due to the high rainfall and base-poor parent materials. The dominant soils on the 1:250000 map are units 503, 504, 506 and 507 with 18%, 11, 18% and 15% of the area of the association respectively. Unit 503 includes humus-iron **podzols** and **brown forest soils** on well drained sites and noncalcareous and humic **gleys** in hollows. The unit occurs principally on sandy loam morainic materials in valleys and footslopes in association with acid grasslands. Unit 504 comprises mainly **peaty podzols** with some peats and peaty gleys, developed on hummocky moraines. Parent materials are sandy loams and loamy sands, with indurated horizons frequently present. Unit 506 includes humus-iron and peaty **podzols** over shallow stony drift on hill and valley slopes. Land is mainly heather moor and *Nardus stricta* grassland used for rough grazing. Unit 507 includes **peaty gleys**, **peaty podzols** and **peat** and is found in the higher rainfall northwestern part of the area. Bog and Atlantic heather moor and blanket bog dominate the unit and grazing quality is generally poor. Both the Foudland and Strichen associations have a small but significant proportion of **subalpine soils**. These are often thin with limited chemical weathering and occur on mountain summits and ridges at altitudes above 750 m.

LAND CAPABILITY FOR AGRICULTURE

The principles behind the Land Capability for Agriculture (LCA) classification evolved from a framework established by the United States Department of Agriculture in the 1960's and the classification is fully described in Bibby et al (1982). The land capability classification for agriculture is based primarily on physical characteristics of the land and integrates climate, relief and soil information. The LCA class is determined by the presence or absence of limitations to agricultural production, grouped under six limitation types. These are climate, wetness, gradient, erosion, soil properties and soil pattern. A standard of management which is appropriate to the quality of the land being classified is assumed, and those limitations which can be removed or reduced at economic cost are disregarded in the classification.

Seven capability classes are recognised. Land in classes 1-4 is defined as suitable for arable cropping, with class 1 land capable of producing the widest range of crops. Land in class 5 is capable of use as improved grassland, subdivided according to its suitability for reclamation. Land in class 6 is capable of use as rough grazing, subdivided according to pasture quality. Class 7 land has very limited agricultural value. It must be emphasised that LCA classes are not recommendations for land use, nor do they indicate the most economically profitable use for a particular area of land. Rather the classes indicate areas where a particular land use may be carried out most easily, and the classification is mainly for planning purposes. In the present context, the 1:250000 scale map provides a useful overview of the land resources of central Scotland and permits an assessment of their value and limitations for agriculture.

Figure 2 shows the distribution of LCA classes in central Scotland. A very large majority of land to the north and west of the Highland fault line falls into class 6, capable only of use as rough grazing. Limitations including cold and wet climatic conditions, thin soils, and steep slopes restrict the capability of land in this area to rough grazing. Land of very limited agricultural value (class 7) is mapped on mountain tops and steep crags. Class 5 land, capable of use as improved grassland, is found on the floors of the major valleys such as Glen Dochart, and there are very small areas of class 4 land at the western end of Lochs Tay and Earn, on freely drained podzols of the Corby/Boyndie/Dinnet association.

The major upland areas of the Midland Valley show clearly the control of LCA by altitude. Extensive areas of the summit plateaux of the Ochil and Gargunnock/Touch Hills are mapped as class 6 due to the exposure, high rainfall and short growing season. At lower altitudes class 4 or 5 land is found. Here soils are usually too thin and slopes usually too steep for cultivation. Similar limitations of wetness, climate and relief are found in the Highland border area, and here also most of the land is mapped in classes 4 and 5. Soils of the Rowanhill/Giffnock association on the

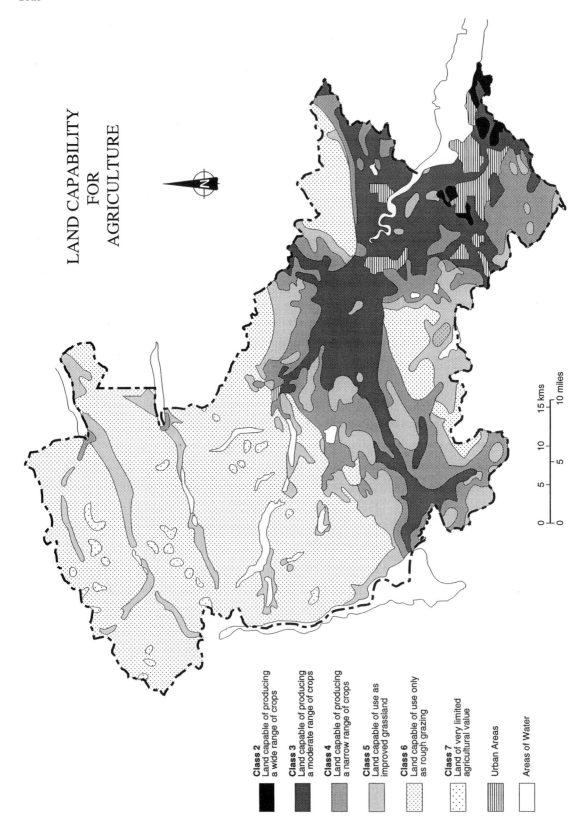

LAND CAPABILITY FOR AGRICULTURE

Class 2
Land capable of producing a wide range of crops

Class 3
Land capable of producing a moderate range of crops

Class 4
Land capable of producing a narrow range of crops

Class 5
Land capable of use as improved grassland

Class 6
Land capable of use only as rough grazing

Class 7
Land of very limited agricultural value

Urban Areas

Areas of Water

Figure 2 Land capability for agriculture (LCIA) - Distribution of classes, central Scotland

Slammanan plateau to the south of Falkirk are also grouped in classes 4 and 5, due to wetness and soil drainage limitations.

The best quality agricultural land in the region is found in the valleys of the River Forth and Endrick Water. Class 3 land is suited to arable cropping, and capable of producing a moderate range of crops. A large area of class 3 land sweeps in an arc from the southeastern corner of Loch Lomond to the estuary of the Forth. The dominant soil in this area is the Stirling association **(Figure 1)**. The soils of the Carse are good agricultural soils and the land is flat and well suited to agriculture. However, land capability is limited by wetness and heavy texture which make production of a seed bed for crops difficult. Class 2 land is capable of producing a wide range of arable crops, but only a small area is found in the region. Soils of the Dreghorn and Darvel associations around Falkirk derived from sandy textured parent materials are mapped in class 2. The only other area occurs on soils of the Rowanhill association east of Bo'ness, where climatic conditions are the warmest and driest in the region.

Table 3   Percentage by area of each LCA class within Central Region and within Scotland.

LCA	class	% Central		% Scotland	
7		1.5		3.3	
6		52.1		48.4	
	6.3		30.0		39.3
	6.2		13.5		7.1
	6.1		8.6		2.0
5		15.9		18.5	
	5.3		6.9		8.5
	5.2		8.2		7.6
	5.1		0.8		2.4
4		12.9		10.7	
	4.2		6.9		5.9
	4.1		6.0		4.8
3		17.4		15.2	
	3.2		16.1		9.3
	3.1		1.3		5.9
2		0.7		2.2	
1		0.0		0.1	

For summary definitions of LCA classes see legend to Figure 2.

Table 3 gives the percentage area of each LCA class in the region and provides a useful summary table of the quality of the land resources of Central Region. The data were obtained using the same point counting method as was used previously for the areas of the soil associations. Overall the area of land suitable for arable cropping represents 31% of the region. Due to climatic limitations there is no class 1 land, and less than 1% of the area is in class 2. 17.4% of the area falls into class 3, but the large majority of this is in the less flexible and productive division 3.2. A further 12.9% of the area is class 4 land, capable of producing a narrow range of crops and suitable for enterprises based primarily on grassland with short arable breaks.

More than 50% of the land area of central Scotland falls into class 6, capable of use only as rough grazing, and over half of this land is dominated by vegetation communities of low grazing value (division 6.3). Land capable of use as improved pasture, class 5, accounts for 16% of the area, but the majority of this is in divisions 5.2 and 5.3, where maintenance of the sward may pose problems due to trafficability and poaching difficulties.

Comparison of the areal extent of LCA classes with those for the whole of Scotland **(Table 3)** reveals a striking similarity between the two sets of figures. The very limited area of class 1 and 2 land and the dominance of class 6 land, and of poor quality grazing land within this class, are distinctive features of both Central and Scotland. The only major difference is the relative extent of class 3.2 land which accounts for almost one sixth of the area of central Scotland, reflecting the areal significance of the Carselands within this region.

LAND CAPABILITY FOR FORESTRY

Maps of Land Capability for Forestry at a scale of 1:250000 were published by the Macaulay Land Use Research Institute for the Forestry Commission in 1988. These maps are similar in nature to the LCA maps described above, but show flexibility for the growth and management of tree crops. Land is graded in one of 7 classes ranging from class F1, land with excellent flexibility, to class 7, land unsuitable for producing tree crops.

The basic division within this central region between the Forth valley and the highlands and uplands controls the distribution of land capability for forestry. The most flexible land is found in the valleys, with areas of class F1 land on alluvial soils along the Allan Water and River Devon. Extensive areas of the Balrownie and Rowanhill/Giffnock soil associations are mapped as class F2 and F3, land with very good and good flexibility respectively. Stirling association soils are the least flexible land in the Forth valley, with class F4 mapped on the gley soils and class F6 with very limited flexibility on the basin peats. Land to the north of the Highland Boundary Fault generally falls into classes F5 and F6, with that above 450-500 m in class F7, unsuitable for producing tree crops. However within the uplands there are also areas of more flexible land. Major valleys such as Glen Dochart, Glen Falloch and the lower hills to the south of Loch Ard are mapped as class F4, with moderate flexibility for growth and management of tree crops, and there is also a small area at the western end of Loch Tay where class F2 land occurs on freely drained podzols of the Corby/Boyndie/Dinnet association. The Ochil Hills and the highest parts of the Gargunnock Hills are similarly of limited flexibility or unsuitable for tree crops, but the lower Touch Hills are

Table 4 Percentage by area of each Land Capability for Forestry class within Central Region and within Scotland ˙. ˙ From Dry and Hipkin (1989)

Land Capability for Forestry	% Central	% Scotland
F1 excellent flexibility	1.2	1.0
F2 very good flexibility	15.3	5.3
F3 good flexibility	8.8	8.1
F4 moderate flexibility	18.6	13.2
F5 limited flexibility	12.7	17.6
F6 very limited flexibility	21.4	24.7
F7 unsuitable	18.6	28.1

mapped in class F4.

Table 4 shows the percentage areas of both central and the whole of Scotland in each of the 7 Land Capability for Forestry classes. From these data the flexibility of the land resources of the region for forestry is considerable. When compared with the figures for Scotland as a whole there are larger percentages of the more flexible classes F2 and F4, and consequently smaller percentages class F5, F6 and F7 land. The area of land mapped as unsuitable for forestry is much larger than that mapped as unsuitable for agriculture (1.5%; Table 3), due to the fact that rough grazing is not limited to the same extent as forestry by exposure at high altitudes. Thus much of the land in class 6 of the LCA (suitable for use as rough grazing) is not suited to the growth of tree crops due to exposure.

SOILS AND ACID DEPOSITION

Concern over the effects of acid deposition on streamwater chemistry and on fish biology has led to a considerable research effort in recent years towards understanding the processes which alter the chemistry of water as it passes from precipitation to the stream. Much of this research has focussed on the role of the soil in modifying the chemistry of water passing through it. Where water percolates slowly through soil horizons interaction between the water and soil minerals may be beneficial or detrimental depending on the concentration of neutralising ions in the soil and on the weatherability of the soil minerals. When the soil contains significant quantities of weatherable minerals and is rich in calcium, acid precipitation is neutralised. Problems of acid deposition are most commonly found in streams draining areas dominated by less weatherable granitic rocks and acid peaty soils which can release toxic aluminium to drainage water.

Within this region, streams draining the Ochils and Gargunnock Hills are generally less acid than those draining the Trossachs Hills. **Table 5** gives results of a survey of water quality in March 1992, in which small streams draining the Gargunnock, Menteith and Trossachs hills were sampled under medium flow conditions. Mean pH was one unit greater and mean calcium some three times greater in streams draining the more base rich soils. Differences in magnesium

Table 5 Chemical composition of streams draining three hill areas.

Area, sample size Na	pH K	Ca	Mg
Menteith Hills	**6.3**	**4.1**	**1.0**
6.8	**0.3**		
(n=6)	0.2	1.3	0.3
3.4	0.3		
Gargunnocks	**6.5**	**3.7**	**1.6**
4.9	**0.1**		
(n=6)	0.3	1.1	0.4
0.3	0.1		
Trossachs	**5.5**	**1.4**	**0.7**
4.0	**0.05**		

All values except pH are given as mg/l; upper bold figure is mean, lower figure is standard deviation.

and sodium concentrations were less pronounced, since these elements are also added in rain water. Longer-term studies of streams in the Trossachs draining acid schists, grits and slates indicate mean streamwater pH in the range 4.0-5.0 and calcium concentrations in the range 0.4-2.0 mg/l^{-1}. Streamwater aluminium concentrations of up to 0.45 mg/l^{-1} and an absence of trout from many streams have been reported. Harriman and Morrison (1982) found greatest acidity and aluminium in forested catchments, and more recent research (Miller et al 1990) suggests that Sitka spruce may enhance sulphate concentrations and acidity compared to Norway spruce. The annual mean calcium concentration of 31.4 mg/l in a small stream draining andesites and basalts on the Ochil Hills (Grieve 1986) is more than 10 times that of the Trossachs streams.

The existence of large differences in streamwater chemistry among catchments within a small region indicates that maps of soil and geology may be useful for prediction of likely impacts of acid deposition on streamwaters. Such mapping exercises often use the concept of a 'critical load', the quantity of acidity deposited on an area which that area can tolerate without adverse effects. Soil and rock mineralogy determine critical loads for soil and freshwater acidification, and maps show that critical loads are generally larger for soils (Department of the Environment 1991). The area to the north of the Highland fault has the smallest critical loads, and is thus most sensitive to acidification. More recent maps based on the 1:250000 Macaulay Land Use Research Institute soil database indicates the likelihood of acid waters occurring under different flow conditions (Langan and Wilson, in press). In most of central Scotland south of the Highland fault acid waters will not occur. On the Ochil and Gargunnock Hills acid waters are likely to occur only at moderate to high flows, when flow is derived from the acid soil horizons. North of the Highland fault where soils and rocks are both acid, acid waters are likely to occur under all flow conditions.

CONCLUSION

The distribution of soils and land resources within central Scotland is controlled by the geology and relief of the region. Its most basic division occurs at the Highland Boundary fault. Peats and peaty soils are common to the north of the fault, where soils vary considerably with topography. To the south of the fault, gleys and brown forest soils dominate, except on the highest parts of the Gargunnock and Ochil Hills where soils are similar to those of the Highlands. Land capability for agriculture and for forestry are similarly split, with less flexible land to the north and more flexible land to the south. Sensitivity to acidification is greatest in the north. Central Scotland possesses a diversity of soil and land resources not found in any other region, and from this point of view may thus be said to be a microcosm of Scotland as a whole.

REFERENCES AND FURTHER READING

Reports and Maps

BIBBY, J.S., DOUGLAS, H.A., THOMASSON, A.J. and ROBERTSON, J.S. 1982. Land Capability Classification for Agriculture. Soil Survey of Scotland Monograph, Macaulay Institute for Soil Research, Aberdeen.

BOWN, C.J. and SHIPLEY, B.M. 1982. Soil and Land Capability for Agriculture, South East Scotland. Macaulay Institute for Soil Research, Aberdeen.

DEPARTMENT OF ENVIRONMENT. 1991. Acid Rain - Critical and Target Loads Maps for the United Kingdom. Air Quality Division, Department of Environment, London.

DRY, F.T. and HIPKIN, J.A. 1989. Land Capability for Forestry in South-East Scotland. Macaulay Land Use Research Institute, Aberdeen.

SOIL SURVEY OF SCOTLAND. 1984. Organization and Methods of the 1:250000 Soil Survey of Scotland. Macaulay institute for Soil Research, Aberdeen.

Articles

GRIEVE, I.C. 1986. Controls of concentration and loadings of major ions in a stream draining intermediate igneous rocks. *Earth Surface Processes and Landforms* 11, 287-291

HARRIMAN, R. and MORRISON, B.R.S. 1982. Ecology of streams draining forested and non-forested catchments in an area of central Scotland subject to acid precipitation. *Hydrobiologica* 88, 251-263

LANGAN, S.J. and WILSON, M.J. 1992. Predicting the regional occurrence of acid surface waters in Scotland using an approach based on geology, soils and land use. *Journal of Hydrology*, in press.

MILLER, J.D., ANDERSON, H.A., FERRIER, R.C. and WALKER, T.A.B. 1990. Hydrochemical fluxes and their effects on stream acidity in two forested catchments in central Scotland. *Forestry* 63, 311-331

MOLOPE, M.B., GRIEVE, I.C. and PAGE, E.R. 1985. Thixotropic changes in the stability of moulded soil aggregates. *Soil Science Society of America Journal* 49, 979-983

MOLOPE, M.B., GRIEVE, I.C. and PAGE, E.R. 1987. Contributions by fungi and bacteria to aggregate stability of cultivated soils. *Journal of Soil Science* 38, 71-77

The Carse of Forth, looking westwards from above Bridge of Allan (Drumrie Road). The Carse is said to be the largest flat area of land in Scotland.

Vegetation and Flora

J. Proctor

INTRODUCTION

Central Scotland, considered as the present Central Regional Council area, comprises large parts of the Watsonian vice-counties of Stirlingshire and West Perthshire (with Clackmannan) with a smaller part of mid-Perthshire (VC's 86-88). Much of this area was discussed by Proctor and Bannister (1974) and the aim of the present paper is to up-date their account and to extend it to cover the whole of the Central Region. The vegetation and flora remain difficult to assess accurately because the regional boundaries coincide neither with those of the Watsonian vice-counties nor with the 10 km national grid squares of the 'Atlas of British Flora' (Perring & Walters 1976).

In the nineteenth century much of the region was as well surveyed as any in Scotland largely owing to the efforts of skilled amateur botanists, particularly Robert Kidston of Stirling and Francis Buchanan White of Perth. Kidston is renowned throughout the world for his work on the fossil flora of the Rhynie Chert and much of his earlier work was concerned with the fossil plants of the rocks of the Carboniferous period which are well represented around Stirling. An excellent biographical account of Kidston is that of Edwards (1984). Colonel Stirling of Gargunnock collaborated with Kidston to produce a meticulously compiled Flora of Stirlingshire which was published in parts in the *Transactions of the Stirling Natural History and Archaeological Society* between 1891 and 1900. The area north of the Forth was included in the Flora of Perthshire edited (from Buchanan White's manuscript after his death) by J.W.H. Trail in 1898.

Over the last two decades there have been several publications dealing with the flora. The most readily accessible sources of recent information are: the species distribution maps in Perring and Walters (1976); the check list for Perthshire plants (VC's 87-89) (Smith *et al* 1992) (which includes records from outside and within the Central Region); a check list of plants of the Falkirk district (VC's 84-86) (Stewart 1986); a lively account of the floristic features of Stirlingshire (VC 86) by Mitchell (1983); and the 'Wild Plants of Glasgow' (Dickson 1991) which has many records for part of VC 86. Herbarium specimens of local plants exist in Glasgow University, The Smith Institute and Museum in Stirling, the Perth Museum and Art Gallery, and the Kelvingrove Museum, Glasgow.

The Region has a wide range of vegetation types which include woodlands, cultivated land, waste ground and grassland, heathland, lochs, fens and rivers, bogs and mires, saltmarshes, sub-montane rock outcrops (including dolomitic serpentinite and copper, lead and zinc ores), and montane vegetation. The *Vegetation of Scotland* (Burnett 1964) provides a background to the vegetation although it contains few references to sites specifically in the area.

Nearly all the information in the present paper refers to vascular plants which are named according to Stace (1991). Mosses and liverworts are given Latin names only and these are taken from Smith (1976) for mosses, and Smith (1990) for liverworts. There is some published information on the fungi (Crockhart 1978; and Watling 1980, 1981) which is not dealt with further here.

HISTORY OF THE VEGETATION SINCE THE ICE AGE

All of Scotland was free of glaciers by 8000 BC and much of Central Scotland had lost its ice long before that, perhaps as early as 11000 - 12000 BC (Price 1983). Following the withdrawal of the main ice sheets there began a period of more settled conditions which allowed the development of lake sediments and peat. These deposits contain preserved and still identifiable pollen grains and the changes that have occurred in the vegetation can be deduced from the examination of this pollen from different levels in the sediments. A summary of the earlier pollen analytical work in the area is in Dickson (1977).

Such pollen analyses have shown that sparse vegetation, consisting mainly of grasses, sedges and a few dwarf shrubs with mosses, followed in the wake of the ice. Much rock debris would have been exposed, and continually disturbed by frost action, at this time. The developing vegetation cover increased to a closed tundra but even by about 9000 BC there were still few or no trees. Donner (1957) and Vasari and Vasari (1968) examined the pollen deposits at a small reservoir about four miles north of Drymen. The site is the nearest example with very early, 'Late-glacial' remains. Tree pollen was only a low percentage of the total and it was considered to have been blown in from distant sites. Many species apart from grasses, sedges and heaths have been recorded from these early sediments including 'weeds' such as Docks and Sorrels (*Rumex* spp), Willowherbs (*Epilobium* spp) and aquatic species, Bulrush (*Typha latifolia*) and Alternate Water-milfoil (*Myriophyllum alterniflorum*). Most of the species were recorded in more recent sediments but two genera, Meadow-rue (*Thalictrum*) and Rock-rose (*Helianthemum*) were not. These include light-demanding species which occur on base-rich soils and which can be interpreted as having disappeared in the face of competition from other species and as a result of progressive soil leaching.

The climate became colder again around 9000

BC and there was a return to much frost movement of the soil and extremely open vegetation. This period ended about 8300 B.C. and was followed by a rapid amelioration of the climate and a marked change in vegetation. There are a number of pollen samples within the area for this later period. Recent work includes that of Stewart, Walker and Dickson (1984) for the Dubh Lochan (near Loch Lomond); Lowe (1982) for a site near Callander; and Lowe & Walker (1981) for a site near Tyndrum. A detailed comparison of these studies is beyond the scope of the present paper but the general picture remains similar to that outlined by Durno (1956) from work on samples from Flanders East Moss and Darnrigg Moss. Following the climatic amelioration there was a rapid invasion of trees. (Birks (1989) has given a detailed account of the spread of tree species following their invasion of Britain.) Birch (*Betula* spp) was dominant, together with some Scots Pine (*Pinus sylvestris* ssp. *scotica*) and a sporadic occurrence of Alder (*Alnus glutinosa*). Around 7000 BC there was a great increase in Hazel (*Corylus avellana*); Oak (*Quercus* spp) and Wych Elm (*Ulmus glabra*) increased to some extent but less than in England and Wales. Around 5500 BC there was a rapid increase in Alder and a decrease in Birch and Scots Pine. Stewart (1983) has described the occurrence of Alder remains dating from about 4200 BC in the peat of the Campsie Fells. Up to about 3500 BC forest was at its greatest extent; in low-lying areas on good soils there was forest of Oak, Ash (*Fraxinus excelsior*), Elm and Alder with varying proportions of Birch; on the lower and middle slopes of the hills there were Birch, Alder, Aspen (*Populus tremula*), Rowan (*Sorbus aucuparia*), Willow (*Salix* spp), and Hazel, with probably a zone of Birch and Willow at higher altitude. The amount of Scots Pine in these forests was probably greatest on the poorer soils and this species would have been most common in the north and west of the region. (Dickson (1992a) has provided an account of the complex history of Scots Pine in Scotland). The altitudinal limit of trees at this time was about 1000 m, much higher than at present. In the few areas above the tree line there may have been a zone of heath, and above this, montane grassland communities. The only lowland areas without forest would have been developing raised bogs and saltmarshes.

There was a sudden decline in Elm pollen around 3000 BC which may have been connected with the first influence of man, since there is evidence that Elm was selectively used as a fodder plant (Pennington 1969). Rackham (1980) suggested that a disease may have caused the Elm decline and it is possible that both a disease, and the activities of man who helped to spread it, combined to cause the decline. Extensive forest clearances by man followed so that by the time the Romans arrived much of Scotland was deforested (Dickson 1992a). (Earlier ideas of widespread forest clearance by the Romans themselves have now been abandoned). Detailed pollen analyses from Flanders Moss (Turner 1965) indicate that, about 2000 years

ago, there was much clearance of forest. The Dubh Lochan site of Stewart, Walker and Dickson (1984) seems exceptional for the region in showing no substantial deforestation until the last 1000 years.

An interesting account of the remains of edible plants from the Iron Age broch, at Fairy Knowe, near Buchlyvie, has been given by Boyd (1983). The broch (or its predecessor, a timber roundhouse) was occupied from sometime during the first century AD until about 200 AD. Boyd reported finding the remains of cereals (including species and varieties no longer cultivated in Britain): principally Six-rowed Barley (*Hordeum vulgare*) but also Wheat (*Triticum dicoccum* and *T. compactum* or *T. aestivum*) and Bristle Oat (*Avena strigosa*). Further evidence suggested that the cereals were locally processed and cultivated nearby. There were also several weed species, most of which are generally regarded as contaminants of cereal crops. Finally, two further plant remains suggested that the broch's inhabitants had some dependence on woodlands. Hazel nut fragments were very abundant and the nuts were probably collected from the wild, although there was perhaps some management of the Hazel. Ramsons (*Allium ursinum*) remains suggest that this plant also was being eaten or at least used for medicinal or religious purposes and this is discussed further by Dickson (1992b).

The extensive forest clearance was followed by a period in which the lowland forest largely recovered, although a climatic deterioration beginning about 500 BC had probably favoured the replacement of the upland forest of flat areas by blanket peat. However, an exploitation of primeval forest that was to end in its almost total destruction began early in the medieval period. During the 12th and 13th centuries there is evidence that many trees were felled to provide fuel for the making of salt. At this time in Scotland "The greatest concentration of salt-works was on the carses bordering the River Forth, from Kalentyre (Callander) up to Stirling" (Anderson, 1967). With the destruction of wolves, deer preservation became increasingly popular and sheep farming expanded enormously, no doubt at the expense of the remaining high level forest. Deliberate clearance of the lowlands for timber and farming also continued. Evidence is beginning to emerge however, as at Mugdock Wood near Milngavie, of ancient woodsmanship (Stevenson 1990) and this may have maintained some woods for centuries against a background of general woodland decline. In the 17th and 18th centuries some of the remaining forest was probably removed for charcoal for iron smelting.

Besides forest, man has influenced every other habitat. Much of the raised bog was reclaimed in the late 18th and early 19th century by the activities initiated by Lord Kames (Cadell 1913); sheep grazing and fires have modified all the habitats above the primeval timberline with the possible exception of the very highest mountain vegetation, and even the salt marshes have been subjected to severe grazing pressures.

The area has a long history of tree planting which has offset the general woodland decline to some extent. Planting on a small scale began over 500 years ago. There was an orchard at Dunmore in 1438 (Anderson 1967), and by the end of that century there are references to the planting of trees other than fruit trees. In February 1501, 15 shillings were paid to George Campbell, gardener of Stirling, to buy sauchs (Willows) and to set them (ibid). Tree planting on private estates reached a maximum between 1750 and 1850. The plantations varied in size from large forests to belts planted for ornament and shelter. For example, the *New Statistical Account* (1845) mentioned luxuriant plantations totalling over 1800 acres (720 hectares) in the Parish of Falkirk. Substantial areas of oak woodland were planted on the east side of Loch Lomond in the eighteenth century to meet the demand for oak bark for the tanning industry (Tittensor 1970). Many details about plantations in Stirlingshire are given in Graham (1812). Since the nineteen twenties the rate of planting has been greatly accelerated, especially by the Forestry Commission, and introduced conifers are now a striking component of the vegetation.

In brief, the present vegetation of the Stirling region is similar to all other areas in Britain in that it reflects the overriding influence of man.

Woodland

There are very many woodlands, from tiny copses to forests of several hundred hectares, which are always a conspicuous part of the lowland landscape. There is much useful information about the woodlands of the survey area in Anderson (1967) and in Edlin (1969).

Roberts (1986) estimated Stirling's total woodland area as about 32000 hectares, or 15% of the total land area. Over half of this is conifer plantations established over the last 60 years, principally by the Forestry Commission. The largest of these forests are the Queen Elizabeth Forest Park, Strathyre Forest, and Carron Valley Forest. The main species planted are Sitka and Norway Spruce (*Picea sitchensis* and *P. abies*), Scots Pine, European and Japanese Larch (*Larix decidua* and *L. kaempferi*) and smaller quantities of Douglas Fir (*Pseudotsuga menziesii*), Western Hemlock-spruce (*Tsuga heterophylla*), European Silver-Fir (*Abies alba*), and Lodgepole Pine (*Pinus contorta*).

Roberts' survey of older woods (excluding those of less than 2 hectares) showed that they accounted for 12265 hectares. Of these, 266 individual sites were classed as 'ancient woodland', i.e. with a proven continuity of cover back to at least 1750. They had a total area of 3746 hectares but most are small (<11 hectares) with only three sites exceeding 101 hectares. Of this ancient woodland area however, about 40% (1475 hectares) has been converted to plantations so that only 2271 hectares remain in a semi-natural state. Long-established (i.e. between 1750 and 1860) woodland accounts for 7156 hectares of which 1914 are of semi-

natural origin and 5242 are of plantation origin. Some present-day woodlands were known to occur in 1750 but had apparently disappeared by 1860 and have been replanted later. These account for 1327 hectares and are now nearly all under plantation forests. A final category in the Roberts' survey was 'Other woodland' which accounts for 36 hectares for which no historical evidence exists but which may include ancient fragments of woodland (e.g. in narrow valleys).

The older woods are in many ways the most interesting category and Keymer (1981) has produced a classification of them based on the composition of the tree canopy. This classification (A to H) is reproduced here with notes on some of the woodland types.

A OAKWOODS

This category includes the Oak woods of the west of the Region which consist almost entirely of Oak, sometimes with Birch and which occur on very acidic soils. Many of these woodlands were coppiced in the 18th and 19th centuries to provide bark for the tanning industry. They may include some Oaks planted in the later part of the eighteenth century. Because Oak bark and timber were so valuable, other tree and shrub species were removed: hence the present uniformity of the tree species composition. There are very few large standard Oaks. The species of Oak is somewhat indeterminate and the population is dominated by intermediates between *Quercus robur* and *Q. petraea* (Cousens 1963). (Some of the purest *Q. petraea* collected by Cousens in Scotland was from Menstrie Glen in the Ochils.) Details of coppice management in Scotland are given by Lindsay (1975). Good examples of this type of wood occur on Loch Lomondside where they have been described by Tittensor (1970), Tittensor and Steele (1971) and Bannister (1978).

Keymer lists three other types of more local Oakwood which all occur on better soils and which have more species.

B MIXED VALLEY WOODS

These woods occur largely on the more nutrient-rich sandstones, limestones and basaltic lavas. They usually occur in valleys and may have Ash, Alder, Wych Elm, Oak, and Silver Birch and Downy Birch (*Betula pendula* and *B. pubescens* ssp. *tortuosa*) in the upper canopy and Hazel and Bird Cherry (*Prunus padus*) in the understorey. Some of these woodlands have a species-rich ground flora and that at Kippenrait Glen, Bridge of Allan, provides a good example. Its ground flora includes, among many other species of fern and flowering plant: Alternate-leaved Golden-saxifrage (*Chrysosplenium alternifolium*), Broad-leaved Helleborine (*Epipactis helleborine*), Bird's-nest Orchid (*Neottia nidus-avis*) **(Figure 1)**, Herb Paris (*Paris quadrifolia*) **(Figure 2)**, Wood Vetch (*Vicia sylvatica*) and Beech Fern (*Phegopteris connectilis*).

The Wych Elms in many of these woodlands have been affected by Dutch Elm disease (Greensill 1977, Neiland and Shepherd 1990).

Figure 1   Bird's-nest Orchid (*Neottia nidus-avis*): a rare woodland plant which has no chlorophyll and lives parasitically off a fungus which infects its roots.   (Bridge of Allan)

Figure 2   Herb Paris (*Paris quadrifolia*): a rare woodland plant which has unusual green petals and stamens. (Bridge of Allan)

C   MIXED ALDER WOODS

This type has some similarities with the last but occurs on wet sloping sites chiefly in the north of the region. Ash, Alder, Oak and Birch are usually present with Hazel often forming a shrub layer. The ground flora has soligenous mire species such as Remote Sedge (*Carex remota*), Marsh Thistle (*Cirsium palustre*), Marsh Hawk's-beard (*Crepis paludosa*), Common Marsh-bedstraw (*Galium palustre*), Tufted Hair-grass (*Deschampsia cespitosa*), Creeping Buttercup (*Ranunculus repens*), Yellow Pimpernel (*Lysimachia nemorum*) and Bugle (*Ajuga reptans*). A good example of this woodland type occurs at the base of Conic Hill near Balmaha.

D   ALDER WOODS

Alder occasionally forms pure stands which are large enough to be called woods.

E   BIRCH WOODS

Birch is abundant and occurs in almost all the woodland types as well as forming pure stands. Birch is a pioneer tree and most of its woodland is of relatively recent origin and likely to change by invasion of other species such as Oak and Rowan. It occurs extensively on raised bogs as at Dunmore Moss and Flanders Moss where it may be favoured by the artificially lowered water tables.

F   PINEWOODS

Native Scots Pine reaches its southern limit in the Stirling region and there are two native pinewoods, at Coille Coire Chuilc and Glen Falloch. These woods have been described by Steven and Carlisle (1959). Scattered native Scots Pine may occur elsewhere (Proctor and Bannister 1974) but the putatively native wood, just outside the Central Region at Braco Castle, has been shown to be an 18th century plantation (Blaxter and Proctor 1984).

G   JUNIPER WOODS

These occur as scattered bushes and thickets. Keymer regarded Common Juniper (*Juniperus communis* ssp *communis*) individuals as nowhere continuous enough to be called a wood, nor do they form an understorey in another woodland type. The age of the central Scotland Juniper patches may not be great.   Forbes and Proctor (1986) working a few kilometres outside the Central Region at Glen Artney, where there is a very large stand of Juniper, found it to date almost certainly from the late 19th century.

H   POLICY WOODS

This category includes the majority of the deciduous or mixed woodlands, especially those on large estates or in the grounds of large houses in the south of the region. Good examples of such woodlands are those of Airthrey, Blairdrummond, Callendar near Falkirk, Doune Lodge, Keir, Lanrick Castle, Leny, and Touch. These woodlands are very variable and often include exotic broadleaves and conifers. They can be entirely planted or modified versions of ancient woodlands.

Cultivated Land and Grassland

Much of the survey area is farmland and is discussed in the Agriculture chapter of the present book. Very briefly, the best agricultural land, such as the Stirling carse land, is arable and Oats, Wheat,

Barley, Potatoes (*Solanum tuberosum*) and Turnips (*Brassica rapa* ssp *rapa*) are grown. Hay, in which Timothy (*Phleum pratense*) predominates is another important crop of the better land. These arable lands are important for the botanist because they provide a reservoir, albeit a diminishing one, of agricultural weeds. Weeds are of course a common component of gardens and Proctor and Bannister (1974) have listed many of the species which occur in gardens in the Dunblane area. An important habitat, often very rich in the same weedy species found in cultivated ground and waste places, is roadside verges. Also found among the common plants of this habitat are the legumes Meadow Vetchling (*Lathyrus pratensis*), Common Birds's-foot-trefoil (*Lotus corniculatus*), Tufted Vetch (*Vicia cracca*), Hairy Tare (*V. hirsuta*) and Bush Vetch (*V. sepium*) and the umbellifer Cow Parsley (*Anthriscus sylvestris*). A delightful umbellifer which appears restricted to roadsides in the region is Sweet Cicely (*Myrrhis odorata*). This may be an old introduction and it is certainly commoner on verges near houses. Its leaves smell very strongly of aniseed and it may have had an ancient culinary use. An intriguing record of female plants of Butterbur (*Petasites hybridus*) was made from a roadside verge near Buchlyvie by Mitchell (1982). The male plants of this species are common but the females are much more local and generally regarded as being restricted to parts of northern England.

A stimulating paper which conveys much of the potential interest to be found in weedy species was written by Cook (1979). During the warm summer of 1977 an eruption of unusual plants occurred in the village of Menstrie on a 0.5 hectare piece of derelict land. Of the over one hundred species which occurred, twenty-six were unusual. Thirteen of the twenty-six were British plants which were rare or not recorded locally. These included Wild Mignonette (*Reseda lutea*), Hairy Buttercup (*Ranunculus sardous*), Henbane (*Hyoscyamus niger*), and Rough Marsh-mallow (*Althaea hirsuta*). Others were alien species and included the very unusual Dragonhead (*Dracocephalum parviflorum*) and the Scentless Mignonette (*Reseda inodora*). The former is a native of North America, the latter a native of south-east Europe and west Asia. The explanation of this unusual flowering event is that the area had been the site of an old rubbish tip and later a place for dairy cattle and then a chicken run. The site had been levelled in 1976 and the surface scarified, without the introduction of new soil. The treatment caused the seeds to germinate and aided by the good weather the proliferation of plants was produced. Cook's paper demonstrated how rich unlikely sites can turn out to be and the study of such sites will help us understand the composition of our changing flora.

On many farms on flatter areas there are grass fields which are ploughed every 7-10 years. Usually a crop is then taken off and they are reseeded for grassland. In addition there is much permanent grassland on less easily worked, sloping and rocky ground. The species composition of permanent grassland is closely correlated with soil type (King and Nicholson, 1964). On the better brown earth soils Common Bent (*Agrostis capillaris*) and Sheep's-fescue (*Festuca ovina* agg.) are characteristic and are accompanied by such species as Red Fescue (*Festuca rubra*), Ribwort Plantain (*Plantago lanceolata*), Wild Thyme (*Thymus polytrichus* ssp *brittanicus*) and White Clover (*Trifolium repens*). Velvet Bent (*Agrostis canina*), Sweet Vernal Grass (*Anthoxanthum odoratum*), Heath Bedstraw (*Galium saxatile*) and Tormentil (*Potentilla erecta*) occur and are increasingly common in the grassland of more acid brown earth soils. A good example of rare neutral unimproved lowland grassland occurs at Dalveich Meadows near Lochearnhead. This has a number of species indicative of neutral or basic conditions including Glaucous Sedge (*Carex flacca*), Field Gentian (*Gentianella campestris*), Fairy Flax (*Linum catharticum*) and Burnet-saxifrage (*Pimpinella saxifraga*) (R. Keymer unpublished).

The grasslands on brown earths are found mainly at lower altitudes and grade into grassland types of poorer soils. Such soils are often strongly leached and acid and may have a thick layer of mor humus which grades into peat. Common Bent and Sheep's-fescue usually persist on these soils, but are frequently replaced as dominant species by less palatable grasses such as Wavy Hair-grass (*Deschampsia flexuosa*), Purple Moor-grass (*Molinia caerulea*) and, in particular, Mat-grass (*Nardus stricta*). Other characteristic higher plant species in these poor grasslands are Bilberry (*Vaccinium myrtillus*), Brown Bent (*Agrostis vinealis*), Sweet Vernal Grass, Green-ribbed Sedge (*Carex binervis*), Heath Bedstraw, Heath Rush (*Juncus squarrosus*), and Tormentil.

Large areas of former grassland have been invaded by Bracken (*Pteridium aquilinum*), as a result of neglect over the last hundred years (e.g. on the southern slopes of the Ochils). Bracken is a serious weed since it tends to occupy the better soils, often to the exclusion of all other species. It is virtually inedible (except for the very young fronds) and poisonous to stock. Gorse (*Ulex europaeus*) and Broom (*Cytisus scoparius*) are also common plants of neglected pastures on better soils.

Heathland

Extensive areas of heath, dominated by Heather (*Calluna vulgaris*), so characteristic of hillsides in many parts of eastern Scotland, are not a conspicuous feature of the region. Such heath was probably much more widespread than it is now, particularly immediately after the initial forest clearances. It seems likely that heath has much diminished under the influence of grazing and excessive burning and has been replaced by various types of grassland (and more recently reafforested). Pollen analyses (Durno 1956) show no fall in Heather pollen which might correspond with the reduction of heathland. They include, however, the contribution from the Heather which has expanded greatly on bogs which have been drained by man. The Heather dominated communities of bog sites are discussed briefly later in this chapter.

Heather moor in the area includes sites north of the Highland Boundary Fault, such as on the eastern slopes of Meall Mor (which has now been planted with trees) and on the opposite side of the valley on Ben Each.   Scattered areas of heath occur south of the Highland Boundary Fault in the Menteith Hills, on the northern and western slopes of the Ochils, and to a lesser extent on the Gargunnock and Fintry Hills. In several places there is a 'Vaccinium edge' (Gimingham, 1964; Pearsall, 1950), e.g. on Callander Craig, of Heather and Bilberry with Crowberry (*Empetrum nigrum*) and Bell Heather (*Erica cinerea*).   Black Hill in the northern Ochils provides an easily accessible example of heath, burned for sheep and grouse. The dominant species is Heather although there are scattered individuals of Green-ribbed Sedge, Bell Heather, Tormentil and Bilberry. *Hypnum cupressiforme* is the dominant moss. Grasses are relatively abundant and are often dominant in depressions in the microtopography. They include Common Bent, Brown Bent, Wavy Hair-grass, Sheep's-fescue, Purple Moor-grass and Mat-grass. Cross-leaved Heath (*Erica tetralix*), Heath rush, Purple moor-grass and the moss *Polytrichum commune* become more abundant in the wetter areas. The many grasses suggest the gradual replacement of the heathland by grassland which is the dominant vegetation of the Ochils.

Lochs, reservoirs, fens, rivers

There is a large variety of lochs varying from the internationally renowned Loch Lomond which combines features of both lowland lakes and highland lochs, to smaller lowland lakes (e.g. the Lake of Menteith) and highland lochs (e.g. Loch Voil). Some freshwater bodies are reservoirs with an artificially raised water level (e.g. Loch Katrine), others are completely artificial (e.g. North Third Reservoir). The microscopic plant life of Loch Lomond has been described by Boney (1978) whilst the larger aquatic plants, recorded within the Loch Lomond National Nature Reserve, are given in the checklists by Idle (1978) and Mitchell & Stirling (1980). Low water levels in Loch Lomond in 1968 enabled Idle, Mitchell & Stirling (1970) to record the diminutive Eight-stamened Waterwort (*Elatine hydropiper*), new to Scotland, in the exposed mud. The species is now recorded from several other sites in the region (Keymer & Mitchell 1980; Newbold & Palmer 1983; Mitchell 1985), the opinion being that it is spreading eastwards across Central Scotland, perhaps by seeds in mud adhering to the feet of wildfowl. An intriguing record of the tropical aquatic Water Fern (*Azolla filiculoides*) has been made for Airthrey Loch, Stirling by Lassiere (1992). The rare native aquatic fern Pillwort (*Pilularia globulifera*) is recorded from Loch Lubnaig and Doune Ponds.

An example of a lowland reservoir is that at Pendreich near Bridge of Allan. The following submerged and floating species have been recorded there: Broad-leaved Pondweed (*Potamogeton natans*), Red Pondweed (*P. alpinus*), Common Water-crowfoot (*Ranunculus aquatilis*), Shoreweed (*Littorella uniflora*) and Amphibious Bistort (*Polygonum amphibia*). Regionally uncommon species such as Least Bur-reed (*Sparganium natans*) and Mudwort (*Limosella aquatica*) are to be found in the Carron Valley and Upper Glendevon Reservoirs respectively.

Vegetation types, transitional between open water and dry land, are associated with the margins of lochs, and for these I have adopted the terminology of Ratcliffe (1964) and called them fens. They are well developed where the sides of the loch are not very steep and where there has been deposition of silt. There is very good wetland vegetation by the southern banks of Loch Lomond. This has been briefly described by Mitchell (1983) and includes: a large colony of Scottish Dock (*Rumex aquaticus*); Elongated Sedge (*Carex elongata*) and Summer Snowflake (*Leucojum aestivum*) in waterlogged woods by the River Endrick; Whorled Caraway (*Carum verticillatum*), Cowbane (*Cicuta virosa*)

Figure 3   Heath Spotted Orchid (*Dactylorhiza maculata* spp. *ericetorum*): a frequent plant of peaty soils but absent from raised and blanket bogs.   (Ochils near Bridge of Allan)

and Tufted Loosestrife (*Lysimachia thyrsiflora*) on wet open ground;   Thread Rush (*Juncus filiformis*) in grassland near the loch shore; and Lesser Water-plantain (*Baldellia ranunculoides*) and Awlwort (*Subularia aquatica*) at the loch-side edge.

Around the margins of Pendreich Reservoir the following species have been recorded: Sneezewort (*Achillea ptarmica*), Marsh-marigold (*Caltha palustris*), Heath Spotted-orchid (*Dactylorhiza maculata* ssp. *ericetorum*) **(Figure 3)**, Marsh Horsetail (*Equisetum palustre*), Soft-rush (*Juncus effusus*), Ragged-Robin (*Lychnis flos-cuculi*), Creeping Forget-me-not (*Myosotis secunda*), Lesser Spearwort (*Ranunculus flammula*) and Yellow-rattle (*Rhinanthus minor*).

A rich fen occurs at the head of Loch Lubnaig and the late A. W. Robson provided the following details. White Water-lily (*Nymphaea alba*) is conspicuous in the deeper water, which in some places is fringed by large colonies of Common Club-rush (*Schoenoplectus lacustris*). In shallower waters there is an extensive sedge bed. The sedges forming distinct zones are Water Sedge (*Carex aquatilis*), Slender Sedge (*C. lasiocarpa*), Bottle Sedge (*C. rostrata*), and Bladder-sedge (*C. vesicaria*). In progressively drier ground occur White Sedge (*Carex curta*), Common Sedge (*C. nigra*) and Oval Sedge (*C. ovalis*). Shoreweed occurs in suitable places. There are some very attractive wet ground species in this locality such as Skullcap (*Scutellaria galericulata*), Water Forget-me-not (*Myosotis scorpioides*), Northern Marsh-orchid (*Dactylorhiza purpurella*), Early Marsh-orchid (*D. incarnata*), Purple-loosestrife (*Lythrum salicaria*), Greater Butterfly-orchid (*Platanthera chlorantha*), and Lesser Butterfly-orchid (*P. bifolia*). The wet ground grades into meadows through which the river, with Alders lining its banks, flows.

The rivers vary from fast-flowing mountain streams to wide, slower-flowing, meanders (e.g. the Forth above Stirling). The Allan Water at Dunblane is a good example of a rocky fast flowing stream in which the current is too swift to allow the establishment of completely submerged vascular plants. The mosses *Fontinalis antipyretica*, *F. squamosa*, *Rhynchostegium riparioides* and *Cinclidotus fontinaloides* are common submerged species. A channel, from the old mill, where the water is almost still has much Blunt-leaved Pondweed (*Potamogeton obtusifolius*). On the river margins or on rocks which are occasionally submerged the following are encountered: New Zealand Willowherb (*Epilobium brunnescens*), Tall Fescue (*Festuca arundinacea*), Monkeyflower (*Mimulus guttatus*), Pink Purslane (*Claytonia sibirica*), Water Forget-me-not, Reed Canary-grass (*Phalaris arundinacea*), Water-cress (*Rorippa nasturtium-aquaticum*), and Brooklime (*Veronica beccabunga*). Giant Hogweed (*Heracleum mantegazzianum*) is a common plant of the river banks here and its occurrence on the Allan Water and several aspects of its natural history and control were discussed by Neiland *et al* (1985).

The Teith at Callander is an example of less turbulent though still fast-flowing river. Here Alternate Water-milfoil is frequent and also present are Shoreweed, Lesser Marshwort (*Apium inundatum*) and a Water-starwort (*Callitriche* sp.) Purple Loosestrife is an attractive member of the river bank flora.

There are extensive beds of Common Reed (*Phragmites australis*) which fringe the Forth between Stirling and Alloa.

Bogs and mires

Raised bogs formerly covered much of the carse land around the Forth. They were extensively drained and literally washed down the river during the late 18th and early 19th century reclamation initiated by Lord Kames (Cadell 1913). Nevertheless the series of raised bogs, collectively known as Flanders Moss, in the upper part of the Forth Valley is still the most extensive

Figure 4   Round-leaved Sundew (*Drosera rotundifolia*): a frequent, insectivorous species, which occurs in wet peaty places.   (Flanders Moss)

Figure 5 Labrador-tea (*Ledum palustre* spp. *groenlandicum*): a celebrated introduction, formerly the subject of much speculation about its possible native status. (Flanders Moss)

area of raised bog in Britain. West Flanders Moss has been afforested but East Flanders Moss still provides an extensive area of less disturbed continuous raised bog of about 10 km². This is substantially intact albeit much altered by drainage and burning.

The vegetation of the southern section of the Moss was described by Bannister (1977) and this work, together with new data from the northern part of the moss, has been used to describe the vegetation of the whole site (Booth 1988). It now seems that the southern section of the bog is more disturbed than the north (it used to be thought that the opposite applied, Proctor and Bannister 1974). However, the northern zone itself has been modified and is still undergoing change at present. It seems that the hydrology of the whole of the East Flanders Moss is still intact and that with management (e.g. using the principles discussed by Booth 1988) the future of this internationally important area can be made secure. A substantial part of the Moss is now a National Nature Reserve and another part is a Scottish Wildlife Trust Reserve.

The Moss has several types of vegetation including some expanding Birch woods which are giving cause for concern since tree cover is likely to be related to a lowering of the water table and a destruction of some of the unusual habitat types. The main bog areas have Heather, Cross-leaved Heath, Hare's-tail Cottongrass (*Eriophorum vaginatum*), *Odontoschisma sphagni*, and *Sphagnum capillifolium* as constant species with Common Cottongrass (*Eriophorum angustifolium*) and several other *Sphagnum* species being frequent. In many places, Cranberry (*Vaccinium oxycoccus*) and Round-leaved Sundew (*Drosera rotundifolia*, **Figure 4**) are common and more locally, White Beak-sedge (*Rhynchospora alba*) and the nationally rare Bog-rosemary (*Andromeda polifolia*). Apart from one isolated outlier, this last-mentioned species reaches its northern limit in Britain in this area. Labrador-tea (*Ledum palustre* ssp. *groenlandicum*) **(Figure 5)** is an intriguing species of Flanders Moss, which occurs locally with the species just listed, and its status on the Moss is discussed by Ribbons (1976) and Christie (1991).

Smaller raised bogs, variously disturbed, occur for example at:

(i)   Dunmore Moss; a severely disturbed bog but noteworthy for harbouring a large population of Labrador-tea on the afforested part.
(ii) Shirgarton Moss; this has been subject to some drainage but is relatively intact. It does have White Beak-sedge in one locality.
(iii) Killorn Moss; is much modified by drainage yet still harbours a large range of raised bog communities. It also has White Beak-sedge.

Blanket bog tends to be developed on all flat or gently sloping land above about 260 m in this region. Large areas of this bog occur on the plateaux of the Fintry and Gargunnock Hills, the Ochils and to the north and east of Callander. The present vegetation is probably derived from a much less disturbed bog dominated by *Sphagnum* which accumulated on the site of former woodland. Remains of trees at the base of the peat have been seen in a number of places. The change from woodland to bog was brought about by a combination of prehistoric clearances and climatic deterioration.

The typical blanket bog community is now dominated by Heather and Deergrass (*Trichophorum cespitosum*) with varying proportions of *Sphagnum* spp. In general they are very species poor and apart from the two dominants, the only common higher plants are Cross-leaved Heath, Common Cottongrass and locally Bog Asphodel (*Narthecium ossifragum*). The blanket bogs are regularly burned. Excessive burning and grazing tend to eliminate Heather and the community becomes dominated by Deergrass. In several places there is severe erosion or 'Hagging' of the peat, presumably another symptom of excessive disturbance. Cloudberry (*Rubus chamaemorus*) is notably abundant in blanket bog on the Campsies and occurs there in drier situations also. An exceptionally large population (2km²) of this species occurs in the western Ochils (Blake 1976).

Soligenous mires, where the wetness of the ground is maintained by lateral seepage of ground water, occur in suitable situations throughout the survey area. They are common in hill country, in channels and hollows or where slopes flatten out, especially in valley floors. The nutrient status of these mires depends on the mineral content of the soil through which the water has flowed.

Nutrient-poor mires are usually dominated by Soft-rush (*Juncus effusus*) or Sharp-flowered Rush (*J. acutiflorus*) and the mosses *Sphagnum* spp. and *Polytrichum commune* and usually have Common Sedge, Heath Bedstraw, and Tormentil as associated higher plants. Mires dominated by Purple Moor-grass and Bog-myrtle (*Myrica gale*) occur locally in the western parts of the region, e.g. by the road from Loch Katrine to Aberfoyle.

In mires of higher nutrient status the dominant plants are Sharp-flowered Rush and bryophytes of which *Calliergon cuspidatum* is a constant. There are usually associated characteristic species such as Sneezewort (*Achillea ptarmica*), Carnation Sedge (*Carex panicea*), Marsh Hawk's beard, Marsh Willowherb (*Epilobium palustre*), Yorkshire-fog (*Holcus lanatus*), Selfheal (*Prunella vulgaris*), Meadow Buttercup (*Ranunculus acris*) and the mosses *Bryum pseudotriquetrum* and those *Sphagnum* spp. which are characteristic of more nutrient-rich situations.

Maritime vegetation

There are no shingle beaches, sand dunes or maritime cliffs in the survey area and the only vegetation that is directly influenced by the sea is saltmarsh. This is best developed on the south side of the Forth estuary below Stirling, and has been described by Proctor, Fraser and Thompson (1983) and Proctor (1987). Its most notable feature is its species poverty. The Stirling saltmarshes lack plants of more southern affinities such as Sea-lavender (*Limonium* sp.) and Sea-purslane (*Atriplex portulacoides*) although there is a recent record of Cord-grass (*Spartina* sp.).

The saltmarsh vegetation is developed on silty material deposited by the river. Often large expanses of this silt are scarcely colonized by plants and extensive 'mud flats' occur e.g. around Grangemouth. Saltmarsh brown sea weeds are very little in evidence.

An easily accessible part of saltmarsh is that near Kincardine Bridge. Here, in the lower parts Common Saltmarsh-grass (*Puccinellia maritima*) together with Sea Arrowgrass (*Triglochin maritima*) and Sea Aster (*Aster tripolium*) are important. A small quantity of Glasswort (*Salicornia* sp.) is present but it never appears as a dominant pioneer. Sea Plantain (*Plantago maritima*) together with Sea-spurrey (*Spergularia* sp.) is more abundant higher up the marsh; Thrift (*Armeria maritima*) is infrequent. Towards the top of the marsh Common Saltmarsh-grass is replaced as the dominant grass by Creeping Bent (*Agrostis stolonifera*) and Red Fescue and Saltmarsh Rush (*Juncus gerardii*) is abundant. Other characteristic saltmarsh plants recorded include Common Scurvygrass (*Cochlearia officinalis*), Sea-milkwort (*Glaux maritima*) and Grass-leaved Orache (*Atriplex littoralis*).

Submontane rock outcrops

Serpentine rock outcrops in a few places associated with the Highland Boundary fault. This metamorphic rock has high concentrations of magnesium and relatively high concentrations of chromium and nickel. The Stirling examples are unusual for this type in that they have high concentrations of calcium. In at least two places there is marked influence on the vegetation. At Conic Hill there are flushes which harbour basiphilous species such as the Yellow-sedge (*Carex viridula* ssp. *brachyrrhyncha*), Broad-leaved Cottongrass (*Eriophorum latifolium*), Black Bog-rush (*Schoenus nigricans*) and Lesser Clubmoss (*Selaginella selaginoides*) (Stirling 1974). At Lime Hill, in Loch Ard forest, the serpentine has basiphiles such as Green Spleenwort (*Asplenium trichomanes-ramosum*) and an abundance of an unusual serpentine form of Black Spleenwort (*Asplenium adiantum-nigrum*) (Figure 6). The Lime Hill vegetation has been described briefly by Johnston & Proctor (1979) who included several plant and soil chemical analyses from the site. Both areas are included in a general survey of British serpentine vegetation by Proctor (1992).

There are conspicuous cliffs and rock outcrops on the Campsie/Fintry Hills. Although there is no serpentine, there are occasional outcrops of calcareous rocks. The north-facing twin Corries of Balglass have basaltic cliffs and flushes with Frog Orchid (*Coeloglossum viride*), Chickweed Willowherb (*Epilobium alsinifolium*), and Northern Bedstraw (*Galium boreale*). On a south-facing cliff elsewhere, there is a basic outcrop which supports the following very uncommon (in Stirlingshire) calcicole plants: Kidney Vetch (*Anthyllis vulneraria*), Common Rock-rose (*Helianthemum nummularium*), Vernal Sandwort (*Minuartia verna*), and Spring Cinquefoil (*Potentilla neumanniana*). Elsewhere the limestone exposures often give no hint, in their flora, of calcium-rich rocks. In general, the species of non-calcareous rock outcrops of the Campsie/Fintry hills are common ones, and many are characteristic of other habitats (Proctor and Bannister 1974). Apparently the rocky outcrops provide a suitably diverse environment in which plants of differing requirements grow in close proximity.

The Ochil Hills also have a number of cliffs and rock outcrops. These have many characteristic species in common with those of similar localities in the Campsie/Fintry Hills and include some Ochil specialities which have been described by Blake (1976). Particularly noteworthy is the Sticky Catchfly (*Lychnis viscaria*), nearing its northern limit in the British Isles, and with its largest British population between Blairlogie and Alva on the south-scarp of the Ochils. Its occurrence there was described in a preliminary way by Blake, Proctor and Wallis (1976) and news of its rediscovery on Abbey Craig was given by Stewart (1987).

A further feature of the Ochils is the presence of spoil heaps from former ore workings. Most of these have a flora with no special features (Proctor and Bacon 1977) but the spoil heaps at Jerah (Heaney and Proctor 1983) and particularly at the Burn of Sorrow (Thompson and Proctor 1983) have an interesting flora which include metal-tolerant races of grasses. The Burn of Sorrow spoil has the rare liverwort *Cephaloziella stellulifera*.

Figure 6 Black Spleenwort (*Asplenium adiantum-nigrum*): the unusual form which occurs on serpentine rocks. (Lime Hill)

Figure 7 Fir Clubmoss (*Huperzia selago*): a frequent species of higher ground on mountains.   (Ben Ledi)

Metalliferous spoil heaps occur elsewhere in the area and there is a large and spectacular lead mine at Tyndrum. This site provided the first Scottish record for the rare moss *Ditrichum plumbicola* which is restricted to lead-mine spoil in Britain, and plant and soil analyses - many revealing a startlingly high lead concentration - from this site have been published by Johnston & Proctor (1977).

Montane vegetation

The survey area contains much land over 700 m in the Ochils and in the region beyond the Highland Boundary Fault. The highest points are the summits of Ben Lui (1134m), Stob Binnein (1165m), and the botanically dull Ben More (1178m).

Although they have some impressive cliffs and crags at lower altitudes the highest parts of the Ochils are on relatively gently sloping ground and are continuously vegetated. The vegetation is not usually of a distinctly montane type but rather a continuation of the blanket bog and grassland that occur at lower altitudes. Blake (1976) briefly described the summit flora of Ben Cleuch (721 m), the highest point in the Ochil Hills. Among other species there, he found fascinating and isolated occurrences of the montane species Stiff Sedge (*Carex bigelowii*), Alpine Bistort (*Polygonum viviparum*), and Dwarf Willow (*Salix herbacea*).

On the higher mountains in the northern and western parts of the survey area there are many types of montane vegetation and topographic features which are typical of mountains such as steep slopes, scree, cliffs, corries and peaks.

Much of the mountain slopes are covered with a montane heath or grass land type vegetation in which Bilberry is often abundant. Sheep grazing has probably favoured the dominance of Bilberry. The following species were noted in a sheep-grazed stand near the summit (879 m) of Ben Ledi: Common Bent, Wavy Hair-grass, Crowberry (*Empetrum nigrum* ssp. *hermaphroditum*), Sheep's-fescue, Heath Bedstraw, Fir Clubmoss (*Huperzia selago*) **(Figure 7)**, Cloudberry, Bilberry and Cowberry (*Vaccinium vitis-idaea*). The mosses *Andreaea rupestris, Hylocomium splendens, Pleurozium schreberi* and *Sphagnum* spp. and several fruticose lichen species were also present. At higher altitudes lichens and mosses often become an increasingly important part of the vegetation. In suitable situations there are high altitude mires and bogs in which Cottongrasses are a striking component.

A most characteristic mountain vegetation (although isolated examples occur at lower altitudes) is associated with springs and flushes, which are soligenous and similar to mires, but which cover a smaller area and have a more localised and rapid flow of water. Springs are typically canalised into small rills whilst in flushes the water spreads out, giving a more diffuse flow. There is intergradation between springs and flushes and mires. A common spring vegetation is dominated by the moss *Philonotis fontana* associated with *Dicranella palustris* and Starry Saxifrage (*Saxifraga stellaris*). Yellow Saxifrage (*Saxifraga aizoides*) is a characteristic plant under slightly more base-rich conditions, when spring and flush vegetation is often floristically rich, as in at least one spring on Ben Ledi where Yellow Saxifrage is associated with Moss Campion (*Silene acaulis*), Alpine Meadow-rue (*Thalictrum alpinum*) and Alpine Bistort.

Ben Lomond (974 m) is one of Stirlingshire's most celebrated botanical localities and some of its features are briefly described by Mitchell (1983). The mountain still has, locally, notable species such as Alpine Mouse-ear (*Cerastium alpinum*), Three-flowered Rush (*Juncus triglumis*), Purple Saxifrage (*Saxifraga oppositifolia*), Sibbaldia (*Sibbaldia procumbens*), and Moss Campion which have been known since John Lightfoot botanized there in 1772. Some species, although their former occurrence can be confirmed from herbarium specimens, have not been seen for years. The most intriguing of these is Arctic Bramble (*Rubus arcticus*) which now seems to be extinct in Britain.

Relatively recently discovered botanically are the high-level outcrops of Loch Tay limestone in the Braes of Balquhidder. Here the following are among the species recorded by Roger (1968): Kidney Vetch, Hairy rock-cress (*Arabis hirsuta*), Green Spleenwort, Moonwort (*Botrychium lunaria*), Dioecious Sedge (*Carex dioica*), Hoary Whitlowgrass (*Draba incana*), Alpine Willowherb (*Epilobium anagallidifolium*), Northern Bedstraw, Wood Crane's-bill (*Geranium sylvaticum*), Meadow Oat-grass (*Helictotrichon pratense*), Three-flowered Rush, Early- purple Orchid (*Orchis mascula*),

Black Alpine-sedge (*Carex atrata*), Hair Sedge (*Carex capillaris*), Downy Willow (*Salix lapponum*), Whortle-leaved Willow and Net-leaved Willow (*Salix reticulata*). On the calcareous mica-schist on the south-east slopes of Stob Garbh, Roger (1962) recorded another rich flora which included several of the species he listed for Creag Mhor and additionally Mountain Willow (*Salix arbuscula*) and Alpine Saw-wort (*Saussurea alpina*). The northern cliffs of Ben Lui have an extremely rich calcicolous montane flora which occurs at a relatively low altitude (460-600m) (Ratcliffe 1977). There is a notable abundance of Mountain Avens, Mountain Willow, Mountain Bladder-fern (*Cystopteris montana*), Rock Whitlowgrass (*Draba norvegica*), Alpine Bartsia, and the moss *Orthothecium rufescens*. A few species such as Northern Rock-cress (*Arabis petraea*) occur on Ben Lui but not on the mica-schist further east. The curtains of vegetation which cover the vertical faces are a special feature of Ben Lui and there is a fine development of tall-herb ledges with Roseroot, Mountain Sorrel (*Oxyria digyna*), Alpine Saw-wort, Round-leaved Wintergreen (*Pyrola rotundifolia*) and Globeflower (*Trollius europaeus*). The rocks become less calcareous above about 760 m, so that the higher parts of the mountain have more acid-loving vegetation with very few rarities but which includes a good range of late snow - bed communities.

CONCLUDING REMARKS

Central Scotland has a rich flora owing to the diversity of its vegetation types. I have discussed much of the published information on the vegetation and flora but there are many unpublished data resulting from field surveys undertaken by Scottish Natural Heritage (formerly the Nature Conservancy Council) and others.

It remains a major task, beyond the scope of the present work, to draw all the data together and to relate the whole to the recent National Vegetation Classification. Hopefully this will be done eventually in the form of a Flora for each consitituent vice-county but these Floras are unfortunately unlikely to be published for a number of years.

It is pleasing that several plants, reported by Proctor and Bannister (1974) as not having been seen in the region since before 1930, are now known to be extant. The Yellow Star-of-Bethlehem (*Gagea lutea*) was rediscovered near Stirling (Crockhart 1977). Other species which have been reinstated (J. Mitchell personal communication), some as a result of extending the area considered by Proctor and Bannister (1974) are: Lesser Water-plantain, Nodding Bur-marigold (*Bidens cernua*), Trifid Bur-marigold (*Bidens tripartita*), Autumnal Water-starwort (*Callitriche hermaphroditica*), Smooth-stalked Sedge (*Carex laevigata*), Six-stamened Waterwort (*Elatine hexandra*), Broad-leaved Cottongrass, Bog Orchid (*Hammarbya paludosa*), Tunbridge Filmy-fern (*Hymenophyllum tunbrigense*), Chestnut Rush (*Juncus castaneus*), Tufted Loosestrife, Round-leaved Wintergreen, Greater Spearwort (*Ranunculus lingua*), Creeping Yellow-cress (*Rorippa sylvestris*), and Marsh Stitchwort (*Stellaria palustris*).

ACKNOWLEDGEMENTS

Dr J. H. Dickson, Mr J. Mitchell and Dr R.E. Thomas are thanked for their very helpful comments on the manuscript.

REFERENCES AND FURTHER READING

ANDERSON, M.L. 1967. A History of Scottish Forestry, (2 vols). Edinburgh. Nelson

BANNISTER, P. 1977. A vegetation survey of East Flanders Moss SSSI. *Forth Naturalist and Historian* 2, 54-68

BANNISTER, P. 1978. A brief survey of South Craigroyston Wood. *Transactions of the Botanical Society of Edinburgh* 43, 41-53

BIRKS, H.J.B. 1989. Holocene isochrone maps and patterns of tree-spreading in the British Isles. *Journal of Biogeography* 16, 503-540

BLAKE, E.A. 1976. Ecological aspects of some of the more local flowering plants of the western Ochil Hills. *Forth Naturalist and Historian* 1, 107-116

BLAKE, E.A., WALLIS, P.R. and PROCTOR, J. 1976. The Red German Catchfly on the western Ochil Hills. *Forth Naturalist and Historian* 1, 117-121

BLAXTER, C.M. and PROCTOR, J. 1984. The Braco Pinewood. *Transactions of the Botanical Society of Edinburgh* 44, 177-185

BONEY, A.D. 1978. Microscopic plant life in Loch Lomond. *Glasgow Naturalist* 19, 391-402

BOOTH, A. 1988. A Management Plan for East Flanders Moss. Unpublished ms. Nature Conservancy Council.

BOYD, W.E. 1983. Botanical remains of edible plants from pre Iron Age broch at Fairy Knowe, Buchlyvie, near Stirling. *Forth Naturalist and Historian* 7, 77-83

BURNETT, J.H. Editor 1964. The Vegetation of Scotland. Edinburgh. Oliver and Boyd.

CADELL, H.M. 1913. The Story of the Forth. Glasgow. Maclehose.

CHRISTIE, I.C. 1991. *Ledum* on Flanders Moss. *Glasgow Naturalist* 22, 41-46

COOK, R. 1979. Some unusual plant records from Menstrie. *Forth Naturalist and Historian* 4, 87-93

COUSENS, J.E. 1963. Variation of some diagnostic characters of the sessile and pedunculate oaks and their hybrids in Scotland. *Watsonia* 5, 273-286

CROCKHART, I.B. 1977. A note on the Yellow Star-of-Bethlehem. *Forth Naturalist and Historian* 2, 69-70

CROCKHART, I.B. 1978. Preliminary list of fungi in the Stirling District. Forth Naturalist and Historian 3, 78-80

DICKSON, J.H. 1977. Guidebook for Excursion C13. Western Scotland II. International Union for Quaternary Research X Congress, Norwich. Geo Abstracts.

DICKSON, J.H. 1991. Wild Plants of Glasgow. Aberdeen. Aberdeen University Press.

DICKSON, J.H. 1992(a). Scottish Woodlands: their ancient past and precarious present. Botanical Journal of Scotland 46, 155-165

DICKSON, J.H. 1992(b). Some recent additions to the Quaternary flora of Scotland and their phytogeographical, palaeoclimatic and ethnobotanical significance. *Act Botanica Fennica* 144, 51-57

DONNER, J.J. 1957. The geology and vegetation of late glacial retreat stages in Scotland, *Transactions of the Royal Society of Edinburgh*, 63, 221 - 264

DURNO, S.E. 1956. Pollen analysis of peat deposits in Scotland, *Scottish Geographical Magazine* 72, 178 - 187

EDLIN, H.L. 1969. Forests of Central and Southern Scotland. *Forestry Commission Booklet* No 25. Edinburgh. HMSO.

EDLIN, H.L. (ed) 1974. Queen Elizabeth Forest Park. *Forestry Commission Guide.* Edinburgh. HMSO.

EDWARDS, D. 1984. Robert Kidston: the most professional palaeobotanist. *Forth Naturalist and Historian* 8, 64-93

FORBES, A.R.D. and PROCTOR, J. 1986. The Glen Artney Juniper wood. *Transactions of the Botanical Society of Edinburgh* 45, 63-72

GIMINGHAM, C.H. 1964. Dwarf shrub heaths. In J.H. Burnett Editor. *Vegetation of Scotland.* pp. 232 - 282

GRAHAM, P. 1812. General view of the Agriculture of Stirlingshire. Edinburgh.

GREENSHILL, E.N. 1977. Dutch Elm disease in Central Scotland. *Forth Naturalist and Historian* 2, 71-78

HEANEY, A. and PROCTOR, J. 1983. Vegetation and soil factors on the Jerah Mine, Scotland. *Transactions of the Botanical Society of Edinburgh* 44, 107-114

IDLE, E.T. 1978. The Flora of the Loch Lomond National Nature Reserve. Glasgow Naturalist 19, 403-421

IDLE, E.T., MITCHELL, J. and STIRLING, A.McG. 1970. *Elatine hydropiper* L. - new to Scotland. *Watsonia* 8, 45-46

JOHNSTON, W.R. and PROCTOR, J. 1977. A comparative study of metal levels in plants from two contrasting lead-mine types. *Plant and Soil* 46, 251-257

JOHNSTON, W.R. and PROCTOR, J. 1979. Ecological studies on the Lime Hill serpentine, Scotland. *Transactions of the Botanical Society of Edinburgh* 43, 145-150

KEYMER, R. 1981. The extent and composition of native woodlands in Central Region. *Forth Naturalist and Historian* 6, 83-96

KEYMER, R.J. and MITCHELL, J. 1980. *Elatine hydropiper* at Loch Watston, West Perth. *Glasgow Naturalist* 20, 86-87

KING, J. and NICHOLSON, I.A. 1964. Grasslands of the Forest and Sub-alpine zones. In J.H. Burnett Editor. *The Vegetation of Scotland.* pp. 168 - 231

LASSIERE, O. 1992. Tropical water fern *Azolla filiculoides* Lamarck on Airthrey Loch, Stirling University. *Forth Naturalist and Historian* 15, 55-56

LINDSAY, 1975. The history of oak coppice in Scotland. *Scottish Forestry* 29, 87-93

LOWE, J.J. 1982. Three Flandrian pollen profiles from the Teith Valley, Perthshire, Scotland I. Vegetational History. *The New Phytologist* 90, 355-370

LOWE, J.J. and WALKER, J.C. 1981. The early Postglacial environment of Scotland: evidence from a site near Tyndrum, Perthshire. *Boreas* 10, 281-294

MITCHELL, J. 1982. Female flowers of Butterbur. *Glasgow Naturalist* 20, 263

MITCHELL, J. 1983. The botanists' Scotland: Stirlingshire VC86. *The Newsletter of the Botanical Society of Edinburgh* 37, 2-7

MITCHELL, J. 1985. *Elatine hydropiper* at the Carron Reservoir. *Botanical Society of the British Isles Scottish Newsletter* 7, 6-7

MITCHELL, J. and STIRLING, A.McG. 1980. The flora of the Loch Lomond National Nature Reserve. A supplement. *Glasgow Naturalist* 20, 77-81

NEILAND, R. and SHEPHERD, J.W. 1990. Dutch Elm disease in Central Scotland. *Forth Naturalist and Historian* 12, 53-66

NEILAND, R., PROCTOR, J. and SEXTON, R. 1985. Giant Hogweed (*Heracleum mantegazzianum* Somm. and Lev.) by the River Allan and part of the river Forth. *Forth Naturalist and Historian* 9, 51-56

NEWBOLD, C. and PALMER, M. 1983. *Elatine hydropiper* - a recent record for the Lake of Menteith. *Glasgow Naturalist 20*, 376-377

THE NEW STATISTICAL ACCOUNT OF SCOTLAND 1845. 8. Dunbarton - Stirling - Clackmannan. and 10. Perth. Edinburgh. Blackwood.

PEARSALL, W.H. 1950. Mountains and Moorlands. London. Collins.

PENNINGTON, W. 1969. The History of British Vegetation. London. English University Press.

PERRING, F.H. and WALTERS, S.M. Editors 1976. Atlas of the British Flora. 2nd edition London. Nelson.

PRICE, R.J. 1983. Scotland's Environment during the Last 30,000 Years. Edinburgh. Scottish Academic Press.

PROCTOR, J. 1987. Saltmarsh vegetation in the Forth estuary, Scotland. *Proceedings of the Royal Society of Edinburgh 93B*, 355-361

PROCTOR, J. 1992. Chemical and ecological studies on the vegetation of ultramafic sites in Britain. In B. A. Roberts and J. Proctor Editors. The Ecology of Areas with Serpentinized Rocks. A World View. 135-167. Dordrecht. Kluwer Academic.

PROCTOR, J. and BACON, M.E. 1977. The Plants and soils of two mineral workings in the Ochil Hills. *Forth Naturalist and Historian* 3, 71-77

PROCTOR, J. and BANNISTER, P. 1974. Vegetation and Flora. In D.W.G. Timms Editor. The Stirling Region, pp. 87-114. U.K. Stirling University.

PROCTOR, J., FRASER, M.J. and THOMPSON, J. 1983. Saltmarshes of the Upper Forth Estuary. *Transactions of the Botanical Society of Edinburgh* 44, 95-102

RACKHAM, O. 1980. Ancient woodland: its history, vegetation and uses in England. Edward Arnold.

RATCLIFFE, D.A. (ed.) 1977. A Nature Conservation Review, 2 volumes. Cambridge University Press.

RATCLIFFE, D.A. 1964. Mires and bogs, In J.H. Burnett Editor. The Vegetation of Scotland. pp. 426 - 478. Edinburgh. Oliver and Boyd.

RAVEN, J. and WALTERS, M. 1956. Mountain Flowers. London. Collins.

RIBBONS, B.W. 1976. *Ledum* in Britain. *Glasgow Naturalist* 19, 219-233

ROBERTS, A.J. 1986. Inventory of Ancient, Long-established and Semi-natural Woodland (Provisional). Stirling District. Nature Conservancy Council unpublished ms.

ROGER, J.G. 1962. Report of the Alpine Section, 1961. Day excursion to Stob Garbh, S.W. Perthshire. *Transactions of the Botanical Society of Edinburgh* 39, 346

ROGER, J.G. 1963. Report of the Alpine Section, 1962. Day excursion to Creag Mhor (3387 ft), head of Glen Lochar, Perthshire. *Transactions of the Botanical Society of Edinburgh* 39, 444-445

ROGER, J.G. 1968. Report of the Alpine Section. Day excursion to the head of Kirkton Glen, Balquhidder, Perthshire. *Transactions of the Botanical Society of Edinburgh* 40, 471-472

SMITH, A.J.E. 1976. The Moss Flora of Britain and Ireland. Cambridge University Press.

SMITH, A.J.E. 1990. The liverworts of Britain and Ireland. Cambridge University Press.

SMITH, R.A.H., STEWART, N.F., TAYLOR, N.W. and THOMAS, R.E. 1992. Checklist of the Plants of Perthshire. Perthshire Society of Natural Science.

STACE, C. 1991. New Flora of the British Isles. Cambridge University Press.

STEVEN, H.M. and CARLISLE, A. 1959. The Native Pinewoods of Scotland. Oliver & Boyd.

STEVENSON, J.F. 1990. How ancient is the woodland of Mugdock? *Scottish Forestry* 44, 161-172

STEWART, D.A. 1983. The history of Alder *Alnus glutinosa* (L.) Gaertn, in the Campsie Fells. *Glasgow Naturalist* 20, 333-345

STEWART, D.A., WALKER, A. and DICKSON, J.H. 1984. Pollen diagrams from Dubh Lochan, near Loch Lomond. *New Phytologist* 98, 531-549

STEWART, N.F. 1986. A provisional list of vascular plants growing in Falkirk district. *Forth Naturalist and Historian* 10, 53-79

STEWART, N.F. 1987. The Sticky Catchfly (*Lychnis viscaria* L.) on Abbey Craig. *Forth Naturalist and Historian* 11, 83-84

STIRLING, A.McG. 1974. Conic Hill, Balmaha. *Glasgow Naturalist* 19, 140

STIRLING, Col and KIDSTON, R. 1892-1900. Notes on the flora of Stirlingshire, a series of 10 reports. *Transactions of the Stirling Natural History and Archeological Society* 13, 88-102; 14, 74-102; 15, 109-113; 16, 88-92; 17, 80-86; 18, 137-9; 19, 103-6; 20, 134-5; 21, 166; 22, 67

TITTENSOR, R.M. 1970. History of the Loch Lomond oakwoods. I. Ecological history and II. Period of intensive management. *Scottish Forestry* 24, 100-118

TITTENSOR, R.M. and STEELE, R.C. 1971. Plant communities of the Loch Lomond oakwoods. *Journal of Ecology* 59, 561-582

THOMPSON, J. and PROCTOR, J. 1983. Vegetation and soil factors on a heavy metal mine spoil heap. *New Phytologist* 94, 297-308

TURNER, J. 1965. A contribution to the history of forest clearance. *Proceedings of the Royal Society* 161, 343-353

TRAIL, J.W.H. Editor. 1898. Flora of Perthshire. Blackwood (reprinted in 1978 by EP Publishing, Wakefield).

VASARI, Y. and VASARI, A. 1968. Late and post-glacial macrophytic vegetation of the lochs of northern Scotland. *Acta Botanica Fennica 80, 1 - 116*

WATLING, R. 1980. Larger fungi of the Stirling Area. *Forth Naturalist and Historian* 4, 95-110

WATLING, R. 1981. Notes on the fungi of Ochtertyre Moss. *Forth Naturalist and Historian* 6, 75-82

Birds

D.M Bryant, M.V Bell, C.J Henty, S.F Newton

Introduction

Central Scotland harbours an impressive variety of birds. They find a place within the region's rich mosaic of habitats, which range from an estuary in the east to a craggy mountain wilderness in the west. The flocks of wintering grey geese, ducks on lowland lochs, breeding and wintering waders, oakwoods with a profusion of summer migrants, impressive populations of predators and healthy communities of familiar species of field and wood, are outstanding amongst the area's birds. Several species also find a home close to the northern limit of their breeding range in Britain, while others have established a toe-hold on their southern fringe. The principal marker for this division is the Highland Boundary Fault, which splits the region and so separates the uplands and its birds from the more sheltered terrain of the Forth valley. To the northwest of the Fault it becomes difficult to find some breeding species which are widespread in the central lowlands: Partridge, Moorhen, Coot, Blackcap, Goldfinch, Tree Sparrow and Magpie are examples. Great Crested Grebe, Ruddy Duck, Nightjar, Kingfisher, Green Woodpecker and Hawfinch are also very thinly scattered or absent in the Highlands but more frequent to the south. Red and Black throated Divers, Golden Eagle, Ptarmigan, Capercaillie, Greenshank and Hooded Crow, on the other hand, are not found as breeders in the Forth valley, and yet they find a place in the remoter uplands of the region and further north. These features lend a special interest to the status of breeding birds in central Scotland and to their different responses to changes in land use and climate.

Typical birds in the main habitats of the region are first described, and the overall balance of their fortunes is then reviewed. Fortunately there is a firm baseline against which to judge recent changes, thanks to the pioneer work of Rintoul and Baxter (1935) on the birds of the Forth Basin. Since this classic work there have been five projects which have considered the status of local species. Bryant (1974) reviewed the birds of the region, while the Breeding Atlas (Sharrock 1976) and Winter Atlas (Lack 1986) stimulated a quite unprecedented interest in bird distributions within the area. Thom (1986) summarised these results in a Scottish context. The forthcoming New Breeding Atlas of the British Trust for Ornithology, due for publication in the next few years, and coming 20 years after the first, will certainly extend our knowledge of recent changes. Monitoring of wildfowl, wader and raptor populations continues under the National Wildfowl Count scheme, Birds of Estuaries Enquiry, and Raptor Study Group and contributes vital information on some important populations of the region. Finally, Henty and Brackenridge (1992) have compiled a species list which brings the record right up to date. Further changes can be followed through the Forth Area Bird Report, published annually by the *Forth Naturalist and Historian*.

Estuary

The estuary of the Firth of Forth lies between the bridges at Queensferry to the east and Stirling in the west. The southern shore of the Forth between Blackness and Kincardine Bridge and both shores west of this point, encompass the estuarine habitats of central Scotland. They consist of a variety of sheltered beaches, saltmarshes, flats and shoals, ranging from the rocky point on which Blackness Castle stands to the glutinous mud at Kinneil. Between Blackness and Carriden the shore is mainly firm with a mix of sand, shingle and exposed rock. From Grangepans to Alloa there are soft muddy flats, with notably wide shores near Grangemouth. Further upriver the intertidal is at first broad and backed by saltmarshes, but towards Alloa it becomes steeper and the water less salty, until at Stirling the river is fresh, backing up at high tide. The changes in the physical nature of the estuary when moving westwards from the open Firth have much influence on the shorelife and therefore on the birdlife. The influence of man can also be strong, via his industrial activities, waste disposal, agriculture, recreation or hunger for claiming land from the sea.

There are three overlapping groups of birds which share a marked seasonality of habit and prefer to use the estuary mainly in winter whilst breeding elsewhere. One group lives offshore and lives mainly by diving for food, a second depends on mudflats exposed at low tide, where they seek a diet of shellfish, and the final is associated with the salt-marshes and the hinterland claimed from the sea, which lies above the high water mark and skirts the intertidal zone. The first group comprises the grebes, divers, seabirds and saw-billed ducks. Divers occur in winter, with both Red and Black-throated regular in small numbers. Great-northern Divers are much scarcer, with only occasional records. The Great Crested Grebe is mainly present in autumn and winter; its population is one of the most important in Britain, with 850 recorded in the mid 1980s, although peaks of 200-500 are commoner. They are usually in a large flock off Kinneil in autumn and early spring but scatter more widely during the mid-winter months. The presence of an occasional Red-necked Grebe in the flock, could perhaps indicate a Scandinavian origin for some of the grebes. Both Slavonian and Black-necked Grebes have been recorded in winter but are very scarce, along with a few sea-going Dabchicks. Cormorants occur in large numbers, not uncommonly being seen at the surface struggling with a large eel or flounder. There is a long-established roost at South Alloa where over 100 birds may assemble, as well as many smaller gathering points on offshore mudbanks and structures. The numbers involved, over 500, make the estuary one of the most important in Britain as a wintering site for this species. The Shag is only occasionally seen, although is common along the coast to the east of the region. Diving ducks generally occur in small numbers during mild weather, but can become numerous during prolonged winter cold when local freshwaters are ice covered. Pochard and Tufted Duck occur, with a small flock of Scaup often at Kinneil in late winter. Eider have become commoner over the last few years, again with late winter and spring being the main months, but with records largely restricted to the Grangemouth-Blackness shore. Goldeneye are seen in large numbers in cold weather with the river at Cambus and Cambuskenneth being favoured sites. Long-tailed Duck and Common and Velvet Scoters are infrequent visitors. Red-breasted Mergansers appear to have declined in recent years, but they remain widespread, mainly east of Alloa, while Goosanders, usually more scattered, are found westward to Stirling.

Seabirds come into the Forth, usually to feed, quite often while escaping gales. Surprisingly, some move through on their way from east to west coasts, perhaps as part of wider wanderings in search of food or to avoid heavy seas. The largest is the Gannet, with adults and immatures regular in small numbers. They are mainly found east of Kincardine Bridge in the deeper waters. Manx Shearwaters occur occasionally in autumn along with many terns and attendant skuas. All the five sea tern species occur, although Little and Roseate are rare. The numbers of Sandwich and Common Terns in August and September can be very large, attracting Arctic and Great Skuas, with Pomarines generally occurring later in the year. Otherwise, Kittiwakes and Fulmars are the commonest visiting seabirds, with hundreds of the former sometimes on the estuary, once in a while striking off inland to the west but more often returning to the Firth to the east. Gannet, Arctic Skua and Fulmar have been seen inland on their cross country flights across the central belt. In winter Guillemots may be common on the estuary, with a few Razorbills and the occasional gale-driven Little Auk. There is a possibility that Guillemots have recently become commoner in winter and have also been stranded inland following gales in a number of recent years.

The mudflats of the estuary hold the most important assemblages of birds in central Scotland. Ten species occur in numbers which qualify them as nationally significant (Bryant 1987). The Shelduck is outstanding (**Figure 1**), with internationally important wintering and moulting populations and a breeding population larger than any other in Scotland (**Table 1**). The wintering population is spread between Cambus and Bo'ness with a focus around Grangemouth. The breeders reach further up the estuary to the outskirts

Figure 1 Shelduck on the Forth Estuary: Internationally important populations moult and winter near Grangemouth. Also found upriver to Stirling, particularly during the breeding season. Inland breeding occurs by the Endrick Mouth, Loch Lomondside   (David Bryant).

of Stirling. The moulting flock is very restricted, however, being confined to Kinneil. Only two other sites in Britain hold comparable numbers of moulting Shelduck and Kinneil with over 4000 birds in 1992, is currently the largest in Europe away from the Knechtsand. The wintering flock of Pintail, now with under 100 birds, tends to favour Skinflats. Teal, Mallard and Wigeon form large flocks on the estuary, with small parties of Shoveler appearing in autumn.

The wading bird community is numerically dominated by Dunlin and Knot, with up to 6000 of each species present in some recent winters (**Table 1**). Both species have declined from peaks of over 10000 in the 1970s. Redshank occur in internationally important numbers, with Curlew, Oystercatcher and Bar-tailed Godwit also numerous. Ringed and Grey Plover winter in small numbers but are generally commoner on passage: over 300 Ringed have been seen in May at Skinflats, with much smaller numbers of Greys peaking in October.

Turnstone and sometimes single Greenshank and Spotted Redshank also winter, but the two shanks are more frequent on passage. A wide range of species is largely restricted to the spring, or more often, autumn passage: Sanderling, Ruff, Whimbrel, Green Sandpiper, Wood Sandpiper, Curlew Sandpiper and Little Stint for example. The Curlew Sandpiper tends to be commoner every third year or so, as a result of their variable

Table 1 Numbers of some wintering waterfowl and waders in the Grangemouth area during the 5-year period: 1986/87 - 1990/91.

	Kinneil		Skinflats	
	Average annual maximum	Maximum count	Average annual Maximum	Maximum count
Great-crested Grebe	344	470	10	24
Cormorant	32	38	261	600
Shelduck	2621	3580	680	1057
Teal	1510	1830	79	203
Pintail	11	28	62	72
Red-breasted Merganser	28	39	64	123
Oystercatcher	97	139	57	70
Lapwing	732	1006	1093	1220
Knot	3387	6440	1214	3650
Dunlin	1398	2000	2610	5150
Black-tailed Godwit	32	70	1	3
Bar-tailed Godwit	267	350	27	84
Curlew	546	600	303	426
Redshank	1201	1410	995	1175

success on arctic breeding grounds (**Figure 2**). Scarcer passage waders have also been recorded such as Grey and Red-necked Phalaropes, Temminck's Stint, Pectoral Sandpiper, Killdeer and American Golden Plover, mainly at Skinflats, Kinneil and Cambus Pools.

The third group of birds mainly associates with the estuarine perimeter, using inflowing creeks, saltmarshes, lagoons and low lying fields, or just roosting on the open waters of the estuary. A small number of Mute Swans is present above Alloa, while in winter Whoopers roost on the Forth between Skinflats and Stirling. There are now two important goose roosts, holding principally Pink-footed Geese at Skinflats and both Pinkfeet and Greylags on the Alloa Inches. They commute from their roosts to feed on farmland by the estuary or further afield. Pinkfeet have risen above 2000 in recent years with hundreds lingering at Alloa into May. Of the scarcer geese, Brents and Barnacles are recorded in small numbers, often mingling with the commoner grey geese, or in the case of Barnacles, are seen overhead on their way south towards their Solway haunts. Lapwing and Golden Plover are prominent amongst the waders, numbering thousands in the autumn and winter, although with the onset of cold weather they make increasing use of the mudflats or seek milder climes to the south and west. Snipe, and much less commonly, Jack Snipe, are found on damp ground around the estuary, on passage or in winter. Herons feed in creeks and pools and use the estuary as a retreat during cold weather. The smaller birds include a wide range of finches and other species exploiting the strand-line, notably Twite, Snow Buntings and occasional Lapland Buntings and Rock Pipits.

The Yellow Wagtails that formerly nested near Grangemouth are now gone, this being one of only two breeding species certainly lost from central Scotland

Figure 2 Migrant wading birds are found at muddy wetland margins, mainly by the Estuary in autumn. Here Dunlin and Turnstone, both retaining their summer plumage, and a juvenile Curlew Sandpiper, feed together. Relatively small numbers of Dunlin and Turnstone moult on the Estuary but much larger numbers winter. The Curlew Sandpiper, in contrast, occurs only as a passage migrant   (David Bryant)

over the past 20 years. Breeding birds around the estuary do include, however, a thriving colony of Common Terns as well as Ringed Plover, Redshank, Lapwing, Meadow Pipit, Sedge Warbler and Reed Bunting. Gulls are a prominant feature of the Forth, although the most impressive numbers arrive only to roost after feeding on fields or waste tips nearby. In excess of 10000 gulls may fly in to the main areas of the Forth to roost, with particular concentrations at Skinflats, Kinneil, Dunmore, Cambus and Fallin. These include Great and Lesser Black Backs, Herring, Common, and Black-headed Gulls. By mid-winter, however, of the Lesser Black Backs only a few remain. Occasional Glaucous or Iceland Gulls are also seen. Little Gulls and Black Terns occur in small numbers on passage, although the former is also seen in winter.

The Forth above Cambus is lined by extensive reedbeds, as the mainly saline waters, encouraging saltmarsh development, give way to a predominantly freshwater environment. Small parties of Mallard and Teal haunt the reedy fringes of the 'windings' up to Stirling. The reed beds themselves do not appear to harbour a rich bird fauna, probably due to their deep litter layer and frequent flooding, but they remain rather poorly known.

The abundant birdlife of the estuary attracts a wealth of predatory birds outside the breeding season, with the number and variety of falcons being particularly notable. Peregrine, Merlin and Kestrel are frequent, as are Sparrowhawk and Short-eared Owl. The Hen Harrier is occasional with a recent record of Marsh Harrier. The falcons and Sparrowhawk make a good living chasing the smaller waders, with Redshank and Dunlin the usual victims.

The estuary is notable for the variety of species recorded. Over 200 species have been noted; about 80% of the area's total. This comes from the mix of waterfowl, seabirds and landbirds brought together by the juxtposition of sea and river, marsh and field. Skinflats, with 163 species on record since 1950, has the longest recent site list, but Kinneil comes close behind, and both sites outpace any others in the region

Freshwater Lochs

The majority of the wintering wildfowl in the region are found in the lowlands around the Forth estuary, in the lower Devon and Forth valleys and by Loch Lomond. The reservoirs in the Touch/ Gargunnock/Campsie Hills are less valuable than 20 years ago but still hold regionally important numbers of duck. The large and deep oligotrophic lochs in the north-west, however, rarely hold more than a few wildfowl though small herds of Whooper Swans occur at a few sites. The wildfowl count data used for these assessments are from the programme of counts organised by the Wildfowl and Wetlands Trust. Unfortunately coverage in this area was poor between the 1985/86 and 1991/92 winters and only Airthrey Loch, Lake of Menteith and the Endrick Mouth have

complete coverage over this period. The 'regular' count is, by common convention, the average of the three highest mid-monthly counts each winter.

The two most important freshwater sites for wintering duck are found at the eastern and western extremes of the area, Gartmorn Dam at Alloa and the Endrick Mouth on Loch Lomondside. Gartmorn Dam is a redundant reservoir and since 1978 has been a Local Nature Reserve. Gartmorn is the most important site for Mallard in the region, with over 1000 at times (**Table 2**). Wigeon have benefited from the active management of a small grass field on the north shore; a peak of over 1350 was recorded in the 1991/92 winter. Numbers of Teal fluctuate depending on the amount of exposed mud. In contrast to the healthy populations of dabbling duck, Pochard and Tufted Duck have declined with recent peaks of 176 and 192 respectively compared with 493 and 807 between 1970-1982. The flock of Coot at Gartmorn is the largest in the area with up to 820 in recent years. Small numbers of Great Crested and Little Grebes, Cormorant and Mute Swan are also regular. Numbers of Whooper Swans fluctuate considerably, 61 being the largest flock in recent winters; under 20 is more usual. The Whooper Swans roost at Gartmorn and feed on arable farmland in the Devon valley but the numbers are generally lower than 10 years ago. Since the 1990/91 winter Greylag have roosted in larger numbers than formerly with 1600 in November 1990. Small numbers of Pinkfeet also occur. Unusual species can turn up at Gartmorn, the difficulty is finding them amongst the masses of common waterfowl. Perhaps the American Wigeon and Smew which were present in the 1991/92 winter will encourage more birdwatchers to visit the Dam. It is an outstanding example of a successful Local Nature Reserve making a major contribution to conservation.

In late winter floodwater in the Devon valley can hold appreciable numbers of duck. The floods at Alva held Mallard, Wigeon and small numbers of Teal in 1990; Pintail and Shoveler have also been recorded there. Some stretches of the river Devon also hold Mallard, Goldeneye and Goosander, the latter species becoming more abundant on the upper reaches. Castlehill Reservoir, just over the regional boundary in Perth and Kinross District, is used as a day roost by Mallard and Goosander which feed on the Devon.

Airthrey Loch on the campus of Stirling University regularly holds 300 Mallard, 50 Tufted Duck and 70 Coot in winter (**Table 2**). Mallard have become more numerous in recent years with 602 present in January 1992, though peak numbers usually occur in late summer. By contrast, the flocks of up to 450 Tufted Duck are now a distant memory. Numbers of Little Grebe are usually highest in September. After successful breeding seasons over 50 Moorhens can be present. Other species are rather scarce at Airthrey with occasional Pochard and Goldeneye and more rarely Wigeon, Teal, Shoveler and Pintail. The almost continuous presence of people along the shore

Table 2 Regular counts of wintering wildfowl; maxima 1970-82 in brackets; 1985-92 under max. Whoopers counted in daytime.

a. **Gartmorn Dam**	1970-82	85/86	86/87	89/90	90/91	91/92	max
Great-crested Grebe	NC	2	0	5	6	4	6
Little Grebe	NC	NC	NC	2	11	9	14
Cormorant	NC	NC	NC	32	3	5	36
Mute Swan	10(63)	21	29	5	10	21	47
Whooper Swan	7(67)	0	16	0	0	11	40
Wigeon	96(592)	370	154	784	567	1069	1350
Teal	128(380)	467	172	375	175	93	510
Mallard	781(1531)	1247	794	713	804	715	1290
Pochard	108(493)	108	132	41	23	92	176
Tufted Duck	284(807)	118	120	148	162	230	244
Goldeneye	35(81)	29	39	67	50	45	79
Coot	NC	379	461	712	489	694	820

b. **Airthrey Loch**	1971-82	87/88	88/89	89/90	90/91	91/92	max
Little Grebe	NC	9	4	8	10	12	17
Mute Swan	6(15)	5	7	6	7	9	11
Mallard	132(167)	242	263	353	421	495	602
Tufted Duck	137(454)	48	78	58	58	63	84
Coot	NC	83	84	78	75	90	97
Moorhen	NC	24	29	29	54	59	62

c. **Lake of Menteith and Loch Macanrie**	1978-82	86/87	87/88	88/89	89/90	90/91	max
Great-crested Grebe	NC	6	4	8	6	4	10
Cormorant	NC	3	10	6	19	12	26
Mute Swan	2(6)	2	4	3	4	5	7
Wigeon	4(13)	0	5	10	4	25	32
Teal	6(14)	76	70	63	171	47	200
Mallard	91(185)	153	95	164	101	76	323
Pochard	16(55)	11	13	6	18	12	27
Tufted Duck	75(160)	32	42	20	38	30	72
Goldeneye	29(44)	41	37	32	35	29	52
Goosander	3(14)	23	4	4	8	10	42
Coot	NC	193	285	123	198	252	342

d. **Endrick Mouth**	1971-79	87/88	88/89	89/90	90/91	91/92	max
Great-crested Grebe	NC	8	0	0	5	NC	15
Mute Swan	8(47)	14	14	12	12	15	19
Whooper Swan	27(56)	0	8	10	10	12	27
Gr. Whitefront	-	215	315	275	350	350	350
Greylag Goose	-	950	533	417	917	600	1500
Canada Goose	-	0	14	5	5	7	15
Wigeon	502(647)	483	583	450	667	683	800
Teal	303(500)	333	400	300	450	483	1000
Mallard	345(667)	150	200	200	217	250	384
Shoveler	21(100)	2	0	9	7	0	20
Pochard	13(35)	0	5	17	11	34	30
Tufted Duck	25(36)	22	19	18	20	31	35
Goldeneye	16(37)	18	11	8	18	21	20
Red b. Merganser	2(7)	4	0	3	6	1	9
Goosander	1(14)	4	2	4	14	6	17

e. **Carron Reservoir**	1970-82	85/86	86/87	87/88	89/90	90/91	max
Great-crested Grebe	NC	3	2	-	5	-	
Cormorant	NC	NC	8	-	9	-	11
Whooper Swan	5(15)	0	5	-	6	-	8
Wigeon	13(73)	48	142	-	57	-	174
Teal	244(744)	305	569	-	55	-	687
Mallard	216(483)	486	570	-	113	-	593
Pochard	16(62)	3	2	-	37	-	44
Tufted Duck	24(77)	49	102	-	32	-	185
Goldeneye	13(75)	1	6	-	7	-	11
Goosander	3(8)	6	2	-	4	-	11

Figure 3 Whooper Swans are found in largest numbers on lowland lochs and farmland. Small groups also occur by highland lochs, such as Loch Dochart near Crianlarich (Helen Riley).

undoubtedly limits numbers of the shyer species.

The flat carselands of the Forth valley which extend westwards from Stirling and Bridge of Allan to Flanders Moss is the most important feeding site in the region for Whooper Swans and geese (**Figure 3**). The first Whoopers can be seen at the end of September, peaking from the second half of November to January. Numbers are very variable between winters (**Table 3**) but with over 100 present at some stage in most winters. The largest recent count was 191 in November 1988. Occasional Bewick's Swans occur in the flocks of Whoopers.

The flocks of Pink-footed geese wintering in the Forth and Teith valleys are of international importance (**Table 3**). In autumn the main roost is Loch Mahaick on the Braes of Doune with peak numbers varying from only 1855 in 1991 to 6500 in 1988. This roost is occupied from early October but may be deserted by December. Large numbers of Pinkfeet from roosts in Strathallan can be found feeding at the eastern end of the Carse in winter, but they can forage as far west as Thornhill. Up to 4000 birds may commute into the Forth valley between December and February. The Forth valley often remains free of snow when Strathallan and sites further north and east are snowbound and frequently holds its largest flocks at this time. Pinkfeet roosting at Lake of Menteith tend to feed round the periphery of Flanders Moss rarely flighting east of Thornhill until February or March. Shooting at Lake of Menteith and on the Carse probably limits the numbers of geese using the area between November and January so it is no coincidence that the largest numbers tend to occur after the shooting season in February and March.

Greylag occur on the Carse in much smaller numbers than Pinkfeet and are now less numerous than a decade ago (**Table 3**). Flocks are often under a 100 birds and can be difficult to find, particularly where there is much dead ground. Greylag arrive in the second half of October and usually depart in the first week of April. In some winters only 100-250 occur but more often flocks total over 500 and sometimes a 1000. Recently a flock of up to 400 Greylag has appeared in the Callander area and these are thought to roost on the nearby gravel pit. The extent to which the Teith valley between Callander and Doune is used by geese is uncertain since visibility is restricted by the topography and numerous plantations.

Small numbers of Barnacle Geese are sometimes found in the flocks of Pinkfeet, usually in October and November. They were particularly abundant in autumn 1990 with 41 at Thornhill in October. One or two Greenland Whitefronts are recorded most years on the Carse. Other geese are rare but Snow Geese, Beans and Brents are on record.

The Lake of Menteith, together with the adjacent Loch Macanrie, is the most important inland site for duck in the Forth valley (**Table 2**). Small numbers of Great Crested Grebe winter and Cormorant have recently increased. There is a regular population of about 100 Mallard. Goldeneye peak at 30-50 in late winter and Coot number up to 300. Loch Macanrie holds most of the Teal with a peak count of 200. Other species are surprisingly scarce. The low numbers of duck are probably due to disturbance from trout fishing which continues to the end of November and from shooting. Other scarce species recorded at Lake of Menteith include single Shoveler, Scaup, Long-tailed Duck and Smew. Red-breasted Mergansers are also occasional winter visitors. Loch Rusky, holds few duck because of disturbance from fishing. Loch Watston, Loch Mahaick and Loch Laggan and Muir Dam at Kippen all hold disappointingly few birds. Mallard are the most numerous with 50-100 a respectable total for each site. Wigeon, Teal, Pochard, Tufted Duck and Goldeneye occur at all these sites in small numbers with varying degrees of regularity. Pintail and Long-tailed Duck have been recorded at Muir Dam. The numerous shooting ponds on the Cromlix estate at the east end of the Braes of Doune are probably collectively more important than some of the larger lochs which seem too disturbed. Up to 2500 Pinkfeet have roosted on the largest of these pools in recent winters. Blairdrummond gravel pit may also be important for duck but again there is little information on this site.

Table 3 Maximum winter counts of swans and geese in the Forth and Teith valleys.

	1985/86	1986/87	1987/88	1988/89	1989/90	1990/91
Whooper Swan	140	116	165	157	91	104
Pink-footed Goose	4350	5070	5000	7000	7465	7855
Greylag Goose	1030	980	260	120	696	775

Figure 4 Loch Voil is one of several highland lochs which hold only a few ducks in winter: Mallard and Goldeneye can usually be seen. Most wintering wildfowl in the region are found by lowland waters and on the coast   (Olivia Lassiere).

Figure 5 The second largest flock of Bean Geese in Britain is found in the south of the region. They moved from Carron Valley Reservoir after water levels were raised   (Helen Riley).

Duck are also found on the Teith and Forth and the rivers are particularly important for Goosander. There have been no recent systematic counts of the rivers but small flocks of up to a dozen Goosander have occured on all the lochs at times giving some indication of the local population.

Endrick Mouth National Nature Reserve straddles the border of Central and Strathclyde Regions and supports a diverse population of wintering wildfowl (**Table 2**), notably one of the few mainland flocks of Greenland White-fronted Geese in Scotland, increasing steadily since 1962, with 350 present in the 1990/91 winter. Greylag increased to 2000-3000 in the late 1970s but had fallen back to 500-100 by the late 1980s following a large reduction in the acreage of barley. Occasional Pink-footed and Barnacle Geese are found with Whitefronts and Greylags while there is a resident flock of Canada Geese. Small numbers of Great Crested Grebe, Little Grebe, Cormorant, Mute Swan and a dozen Whoopers are regular. Wigeon and Teal are the most numerous duck with recent peaks of 800 and 1000 respectively. This is the best site in the region for Shoveler with flocks up to 50, peak numbers occurring in autumn and spring. Pochard, Tufted Duck, Goldeneye and Goosander are regular. Shelduck and Red-breasted Merganser return in late winter to breed. Lochs Venachar and Achray are the most important of the Trossachs Lochs for wintering wildfowl though the

only recent winter count data was 1986/87.
When Mallard numbered up to 380 in December and Wigeon, Teal, Pochard and Goldeneye were noted but surprisingly no Tufted Duck. Small flocks of Whooper Swan and Greylag may be present.

Limited data from Loch Lubnaig suggests small numbers of Little Grebe, Mallard, Pochard, Tufted Duck, Goldeneye and Whooper Swans at the shallow northern end of the loch. Lochs Voil and Doine, Balqulidder, hold few birds (**Figure 4**). The west end of Loch Tay at Killin holds some duck but no quantitative information is available. Further west Loch Dochart is a regular wintering site for 20-30 Whooper Swans and a few common duck.

The reservoirs in the hills to the south of the Carse of Stirling have declined in importance. Numbers of Mallard at North Third are much reduced from peaks of 500-700 twenty years ago, with the regular population now under 100. Small numbers of the other common species are found more or less regularly. Disturbance from fishing is the most likely cause of the decline. The more exposed Loch Coulter holds similar numbers of duck with up to 180 Mallard and 40 Wigeon. Roosting Greylag are a notable feature here; small numbers sometimes feed round the the reservoir but most commute into the Forth valley. Limited data suggest that the sheltered Touch Muir reservoir can sometimes hold substantial numbers of duck.

Table 4   Maximum monthly counts of Bean Geese on the Slamannan plateau (unpublished observations of J.Simpson

	Sep	Oct	Nov	Dec	Jan	Feb	Mar
1989/90	-	86	-	116	120	120	-
1990/91	27	140	140	147	130	-	129
1991/92	40	101	146	85	90	113	74

Carron Valley Reservoir lies on the watershed of the rivers Carron and Endrick and has been one of the most important freshwater sites for wildfowl in central Scotland. Unfortunately the water level of the reservoir was raised about 1 metre in the 1987/88 winter which pushed the shoreline closer to the surrounding conifer forest and eliminated shallow feeding areas favoured by dabbling duck. Numbers have declined dramatically with the annual peaks of Teal and Mallard each falling from 600-700 to about 100. Numbers of Wigeon, Pochard and Tufted Duck are very variable between winters. Great Crested Grebe, Whooper Swan, Goldeneye and Goosander all occur in small numbers but Goldeneye appear much scarcer than a decade earlier. Occasional flocks of Pink-footed and Greylag geese are recorded. The reservoir's main claim to ornithological fame was as one of Britain's few sites for Bean Geese which numbered up to 150 in the 1980s (**Figure 5**). Their appearance was always somewhat erratic, often they appeared early in the autumn from mid-September to early October then disappeared only to reappear in late winter. Sometimes they grazed the reservoir margins (now flooded) but often appeared to use the site just for loafing. In February 1988 three of the birds were observed to be colour-ringed and it transpired that they were Swedish birds involved in a reintroduction programmme.

The flock of Bean Geese disappeared from the Carron valley when the reservoir was raised but was subsequently discovered on the Slammanan plateau south of Falkirk around Lochs Ellrig and Fannyside (**Table 4**). Unfortunately, their future is in some doubt: a clay-pigeon shoot on one of the main feeding areas, quarrying, open-cast mining, plans for forestry and over-grazing of some favoured feeding sites by sheep may yet lead to their demise. Small numbers of Pinkfeet and Greylag are sometimes seen in the Slammannan area and seem to be increasing. Greenland Whitefronts were also present in 1991 and 1992.

There are no recent data for the other waters in the region, including Carron dam at Stenhousemuir, two reservoirs near Denny and the Earlsburn reservoirs in the Gargunnock hills. However these sites are either too small and disturbed or too exposed to hold many birds.

There is rather little information on breeding waterfowl in the region. One exception is Airthrey Loch where a detailed study of the breeding waterfowl has been undertaken.

Airthrey had 5 pairs of Little Grebe (**Figure 6**), 1 pair of Mute Swan, 21-28 pairs of Mallard, 7-8 pairs of Tufted Duck, 20-26 pairs of Coot and 9-18 pairs of Moorhen annually during the study. Despite its small size Airthrey is probably one of the most important inland sites in the region for breeding waterfowl but it is atypical in many respects.

The remainder of this section discusses the

Figure 6 The Dabchick or Little Grebe nests on freshwaters throughout the region. Five pairs usually attempt to breed on Airthrey Loch, where a pair recently raised three broods in one season   (David Bryant).

breeding waterfowl by species rather than by site because of the paucity of information on most sites. A pair of Red-throated Divers has nested since 1974 on hill lochs in the west of the area. In 1990 two pairs attempted to breed. Black-throated Divers are present from late March to early July, but low water levels at the nesting lochs have been responsible for several failures.

Great Crested Grebe summer regularly at several sites but nesting is not usually successful. They tend to favour larger water bodies such as Gartmorn Dam, Lake of Menteith and the Carron Valley reservoir. Little Grebe breed on smaller waters and are therefore easily overlooked. Away from Airthrey breeding has only been recorded at Loch Ard and Cromlix in recent years but this is surely a serious underestimate of the population.

Mute Swan nest on most lowland eutrophic waters in the area. At some sites vandalism is a problem but generally they are successful. There are no recent records of Greylag breeding in the Loch Venachar/Achray area following an attempted introduction in the 1970s. Small numbers of Canada Geese occasionally appear at sites on the Carse: a pair nested at Loch Watston in 1991. Given the population at the Endrick mouth it is surprising that there are not more sightings of this introduced species. Numbers of Shelduck nesting at the Endrick mouth are much reduced, following the arrival of mink, with 6 or fewer pairs now normal (Mitchell 1993).

The ubiquitous Mallard is found from sea level to c 500m, frequenting large lochs and reservoirs to small lochans and ponds, rivers and ditches. The other dabbling duck have a much more local distribution.

Wigeon are found at a few sites in the north-east of the area with 1-2 pairs regularly seen at Upper Glen Devon Reservoir, Cromlix and Loch Mahaick. Teal favour the higher moorland areas and can easily be overlooked on small bogs and marshes. In 1987 wader survey teams recorded Teal on Menstrie and Alva mosses in the Ochils, and on the Gargunnock and Earls Hills. They have also been found on moorland near Killin and are probably widespread in the uplands. In 1990 pairs were noted at Loch Katrine and the Venachar/Achray marshes, while up to 7 males have been recorded at Upper Glen Devon Reservoir. Up to 10 pairs of Shoveler breed at the Endrick mouth but away from this site they are surprisingly scarce even during spring passage. Cambus pools is the only other site which attracts the species with any regularity and two pairs may have nested in 1989. A pair of Gadwall nested there in 1990. This species is a surprisingly scarce visitor to the area, especially given the breeding populations in Tayside.

Tufted Duck have increased dramatically at many sites in recent years and may be the most abundant breeding duck at some sites. It is therefore astonishing to find that away from Airthrey broods have only been recorded at Cromlix, Loch Watston and on the river Devon at Alva in the last five years. There are no recent records of summering or breeding Pochard or Pintail. Also, the Common Scoter has not bred on Loch Lomond for several years, and may be lost to the region. Many of the Trossachs Lochs appear suitable for Goldeneye but this species has proved reluctant to breed beyond its strongholds on Speyside although it regularly lingers into May.

The two saw-billed ducks, the Goosander and Red-breasted Merganser are widespread throughout the area in small numbers and are subject to persecution on some fisheries. Mergansers tend to be found on the lower reaches of the river systems, though birds have also been recorded from North Third and Carron Valley reservoirs in the spring. The largest numbers occur at the Endrick mouth. Goosander are found more on the upper reaches of the rivers and can be seen on small burns far into the hills. The Devon valley holds several pairs with broods noted as far downstream as Dollar. They have been recorded on many of the Trossachs lochs and at Loch Voil. A very recent newcomer to the area is the North American Ruddy Duck which bred successfully for the first time at Loch Watston in 1991. This species is now also established at several nearby sites in Tayside.

Coots are found on most lowland eutrophic waters and can reach a high density at favoured sites like Airthrey. Moorhens can be found on almost any wetland from marshy corners of fields, ditches, streams, slow flowing stretches of river and ponds up to large water bodies where there is abundant cover. It would be interesting to know if Moorhens suffer from predation by mink since populations in other areas are reported to have declined where mink are common and a decline was noted on the Devon after 1977, where mink were widespread (Henty 1991).

Figure 7 Colonies of Herons are scattered throughout the area. Birds spread widely after breeding, appearing beside most lochs and rivers. During hard weather many take refuge on the Forth Estuary   (David Bryant).

Herons can be seen on most lochs and rivers throughout the year (**Figure 7**). Some well established heronries are known but in areas where the species is disturbed pairs may nest singly and change sites between years. The many conifer forests and plantations in the area now reaching maturity offer almost unlimited nest sites and it is impossible to arrive at a sensible figure for the local breeding population. Adults attend the colonies from February onwards and the young rapidly disperse after fledging in late May. The local population may be augmented by birds from further north from late summer to late winter.

Farmland

Most of the low ground in the east of the region is devoted to arable farming with an emphasis on cereal production. This gives way to a mixed landscape with cattle and ploughland where the ground rises above Stirling, ultimately giving over to sheepwalk on the Ochils and Campsies and the moors and mountains of the west. This pattern of agriculture has a dominant influence on the birds of the area, though in reality the agricultural landscape is more of a patchwork than this outline suggests. In all areas, for example, some land carries hedgerows or trees while nearby ground lacks even scrub. Equally, pools and small marshes are distributed throughout, although these have become infrequent where agricultural production has been

Figure 8 Corn Buntings could be found on many lowland farms in the 1970s but by the early 1990s they were restricted to a few pairs in the southeast of the region   (David Bryant).

bird of the arable lowlands is the Corn Bunting, characteristically perched on any telegraph wire which passes through its territory (**Figure 8**). It is now only known from a few sites between Falkirk and Kincardine, and could shortly be lost to the region. The cause of its decline remains obscure, since the species has a liking for barren barley plains, so the flight from traditional agricultural practices is not the only possible explanation.

Grassland with berry-bearing hedges provides an ideal refuge for Fieldfare and Redwing on passage or in winter, although these species tend to be commoner before the end of the year and again in early spring. Year round they may be joined by the Mistle Thrush, which may form impressive flocks in autumn. The low carseland stretching to the east, and more particularly, to the west of Stirling, is a haunt of grey geese throughout the autumn and winter. They are one of the most imporant features of the region's birdlife and are described above in relation to their freshwater and estuarine roosts.

The breeding birds of farmland include most of the familiar species of the countryside and garden. The most striking assemblage, due to their conspicuousness and importance for conservation, is that of the breeding waders. Lapwing and Oystercatcher are widespread, with the former showing some signs of retreat from formerly favoured sites as farming intensifies, while the latter continues to expand beyond the confines of the riverside. Curlew, Redshank and Snipe can also be found throughout where grassland is dominant, although the Redshank is more limited to moist lower ground. A former visitor to the region was the Corncrake, particularly to the carse to the west of Stirling. Sadly they now appear to have retreated along with the bulk of the Scottish mainland population. Unless this wider decline is reversed as a result of changing agricultural priorities, the Corncrake is probably already a permanent loss to the region. Another species relying on grassland which is in decline is the Barn Owl. Formerly widespread, with road casualties a sadly common sight, the species has now become very scarce. The virtual absence of recent road casualties is no compensation for the demise of a species, almost certainly due primarily to ploughing and reseeding of traditional meadow haunts and tidying of field edges and corners.

The commoner resident birds of woodland, such as Blackbird, Robin, Wren and Chaffinch can be found breeding throughout much of the farmland of central Scotland. Migrants are more thinly distributed but include Willow Warbler, Whitethroat, Sedge Warbler and Spotted Flycatcher where the cover is suitable. Grasshopper Warblers are much scarcer, however, with the Lesser Whitethroat a possible future colonist, given their frequency to the south of the Region.

It will be of great interest to see if the decline of species associated with the farmed landscape is slowed or halted by the recent 'greening' of attitudes amongst farmers, governments and consumers. A consolidation

greatest. The intensively farmed lowlands hold only a thinly distributed breeding bird community, whereas it is more richly developed with a larger element of woodland species on most mixed farms. The rough grasslands resulting from extensive sheep grazing on the higher ground is also rather poorly populated by birds, to the extent that in winter a visit can reveal a landscape largely devoid of birds apart from a wandering crow or scavenging Great Black Back. The birds of this upland habitat are dealt with later in the moorland section.

The winter scene on open farmland is characterised by flocks of finches, including Chaffinch, Greenfinch and Linnet with fewer Goldfinch and Brambling, along with some Yellowhammers and Tree Sparrows and occasional Twite. House Sparrows are also common around farms while the fields hold Skylark, Wood and Feral Pigeons, Rook, Jackdaw, Lapwing, Starling, Common and Black-headed Gulls and Grey Partridge. Golden Plovers occur, but away from the estuary have usually moved on by the end of the year. In a few places Red-legged Partridges (and more recently hybrids with the Chukar) have been introduced, but they do not appear to flourish. Other widespread species, especially where there is some tree cover, include Stock Dove, Pheasant, Carrion Crow and Magpie. A range of predatory birds is present, rather more thinly spread than around the estuary, but more often including Buzzard and Hen Harrier, and increasingly so towards the west. A formerly widespread

of more traditional methods, or more likely an avoidance of an ever greater productivity spiral, are likely to underlie any stabilization of prospects for the breeding and wintering birds of farmland.

Woodland

Viewed from any vantage point around the Carse of Stirling, much of the region appears well wooded with conifer plantations especially prominent on the rising ground, and more varied mixed deciduous woodland usually within the larger estates. At the maximum extent of natural forest, in the postglacial period before the influence of man, the lower ground would have been covered with Oak, Alder and Elm, with Birch, Willow and Aspen becoming prominent higher up and a belt of Scots Pine mainly in the north and west. With the clearance of forest for agriculture, tree cover reached a minimum in the 17th century. Systematic planting was widespread in the 18th century with Larch coming into prominence and Beech and Sycamore conspicuous in amenity planting. This century has seen an enormous expansion of conifer forest with Sitka Spruce a dominating introduction. The original forest persists, however, in general nature if not historical continuity, as small areas of hill oakwood, modified by a long history of coppicing and grazing, and some relics of heavily grazed hillside pinewoods and Alders.

In midwinter the hill oakwoods and the large conifer plantations are similar in that very few birds remain (**Table 5**). It is easy to spend several hours and see only a few Wood Pigeons, Wrens, Robins, Coal Tits and Bullfinches. Chaffinches largely winter on farmland and most Siskins move farther south. However the mixed deciduous woodlands on lower ground, such as Mine Wood or Hermitage Wood, often have a full complement of resident species. In addition to those mentioned above, Great and Blue Tits are frequent as are Blackbirds, Song Thrushes and Dunnocks; a species mix very similar to that found in suburbs with plenty of cover. Relatively few species come to feed in numbers as winter visitors, in hard weather flocks of Redwings can be found foraging in leaf litter whilst Goldfinches and Siskins may prospect large Birch trees and after a good mast year large parties of Woodpigeons feed under Beeches. The occurrence of dense patches of young Rowan within oakwoods suggests seed distribution through the roosting of flocks of migrant Redwings or Fieldfares.

By early March in most years the woodlands are filled with Chaffinch song and in conifer plantations Goldcrests and Coal Tits are frequent but it is not until mid-April or early May that most of the long distance summer migrants are in place. The three leaf warblers illustrate some of the subtleties of habitat selection in woodland birds. The Willow Warbler is by far the commonest species but is absent where there is a high canopy, preferring open woods, edges, young plantations or strips of trees along burns, often high into the hills.

By contrast the Chiffchaff prefers tall deciduous trees with a rich shrub layer, often in the grounds of large houses which led the late Professor Meiklejohn to smear it as a 'snob' species. However, some individuals sing in tall spruce plantations. Wood Warblers are one of the few woodland species that normally require extensive woods with a dense canopy, typically areas of beech or semi-natural oak. In both cases the shrub layer is sparse. Blackcaps have similar requirements to Chiffchaffs whereas Garden Warblers are usually found in lower, bushier situations. Whitethroats avoid a tall canopy and hence are only in clearings whilst Lesser Whitethroats are almost unknown in our area. The distribution of Pied Flycatchers is largely within that of the Wood Warbler but it is even more characteristic of western districts and is very much affected by the presence of nest boxes. A nestbox project was started in the Trossachs in 1973 and in 1991 58 pairs raised 317 young. However, nesting in boxes can be an advertisement to predators; at the RSPB Reserve at Inversnaid in 1991 Pine Martens raided most of the 17 pairs of Pied Flycatcher. Redstarts also benefit from the provision of nestboxes (26 in the Trossachs project in 1991) but can be found occasionally in open conifers and are characteristic of hill birchwood. The last two species are traditionally associated with Tree Pipits largely due to their common liking for grazed oakwoods with a relatively low canopy and little undergrowth, The Tree Pipit, however, is found more widely in sparse woodland and in young conifer plantations provided there are songposts (Henty 1976).

Most common species are found in all types of woodland, though the less common species mentioned above are very scarce in conifer woods, in particular there are few species that are conifer specialists - even Coal Tit, Goldcrest and Siskin can be found regularly in deciduous areas. However, the two conifer specialists, Crossbill and Capercaillie, are particularly interesting. Crossbills are now widespread in the extensive western spruce forests here although the first breeding was not proven until 1977 (Mitchell 1977). They belong to the Continental form *Loxia curvirostra* and at times irrupt in large numbers from abroad. This happened in the autumn of 1990 and parties were still frequent in Loch Ard Forest through the following summer. Crossbill (and Siskin) are difficult to census but there is little doubt that they have increased as breeding species in recent years. Siskins were for example only recorded as 'probably breeding' in Carron Valley Forest during the 1968-73 Breeding Atlas, but there were possibly 100 pairs in 1977 whilst in a mixture of oak and conifer forest in Loch Ard Forest in 1992 Siskins were as frequent as Great Tits. The largest British gamebird, the Capercaillie, is also a colonist of conifers having spread into this area between 1856 and 1875, after the species had become extinct in Scotland and then been reintroduced to Tayside in 1837 (Rintoul and Baxter 1935). However, it has never become common locally, unlike the Pheasant whose numbers are admittedly boosted by release of reared birds but also flourishes in

Table 5   Bird communities in the woodlands of central Scotland. Figures show the percentage frequency/relative abundance of each species.

| | SUMMER | | | WINTER | | |
| | Deciduous | | Conifer | Deciduous | | Conifer |
	Mine Wood	Lomondside Oaks		Lowland	Hill Oaks	
Gt sp Woodpecker	0.6	0.1		1.1	2.0	
Green Woodpecker	0.4	0.5			1.0	
Tree Pipit		1.4				
Wren	8.1	16.4	13.8	5.6	7.8	6.1
Dunnock	3.4	0.9	1.8	1.1	1.0	0.8
Robin	9.2	11.1	6.4	4.4	2.9	0.8
Redstart		1.2				
Blackbird	11.3	6.6	0.9	9.2	2.0	
Song Thrush	2.1	3.7	0.9	0.7	1.0	
Mistle Thrush	0.9	0.5	1.8	0.4	1.0	
Whitethroat		0.2				
Garden Warbler		3.0				
Blackcap	0.9	0.6				
Wood Warbler	4.1	1.9				
Chiffchaff	+					
Willow Warbler	4.3	11.8	3.7			
Goldcrest	0.9	1.4	17.4	0.4	1.0	5.3
Spotted Flycatcher	1.1	0.6				
Pied Flycatcher		0.1				
Long-tailed Tit	0.2	1.7		8.5	17.6	
Coal Tit	1.3	3.6	17.4	6.0	28.4	78
Blue Tit	13.7	4.9	0.9	22.6	9.8	
Great Tit	5.3	3.6		13.2	2.9	
Treecreeper	1.5	2.6		3.0	3.9	
Jay		0.3	1.8	0.5	6.9	0.8
Magpie				1.1	1.0	
Starling	14.7	0.5				
Chaffinch	14.1	19.3	26.6	7.6	1.0	1.5
Greenfinch	0.9					
Goldfinch				5.1	1.0	
Siskin			3.7	8.8	4.9	0.8
Redpoll		0.3		0.2	1.0	
Bullfinch	1.1	1.0	2.8	0.7	2.0	4.5
Total Records	468	858	109	569	87	131
Records per hour	-	-	-	57.2	12.1	11.3

NOTES: Summer:-   Mine Wood (9.3ha) - from detailed mapping survey by G.Shaw in 1974, 75, 76. Lomondside Oaks (101ha) - summary of detailed mapping surveys, Williamson 1974. Conifer Summer (3 woods 1975-78) and all winter data from transect counts (Henty, unpublished)
Winter :- Deciduous Lowland: 4 woods 1990-92; Deciduous Hill Oaks: 4 woods 1991/92; Conifer: 6 woods 1991/92.

completely wild situations. Another gamebird is the only woodland wader, the Woodcock, which is widespread throughout the region. Two birds of prey are characteristic of woods, Sparrowhawks can be seen almost anywhere, whereas the Buzzard is very scarce as a breeding bird east of Stirling. The other main predators of woodland are owls, but they are poorly documented although it is clear that Tawny Owls are widespread and frequently heard, whereas Long-eared Owls are much scarcer and most often in conifers. Barn Owls are scarce and enter woodland only at the fringes. In Queen Elizabeth Forest Park (QEFP) the Forestry Commission have put up 101 nest boxes, but by 1992 Barn Owls have only used them for autumn roosting although several Tawnies have bred. Both woodpeckers have spread in historical times in Scotland; Great Spotted Woodpeckers since the late 1800s and they are now widespread in all types of woodland though scarce in summer east of Stirling. Green Woodpeckers first nested in Scotland in 1951 and locally in 1960. Now this species is widespread in deciduous woodland although equally characteristic of short grass hillsides with only scattered trees; it is presumably responsible for the excavations in the large wood ant mounds of QEFP. Lesser Spotted Woodpeckers were reported in autumn/winter in Loch Ard Forest in 1968 and 1970. However, the birds were never seen by specialist ornithologists and have never occurred again. Another trunk climber is the Nuthatch which has recently spread into the Borders (Murray 1991), but we have only one record on Loch Lomondside in 1978 (which seems to have been misplotted by Murray to Strathyre, so there is still no acceptable record for the Forth basin). A species perhaps on the verge of extinction is the Nightjar, which was not recorded for 20 years until a singing bird was tracked down in Loch Ard Forest in 1992.

Several species commonly nest in woodland but usually feed in open country: Starling, Carrion Crow, Jackdaw and Rook. However, Jays are true forest birds and are known as specialist buriers of acorns and hence a significant agent in the regeneration and dispersal of oaks. Magpies are regular inhabitants of at least the fringes of woodland, their great increase in numbers in suburbs in the last 20 years has been paralleled by a spread into Loch Ard Forest away from Aberfoyle.

It is particularly unfortunate that there is so little quantitative data on the bird life of local conifer forests since there is such a large and still increasing area of conifer plantation. Contemporary forestry policy is now much more sensitive to conservation issues and there can be no doubt that such actions as leaving burnsides unplanted, and creative inaction in allowing natural regeneration of trees, as well as planting a deciduous complement, will increase the variety and abundance of birds in commercial forests.

(Olivia Lassiere)

Figure 9 The largest tract of montane habitat is the southern Highlands in the northwest of the region where there are several well known Munros; including Ben Lomond and Ben More. The summit of Ben Dubhchraig is shown in late winter, when the area is a haunt of Ptarmigan, hunting Golden Eagles and early-nesting Ravens. In summer, the commonest breeding bird is the Meadow Pipit. Peregrine and Ring Ouzel also occur throughout the area. The hybridization zone of the Carrion and Hooded Crow crosses these mountains, with pure 'Hoodies' to the north and 'Carrions' to the south.

Mountain and Moorland

Mountain and moorland habitats within central Scotland occur in five units, all with different geological and physiographic features. Four units can loosely be classified as montane, namely (1) the Campsies/Fintry/Gargunnock/Touch Hills, (2) the Ochil Hills, (3) Braes o' Doune/Menteith Hills and (4) the southern Highlands proper, extending northwards from Callander and Killin (**Figure 9**). The fifth unit, Flanders Moss, is of upland-type moorland habitat lying in a lowland setting in the Forth Valley.

In the following sections the characteristics of each unit and its typical birds are considered in turn. Since the publication of The Stirling Region in 1974, some upland habitats and species groups have received a considerable amount of attention though, overall, comprehensive ornithological research in upland central Scotland has been scarce. Much of the material presented here draws on the efforts and findings of people engaged in three studies: the Central Scotland Raptor Study Group (CSRSG), the former Nature Conservancy Council's Moorland Bird Survey (MBS) and the University of Stirling's Dipper Group.

The Campsie Fells/Gargunnock Hills (Unit 1) are sandwiched between the River Forth in the north and the greater Glasgow conurbation to the south. There are few discernible summits, though Earl's Seat in the southwest reaches 578m. In general, they

Figure 10 Blackcock at the 'lek'. The species is mainly found in the uplands, often favouring the moorland edge and young conifer plantations. There are no longer birds at a formerly well watched site on Sheriffmuir, and there is concern the decline may be more widespread   (David Bryant).

comprise a rolling plateau of rough grassland and heather moorland at altitudes between 300-500m, very sharply demarked from the surrounding valleys by an escarpment composed of long cliff lines with intervening vegetated talus slopes of more easily erodible strata. The massif is split on an east-west axis by the Rivers Carron and Endrick, both rising in the Carron Valley Reservoir. This area is also heavily afforested.

Upland bird communities can broadly be divided into those associated with either flatter grasslands and moorlands or cliff lines and escarpments. Skylarks and Meadow Pipits occur in moderate to high densities throughout.

Three larger species stand out as typical of moorland areas: Red Grouse, Golden Plover and Curlew, occurring at regionally important densities (Calladine et al 1990). Red Grouse are mostly associated with Heather, whereas habitat choice in waders is governed more by vegetation height than plant species. Golden Plover choose open areas with short vegetation (stunted, high altitude communities or recently burned areas of heather moorland) while the widespread Curlew prefers more cover in areas of taller vegetation such as *Juncus* flushes (ob cit). Other wader species occur patchily at low densities where there is suitable habitat (Lapwing, Snipe and Common Sandpiper). The Dunlin also falls into this category: a very small number of pairs breed in the wettest blanket peat areas in the west of the Campsies.

The cliffs and scarps are perhaps best known for breeding Peregrines. Inter-nest distances are amongst the lowest recorded in Britain (Mitchell and Broad

1987). Scree slopes beneath the cliffs are a favoured breeding habitat of Wheatears; they too can occur at very high densities, although they are also widely distributed in the moorland areas where rocky outcrops and stone walls are present. Breeding groups of Twite appear to have established themselves in the Campsies/Gargunnocks (as well as the Ochils and elsewhere) and, although little is known about their precise requirements, they often favour the transitional ground between moorlands and lower lying agricultural land. Several other typical upland species occur in these hills, including Black Grouse, Short-eared Owl and Ravens. In the early 1970s six Raven territories were known but by 1981 only one remained occupied (Mitchell 1981). This one remaining site was subsequently deserted, but two of the others have since been re-occupied. During winter these hills are relatively quiet but small numbers of Snow Buntings may be found on windswept clifftops such as at Stronend.

A sizeable portion of the Ochil Hills (Unit 2), and certainly the most spectacular part, lies within the region. The south-facing scarp of this massif runs along the line of the Ochil Fault which separates lowland Clackmannanshire, underlain by Carboniferous coal measures, from a thick sequence of Old Red Sandstone volcanic uplands. The Ochils rise from near sea level to 721m at the summit of Ben Cleuch, but the top of the scarp face is usually around 500m above Strathdevon. Away from the scarp, the overall impression is of rolling grassy sheepwalks, incised by a multitude of burns which form steep glens and spectacular gorges when they cut through the Ochil Fault. In a relatively small area habitat can be very variable; however, the broad classification into

Figure 11 Dotterel visit our highest hilltops on passage in spring. A possible former breeder but with no evidence of any recent attempts   (Helen Riley).

either the tops or glens and scarps, is reasonably useful in describing bird communities.

The tops are mostly grassy and dry, though two larger (bog) mosses occur above Alva and Menstrie. These are flat, peaty areas dominated by Heather. Smaller, wet *Juncus* flushes often occur around the headwaters of burns. Unlike the Heather moorland areas on the northwest-facing slopes of the Ochils in neighbouring Tayside, Alva and Menstrie Mosses are not managed intensively and the Red Grouse populations are low. Black Grouse (**Figure 10**) have almost disappeared, but the occasional Greyhen is still seen in areas with a little more cover. At the time of the first Breeding Atlas (1968-72), Golden Plover were reasonably common on the higher summits and ridges with short grass swards, with a population estimated at 20-25 pairs. Nowadays, very few are seen in such areas but small numbers still breed on the mosses. The MBS estimated nine and two pairs respectively in their study areas on Alva and Menstrie Mosses in 1987. Breeding Curlew and Snipe are present in the mosses, although far more Curlew occur in the grasslands and it is, perhaps, the most numerous breeding wader in this upland area. Redshank and Lapwing are patchily distributed, although both can usually be seen on the slopes around Backhills Farm near Upper Glendevon Reservoir. Sometimes, Dotterel turn up on the summit of Ben Cleuch; its alpine-type habitat is too limited and too disturbed by hikers for them to breed at this site, but small numbers probably pass through regularly on migration (**Figure 11**). Breeding raptors are scarce on the summits, though the occasional pair of Merlin is suspected. Otherwise, Peregrines and Kestrels and, less frequently, Buzzards can be seen hunting over the tops. Carrion Crows are the only regular breeding corvid, mostly in trees, but in late summer large mixed flocks of post-breeding and immature corvids (Crows, Rooks, Jackdaws) frequent the tops, often in the company of Starlings. In some summers, fairly large flocks (20-40) of Ravens occur on the tops utilizing sheep carrion, with a roost gathering on the north side of the hills overlooking Strathallan in Tayside. In other years, only occasional singles and duos occur irregularly. Skylarks and Meadow Pipits are often exceptionally numerous in spring and summer, though most of them desert the hills for low-lying agricultural areas in winter, to reappear in March. The Snow Bunting is perhaps the only regular winter visitor to the tops, though it is often only detected when harsh weather brings it down to lower altitudes.

The glens and scarps of the Ochils display a wider diversity of breeding birds and, although several such as Wheatear and Whinchat may occur in suitable patches on the tops, they are present at much higher densities in glen and scarp habitats. The small burns tumbling through the upper reaches of glens have good numbers of Dipper, Grey Wagtail and Wren, though breeding Teal and Common Sandpiper mainly occur on those flowing northwards (**Figure 12**). Mallard are

Figure 12   The Devon near Muckhart. The swift waters draining the uplands typically hold populations of Dippers, Grey Wagtails, Common Sandpipers and Goosanders   (David Bryant).

present throughout and burnside nests may be located at over 500m altitude. Herons occur in the glens at all times of year, though no breeding colonies are presently known.

The south-facing scarp slope between Blairlogie and Dollar abounds in cliffs and crags. These are a haunt of Peregrines and Kestrels. Jackdaws occur quite high up on Dumyat, especially where rock faces are well pitted with holes and niches. Pairs of Ravens are seen regularly on Dumyat and in the vicinity of Craig Leith (above Alva); display has been recorded recently and it is hoped that these corvids will reoccupy their former breeding sites on these spectacular buttresses. Wheatears are most common on crags and screes and small numbers of breeding Twite have been located in three places, also in broken rocky habitat. Numbers of breeding Whinchat seem to vary from year to year but these birds are always most conspicuous in areas with extensive bracken cover, both on the scarp (e.g. between Tillicoultry and Dollar) and in the glens (e.g. Burn of Sorrow, behind Castle Campbell). Stonechat used to be common in the gorse-clad parts of the scarp but after a period of absence a small number have reappeared in the vicinity of the Glendevon Reservoirs and Alva; possible early signs of re-establishment? The Grey Partridge is another bird regularly encountered in glens, especially where there is *Juncus* and bracken cover; in spring pairs are often flushed above 300m. The current status of the Ring

Ouzel gives some cause for concern. This species used to be fairly widespread in the glens and on the scarp, but recent sightings are few and have been confined to steep glensides, especially those with patches of heather. Despite the abundance of suitable hosts on the tops, Cuckoos are more regularly heard (and seen) on the scarp. The Tree Pipit sometimes breeds well above the 'tree-line'. Interestingly, crags and large boulders appear to be adequate alternatives to trees from which to launch song and display flights.

The Braes o' Doune (Unit 3) form a major tract of heather moorland above the Teith Valley, marking the flanks of the southern Highlands proper. However, rather little is known about the area ornithologically, though they undoubtedly support good numbers of breeding waders, especially Curlew, as well as Red Grouse and a few Hen Harriers. Unfortunately, large areas have recently been afforested and typical upland bird communities are at risk. The Menteith Hills have largely disappeared under a blanket of conifers and on the whole can no longer be considered suitable habitat for most mountain and moorland birds.

The southern Highlands (Unit 4) form by far the largest tract of truly upland habitat in the region, with several well known Munros, including Ben Lomond (974m) in the south west and Ben More/Stob Binnein (1174m) in the north. Their bird communities are poorly known, with the exception of raptors, though Meadow Pipits predominate throughout. Montane areas are characterised by the presence of Golden Eagles, Ravens, Ptarmigans and Peregrines (whose breeding success is monitored annually by the Central Scotland Raptor Study Group). This part of central Scotland holds about nine Golden Eagle home ranges, although at present only seven appear to be occupied. In 1991 only two pairs were successful, fledging three young in total. Populations of Eagles, Peregrines and Ravens are fairly stable though breeding success can be very variable, whereas the fortunes of Ptarmigan, at their most southerly outpost, remain something of a mystery. Glens and lower-lying areas with commercial forestry, other woodland, moorland and bogs hold the remaining upland raptors: Buzzards, Hen Harriers and Merlins. However, Merlins are very scarce with only three pairs present in the north of the region in 1990. Given suitable habitat, densities of Golden Plover, and maybe Dunlin, are locally higher than in the Campsies/Gargunnocks and Ochils. Twite are known to breed in the Ben Ledi area and elsewhere near Callander and in the vicinity of Balquhidder.

Flanders Moss (Unit 5) is the most intact lowland raised bog in the area and is one of the best examples of this habitat type in Scotland. However, its fringes have become increasingly afforested and birch scrub is apparently invading some of the remaining open areas. Peat digging is another current threat to the integrity of the site. In the 1970's and early 1980's it was famed for one of the largest inland gull colonies in Scotland, with approximately 8000 pairs of Lesser Black-backed and 500 pairs of Herring Gulls in 1980. The colonies have

Figure 13   Barbush sand quarry near Dunblane held a thriving Sand Martin colony for many years. At one time it was the largest in Scotland with nearly 1000 pairs. The population crashed dramatically in 1984, linked to drought in their African winter quarters, but has now recovered (Olivia Lassiere).

much decreased in recent years with only a few hundred pairs present in 1986 when breeding success was also very poor (six chicks reared). Although reasons are not fully known, there seems to have been a coincident growth in the size of a gull colony in neighbouring Tayside. During winter Hen Harriers frequent Flanders Moss and can often be seen hunting over surrounding farmland, and the site is irregularly used as a Pink-footed Goose roost.

Although the mountains and moorlands of central Scotland do not hold the ornithological riches of some exceptional areas further north (Cairngorms, FlowCountry, northwest Highlands) or in the Hebrides (Islay, Uists), they are of much value. The contrasting images of highlands, lowlands, the Forth Estuary and industry from a single viewpoint often surpasses in variety that from within a wholly upland area and of course, ornithologically, there is still much to be learned.

Urban and Industrial

The most familiar of birds are those which live close to man. Few will fail to register, and many will recognise, the Magpie, Carrion Crow, Black-headed Gull, Starling or House Sparrow, since they are common and conspicuous around towns and villages. Bird table visitors are also well known and are dominated by Blue and Great Tits, Blackbird and Robin, although a well stocked table can also attract a variety of less usual species, sometimes including GreatSpotted Woodpecker, Blackcap and Siskin. The latter has become more frequent over the past decade, to join another relatively recent arrival at many tables, the Collared Dove.All four aerial feeding species have a close association with man and his activities. Swallows avoid towns and nest most commonly on farm buildings or around villages, forming colonies of over 10 pairs where farm practices and buildings remain traditional in style. House Martins are found in many villages and are happy to colonize industrial buildings if left undisturbed. They appear to have suffered a recent decline, but this could be a false impression and just reflect a tendency to nest increasingly in scattered pairs, and therefore less obviously, on new housing estates. The Sand Martin, which chooses mostly sand quarries for nesting, suffered a dramatic fall in numbers in 1984 (**Figure 13**). Many of its smaller colonies became extinct while the larger ones, including the largest in Scotland at the time near Dunblane with 900-1000 pairs, lost the bulk of their birds (Jones 1987). Populations have now recovered, although their success is very dependent on sympathetic treatment by sand quarry operators, and an absence of severe droughts in sub-Saharan Africa. The Swift remains frequent in our older towns and villages, where it can find a wealth of nest sites, with a recent count of 160 birds together in Bridge of Allan for example. Ringed Plovers and other wader species nest in small numbers near some sand quarries and reservoirs (Henty 1991). Colonies of Black headed and Common Gulls also occur at these sites.

Waste tips are a focus for the activities of crows and the larger gulls. While there is an increasing practice of covering organic waste with soil soon after dumping, it remains available for long enough to allow many birds to find food. Crows, Herring and Lesser Black Backs and Starlings are the main scavenging species, but others are also frequent. The gulls form conspicuous parties as they fly or soar between roosts and their feeding or breeding sites.

Discussion

The greatest interest in the status of the region's birds attaches to the fate of breeding species. Since the last review, covering the period 1935-1972 (Bryant 1974)

eight species have been proved to breed for the first time (**Table 6**). The first newcomer was the Black-throated Diver, although colonisation is marred by generally poor breeding success. The first young were not reared until 1982 (Thom 1986), even though eggs were laid in 1974. The Red-throated Diver was proved to breed in 1974 (Thom 1986), although it had been suspected of doing so previously. The Ruddy Duck, a species accidentally introduced from North America and establishing itself in Somerset only in 1960, raised young for the first time in central Scotland in 1991 near Doune. The Common Scoter has nested on Loch Lomond since 1971, right on the edge of the area considered here but numbers have decreased greatly, perhaps to extinction, in the last four years. The Little Ringed Plover has nested on just one occasion, but unfortunately the clutch was destroyed, and while the species was present in the year following, there have been no further breeding attempts. Arctic Terns nested in 1977 on Loch Lomondside. Hawfinch and Crossbill, previously suspected of breeding were also first proved to breed in the 1970s. The Osprey has consolidated a tentative hold by recolonizing Loch Lomondside in 1989. Sadly, the nest was robbed in 1992, but a continued presence of this species seems likely given its steady progress elsewhere in Scotland where over 100 young were raised in 1992. The Kingfisher has also recolonized effectively following a series of mild winters, so it is once again to be found along favoured rivers such as the Devon, Endrick and Allan.

The Yellow Wagtail, and probably the Corncrake and Herring Gull as well, were lost as breeding species during the 1980s. Also, some sporadic breeders have not nested recently; Pintail and Pochard are examples. These losses should be weighed against those species which have either clung on, such as the Nightjar in the Trossachs, or have recently been proved to have very small populations, such as Dunlin and Twite. Some species have shown gratifying increases, colonizing or recolonizing new areas, such as Peregrine and Buzzard. Also, Crossbill and Siskin have benefitted from recent forestry plantings and Pied Flycatchers have taken up residence in the nest-boxes provided for them. Trends amongst commoner species are always difficult to follow without detailed studies, but Tufted Duck, Collared Dove, Magpie and Jay seem to have increased. On the other hand, Barn Owl, Redshank, Lapwing, Capercaillie, Grasshopper Warbler, Ring Ouzel, Stonechat, Tree Sparrow and, outstandingly, the Corn Bunting, have shown signs of decline. Only the last species, however, is close to being lost, although here as elsewhere the cause remains obscure (Marchant et al. 1990).

Table 6 Changes of status for the birds of central Scotland during 1970-1992.

Bred for the first time (n=8)

Black throated Diver (1974)
Red throated Diver (1974)
Ruddy Duck (1991)
Common Scoter (1971)
Little Ringed Plover (1987)
Arctic Tern (1977)
Hawfinch (1973)
Crossbill (1977)

Apparently ceased to breed (n=3)

Corncake (1988)
Yellow Wagtail (1986)
Herring Gull (late 1980s)

Species and sub-species recorded for first time (n=17)

White Pelican (presumed escape, 1973)
White Stork (1982)
Wood Duck (presumed escape, 1980)
Green-winged Teal (N. American subspecies, 1978)
American Wigeon (1992)
Red-crested Pochard (1988)
Ruddy Duck (1991)
Hobby (1989)
Killdeer (1983)
Little Ringed Plover (1983)
Amercian Golden Plover (1977)
Black Guillemot (1983)
Nuthatch (1978)
Red-backed-Shrike (1988)
Bluethroat (1980)
Crested Tit (1981)
Two-barred Crossbill (1985)

Seventeen species (**Table 6**) have been added to the central Scotland list, although their status is sometimes difficult to determine exactly, since recording and vetting of records was largely absent until the *Scottish Bird Report* appeared in the 1960s. The history of commoner species and the occurence of local rarities is therefore likely to remain rather obscure for the period 1940-60s. However, with annual publication of local records in the *Forth Naturalist & Historian* and the Scottish Ornithologists' Club's *Scottish Bird Reports*, there is no longer a problem of accurate record keeping. A total of 17 species has been recorded for the first time since the early 1970s. Two of these (Ruddy Duck, Little Ringed Plover) have bred, whereas the others are apparently vagrants or possible future colonists. Mitchell (1992) notes some additional species just outside the area covered here, to the west of the River Endrick. The regional species list, including Endrick Mouth records, stands at 259 species, up to the end of 1991 (Henty and Brackenridge 1992).

For the most part there are a few immediate threats to the most important breeding, passage and wintering populations of the area. Until recently, however, the best of the Forth estuary was zoned for land-claim and industry, and had this gone ahead it would have largely destroyed its interest. Given the current pressure for development of estuarine shores, it is too early to be confident of the security of the area. Protection of raptors, especially at nest sites, also remains necessary, although a wider acceptance of the place of birds of prey in the countryside seems to be gaining ground. Reconciling the differing interests of farmers and flocks of wintering geese and swans is also a priority. These, in conjunction with more sensitive management of lowland farms, woodland and forest, urban and common ground and the wider uplands, and the development of wetland and other reserves to protect and extend scarce habitats, should ensure that any changes in fortune for the birds of central scotland over the next few decades cannot be blamed on local actions of neglect.

REFERENCES AND FURTHER READING

BAXTER, E.V., and RINTOUL, L. J. 1953. The Birds of Scotland. Edinburgh: Oliver and Boyd.

BELL, M.V. 1993. Productivity of waterfowl breeding at Airthrey Loch, Stirling. *Scottish Birds*, 17, 27-39

BROTHERSTON, W.M. 1875. The birds of Clackmannanshire. *Proceedings of the Alloa Society of Natural Science, 1807 to 1875,* 15-23, 104-111.

BRYANT, D.M. 1974. Birds of the Stirling Region. In Timms, D. Editor. The Stirling Region. BAAS, Stirling, 1974, 123-146

BRYANT, D.M. 1978. Moulting shelducks on the Forth estuary. *Bird Study, 25,* 103-108

BRYANT, D.M. 1980. Birdwatching on the Forth Estuary. *Scot. Birds, 11,* 78-82

BRYANT, D.M. 1987. Wading birds and wildfowl of the estuary and Firth of Forth, Scotland. *Proceedings of the Royal Society of Edinburgh* 93B, 509-520

BRYANT, D.M. 1993. Bird communities in Oak and Norway Spruce woodlands on Loch Lomondside - a long term study. *Forth Naturalist and Historian* 16, 61-71

CALLADINE, J., DOUGILL, S., HARDING, N. and STROUD, D.A. 1990. Moorland birds on the Campsie Fells, Touch Hills, and West Ochil Hills, Stirling: habitats, distribution and numbers. *Forth Naturalist and Historian* 13, 53-69

CRANSWICK, P.A., KIRBY, J.S., and WATERS, R.J. 1992. Wildfowl and wader counts: 1991-92 Published by WWT and BTO.

FORTH AREA BIRD REPORT 1974 - annually by C.J. Henty in *Forth Naturalist and Historian.*

HENTY, C.J. 1976. Habitat selection in the birds of woodland and open woodland of the Stirling area. *Forth Naturalist and Historian* 1, 39-48

HENTY, C.J. 1991. Birds of the River Devon surveyed over 10 years. *Forth Naturalist and Historian* 14, 50-64

HENTY, C.J. and BRACKENRIDGE, W.R. 1992. Check list of the birds of Central Scotland. *Forth Naturalist and Historian* 15, 19-26

JONES, G.J. 1987. Selection against large size in the Sand Martin Riparia riparia during a dramatic population crash. *Ibis* 129, 274-280

LACK, P. 1976. The Atlas of Wintering Birds in Britain and Ireland. Calton, Poyser.

MARCHANT, J.H., HUDSON, R., CARTER, S.P. and WHITTINGTON, P. 1990. Population Trends in British Breeding Birds. Tring, British Trust for Ornithology.

MITCHELL, J. 1977. Breeding of Common Crossbill *Loxia curvirostra* in the Stirling Region. *Forth Naturalist and Historian* 2, 1-10

MITCHELL, J. 1981. The decline of the Raven as a breeding species in central Scotland. *Forth Naturalist and Historian* 6, 35-42

MITCHELL, J. 1986. Summer birds of Loch Lomondside's, semi-natural woodlands. *Loch Lomond Bird Report, 14,* 12-27

MITCHELL, J. 1992. The birds of the Endrick Mouth, Loch Lomond - An update of the annotated check-list up to 1 January 1990. Unpublished Report of Scottish Natural Heritage, 25pp

MITCHELL, J. 1993. Shelduck at the Endrick Mouth, Loch Lomond. *Glasgow Naturalist* 22, 288-9

MITCHELL, J. and BROAD, R.A. 1987. Close nesting of Peregrines in Stirlingshire. *The Glasgow Naturalist* 21, 359

MURRAY, R.D. 1991. The first successful breeding of Nuthatch in Scotland. *Scottish Bird Report* 22, 51-55

OWEN, M., ATKINSON-WILLIS, G.L., and SALMON, D.G. 1986. Wildfowl in Great Britain (2nd edition). Cambridge University Press.

PRATER, A.J. 1981. *Estuary Birds of Britain and Ireland.* Carlton: Poyser.

RINTOUL, L.J. and BAXTER, E.V. 1937. A Vertebrate Fauna of Forth. Edinburgh, Oliver & Boyd.

SCOTTISH BIRD REPORT 1969 and annually by the Scottish Ornithologists Club, Edinburgh.

SHARROCK, J.T.R. 1976. The Atlas of Breeding Birds in Britain and Ireland. Calton, Poyser.

SYMONDS, F.L., and LANGSLOW, D.R. 1984. Geographical origins and movements of shorebirds using the Firth of Forth. *Ringing and Migration, 5,* 145-152

TAYLOR, I.R. 1978. Wader migration in the upper Forth estuary. *Wader Study Group Bull., 22,* 11-16

THOM, V.M. 1986. Birds in Scotland. Calton, Poyser.

WILLIAMSON, K. 1974. Oak wood breeding bird communities in the Loch Lomond National Nature Reserve. *Quarterly Journal of Forestry* 68, 9-2

Caught in the act! A Pine Marten photographed as it attempts to raid a nestbox. Heavy losses of nesting Pied Flycatchers to predators on the RSPB reserve at Inversnaid were eventually traced to this agile predator, which only spread back to the region in the early 1980s.   (Don MacCaskill).

Badgers take a very wide range of food types. Earthworms, small mammals, insects and nuts can be common in the diet in wild country. When they are close to man they sometimes take food offered to birds: this Badger climbs onto a bird table for a meal of peanuts.   (Andre Goulancourt).

Mammals

J.F. Haddow

Introduction

Central Scotland contains a great diversity of habitats and a substantial proportion of the terrestrial British mammals occur within its boundaries. As it includes the upper reaches of the Forth Estuary a large proportion of our marine mammal fauna has also been recorded, but most of these cannot be regarded as residents.

Before the account by Proctor (1974) the last general survey of mammals in the area was published in *A Vertebrate Fauna of Forth* by Rintoul and Baxter in 1935. Since 1974 there have been a number of surveys of particular species of mammal which have added much to our knowledge, but there are still significant gaps. The third edition of *The Handbook of British Mammals*, edited by Corbet and Harris (1991) provides the most detailed and up-to-date general reference. *The Mammals of Britain and Europe* by Corbet and Ovenden (1980) is a readily available and readable book.

Terrestrial mammal species living in Central Region are from six Orders: *Insectivora* (insectivores), *Chiroptera* (bats), *Lagomorpha* (rabbits and hares), *Rodentia* (rodents), *Carnivora* (carnivores) and *Artiodactyla* (deer and goats). There are also mammals from two marine Orders: *Pinnipedia* (seals) and *Cetacea* (whales).

Insectivores

Five species of Insectivore are found in the region. The Hedgehog (*Erinaceus europaeus*) is widespread, its presence most easily noted from road casualties. It is most abundant where there is grassland close to woodland, scrub or hedgerow. Hedgehogs are likely to be present in all lowland habitats where there is sufficient cover for nesting, and occur up to the tree line. The Mole (*Talpa europaea*) is another widespread and common animal noticeable from the molehills it makes when excavating its burrows. Earthworms are the single most important prey, and moles will be more abundant wherever these are plentiful. Mitchell (1981) records moles present on four out of the five major islands in Loch Lomond on the Central Region side of the boundary (Inchcruin, Inchfad, Inchcailloch and Clairinsh), and around the mouth of the River Endrick huge 'fortresses' are built as a response to winter flooding. These can be up to one metre high and established long enough to be well vegetated. The highest point moles have been found in the region is at 700 metres below a south-facing exposure of limestone on Beinn Dubhcraig near Loch Oss.

The Common Shrew (*Sorex araneus*) is found almost everywhere provided some low vegetation cover is available, and consequently may be found even at the summit of the highest mountains in the Region. The Pigmy Shrew (*Sorex minutus*) is equally widespread but generally less abundant. It is found in all types of habitat but mostly where there is plenty of ground cover. The Water Shrew (*Neomys fodiens*) has a more local distribution and is probably under-recorded in the Region. It is mainly found on the banks of clear, fast-flowing, unpolluted rivers and streams, but also by ponds and drainage ditches. Occasionally it is found some distance from water where there is good cover. Water Shrews have become more common recently on the Endrick marshes, due to the creation of shallow lagoons with abundant sedges.

Bats

Four species of bat (*Chiroptera*) are found throughout much of Scotland, and all four are widespread here. All British bats are insectivorous, and are more abundant in any habitat with a rich insect population. Woodland with clearings or rides, pasture with hedgerows, and scrub are good bat feeding areas. The best habitat is near water, particularly along well-vegetated riverbanks or loch sides. Bats now mainly use artificial structures for their summer nursery colonies, and their roosting requirements also influence their distribution.

The Common Pipistrelle (*Pipistrellus pipistrellus*) is widespread **(Figure 1)**, and has summer roosts in every type and age of building, though mainly inhabited ones.

Figure 1 An Adult female Pipistrelle bat in the hand. It is the smallest and commonest of our bats and can be seen throughout the region. (J.F.Haddow)

Female bats form nursery colonies in houses during the summer months, and numbers in this Region vary from 30 to 1200 (a Fintry roost) but typical colony sizes range from 100 to 800 adult females. The Brown Long-eared Bat (*Plecotus auritus*) is also found throughout the area. This species prefers lightly wooded areas, feeding by gleaning insects from tree bark and leaves. Nursery colonies typically number 20 to 50 in this area, though the largest recorded is 132 (1991). These bats often roost visibly in lofts of older, stone built houses and are easily disturbed.

Daubenton's Bat (*Myotis daubentonii*) normally feeds over water, hence its other name, the Water Bat. It can be found particularly over calm stretches of river and lochs with overhanging trees, but emerges to feed late and is less noticeable than the Pipistrelle. Although it is widespread, fewer nursery roosts in houses are known of than any other bat in the area, and this is the general picture in Britain. Occasional records from tree holes suggests that many of the summer roosts are in natural sites. Harvie Brown (1906) includes a photograph of 'Daubenton's bat-rocks on Loch Dochart' where in 1888 "a large colony of bats" had been found and identified as this species. He did not find them when he searched in May 1905, and a more recent survey in the 1970's failed to confirm their presence. The two known nursery colonies in houses in the region number about 70 and 150 females. The first published record for Natterer's Bat (*Myotis nattereri*) in Scotland this century was from an underground hibernation site near Aberfoyle (Placido 1972). Since then this bat has been recorded north to Morayshire and west to Argyll. Only a few summer roosts are known here, so far none north of Callander. Its preference for buildings is similar to the Long-eared Bat and the largest roost found has been 85 females. This is another species preferring to feed in woodland or areas with high hedgerow, and it is difficult to observe in flight.

Although the general impression is that bats have become more scarce in the last 30 years, regular surveys of roosts in this region since 1984 have shown little change overall. This is in contrast with the fall in numbers elsewhere over the same period, which becomes increasingly marked moving southwards in Britain. Wintering habits of bats in Scotland are poorly understood. Until recently so few were found during the winter that it was thought that they migrated southwards. The commonest species, the Pipistrelle, was most difficult to find, but since 1988 a small number of hibernation roosts for this bat have been identified.

Rabbits and Hares

The most common Lagomorph is the Rabbit (*Oryctolagus cuniculus*). Introduced into England by the Normans, it was at one time mainly confined to managed warrens, but wild populations spread from coastal areas and lowland heaths. There are records of rabbit warrens at Crail in Fife in 1264, and the *Old*

Statistical Account of 1795 mentions them in this region though they may have been established here for some centuries. They were not seen on Loch Lomondside until the 1820s (Mitchell 1983). Successive outbreaks of myxomatosis from 1955 resulted in a crash in the population, but there has been a general recovery since then. The Strathblane area, however, has shown a massive rise in numbers. Rabbits are found wherever there are areas of short grasses, with a secure refuge (burrows, boulders, hedgerows, scrub, woodland) in close proximity to feeding areas.

The Brown Hare (*Lepus europaeus*) is widespread in lowland pasture and arable land in the south and east of the region. It can be found up to a height of 700 m (e.g. on Ben Vorlich) but more usually is seen under 300 m, for example, in the highland northwest of the region wherever there is suitable land under grass or arable crops, such as Glen Dochart. The Brown Hare is replaced by the Blue or Mountain Hare (*Lepus timidus*) at higher altitude (**Figure 2**), where the land is dominated by heather (*Calluna vulgaris*) which it uses both for food and shelter.

Figure 2   A Mountain Hare sheltering in a snow burrow. It is mainly found in uplands but also locally on suitable low ground, such as the raised bog at Flanders Moss in the Forth valley.   (D.MacCaskill)

The numbers of this species fluctuate locally, for example the population is high in the Campsie Hills at the present time (1992). Peak numbers occur at roughly ten year intervals. The link with the quality of the heather is emphasised by observations that the Mountain Hare's abundance is matched by the state of the Red Grouse population. An interesting population of this species, belying its common name, is found almost at sea level on Flanders Moss, the largest area of intact lowland raised bog in Britain.

Rodents

Rodents include squirrels, rats, mice and voles. The Red Squirrel (*Sciurus vulgaris*) is thought to have disappeared from this region by the early 18th century, probably because of forest felling. There is good evidence of its spread after reintroductions at the end of the 18th century (Harvie Brown 1878). Red Squirrels are now found in the northern, northeastern and central parts of the region, from Killin in the north, through Callander to Aberfoyle and as far as Blairdrummond, around Doune, Dunblane and Bridge of Allan. They occur by Loch Katrine and in Loch Ard Forest. Now that there is a continuous connecting strip of trees, red squirrels have recently begun to move south from Loch Ard Forest into Garadhban Forest. They were reported in the 1980s from Killearn and in the late 1980s were first noticed in the Carron Valley Forest. To the east, this species has been reported from near Forestmill in Clackmannan District. Red Squirrels are usually found in coniferous forests, though mixtures of tree species provide a more reliable year-to-year seed food supply than single species forests and are therefore probably preferred. Grey Squirrels (*Sciurus carolinensis*) were introduced from North America to three sites in Scotland between 1892 and 1920. The earliest release was at Finnart on Loch Long; they spread eastwards to reach Loch Lomond by 1903, subsequently colonising all the suitable woodlands around the loch and on its islands (Mitchell 1983). The last Red Squirrel reported from Inchcailloch was in 1945. Grey Squirrels are the only species found in much of Falkirk and Clackmannan Districts and are common in Stirling and Bridge of Allan. How much overlap there is between the two species is unclear - in Carron Valley Forest Red Squirrels are on the increase whereas greys are decreasing. Grey Squirrels are found in Fintry, Balfron, Aberfoyle and Brig o'Turk. The Grey shows a preference for deciduous woodland, and in mainly coniferous areas the Red Squirrel appears to compete successfully with it. The Grey is distinctly bolder, more adaptable, and commonly feeds from bird tables in suburban areas. These habits seem likely to allow the Grey to maintain its status in the more populated parts of the region.

The Bank Vole (*Clethrionomys glareolus*) is common wherever there is mature mixed deciduous woodland with a thick shrub or field layer. It is also found in grassland habitats, young deciduous plantations, conifer stands and hedgerows. This species undergoes marked changes in numbers from year to year in the oakwoods on Loch Lomondside. The Field Vole (*Microtus agrestis*) prefers rough, ungrazed grassland, and where a forest has been planted on previously fertile pasture, conditions are ideal, leading to population explosions or plagues. The most striking example of this was in the Carron Valley in the early 1950s (Charles 1956) where numbers peaked at more than 800 per hectare in some places before dropping to a fifth of this level as predation and competition for space restored the balance.

The Water Vole (*Arvicola terrestris*) prefers densely vegetated banks of ditches, rivers and streams, generally where the current is slow and water present throughout the year. During 1990 R.Strachan (in prep.) surveyed 23 sites for presence of this vole as part of a UK wide survey of 1,926 sites (608 in Scotland). Only 3 of the sites (13%) in this region were found to show signs of the Water Vole. This compares with 161 in Scotland (26%) and 711 in the UK (37%). The survey showed that Water Voles are found in the Endrick catchment and Loch Lomond (southern half). General comments about rivers in the Forth catchment (including Avon, Teith, Kelty, Duchray, Katrine, Allan and Devon) are that they show a highly fragmented distribution of Water Voles with many sites negative. Although there is much suitable riparian habitat the species is apparently uncommon. Signs of this species were recorded from Stirling University campus in 1982. Mitchell (1976) describes interesting high-altitude colonies of this vole on Loch Lomond-side. These are on the upper reaches of the Cailness Burn west of the loch (411 metres), and to the north on Lochan Beinn Chabhair (503m), Lochan Uaine (487m) and Loch Oss (640m). A more recent report from 1986 was on Loch Essan above Glen Dochart, at 434m. All these colonies are situated on fairly level ground but with steep slopes below which ensure a rapid run-off of excess water.

The Wood Mouse (*Apodemus sylvaticus*) is widespread, found in most habitats if not too wet (**Figure 3**). It is rarely found above the tree line on high moorland and scree, except where stone walls or buildings give cover. It often enters houses, particularly in late autumn-winter to seek shelter and food. The House Mouse (*Mus musculus*), though widespread is probably less common now than 20 years ago. Though they are most likely to be found in buildings and food stores they can live independently of humans where there is little competition with other mammals. Changes in agricultural practice (corn ricks used to give mice protection during winter) and domestic food storage (more packaging, less loose dried food) have restricted the food supply for house mice. The Brown or Common Rat (*Rattus norvegicus*) is another rodent closely linked with humans. It is typically associated with farms, refuse tips, sewers, urban waterways and warehouses, but occurs in hedgerows around cereal crops and root crops. Brown Rats prefer areas with dense ground cover close to water. This species was introduced to Britain in shipping from Russia in around 1728-29 and gradually replaced the Black or Ship Rat (*Rattus rattus*). Its spread in Scotland was slow - it was described in 1855 as 'recently introduced' in some highland areas.

Carnivores

Among the Carnivores the Fox (*Vulpes vulpes*) is widespread and common. A highly adaptable and versatile species, it is found in all habitats from mountain tops to suburbs. Throughout the region foxes are controlled (mainly by shooting and snaring) by sheep

Figure 3   The Wood Mouse, is common in the region, although usually avoids the highest ground. It is agile, often feeding above ground level and readily enters buildings in autumn and winter to find shelter and food.   (D.M.Bryant)

farmers who frequently regard them as a significant cause of lamb mortality. Studies in Scotland have shown that the proportion of lambs taken by foxes is low (losses of 0.6% to 1.8%), and also there is no evidence that current levels of control have a significant effect on the overall fox population. In one large hill farm in the north of the region the policy is to leave foxes alone completely in order not to upset the balance of fox families and territories, and on that farm (with 2,000 ewes) predation on lambs is considered to be very low. On farms where foxes are actively controlled the most effective policy is considered to be trapping only in the period immediately prior to lambing. There are no longer any fox hunts in the region.

Pine Martens (*Martes martes*) made their return to the region in the early 1980s. Proctor (1974) mentions the last record of one being killed at Balquhidder in 1880 and a sighting at Callander in 1879. The marten was so intensely hunted by gamekeepers and 'sporting gentlemen' that it declined from a species widespread in Britain to one limited to northwest Scotland, north Wales, parts of Ireland and northern England. Velander (1983) charts the spread of the marten from northwest Scotland from the beginning of this century up to 1982, by which time its distribution reached almost to central Scotland.   However one Pine Marten was trapped unintentionally in 1981 in a mink trap set on the Touch estate, and another was seen near Gartmore in 1984. More recently, the Pine Marten has been seen around Strathyre and in Loch Ard forest almost to its southern edge.   One was also seen in the RSPB Reserve at Inversnaid where it had been raiding bird nestboxes (see p76). Pine Martens can clearly be found in a variety

Figure 4   A Stoat emerging from a rabbit burrow. A widespread predator, distinguished from weasel by its larger size and long black-tipped tail. Most individuals retain their brown coat throughout the year but the white, ermine, form also be seen during winter; including some records from the lowlands.   (D.MacCaskill)

of habitats where plenty of cover is available. In Scotland a study has shown a preference for hunting in areas with older conifer cover. The main food items are small rodents and birds, beetles and berries.

The Stoat (*Mustela erminea*) (**Figure 4**) and the Weasel (*Mustela nivalis*) are both widespread and found in most habitats, particularly where there is good cover. Open spaces are avoided by the use of dykes and hedgerows for movement. Stoats are more likely to be seen than Weasels, but the latter are more common as road deaths. There is no consistent pattern regarding the change from the stoat's brown summer pelage to the white (ermine) winter pelage in this area. Although most Stoats in the southern lowland parts remain brown all year, some ermine forms have also been observed there.

The Mink (*Mustela vison*) is a native mammal of North America, but has been bred on fur farms in Britain since 1929. Self-sustaining populations in the wild began to be established from the 1950s, from escapes or releases. In the early 1960s there was a large number of mink farms across Scotland's central belt, with the inevitable result that a wild population became established. By 1988 only two farms existed, one at Kippen which closed that year, another at Ochtertyre which also closed recently. The feral mink is now widespread though patchy in its distribution. It is found in a range of aquatic habitats and may spend some time away from the water where its prey, such as rabbits, are abundant. It also includes a wide variety of mammals, birds, fish, and invertebrates in its diet. Ducks, moorhens and coots are most heavily predated on rivers and lochs. Depending on the area, its most important food may vary between fish, mammals or birds. A survey of selected parts of the region in 1990 (Strachan in prep.) found Mink in 4 out of 25 sites (16%) compared with 27% in Scotland and 34% nationally. Some of the rivers entering Loch Lomond yielded mink signs, and the River Forth catchment also showed patchy distribution. Mink are known to occur near the high altitude water vole population on the Cailness burn.

The Badger (*Meles meles*) was recorded by Rintoul and Baxter (1935) as "Formerly common, now scarce and local". The species still appears to be reasonably common in the west of the area. A survey in 1986/87 of Loch Lomondside by John Mitchell found 28 active setts from Drymen northwards. An additional four setts were not surveyed but Badgers had been present in 1970. There was evidence of decline in active setts to the southwest, outside the Region. Badgers are also found from Callander northwards but many of the known setts in the north east are no longer active. There is little evidence of them existing nearer Stirling. Their range extends eastwards from the Drymen area through Fintry to the Carron Valley and in the south and east of Falkirk District. There have been occasional records from Clackmannan District in the 1980s suggesting that they may be on the increase since Proctor (1974) reported them as extinct there. Badgers show preference for areas where there is adequate cover, well drained and easily dug soil, little disturbance by humans or domestic animals and a varied and plentiful food supply (particularly earthworms).

The Otter (*Lutra lutra*) was the subject of a Scottish survey in 1977-79 (Green and Green 1980). Of the 146 sites surveyed in this area, otter signs were present at 71 (49%). This compares with the Scottish figure of 73% of sites with positive signs. Six of the 10km squares contained no signs at all, comprising about 21% of the total area. Five of these covered the area from Stirling downriver along the Forth estuary, including the lower reaches of the Carron and Avon. The sixth square contained intensive farmland by the Forth near Kippen. The survey, however, suggested that there had been a decline in otter numbers within their range, and the remaining population is densest in the upper reaches of the Forth river system, and the middle and lower Endrick. Otters were recorded as widespread upon the headwaters of the Tay; on the Carron restricted to the reservoir and the main river above Denny; absent from the Avon and the Black Devon; present but "maintain a precarious and isolated existence" on the middle and upper reaches of the Devon; found the length of the Teith down to its junction with the Forth; on the Allan Water signs are only plentiful at the rich lochs of Carsebreck and along the River Knaik. The general picture was one of slow decline at the edges of its main range, and since the survey there has been little evidence of a resurgence in numbers. It is hoped that recent improvements in water quality will be followed by an increase in otter numbers, but a major contributing factor to their decline is human disturbance, and this is on the increase. The availability of secure lying-up and breeding sites may influence distribution. This is supported by their readiness to make use of small otter havens and artificial holts, as has happened on the Loch Lomond National Nature Reserve.

The Wildcat (*Felis silvestris*) disappeared from most of the area before 1850 and may have lingered around Balquhidder into the 1860s (Proctor 1974). This mammal was surveyed in Scotland during 1983-87 (Easterbee, Hepburn and Jefferies 1991). The bulk of the information obtained was based on interviews with gamekeepers, forest rangers, fox-hunters and hill shepherds, since by the nature of their occupations they were most likely to be aware of wildcat presence. Staff of the Nature Conservancy Council and amateur naturalists also provided a significant number of records. Careful comparison with previous surveys which were based mainly on sightings, observations of road casualties and predator control data showed that the population expansion which took place from its minimum about 1914 apparently halted about 1950. There have been local range fluctuations since then, but the majority of areas show either no change or contraction of numbers. Central Scotland straddles the southern limit of the wildcat range in Britain, since it is only found from the Highland boundary northwards. Its main distribution extends southwards on Loch Lomondside as far as Garadhban forest. More centrally it is local north of Aberfoyle. The 1983-87 survey showed that it is not uncommon in highland Tayside which borders the central-eastern part of Central Region, and may occur north of Braco (just in Tayside) and in the carse west of Stirling. The population found in the Carron Valley in the 1960s no longer lives there.

Easterbee et al (1991) expressed concern over the hybridisation of true wildcats with feral domestic cats, and Scottish Natural Heritage is currently considering a study of wildcat genetics to establish their true relationships. Wildcats are found in upland forest and woodland, moorland and hill ground, usually below 500m. Forestry plantations, especially in the early years after planting, are an important habitat, offering shelter and prey such as small mammals and rabbits.

Figure 5   The Red Deer can be found on most open moorland in the northwest of the region. While absent from the east, they have recently increased in the south since being reported from the Carron Valley Forest in the late 1980s. (D.M.Bryant)

Deer and Goats

Artiodactyls include four species of deer and the feral goat. The Red Deer (*Cervus elaphus)* is probably the mammal that most people associate with the Highlands in common with the Golden Eagle amongst the birds (**Figure 5**). The Red Deer is an important part of the economy of large Highland estates.

They can be found on most open moorland areas in the northwest of the region, and the range extends southeastwards to the River Endrick, the confluence of the Forth and Teith, and via the Fintry and Campsie hills to Carron Valley Forest where they have recently increased in number. They began to be reported from Carron valley in the late 1980s, and culling began in 1991. Their occurrence in conifer plantation is influenced by its age and structure. Highest densities tend to be found in open thicket rather than older forests. The introduced Sika Deer (*Cervus nippon*) is expanding its range rapidly in Scotland and its ability to hybridize with the native Red Deer is threatening the genetic integrity of that species (Ratcliffe 1987). A captive herd of Sika was introduced to Carradale, Kintyre, in 1893 and escaped during 1914-18, spreading

northwards to reach the west side of Loch Lomond in 1983. The first reported sighting of a Sika Deer stag on the east side of Loch Lomond was at Inversnaid in 1987 (Trubridge 1990). Another herd was introduced at Tulliallan in Fife, on the Clackmannan district border. Sika Deer escaped from there but remain localised in the adjacent Devilla Forest, though they have been seen near Clackmannan. Sika are more closely associated with forest and woodland than Scottish Red Deer, and are less able to adapt to tree-less conditions.

Fallow Deer (*Dama dama*) were re-introduced to England by the Normans in the 11th Century, having become extinct in Britain during the last glaciation. Fallow in Scotland are likely to have originated from park herds, although through breeding most western Scottish animals are darker than typical park deer. They are established on Loch Lomond-side from the Endrick north to the wooded lower slopes of Ben Lomond, and have been seen on some of the loch's islands. Fallow bucks have been seen in Loch Ard forest from the mid 1980s but as yet there is no established population there. Occasional reports come from the extreme east of the region, on both sides of the Forth. The nearest captive herd is at Hopetoun House, West Lothian, from which some strays may reach Central Region. Fallow Deer show a preference for mature deciduous or mixed woodland with a well established understorey. Roe Deer (*Capreolus capreolus*) became extinct over much of Britain and by the beginning of the 18th century only survived in parts of the Highlands, including the northwest of this area. The increase in woodlands following that time lead to expansion of the range so that roe had reached south to the Borders by 1840. Roe Deer are now found throughout the region, wherever there is open woodland

Figure 6   A Roe Deer in a spruce plantation; the smallest of our deer, it is found in forests, woods and sometimes in more open country, throughout the area. This buck still has its antlers in velvet.   (D.MacCaskill)

or forest, and in plantations up to the pre-thicket stage (**Figure 6**). They can be found in farmland not far from cover, and similarly occupy open moorland above the tree line, particularly where Red Deer are few in number. Roe Deer have been seen up to 760m in the Scottish Highlands.

Feral Goats (*Capra hircus*) originate from domestic stock which were either released or escaped, particularly during the 18th and 19th centuries as people moved from highland areas to obtain employment in the industrial regions of the central belt (Trubridge 1988). At one time there were Feral Goats in a number of highland parts of the region, but now they are restricted to the east side of Loch Lomond from Rowardennan to the north end of the loch. There were some in Loch Ard and Achray forests until the 1950s. This animal is found in mountainous areas where there are cliffs which are used for refuge, shelter, and feeding in the associated shrub communities.

Seals, Whales and Dolphins

Pinnipedes (seals) recorded in central Scotland include the two native British species plus one vagrant. The Common Seal (*Phoca vitulina*) can be seen in the stretch of the River Forth from Alloa to Blackness, though very occasionally will stray as far up river as Stirling bridge. The nearest breeding area is on the north Fife coast. Grey Seals (*Halichoerus grypus*) breed on the Isle of May in the Firth of Forth and on rare occasions individuals reach as far west as Alloa. Harp Seals (*Phoca groenlandica*) breed in the Arctic Atlantic but outside that season can be found off the north Norway coast. There have been a handful of records from the Scottish coast, including two captured at Grangemouth in 1903.

A number of Cetaceans (whales, dolphins, porpoises) have been seen in the Firth of Forth, but only the smallest, the Harbour Porpoise (*Phocoena phocoena*) regularly occurred as far up as Alloa. The *Second*

Statistical Account described porpoises as being a 'constant inhabitant' of the Forth at Alloa. Sightings in recent years have been much less frequent. Other Cetaceans records (mainly strandings) are summarised in **Table 1**.

Other records occur from around Stirling and beyond in the Carse. These date from the time following the last glaciation when the sea extended further west. A Blue Whale (*Balaenoptera musculus*) skeleton was found in 1819 in the grounds of Airthrey Castle, where Stirling University is now sited. Fin Whale bones have been found near Stirling (1863) and Gargunnock (1877) and Humpback Whale bones (*Megaptera novaeangliae*) in the Carse clay at Blairdrummond (1824).

Mammals no Longer Found in Central Scotland

Mammals which are part of the region's historical and prehistorical past include the extinct Mammoth (*Mammuthus primigenius*) and the Aurochs (*Bos primigenius*), the latter extinct in Britain for over 3000 years, and in Europe since 1627. The Elk (*Alces alces*), Reindeer (*Rangifer tarandus*) and Lemming (*Lemmus lemmus*) still occur in northern continental Europe, but no longer occur here, or, with the exception of the Reindeer introduced to the Cairngorms, elsewhere in Scotland. Later extinctions include the Wild Boar (*Sus scrofa*). Apparently no written record remains of this species in central Scotland although several place names indicate that wild boar were found around Aberfoyle and Muckhart (Proctor 1974). They are still widespread in continental Europe. Wolves (*Canis lupus*) were hunted in the neighbourhood of Stirling in the early days of the 17th century and possibly persisted a little longer in the more remote parts of the area. Wolves survived in Scotland until 1740 and are now rare in Europe as a whole. Wild White Cattle (*Bos taurus*) were probably not extinct here until after the 16th century. These cattle were similar to those now

Table 1   Records of Cetaceans on the Forth, 1800-1981   (See references - Evans, Fraser, Herman, Stephen, Maclaren)

Species	Location and date
Fin Whale (*Balaenoptera physalus*)	Alloa 1808
Sei Whale (*Balaenoptera borealis*)	Kinneil 1872
Minke Whale (*Balaenoptera acutorostrata*)	Alloa 1888
White Whale (*Delphinapterus leucas*)	Cambuskenneth 1815
(killed by salmon fishers, for three months was around Alloa)	
another shot after a week in the river	Kildean, Stirling 1932
Northern Bottle-nosed Whale (*Hyperoodon ampullatus*)	Alloa 1845
(the largest female of this species found anywhere in the world);	Grangemouth 1894, 1949, 1969;Skinflats 1981
Common dolphin (*Delphinus delphis*)	Bo'ness 1937, 1952
Bottle-nosed Dolphin (*Tursiops truncatus*)	Alloa 1940 (shot)
White-beaked Dolphin (*Lagenorhynchus albirostris*)	Alloa 1923, 1933
Killer Whale (*Orcinus orca*)	Alloa 1932
(a juvenile female captured because it was thought to have been chasing salmon)	
Risso's Dolphin (*Grampus griseus*)	South Alloa 1919

preserved in a semi-wild state at Chillingham in Northumberland.

Other species disappeared from the area more recently. The Black Rat, or Ship Rat was probably once widespread in human habitation in Britain and Ireland until gradually replaced by the Brown Rat, beginning in the 18th century. The Black Rat's origins are in India and southeast Asia, spreading to north Africa and Europe along trade routes, reaching Britain during Roman times. The *Second Statistical Account* of 1845 records some late survivors e.g. "very seldom seen in Alloa", and "to occur" at St Ninians. The last record appears to be of one killed near Stirling in 1886 (Sword 1908). In the most recent national survey of these rats the only Scottish populations were in Dundee (1988) and Edinburgh (1989) (Twigg 1992). The Polecat (*Mustela putorius*) was common throughout Britain before 1800, but with the rise of the sporting estate was steadily persecuted. It had disappeared from most of this area by 1860. The last known local record is a sighting on Ben Ledi in 1894, with the last definite record for Scotland in 1912. Occasionally animals are found which resemble Polecats but these have always proved to be Polecat Ferrets (*Mustela furo*). These animals were escapes, and there is no evidence in the Region that any feral population has been established. The Harvest Mouse (*Micromys minutus*) is included among the animals of the parish of Alloa in the *Second Statistical Account* and recent confirmation of a population in the south of Edinburgh (the only recent Scottish record) suggests that it could possibly have occurred here at one time.

The Muskrat (*Ondatra zibethicus*) was introduced here when five pairs escaped near Braco in 1927, though one male was later found dead. These animals had been imported from Canada to start a fur farm (Warwick 1934). These Muskrats bred and by 1934 had spread along the Allan Water to the Forth and along the Teith and the Goodie Burn. Isolated individuals were recorded from the Carron and Devon. Its habit of burrowing into banks of rivers and lochs makes the Muskrat very destructive and legislation in 1932 prevented any further imports into Britain. A campaign to eradicate the Muskrat was successful and the wild population in Britain was eliminated by 1937.

The Future

The populations of mammals in central Scotland are of course dynamic, not static, and there will always be change. The reduction in persecution of mammals previously regarded as 'vermin', due in part to new legislation, may allow the Pine Marten to extend its range, and the Wildcat to make some recovery. Mink are likely to spread further before reaching a stable population size, in spite of attempts to control them. The recent legislation increasing protection of Badgers to include the setts may limit disturbance by fox hunters as well as limiting building development near setts. The otter situation is more complex, and a combination of vigilance on pollution and conservation or improvement of riverine habitat will be necessary to halt its decline. Attitudes to bats changed to their advantage during the 1980's thanks to legislation and popular education. There is still, however, misunderstanding and intolerence and the more vulnerable bat species are likely to decline unless roosts and feeding habitats are conserved.

In 1992 the Sika Deer was added to the list of species which cannot be legally released or allowed to escape into the wild, but the existing wild Sikas are likely to continue their spread. Hybridisation with native Red Deer is a concern for the genetic integrity of that species. The Water Vole merits a more intensive regional survey in view of its apparent decline, particularly in view of the spread of the Mink. Not enough is known about another water mammal, the Water Shrew, to comment on any possible changes in its population. This area is on the northern edge of the UK range of some bats, and species such as the Noctule (*Nyctalus noctula*) and the Whiskered Bats (*Myotis mystacinus, M.brandtii*) may yet be recorded here. Indeed a small roost of *mystacinus* was found near Blanefield in July 1993.

ACKNOWLEDGEMENTS

I am grateful to John Mitchell of Scottish Natural Heritage for giving me the benefit of his extensive knowledge of the mammals of this area. Thanks are also due to Alastair Fairweather (Forestry Commission), Jeremy Herman (National Museums of Scotland), Don MacCaskill, and Stewart Pritchard and David Balharry (SNH) for information and assistance.

REFERENCES AND FURTHER READING

ARNOLD, H.R. 1984. Provisional atlas of the mammals of the British Isles. Biological Records Centre, Huntingdon (and additional recent records provided by Henry Arnold of the BRC).

BULLOCK, D.J., HADDOW, J.F., NEVILLE, P.A. and PLACIDO, C. 1986. The Distribution of Natterer's Bat, *Myotis nattereri* (Khul), Scotland. *Glasgow Naturalist* 21, 137-141.

CHARLES, W.N. 1956. Effects of a vole plague in the Carron Valley, Stirlingshire. *Scottish Forestry* 10, 201-204

CORBET, G. and OVENDEN, D. 1980. The mammals of Britain and Europe. Collins, London.

CORBET, D. and HARRIS, S. Editors 1991. The Handbook of British Mammals Blackwell, London

CUTHBERT, J.H. 1973. The origin and distribution of the feral mink in Scotland. *Mammal Review* 3, 97-103.

EASTERBEE, N., HEPBURN, L.V. and JEFFERIES, D.J. 1991. Survey of the Status and Distribution of the Wildcat in Scotland, 1983-1987. Nature Conservancy Council for Scotland.

EVANS, W. 1892. The Mammalian Fauna of the Edinburgh District. McFarlane and Erskine, Edinburgh.

FRASER, F.C. 1934 to 1974. Report on Cetacea stranded on the British Costas, Nos. 11-14. British Museum.

GREEN, J. and Green, R. 1980. Otter Survey of Scotland 1977-79. The Vincent Wildlife Trust.

HADDOW, J.F. Editor 1986 to 1988. Central Scotland Bat Group Report (1984-1987) (also unpublished survey records).

HADDOW, J.F. 1992. Annual roost patterns of bats in Doune castle. In: *Scottish Bats* Volume 1, Edinburgh.

HARVIE BROWN, J.A. 1878. The squirrel in Stirlingshire. *Transactions of the Stirling Natural History and Archaeological Society* 1, 11-13

HARVIE BROWN, J.A. 1906. A Fauna of the Tay Basin and Strathmore. D. Douglas, Edinburgh.

HERMAN, J.S. 1992. Cetacean Specimens in the National Museums of Scotland. National Museums of Scotland Information Series No.13, Edinburgh.

MACLAREN, W.B. 1981. Notes on a stranding of a Bottle-nosed Whale on the mudflats at Skinflats. *Forth Naturalist and Historian* 6, 16-24.

MITCHELL, J. 1976. High Altitude Water-vole colonies on Loch Lomond-side. *Western Naturalist* 5, 112.

MITCHELL, J. 1981. The adaptable Loch Lomondside Mole. *Scottish Wildlife* 17 18-21.

MITCHELL, J. 1983. Strange beasts on the Bonny Banks. *Scottish Wildlife* 19, 20-24.

OLD STATISTICAL ACCOUNT OF SCOTLAND 1795 Blackwood, Edinburgh.

PLACIDO, C. 1972. New records of Natterer's Bat *Myotis natteri* in Scotland. *Western Naturalist* 1, 59-62.

PROCTOR, J. 1974. Mammals In: The Stirling Region. University of Stirling.

RATCLIFFE, P.R. 1987. Distribution and current status of Sika Deer *Cervusnippon* in Great Britain. *Mammal Review* 17, 39-58

RINTOUL, L.J. and BAXTER, E.V. 1935. A Vertebrate Fauna of Forth. Oliver and Boyd, Edinburgh and London.

SPEPHEN, A.C. 1932. Notes on some whales recently stranded on the Scottish coast. *Scottish Naturalist* 1932, 163-7

STRACHAN, R. (in prep.) VWT water vole survey report. The Vincent Wildlife Trust.

SWORD, J. 1908. The vertebrate fauna of King's Park. *Transactions of Stirling Natural History and Archaeological Society* 30, 123-152.

THE SECOND STATISTICAL ACCOUNT OF SCOTLAND 1845. Blackwood, Edinburgh.

TRUBRIDGE, M. 1988. The Goats of the Loch. *The Scots Magazine* New series 129, 179-188.

TRUBRIDGE, M. 1990. Additional record of Sika Deer *Cervusnippon* on Loch Lomond-side. The *Glasgow Naturalist* 21, 615.

TWIGG, G.I. 1992. The Black Rat in the UK. *Mammal Review* 22, 33-42.

WARWICK, T. 1934. The distribution of the Muskrat in the British Isles. *Proceedings of the Zoological Society of London* 110,165-201.

Butterflies and Moths

G. Thomson

Introduction

Central Scotland is predominantly agricultural or urban in the south and east while the west, centre and north have a mix of moors and woodlands. Some rich meadows and pastures in the south and east offer a home for many species, but are very localised, whereas the tracts of moorland and mature coniferous forest elsewhere, while often unsuitable for many species, can be very extensive. Overall, few central Scotland species are not found somewhere in its two main subareas. The most notable exceptions are the Mountain Ringlet, which is restricted to the mountains of the northern, western and central parts, the Pearl-bordered Fritillary, which is found only in one part of the Trossachs in the west, the Scotch Brown Argus, which is restricted to the south east, and the Scotch Argus which is confined to the far west.

Several habitats in the south and east of the region are particularly suited to butterflies. Dry hillsides, such as the scarp of the Ochil Hills above Alva and Menstrie, have slopes which face south, receive more heat from the sun and are usually well drained. South-west facing slopes can often have a mean summer temperature several degrees above adjacent level sites. Bird's-foot Trefoil *(Lotus corniculatus)* frequently grows in these areas and when the soil is also base rich, Rockrose *(Helianthemum chamaecistus)* is often well established. Less productive are hillsides where Gorse or Broom invades the grassland. In lowland and upland areas, where the land is not overgrown with tall herbs, permanent pasture with Trefoil, Vetches *(Vicia species)*, Field Scabious *(Knautia arvensis)*, Plantains *(Plantago species)* and a rich mixture of wild flowers attracts butterflies and moths. Many of our common species colonise such habitats. A limited amount of grazing greatly helps to maintain the pasture in a suitable state. The raised bogs in the centre and south of the region, especially Flanders Moss, are extensive oases where several very local species are found. Even the heavily cut peat bog of Letham still provides a home for some local species. Many butterflies prefer wetland areas. These habitats have an abundance of meadow flowers, including Lady's Smock *(Cardamine pratensis)*, which provide food for both adult insects and their larvae.

In the west, centre and north of the region, the richest butterfly habitats are mixed oak-birch woodlands, especially in the Trossachs area and the foothills of Ben Venue and Ben Lomond. Young coniferous woodlands, usually on acid soils, afford shelter which encourages some species, especially the small Fritillaries *(Boloria species)*. Throughout the region, recently cleared ground, derelict land, rubbish tips, roadside verges and railway embankments, all of which can be called 'wasteland', are places where many of the region's species are found. Wasteland is at least a temporary home to a greater number of butterfly species than any other single habitat in the area, if the fairly regular migrant butterflies such as Painted Ladies are included. The restricted access to the area effectively excludes some coastal species from the region.

What we know about habitat preferences is extensive in butterflies. It is, however, almost entirely lacking for most moths in this region; even if these preferences are known in other parts of Britain it does not necessarily follow that they will be the same in central Scotland. Study of nocturnal species, which form the vast majority of the moth fauna, is largely restricted to identification of samples from light trapping. This tells us very little about the places from which the insects are attracted. There is very little evidence that most moths are restricted to very specific habitat types. Indeed, some less fastidious moths that are usually associated with littoral areas have been found in the Hillfoots, squeezing into the region via the Forth Estuary.

Species and Distributions

Details of the present distribution of butterflies and moths in central Scotland are known from Bryant (1981), Christie & Christie (1980), Coates (1968), Holmes (1982/3), Thomson (1968, 1976, 1977, 1980) and the records held at the Biological Records Centre at Abbots Ripton, Cambridgeshire. The older list of McLaurin (1928-9) is also useful. There is also a very full record of butterfly distribution changes over the past 150 years (see Thomson 1976, 1980). The Lepidoptera in the region appear to have been less adversely affected by climate changes and habitat disturbance than is evident elsewhere in Britain. Several butterflies found throughout the region, some more or less commonly, are the species whose larval foodplants are widespread and common. The Large White *(Pieris brassicae* L.), Small White *(P. rapae* L.), Small Tortoiseshell *(Aglais urticae* L.) and Small Heath *(Coenonympha pamphilus* L.) are found almost anywhere. The Green-veined White *(Pieris napi* L.) is also common but tends to be restricted to damp or marshy ground for the first brood in spring; it is more widespread in the summer. The Small Copper *(Lycaena phlaeas* L.) and Common Blue *(Polyommatus icarus* Rottemburg) are only a little more localised requiring flowery habitats where the larval food plant Sorrel *(Rumex* species) and Bird's-foot Trefoil *(Lotus corniculatus)* respectively are found. The Meadow Brown *(Maniola jurtina* L.) is common in most grassy areas, but is far less so in the north and west in areas where Purple Moor Grass *(Molinia caerulea)* predominates, or at elevations over 300m. The form of the Meadow Brown **(Figure 1)** approaches subspecies *splendida* White, especially in the north of the region. A few species which do not overwinter are

Figure 1 The widespread and common Meadow Brown (*Maniola jurtina*).

Figure 2 The spreading Orange Tip (*Anthocharis cardamines*)

immigrants to the region. They include the Red Admiral (*Vanessa atalanta* L.) and Painted Lady (*Cynthia cardui* L.) which arrive in small numbers most years but can occur widely. The Red Admiral and Painted Lady were particularly common in the region in 1975, 1976, 1980 and 1992. The Peacock *(Inachis io* L.) is seen far less frequently. The Clouded Yellow (*Colias crocea* Geoffroy in Fourcroy) is a rare immigrant, but has been seen in the south of the region in recent years. Exceptional years for the Clouded Yellow in Scotland have been 1933, 1935, 1936, 1941, 1947, 1975 and 1991. Clouded Yellows were seen in central Scotland in 1935, 1941, 1947 and 1991. The largest spring migration of this species to Scotland and to this region, however, was in 1992 when several were seen in May and June and larger numbers in July and August. The Camberwell Beauty (*Nymphalis antiopa* L.) has been seen twice, at Kinlochard in July 1976 and at Dunblane in July 1977. The Large Tortoiseshell (*Nymphalis polychloros* L.) has been noted only once: this was in May 1980 (Biological Records Centre) in mixed woodland with Elm (*Ulmus* species) in the Sauchie Crag area, a few miles south east of Stirling. It is generally believed that all recent records of this butterfly are of immigrants from the continent of Europe. There is no reason to suggest that this individual was anything otherwise. The species has never been a common one and was officially declared extinct in England in 1992.

Distributions of other butterflies found in the region are far more complex. The Orange Tip (*Anthocharis cardamines* L.) **(Figure 2)** was known in the middle of last century in the Stirling and Clackmannanshire areas and parts of the north of the region but became extinct by 1900. About 1950 a great expansion of the range of this species took place from its colonies in southern Scotland and the Spey Valley, Aberdeenshire and Angus. By the 1980s the Orange

Tip had returned to Perthshire. In the last few years it has been recorded in several eastern parts of the region, both in the north and the south. In some areas, for example north of Dunblane on the Central/Tayside border, it is now a well-established resident. The larvae

Figure 3 The local Purple Hairstreak (*Quercusia quercus*)

of the butterfly feed on Lady's Smock (*Cardamine pratensis*) in central and northern Scotland. Adults are found in May and June on marshland, often in areas which flood extensively in the winter.

The Green Hairstreak (*Callophrys rubi* L.) **Figure 3)** flies in April, May and June from the north to the south of the region. It is restricted to habitats which have extensive stretches of Blaeberry (*Vaccinium myrtillis*), often in dry, heath or upland areas. Its close relative, the Purple Hairstreak (*Quercusia quercus* L.), is similarly restricted by the larval foodplant, Oak (*Quercus* species). It is found only in the south and west of the region, from Bridge of Allan to the Trossachs, flying round the tops of Oaks in late July and August. This inconspicuous butterfly could be overlooked in other parts of the region: most of the known colonies in this region were only found in the late 1970s but were undoubtedly established much earlier.

The Scotch or Northern Brown Argus (*Aricia artaxerxes* Fabricius) is restricted to the warm south-facing slopes of the Ochil Hills where its larval foodplant Rockrose (*Helianthemum chamaecistus*) grows. Although it occasionally flies in the low lying land at the foot of the hills, its breeding sites are at an elevation over 200m. The Scotch Brown Argus flies in late June and early July. This is a little earlier than the colonies on the Scottish east coast perhaps reflecting the sunny aspect of its habitat. The Small Pearl-bordered Fritillary (*Boloria selene* Denis and Schiffermuller) frequents damp situations, open woodland, the edges of young coniferous plantations, moorland and marshland. In these localities rush (*Juncus* species) and often Bog Myrtle (*Myrica gale*) are present. It is a fairly local butterfly. In the south of the region it is absent from some more populated areas but further north it can be extremely common. It flies in the last two weeks of June and throughout July at low levels and in the mountains to 800m. The very similar Pearl-bordered Fritillary (*Boloria euphrosyne* L.) **(Figure 4)** is extremely local, being restricted to a few areas in the Trossachs and the

far north of the region. It prefers much drier situations than the Small Pearl-bordered Fritillary, usually in light woodland and in woodland clearings. This species flies in late May and June and the larvae feed on Violet (*Viola palustris*).

The Dark Green Fritillary (*Argynnis aglaia* L.) is common in July and August in remote areas, in open moorland, river valleys and woodland clearings, often in the mountains. It is much more local in the south, but is found in the Stirling and Dunblane areas and the Ochil Hills. Like other fritillaries, the larvae depend on violets.

Mountain Ringlet (*Erebia epiphron* Knoch) colonies are restricted to habitats over 350m, although the butterfly does stray to lower levels. It can be found in late June and July on most high mountains, including Ben Lomond and Ben More, but appears to be absent from Ben Ledi and Ben Vorlich. It is surprising that the Scotch Argus (*Erebia aethiops* Esper) is not more widespread in the region. The butterfly is found commonly in the north, west and south of Scotland in areas where Purple Moor-grass (*Molinia caerulea*) is abundant. Here it is found only in the extreme west of the region, in the Ben Lomond, Brig o' Turk and Tyndrum areas. The Large Heath (*Coenonympha tullia* Mueller) is usually common on raised and blanket bogs in the region, including those in the lowlands such as Flanders Moss and the remnants of Letham Moss. It is also found in damp moorland where its principal larval food plants grow, probably Common Cotton-grass (*Eriophorum angustifolium*) and Purple Moor-grass (*Molinia caerulaea*). Two subspecies of the Large Heath are found in Central, the typical subspecies *tullia* in the south and at low altitudes, and the large, pale form *scotica* Staudinger in the north and in the mountains.

Like the Orange Tip, the range of the Ringlet (*Aphantopus hyperantus* L.) has increased dramatically over the last ten years. The larvae feed on various common grasses and the adults fly in a wide range of grassland biotopes. Although the Ringlet appears to have no very specific requirements, its distribution was discontinuous in the south and west of the region. It was fairly common on various parts of Flanders Moss, between Callander and Doune, some parts of Clackmannanshire (near Dollar and Alloa) and a few sites in the north. Recently, the colonies have spread and in many areas the former by discrete populations have become contiguous. In many parts of the region, especially in south Perthshire, the Ringlet is now a common and widespread butterfly. No Skippers (Hesperiidae) have been recorded in central Scotland.

We know the specific habitats of only a few day-flying moths with any certainty and a few of these are of special note. The Narrow-bordered Bee Hawk Moth (*Hamaris tityus* L.) is a species of remote moorland and is found in such situations in the Callander area. The Orange Underwing (*Achiearis parthenias* L.) was not known in the region until the 1970s. Indeed, before then it was not recorded from anywhere between Cumbria and Rannoch Moor. It is now common on

Figure 4   The rare Pearl-bordered Fritillary (*Boloria euphrosyne*).

both Flanders Moss and in the Callander area and perhaps is overlooked elsewhere. It frequents light Birch (*Betula* species) woodland. Two coastal moths are found in the Ochil Hills, the Narrow-bordered Six Spot Burnet (*Zygaena filipendulae* L.) and the Cinnabar Moth (*Tyria jacobaeae* L.). The Six Spot Burnet has also been found on a railway embankment near Dunblane and by the Ochil Hills at Muckhart.

Central Scotland is fortunate in having within its boundary a high proportion of the Scottish butterfly fauna. Day and night flying moths are also well represented, although they have been only briefly described here. This encouraging situation is due in part to the diversity of habitats across the central lowlands. Whether populations expand or retreat over the coming decades, however, very much depends on how we manage both common and scarce habitats within our landscape and on the vagaries of our fickle climate.

REFERENCES AND FURTHER READING

BRYANT, D. M. 1981. Lepidoptera from the parish of Muckhart south east Perthshire (Central Region). *Forth Naturalist and Historian* 6, 43-52

CHRISTIE, E. R. and CHRISTIE, J.C. 1980. Moths of East Loch Lomondside. Report of Nature Conservancy Council, South West (Scotland) Region.

COATES, D. L. 1968. Lepidoptera from the Stirling area. *Entomologists Record and Journal of Variation* 80, 7-22, 104-109

HOLMES, C. W. N. 1982/3. Lepidoptera of the Falkirk District of Central Region. *Forth Naturalist and Historian* 7, 57-76

McLAURIN, M. and A. 1928-9. The butterflies and moths of Stirling district. *Transactions of the Stirling Natural History and Archaeological Society* 15, 9-12

THOMSON, G. 1968. The macrolepidoptera of Stirlingshire and south Perthshire. *Entomologists' Record and Journal of Variation* 80, 246-249

THOMSON, G. 1976. Our 'disappearing' butterflies. *Forth Naturalist and Historian* 1, 89-105

THOMSON, G. 1977. Migrant butterflies in central Scotland. *Forth Naturalist and Historian* 2, 49-53; 3, 29

THOMSON, G. 1980. The Butterflies of Scotland. A Natural History. Croom Helm, London.

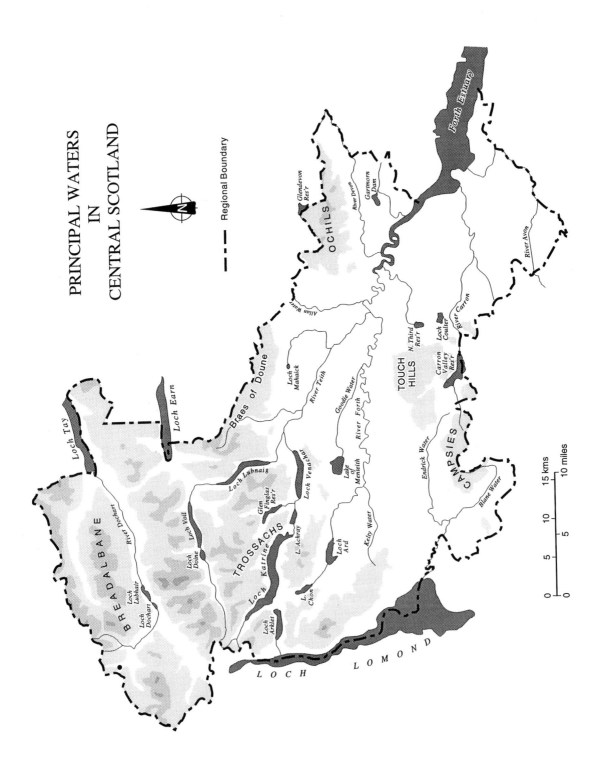

PRINCIPAL WATERS
IN
CENTRAL SCOTLAND

N

– · – Regional Boundary

Forth Estuary

Glendevon Res'r

River Devon

Gartmorn Dam

River Avon

OCHILS

Allan Water

Braes of Doune

Loch Earn

Loch Tay

Loch Mahaick

River Teith

Goodie Water

River Forth

N. Third Res'r

Loch Coulter

River Carron

Carron Valley Res'r

TOUCH HILLS

BREADALBANE

River Dochart

Loch Lubhair

Loch Dochart

Loch Voil

Loch Doine

Loch Lubnaig

Loch Venachar

Glen Finglas Res'r

TROSSACHS

L. Achray

Loch Katrine

Loch Ard

Loch Chon

Lake of Menteith

Kelty Water

Endrick Water

CAMPSIES

Blane Water

Loch Arklet

LOCH   LOMOND

0   5   10   15 kms

0   5   10 miles

Aquatic Life

D. S. McLusky and O. L. Lassiere

INTRODUCTION TO THE HABITATS

The area of central Scotland covered by this book is largely the catchment of the River Forth. Additionally, the northern part, especially the River Dochart, forms part of the headwaters of the Tay catchment, and the southwestern corner embraces the River Endrick, and Loch Lomond, which flow into the Clyde estuary, through the River Leven **(Figure 1)**.

The Forth catchment includes habitats ranging widely from the hill lochs and streams of the highland areas, which feed the major lochs such as Loch Katrine, to the major rivers, the Forth, and perhaps more importantly the Teith, which cross the lowland areas and beyond Stirling become tidal as they mix with salt water from the North Sea to form the Forth estuary. Within this diversity of habitats is found a wide variety of aquatic life.

Lochs and Ponds

The 2640 km² Central Region represents 3.42% of the area of Scotland holding about 5.0% of its population. 2.7% of this area is water including 355 lochs, lochans or ponds, making one water body per 7.4 km² **(Table 1)**.

These water bodies range widely in size with each of the five lochs Katrine, Lomond, Venachar, Earn and Tay, and the Carron Valley Reservoir being over 350 hectares (3.5 km²), but 294 (82.8% of the total) are less than, or equal to, 4 ha in area, including 223 of one hectare or less **(Figure 2)**.

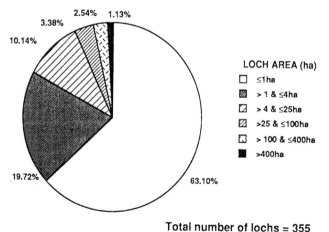

Figure 2   Percentages of lochs in various size categories.

Lochs, lochans and ponds are found at all altitudes, but a clear majority are below 200m **(Figure 3)** The water bodies of central Scotland are thus distributed widely across the area, and no place is far from water.

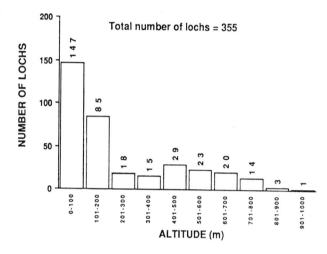

Figure 3   Distribution of lochs by altitude.

In terms of loch density, Central Region compares favourably with its bordering regions, but falls far short of the Western Isles Council area where over 5% of the land area is water **(Table 1)**.

Table 1 Loch numbers in different regions of Scotland

(Data from Lassiere (1992), Smith and Lyle (1979), Maitland (1979), Scottish Development Department (1976), and Scottish Wildlife Trust (1974))

Region	Area (km²)	Lochs	Area (ha)
Central	2640	355	744
Lothian	1755	257	680
Tayside	7500	947	790
Western Isles	2900	6038	48

Within Central Region:

Stirling District	282
Falkirk District	58
Clackmannan District	15

A recent mapping study has shown that the number of water bodies in Central Scotland is increasing, contrary to declines occurring elsewhere in Britain, due in part to the construction of reservoirs, but also to deliberate pond creation for ornamental and other purposes. Since 1896 there have been 188 lochs gained

and present day use, there is less intensive arable agriculture, and relatively few large centres of population.

Figure 5 A man-made loch, Ochlochy Park pond, Dunblane.

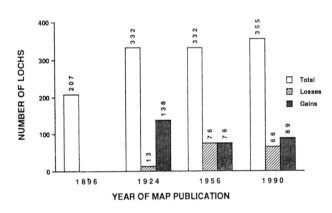

Figure 4   Numbers of lochs in 1896, 1924, 1956, 1990.

and 40 lost, giving a net addition of 148 **(Figure 4)**.

Less than 7% of the gains were of large water bodies, for example the reservoirs at Carron Valley and Glen Finglas, so more than 93% were of smaller lochs. This is very important because it is these sites, with shallow water and varied shorelines, that support the most diverse fauna and flora. If we compare the number of lochs <4ha in the 1890s with the 1990s there has been an overall increase of 86%. Whilst several water bodies have disappeared in this time some of the appearances are due to improved mapping techniques. This region has fared much better in this regard than other areas of Britain **(Table 2)**.

Table 2   Some lochs and pond losses over the last 100 - 150 years. (Adapted from Jeffries and Mills, 1990)

Area	% loss,	% gain	General land use
Central Region		+86	Upland & arable
Edinburgh	-6		Urban
Midlothian (Scotland)	-23		Arable & pasture
Clywd (Wales)	-32		Arable & pasture
Leicestershire (England)	-60		Intensive arable
Bedfordshire (England)	-82		Intensive arable

This may be in part because its lochs and ponds are extremely variable in terms of their catchment, origin

Figure 6   A natural loch, Loch Ard forest.

Of the 355 water bodies on present day maps, c 65 are man-made **(Figure 5)** and c 150 are natural **(Figure 6)** Natural waters include hill lochs, oxbow lakes, glacial cut lochs, brackish pools close to the estuary, and lochs on the remainder of Flanders moss. The majority of the man-made are reservoirs for a wide variety of purposes, including drinking water, whisky distilling, power generation and yeast production, others include town ponds with concrete edges, curling ponds, garden and park ponds, industrial settling tanks, gravel pits, quarries and shooting ponds.

The Larger Lochs

The largest loch wholly within the area is Loch Katrine, which with a volume of 818 million m³ is the tenth largest Scottish loch by volume. Together with Lochs Arklet, Venachar, Achray and the Glen Finglas Reservoir, Loch Katrine is the principal drinking water reservoir for Glasgow, linked to the city by a twin aqueduct via holding reservoirs at Mugdock, near Milngavie. Its use as drinking water with only minimal treatment for a large proportion of the population of Scotland shows the vital role of the freshwaters of this central region. The Carron Valley Reservoir and Loch Lomond are also used for drinking water supply, and together with Loch Turret in Tayside, are all now linked through the imaginative Central Scotland water scheme which forms a supply grid to ensure a plentiful supply of water for drinking and industry, especially the large petro-chemical industries of Grangemouth.

Beyond Kingshouse, between Strathyre and Lochearnhead, is the catchment of the Tay. Loch Earn, the 13th largest loch in Scotland by volume, is largely in Tayside and outwith the context of this chapter as is Loch Tay which is the 4th largest water body in Britain by volume, its volume only being exceeded by Lochs Ness, Lomond and Morar **(Table 3)**.

Table 3   Large lochs - length, area, depth and volume

Loch	Length (km)	Area (km²)	Depth max (m)	Depth min (m)	Volume (m³.10⁶)
Central Scotland:					
Lomond	36	71	190	37	2628
Katrine	13	12	151	61	818
Earn	10	10	88	42	433
Tay	23	26	155	61	1697
Other large lochs:					
Awe	41	39	94	32	1230
Ness	39	57	230	132	7452
Morar	19	27	310	87	2307
Shiel	28	20	128	41	793

At the western margin of central Scotland lies Loch Lomond, which in terms of surface area (71 km²) and shoreline length (153 km) is the largest water body in Britain, and in terms of volume the 2nd largest, being only exceeded by Loch Ness. Loch Lomond has been fully described elsewhere (Tippet 1974, 1993; Maitland

1981). It is a unique blend of a deep fiordic loch in the northern half, a shallow broad loch studded with islands in the southern half, and is the only large loch to straddle the Highland Boundary Fault Line. The northern part is 18 km long and narrow, <1.5 km wide, but extends down to 190 m depth. Since the surface is at about 9 m above sea level, most of its water is below sea level. The southern part, studded with islands, is approximately 7 km by 11 km, and less than 18 m deep throughout. The eastern shore and islands lie within the jurisdiction of Central Region, and the western shore and islands within Strathclyde Region. The loch is managed by the Loch Lomond Park Authority, who as well as interests in wild and aquatic life, has to deal with the many people who use the loch for recreation, ranging from anglers to speed-boat owners.

Rivers and Streams

The main river in terms of flow is the Teith, which drains Lochs Katrine, Venachar and Lubnaig passing Callander and Doune en route to Stirling. The long term average flow of the Teith as it enters the Forth estuary is 25.03 m³ s⁻¹, being approximately 40% of the freshwater entering the estuary **(Table 4)**.

Table 4   The catchments of Central Scotland (Data from Forth River Purification Board, and Leatherland, 1987).

Name	Catchment Area (km²)	Mean Flow m³ sec⁻¹	Length km
Forth :			
Devon	201	4.86	50
Allan	218	5.10	47
Teith	586	25.03	63
Forth	397	14.77	112
Carron	173	4.70	39
Avon	195	3.62	37
Clyde :			
Endrick	267	8.20	49
Tay :			
Tay (entire)	4590	163.80	148
Dochart	234	16.30	23

The Teith is especially important under low flow conditions, when its 4.01 m³ sec⁻¹ comprises half of all the region's river waters, due to its large headwaters catchment, incorporating Lochs Katrine, Venachar, Lubnaig, Voil, and their feeder streams, as well as the rivers Balvag and Leny. Even though a large part of the waters of Loch Katrine are diverted by pipeline to Glasgow enough remains to give the Teith domination. The cleanliness and purity of the water in its upper reaches are outstanding.

The second most important river is the Forth itself, which mainly drains from the Loch Ard forest area and the Lake of Menteith. Other key rivers are the

Allan and Devon which enter the Forth estuary above and below Stirling respectively, the Carron which runs from the Carron Valley Reservoir down through Denny and Falkirk to reach the estuary at Grangemouth, and the Avon which enters the Forth near Bo'ness **(Table 3)**. In the west the Endrick enters Loch Lomond near Balmaha, contributing 22% of the inflowing water to the loch.

The River Tay is the largest river in Britain by flow volume. It commences within this area as the Dochart (Tay) at 625 m near Tyndrum, descending to 140 m at Killin to enter Loch Tay. The river has a typical convex curve, changing from a descent of 115 m km^{-1} initially, to a descent of 2.2 m km^{-1} before Killin. Beyond Loch Tay, towards Perth, it averages a descent of 1.4 m km^{-1}. Over the length of the Dochart the land use changes from rough grazing, to a mixture of rough grazing, with increasing proportions of arable and forestry use. The bed of the river starts off as 40% rock,

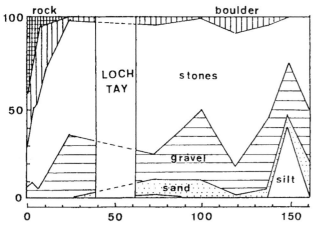

Figure 7 Vertical section of the Tay River system (After Maitland and Smith, 1987)

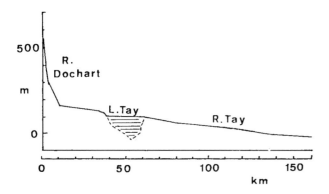

Figure 8 Bed materials composition along the Tay River system. (After Maitland and Smith, 1987)

descending to an increasing proportion of stones, gravel and sand. **(Figures 7,8)**.

Canals

Canals form important aquatic habitats in the area. The Forth and Clyde extends from Bowling on the Clyde to Grangemouth on the Forth. Despite its blockage at several points, due mainly to new road schemes, much of the canal remains intact. The Union Canal from Falkirk to Edinburgh is also largely intact.

The Forth Estuary

At the eastern margin of the area is the Forth estuary, one of the major estuaries of the British coastline, stretching for approximately 48 km from its head at the tidal limit above Stirling (at Craigforth, near the M9 motorway bridge) to its mouth at Queensferry, where it is straddled by the Forth Road and Rail Bridges. Eastward of the Bridges is the Firth of Forth, outwith the subject area of this book. Throughout its length the estuary is subject to regular tidal fluctuations, with a tidal amplitude of 5 m from Queensferry to Alloa, reducing to 3 m at Stirling (McLusky 1987). Before the Second World War there was regular shipping traffic up the estuary, as far as the quay at Riverside in Stirling. This has long ceased, although some traffic continued to reach Alloa until the 1960s. This port too has been abandoned, although a proposal to reopen it in 1992 received strong local support. Otherwise, shipping traffic now comes into the estuary as far as Grangemouth, one of the key ports for Scotland, with a busy traffic in timber, refined oil products, and general goods, particularly across the North Sea to mainland Europe.

Along the estuary there is a gradation in salinity from fresh water at Stirling to sea water at Queensferry. The upper part of the estuary (Stirling to Alloa), known locally as 'The Windings' is narrow and meandering and dominated by fresh water entering from the Rivers Forth and Teith. The main mixing zone between salt and fresh water, the so-called 'freshwater/seawater interface', occurs in the Cambuskenneth - Fallin - Cambus reach, characterised by turbid waters as the fine material carried by both river and tide are continually maintained in suspension. This region experiences a marked oxygen sag, as decomposition processes utilise the oxygen available in the water. This natural sag is exacerbated by organic waste discharges as described later. Below Alloa the estuary begins to widen substantially as it passes Dunmore and Airth, and under Kincardine Bridge, widening further, by Grangemouth and Bo'ness. Here salinity increases from approximately 25% sea water at Alloa, to 95% sea water at Bo'ness. In the upper part of the estuary the intertidal mudflats are narrow, short and steep, but in the central part below Alloa the mudflats widen, and beyond Kincardine they form large expanses at Skinflats, Kinneil, Culross and Torry Bay which are vital habitats

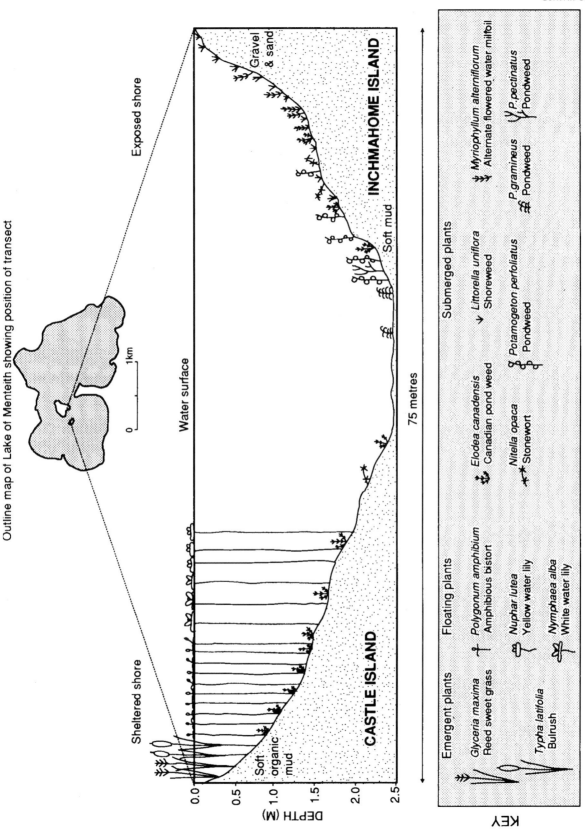

Figure 9 Vertical profile of plants between Castle and Inchmahome islands, Lake of Menteith (After Ogden, 1975).

for many forms of wildlife, especially wading birds which visit the area in winter time.

AQUATIC LIFE

Not only are the standing and flowing waters of this central region important features of the landscape they are also home to many species of bacteria, fungi, plants and animals. More than a quarter of all notified wildlife sites in the area have some form of aquatic habitat within their boundaries, including streams, river banks, canals, flooded quarries, lochs, wetlands, mires and fens.

Plants

The plants associated with these waters are many and varied, including microscopic algae, mosses, liverworts, ferns and flowering plants. They may be found bordering the waters edge, floating on the surface, submerged, in the water column, encrusting rocks or sand grains and some even living on the surface of larger plants, as epiphytes on larger plants. It is beyond the scope of this chapter to describe all the plants in detail, but some are given as examples in the context of describing different aquatic habitats.

LOCH FLORA

A first glance at a loch will reveal that there is a distinct pattern of plant zonation. Terrestrial plants merge into marsh species, which in turn merge into emergent plants bordering the waters edge with truely aquatic plants in the open water itself. As lochs gradually become infilled through the process of siltation the flora will eventually become entirely terrestrial again. **Figure 9** is an example of a loch profile showing the plants occuring along a transect in the Lake of Menteith.

Other lochs in Central Region will have some of the following species in the different zones **(Table 5)**.

Table 5   Plant species by plant zones in and around lochs in central Scotland

Marginal and emergent	Floating	Submerged
Branched bur-reed (*Sparganium erectum*)	White water lily (*Nymphaea alba*)	Canadian pond weed (*Elodea canadensis*)
Water forget-me-not (*Myosotis scorpioides*)	Yellow water lily (*Nuphar lutea*)	Spiked water milfoil (*Myriophyllum spicatum*)
Brooklime (*Veronica beccabunga*)	Broad leaved pondweed (*Potamogeton natans*)	Starworts (*Callitriche spp.*)
Water mint (*Mentha aquatica*)	Amphibious bistort (*Polygonum amphibium*)	Pond weeds (*Potamogeton spp.*)
Sedges (*Carex spp.*)	Duckweeds (*Lemna spp.*)	Quillwort (*Isoetes lacustris*)
Water horsetail (*Equisetum fluviatile*)	Bladderworts (*Utricularia spp.*)	Water lobelia (*Lobelia dortmanna*)
Marsh marigold (*Caltha palustris*)	Filamentous algae	Stoneworts (*Chara & Nitella spp.*)
Bog Bean (*Menyanthes trifoliata*)	Flote grass (*Glyceria fluitans*)	Common water crowfoot (*Ranunculus aquatilis*)
Soft rush (*Juncus effusus*)		
Common spike rush (*Eleocharis palustris*)		

FLOWING WATER FLORA

In fast flowing streams larger plants may be entirely absent, but where the flow is moderate a number are able to establish themselves, particularly along the edges of the main channel. Various species of bryophyte, Bur-reeds (*Sparganium* spp.), Lilies (*Nuphar lutea, Nymphaea alba*), Alternate-flowered Milfoils (*Myriophyllum alterniflorum*), Pondweeds (*Potamogeton* spp.) and Reeds (*Phalaris arundinacea*) are examples of such plants in Central Region rivers. A recent survey of plants in the River Teith found numerous species including Yellow Irises (*Iris pseudacorus*), Reed Sweet Grass (*Glyceria maxima*), Water Plantain (*Alisma plantago-aquatica*), Shoreweed (*Littorella uniflora*), Curled Pondweed (*Potamogeton crispus*), Willow Moss (*Fontinalis antipyretica*) and Starworts (*Callitriche* spp.) in the main river channel.

The river banks provide a habitat for a characteristic flora, for example, along the banks of the River Teith trees like Alder (*Alnus glutinosa*), Ash (*Fraxinus excelsior*), Willow (*Salix* spp.) Sycamore (*Acer pseudoplatanus*), Oak (*Quercus robur*), Beech (*Fagus sylvatica*) Hazel (*Corylus avellana*), Birch (*Betula* spp.) and Hawthorn (*Crataegus monogyna*) flourish. Other plants on the banks include Common reed (*Phalaris arundinacea*), Meadowsweet (*Filipendula ulmaria*), Ferns (e.g. *Dryopteris* spp), Globe flower (*Trollius europaeus*) and Soft rush (*Juncus effusus*).

AQUATIC RARITIES

In central Scotland at least 277 (24%) of the 1156 recorded taxa of ferns and flowering plants are found in either aquatic or wetland habitats. Most of these are quite common but there are a few rare species in need of protection. A Nature Conservancy Council survey of the status of aquatic plants in Britain was conducted on a River Purification Board area basis. In this central area, which is served by the Clyde, Forth and Tay River Purification boards, as many as six nationally rare, 22 nationally scarce and 42 locally rare species are found **(Table 6)**.

Two of the six national rarities are found associated with standing water habitats. The Loch Lomond Dock (*Rumex aquaticus*) **(Figure 10)** is only found in 3 of the 2,600 10x10km grid squares in Great Britain and as such is included in the British Red Data book of rare plants. It was discovered in 1935 near Balmaha. Although widely distributed throughout

Figure 10 The Loch Lomond Dock (*Rumex aquaticus*): a national rarity found on the shores of Loch Lomond. (Courtesy of John Mitchell)

Table 6 Numbers of rare species of aquatic plaants in Tay, Forth and Clyde River Purification Board Areas, in need of protection. Data from British Red Data Book (1983) and Palmer & Newbold (1983).

Distribution category	Tay RPB	Forth RPB	Clyde RPB
National Rarity (in <16 of GB 10x10 km squares)	4	2*	6
Nationally Scarce (in 16-100 of GB 10x10 km squares)	21	22	23
Locally Rare (in >100 of GB 10x10 km squares)	36	42	28

* National rarities in Forth RPB area: *Elantine hydropiper* (Eight-stamened waterwort) *Najas flexilis* (Slender naiad)

Central and Northern Europe, it was previously unrecorded in Britain. It differs from the common Great Water Dock in having spear-shaped leaves and protuberances on the fruit.

The Eight-stamened Waterwort (*Elantine hydropiper*) **(Figure 11)** is a small plant which grows submerged on sandy substrata. It can be seen during exceptionally dry periods when normal water levels are reduced significantly. It is a national rarity, being found in only six 10km squares in Great Britain, but is a poor competitor and in normal conditions is outgrown by faster growing, larger macrophytes. It is usually found at sites moderately rich in nutrients and the first

Figure 12   The Monkey Flower, introduced, commonly found around lochs and along some river banks.

Figure 11 The Eight-stamened Waterwort, one of the smaller aquatic rarities   (Courtesy of John Mitchell).

record of the species in Scotland, outside the Clyde area, was at Loch Watston, south-west of Doune, in July 1980. Since then it has also been recorded in the Carron Valley Reservoir and the Lake of Menteith.

The region has a number of Sites of Special Scientific Interest (SSSI) which have been notified because their associated aquatic flora is of interest. For example, Carbeth Loch, just north of Milngavie, is home to the Greater Spearwort (*Ranunculus lingua*) and the nationally rare species, the Least Yellow Water Lily (*Nuphar pumila*) is found in Lochan Lairig Cheile, north west of Lochearnhead. Some of the more common species are introductions. The Monkey Flower (*Mimulus guttatus*)**(Figure 12)** was first recorded in Britain in 1830 and is often found bordering lochs or along river banks and is now found in 18 of the 49 10km squares of the region. The Giant Hogweed (*Heracleum mantegazzianum*)**(Figure 13**, and Nieland et al 1987) which originates from the Caucasus Mountains, It is often found growing next to waterways. The banks of the Allan Water have become extensively colonized

Figure 13 Giant Hogweed, introduced species found along some river banks.

with this plant which can reach heights of over 3.5 metres. It is thought that they are the descendants of plants introduced to the Cromlix House Estate at the turn of the century. This species can cause problems because the sap contains chemicals which sensitize human skin to strong sunlight. They can restrict public access to loch shores and river banks and may cause erosion since they often replace existing vegetation which stabilizes the soil.

The flora associated with river banks and main channels can be useful indicators of both water and substrate chemistry. Floral surveys along the banks of the rivers Teith and Endrick have shown them to be oligotrophic (low in nutrients) in their upper reaches and mesotrophic (medium range in nutrient levels) in their lower reaches. These rivers may be compared with rivers in the south east of England which were all eutrophic (nutrient rich).

Water plants can also be used to assess the quality of standing water bodies, for example the large Trossachs lochs and Loch Lomond are oligotrophic with characteristic plants like *Sphagnum* mosses, Shoreweed (*Littorella uniflora*), Water Lobelia (*Lobelia dortmanna*), Broadleaved Pondweed (*Potamogeton natans*) and Willow Moss (*Fontinalis antipyretica*). The Lake of Menteith is a mesotrophic loch with many associated species including Alternate-flowered Water-milfoil (*Myriophyllum alterniflorum*), Stoneworts (*Nitella* spp.), White Water Lily (*Nymphaea alba*) and Canadian Pondweed (*Elodea canadensis*).

CANAL FLORA

The habitat of the Forth and Clyde and the Union Canals can in many ways be regarded as elongated ponds. In the absence of traffic, the water is often undisturbed, and encroachment by shore plants and siltation can become major problems when not controlled. Along a section of the Union Canal, 44 species of macrophyte (larger aquatic plants) were found in 1987. Of these, 50% were species that are uncommon or rare in Scotland. A survey of the Forth and Clyde between Bowling and Falkirk recently recorded 102 species of macrophyte. Some like the Duckweeds (*Lemna minor*, *Lemna trisulca*) were very common, along with Reed Sweet Grass (*Glyceria maxima*), Water Mint (*Mentha aquatica*) and Stinging

Table 7 Animal life in freshwaters.

Without backbones	Invertebrates
Common group name	Scientific name
Single celled animals	Protozoa
Sponges	Porifera
Freshwater Anemone	Cnidaria, Hydrozoa
Flatworms	Platyhelminthes, Tricladida
Ribbon worms	Nemertea
Round worms	Nematoda
Wheel animalcules	Rotifera
Hairybacks	Gastrotricha
Worms	Annelida, Oligochaeta
Leeches	Annelida, Hirudinea
Moss Animals	Bryozoa
Snails, Limpets & Mussels	Molluscs
Water bears	Tardigrada
Spiders & Mites	Chelicerata
Shrimps, Water fleas	Crustacea
Insects	Uniramia, Hexapoda
Springtails	Collembola
Stoneflies	Plecoptera
Mayflies	Ephemeroptera
Dragonflies & Damselflies	Odonata
Water bugs	Hemiptera
Water beetles	Coleoptera
Alderflies	Megaloptera
Caddis flies	Trichoptera
True flies	Diptera
Moths & Butterflies	Lepidoptera
Ants	Hymenoptera
Fish	Pisces
Amphibians	Amphibia
Reptiles	Reptilia
Birds	Aves
Mammals	Mammalia

Nettles (*Urtica dioica*). Others like the Marsh Marigold (*Caltha palustris*), the RaggedRobin (*Lychnis flos-cuculi*) and Frogbit (*Hydrocharis morsus-ranae*) were very rare.

Aquatic plants form an integral part of the flowing and standing water communities in the area. They oxygenate the water, provide a food source for some animals and create three dimensional living spaces for the animals to inhabit, e.g. dragonflies lay their eggs on aquatic vegetation and newts and toads their spawn.

Animals

Over 3800 species of animals, excluding protozoa and parasites inhabit the freshwaters of Britain, most familiar being the vertebrates like fish, amphibians, waterfowl and mammals. But these only represent a small proportion of the entire list **(Table 7)**. The vast majority are invertebrates which include microscopic single celled animals like *Amoeba* and *Euglena* and the macroscopic sponges, small anemone-like creatures (*Hydra*), worms, molluscs, leeches, crustaceans, water mites and insects. Insects are by far the largest group and include the water bugs, water beetles, alderflies, mayflies, stoneflies, caddis flies, dragonflies and true flies. Of 1863 species of aquatic insect in Britain, 1138 are the true flies (Diptera), which include the dancing, non-biting midges as well as the biting midges. In central Scotland, examples from all of these groups can be found in the varied aquatic habitats already described. **Table 8** shows the numbers of species in various aquatic animal groups in central Scotland compared to Great Britain as a whole. **Figure 14** pie charts illustrate the groups of 'all animal' and 'insects' in central Scotland lochs and ponds.

Five species of amphibian have been recorded in the region: the Common Frog (*Rana temporaria*), the Common Toad (*Bufo bufo*) and three species of Newt, the Palmate (*Triturus helveticus*), Smooth (*Triturus vulgaris*) and the Great Crested (*Triturus cristatus*). A survey in 1992 of amphibian distribution attempted with the aid of over 250 volunteers to look at their

Table 8   Number of species in ten freshwater animal groups in central Scotland and the United Kingdom.

Group	No. of species in central Scotland	No. of Species in U.K.	Reference
Leeches	10	16	Elliot & Tullett 1982
Molluscs	43	71	Kerney 1976
Hoglice (*Asellus*)	2	3	Moon & Harding 1981
Stoneflies	26	30	Hynes 1984
Dragonflies & damselflies	11	39	Gardner 1983 and Chelmick et al. 1980
Water bugs	36	64	Savage 1989
Blackflies	5	34	Davies 1968
Fish	21	55	Maitland 1972
Amphibians	5	6	Arnold 1983

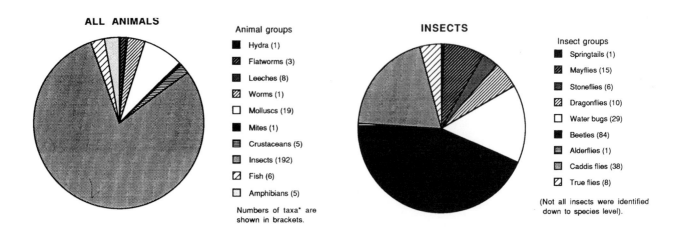

Figure 14 Pie charts of the range of all animals and insects found in central Scotland lochs and ponds.

distribution in all 49 10x10 km squares in Central Region. This survey showed that the Common Frog is found throughout the region and spawns in nearly every available aquatic habitat from lowland lochs and garden ponds, to roadside puddles and mountain peaty pools. Toads are quite common in the lowland areas, choosing to spawn in waters where there are aquatic plants around which they wrap their strings of eggs. Smooth and Palmate Newts are apparently far less common, but have been found in a range of sites including flooded quarries, curling ponds and canals. The Great Crested Newt has not been seen in the region since the 1970s.

In central Scotland there are no native species of reptile which are truly aquatic, however, adders do occur and may be found in the water resting or heading towards the refuge of a loch island. There is anecdotal evidence for terrapins surviving in the Forth and Clyde canal, most probably rejected pet red-eared terrapins; although they survive, the low temperatures make it impossible for them to breed successfully.

The birds and mammals of the area, including several associated with aquatic habitats, for example Dipper, Otter and other species, are described in separate chapters within this book.

The general picture, allowing for recent changes in distribution, is that this region provides suitable habitats for most of the animal groups. In addition to the free living fauna, there are many parasitic species, animals - flukes, tapeworms, spiny-headed worms and crustaceans, and microorganisms- viruses, bacteria, fungi.

Life in Ponds

A survey of the lesser open water bodies (ponds!) in the region was conducted in 1991 as part of the Operation Brightwater campaign. The water chemistry, flora and fauna of 30 representative sites, both natural and man-made ponds were surveyed. These smaller aquatic habitats were found to be extremely important for wildlife, with 240 plant and 241 animal taxa. These included some plant species noted as being rare in the area e.g. the Ivy-leaved Duckweed (*Lemna trisulca*) Cowbane (*Cicuta virosa*). The locally rare, North American Freshwater Shrimp, *Crangonyx pseudogracilis*, first recorded in Scotland in 1959 at Grangemouth in ponds used for seasoning timber, was found in Airthrey Loch, Stirling University. In general, animals found were dominated by insects with more than 54 species of water beetle, 37 species of caddis fly and 25 species of water bug being recorded. The water quality varied considerably from nutrient poor acidic bog pools, fringed with *Sphagnum* moss and inhabited by a few beetle and dragonfly species, to enriched alkaline garden ponds supporting many species of both plants and animals. These smaller waters are also favoured breeding sites for amphibians. A number of sites in the region are suffering from neglect manifested as reduced water supply, rubbish dumping and infilling, among other problems. Their small size also makes them very susceptible to the effects of changing land use. These small waters are important refuges for aquatic life, and as such should be safeguarded for future generations to enjoy.

Life in the Large Lochs

Loch Lomond, the largest water body in the British Isles, judged by its surface area and shoreline length, has a wide variety of all forms of aquatic life. Suspended in the water are phytoplankton, the microscopic algae, and the zooplankton which feed upon the phytoplankton. Phytoplankton are restricted to the top 5 - 10 m of water where sufficient light penetrates to sustain photosynthesis. In addition to light, the phytoplankton needs nutrients, especially phosphates and nitrates, in order to grow. The land surrounding the northern part of the loch which is composed of ancient metamorphic rocks (see Geology chapter) and supports only a limited amount of agriculture, supplies 78% of the water entering the loch, and therefore the quantity of nutrients entering from the land is very low. The northern waters of the loch are therefore classified as oligotrophic, meaning poorly fed, and the production of phytoplankton is accordingly restricted. By contrast, the southern waters of the loch receive more nutrients from the River Endrick, which is draining lowland sedimentary rocks, with some good agricultural land. This southern inflow only represents 22% of the total, however, and the large overall volume of water effectively dilutes the nutrients so that Loch Lomond can never be regarded as over-enriched or eutrophic.

The waters of the northern part of Loch Lomond become stratified, or layered, during the summer months, because of its great depth. Without any mixing this effectively this confines the phytoplanktonic algae to the surface layers, which become nutrient depleted, restricting the growth of such algae to a brief spell in the spring. In the shallower southern waters the mixing of nutrients can occur all summer long, and the growth of phytoplankton can thus be sustained for a longer period. As a result, the northern part of the loch is considered to be unproductive, and the southern part to be productive.

Phytoplankton supports animals in two ways. Firstly they are consumed directly by zooplankton, including rotifers and small crustaceans, principally *Daphnia hyalina* and *Diaptomus gracilis* (Water Flea and Copepod). Secondly, as the phytoplankton die they fall to the bottom of the loch to support bottom-dwelling, or benthic, animals such as Chironomid larvae (the non-biting midges). In turn the zooplankton are fed upon by surface dwelling fish, of which the most important in Loch Lomond is the Powan (*Coregonus lavaretus*). In Scotland, the Powan is only found in Loch Lomond and Loch Eck. Powan are members of the salmonid family, and as whitefish are thought to be a part of the scattered remnants of a more widespread population of *Coregonus* which existed just after the last Ice Age. For many years they have been the most abundant fish in the Loch, with Trout (*Salmo trutta*) as the second commonest (the British record sea trout was taken from Loch Lomond in 1986). The next most important fish used to be the Perch (*Perca fluviatilis*). In 1982 the Ruffe (*Gymnocephalus cernua*) appeared in the Loch, more than 100 km north of any previous records. It is believed to have been introduced to Loch Lomond by anglers from England, who use these small fish as live bait when fishing for pike. Since its introduction, the Ruffe has steadily increased in abundance and the Perch has declined dramatically. The Ruffe also poses a major threat to the Powan, whose eggs it eats in large numbers at spawning time.

In the shallow margins of the loch, a range of benthic animals are found feeding upon rooted vegetation, decaying organic matter and smaller animals. These animals, which can be readily seen by examining the surface of stones, or by using a pond net in shallow waters, include a wide variety of insect larvae such as mayflies, caddisflies, stoneflies and midges (Ephemeroptera, Trichoptera, Plecoptera, Diptera), as well as adult insects, such as water-bugs and beetles (Hemiptera, Coleoptera). Also present are molluscs, leeches, sponges, and hydroids. The water level of loch Lomond fluctuates by a mean of 0.76 m monthly, with an extreme range of 2.24m. Such fluctuations affect the shore life, especially where the shore gradient is shallow, for example in the southern basin. Here these vertical water movements may represent horizontal movements of 25.6 - 65.3 m. Thus, during a dry spell these shore animals must endure exposure, which may lead to death. The fluctuating water level also restricts the growth of marginal vegetation, so the typical shore of Loch Lomond is a band of virtually bare stones and rock, providing a vivid contrast to the profusion of plants and animals which are found on the shores of the smaller lochans and ponds elsewhere in the region.

At greater depths, where light cannot penetrate and there is no direct plant production, the benthos becomes much less varied and often consists only of Chironomid larvae, bivalve molluscs (especially *Pisidium*) and oligochaete worms (especially Tubificidae) which feed upon decaying plant material which falls down from surface waters. This deeper habitat, which can only be sampled with a grab or similar device, may also suffer from oxygen depletion, or anoxia, as the vegetation decaying bacteria consume the available oxygen.

Life in Rivers and Streams

A detailed study of the animals living in the streams within the Loch Ard forest area, which are the head waters of the River Forth, has been made by Morrison (1989). These streams, e.g. the Kelty, have been a major test site of the effects of acidity as they arise on naturally acidic rocks north of the Highland Boundary Fault. The animals living in acid streams have been compared to those living in nearby, but neutral, streams, such as the Corrie, which arise south of the Highland Boundary Fault **(Table 9)**.

Table 9 Numbers of types of animals found in neighbouring neutral and acid streams of the headwaters of the River Forth. From Morrison (1989)

Taxa	Corrie Burn (neutral)	Kelty Burn (acidic)
Worms (Oligochaetes)	5	2
Limpet (*Ancylus fluviatilis*)	1	0
Shrimp (*Gammarus pulex*)	1	0
Mayflies (Ephemeroptera)	5	1
Stoneflies (Plecoptera)	9	8
Caddisflies (Trichoptera)	3	4
Fly larvae (Diptera)	3	3
Beetles (Coleoptera)	6	3
Fish (*Salmo trutta*)	1	0
Total	34	21
pH	6.5	4.5

Particular absences from the acid streams are snails, shrimps and mayflies, whilst stonefly and caddisfly larvae are much less affected.

The downstream sequence of animals and plants in the River Tay (Dochart) has been described by Maitland and Smith (1987). Mosses are the only large plants found on rocks in the upper-most reaches, but as the gradient starts to lessen, oligotrophic species (*Littorella uniflora, Myriophyllum alterniflorum* and *Elodea canadensis*) appear **(Figure 15)**.

The distribution of the invertebrates in the river indicates a clear succession down the river. Among the non-insect animals only one species, the Flatworm *Crenobia alpina*, occurs near the source. The insects are dominated by the mayfly, stonefly and caddisfly larvae (Ephemeroptera, Plecoptera and Trichoptera respectively) with a clear succession which includes the Stonefly *Perla bipunctata* and the Mayfly *Ameletus inopinatus* restricted to the uppermost reaches, and then an increasing variety of species as the Dochart approaches Killin. The fish show a succession down the river with trout reaching the furthest inland point, but not quite the source, followed in succession by eel, salmon, minnow, stone loach, perch, 3-spined stickleback, arctic charr and pike **(Figure 16)**. Another

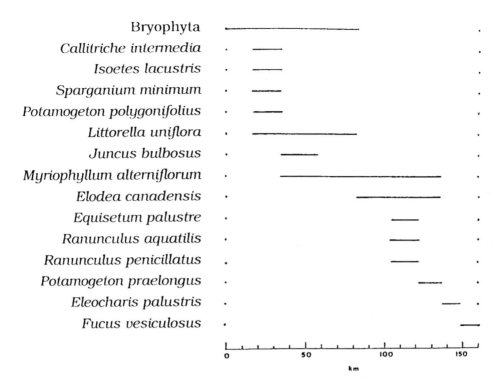

Figure 15 Macrophyte plants along the Tay River system. (After Maitland and Smith, 1987)

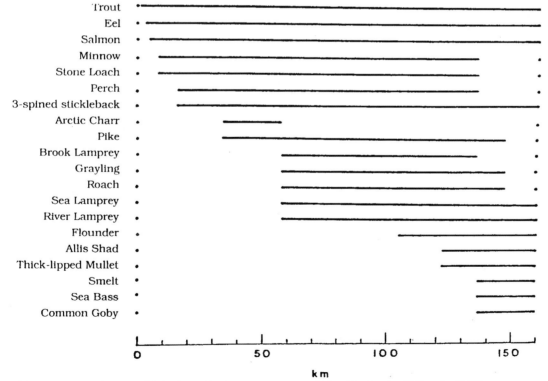

Figure 16 Distribution of fish along the Tay River system. (After Maitland and Smith, 1987)

11 fish species occur below Loch Tay, but do not reach the Dochart.

Life in the Forth Estuary

The upper Forth estuary, from Stirling to Alloa, is characterised by narrow intertidal areas, and turbid waters where salt and fresh water meet. The fauna of the muddy sediments of the intertidal and subtidal is dominated by large populations of oligochaete worms. These, so-called, sludge worms thrive in many habitats, but become particularly abundant in habitats which suffer organic pollution and oxygen depletion. Along the estuary from Riverside in Stirling down to Cambus and Alloa, they are usually the only animals living in the muds, but in large numbers, often up to 100,000 in one m². In the uppermost part of the estuary, from Craigforth down to Cambuskenneth, typical freshwater animals, such as insect larvae may be found, but the number and variety of these diminish approaching the salty water further down the estuary **(Figure 17)**.

Below Alloa, the sediments of the estuary are inhabited by a variety of estuarine animals. The variety of these increases as one progresses seaward. The first to appear is the Rag Worm (*Nereis diversicolor*), particularly abundant at Dunmore, and elsewhere between Alloa and Kincardine. As conditions in the upper estuary have begun to improve so the rag-worm has moved above Alloa, so far reaching up to Cambus.

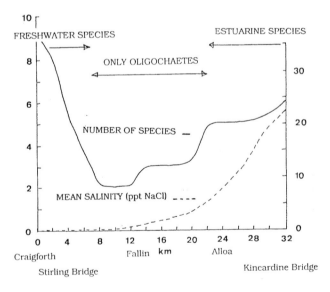

Figure 17 Penetration of animal species into the upper Forth estuary.

The next species to appear seawards are an Amphipod Shrimp (*Corophium volutator*), a bivalve mollusc, the Baltic Tellin (*Macoma balthica*) and a small Gastropod Snail (*Hydrobia ulvae*). These animals all appear between Alloa and Kincardine, and there is evidence that as the estuary has been cleaned up, so they have moved further upstream. They are however most abundant below Kincardine, forming large populations, especially in the intertidal areas of Skinflats and Kinneil.

The animals living within the mudflats form essential food for the birds which visit the area during winter. They are also fed upon by the Brown Shrimp (*Crangon crangon*), the Shore Crab (*Carcinus maenas*) and many species of fish, most notably the Eel-pout (*Zoarces viviparus*) and the Flounder (*Platichthys flesus*) which live in the estuary throughout the year, as well as large stocks of juvenile haddock and whiting which periodically move into the estuary to feed. The success of many species of birds and fish thus depends on the maintenance of the large stocks of inter-tidal animals, and it is for this reason that Skinflats and Kinneil are recognised as Sites of Special Scientific Importance (SSSIs) by Scottish Natural Heritage (see also Conservation chapter).

As well as animals living in the sediments of the estuary, the benthos, there are many animals living within the water. There is a clear gradation down the estuary, with more species at the seaward end. Particularly important is the zooplankter *Eurytemora affinis* which is the sole species occurring in low salinity waters, especially at the freshwater/ seawater interface. The breakdown processes which occur in the water at these low salinities support large populations of bacteria and rotifers, which are fed upon by the *Eurytemora*. Feeding upon the zooplankters in the estuary are pelagic fish such as Herring (*Clupea harengus*) and Sprat (*Clupea sprattus*), large shoals of which regularly reach as far as Alloa. More recently they have been rejoined by the Smelt (*Osmerus eperlanus*) which has returned to the Forth estuary after many years absence, clear evidence of pollution abatement.

Also passing through the estuary, but not feeding in it, are migratory fish, especially the Salmon (*Salmo salar*) and the Eel (*Anguilla anguilla*). Even during its most polluted period the estuary had Salmon passing through for part of the year, the problem being that during the summer months the pronounced oxygen sag effectively blocked their migration. Whilst an oxygen sag remains, it is now briefer and less severe and the numbers of Salmon in the estuary and rivers have clearly increased. To assist their passage much of the Salmon netting on the estuary, legal and otherwise, has now been halted.

Within an estuary most of the animal production depends on detritus, that is the decaying remains of plant and animal life, supplied from rivers, salt marshes and the sea. Thus a highly productive estuary, such as the Forth, depends in large part on production elsewhere, transported to it by water movements.

POLLUTION AND OTHER PROBLEMS

The primary responsibility for the maintenance or improvement of water quality in the area is with the Forth River Purification Board (FRPB) and within their catchments the Clyde and Tay RPBs. In order to discharge this responsibility the River Boards regularly monitor all features of the waters within their areas, such as water flow, dissolved oxygen, nutrient and pollutant content, and the aquatic life present.

In all rivers and lochs the animals and plants present reflect the variety of environmental conditions. They are also a good indicator of water quality, since each individual species has its own tolerance limits to disturbance. The variety of insects and other invertebrates in a stream will depend on water chemistry and also on how clean the water is. The Forth River Purification Board, as the main pollution watchdog in this area, uses sampling of the animals in streams and rivers to assess the quality of the waters. Some groups of animals (such as mayflies, stoneflies and caddisflies) are extremely sensitive to organic pollutants, while others such as Oligochaetes, Chironomid larvae and the Hog-louse (*Asellus*) will survive even in polluted waters. By examining the numbers of pollution sensitive and pollution insensitive species the water quality can be assessed. This animal based system has considerable advantages over chemical equivalents, because often a chemical will be washed downstream before there is an opportunity to collect a water sample. Although this scheme, known as the BMWP score (Biological Monitoring Working Party), has been mainly used to identify organic pollution, such as sewage, it can also be adapted to identify other problems. For example in acid, but otherwise clean, waters stoneflies survive and mayflies disappear. The Forth River Purification Board samples animal life at many locations all over the area with, for example, nine sample locations on the River Teith, each visited at least twice a year. The results of such surveys, presented in the annual reports of the FRPB, overwhelmingly show that the waters in central Scotland are of excellent quality. There are however some exceptions and these clearly point the way to the need for remedial action.

The River Black Devon, which flows from the Cleish Hills towards Alloa is partially affected by mine-water discharges, especially in its tributaries, but the main river is generally clean. The Brothie Burn flows from the Gartmorn dam to Alloa harbour, and is adversely affected by sludge from a water treatment works and by urban run-off, including the wastes from choked sewers. Depite progress the Brothie remains in an unsatisfactory condition. The River Devon used to be polluted by sewage from the towns of Dollar, Tillicoultry and Alva, but major improvements to their sewage works in the 1980s have largely solved this problem. The Dams Burn, however, which joins the Devon at Menstrie, has recently suffered from chemical spillage and septic tank waste which have caused pollution problems in the Devon.

In its upper reaches the Allan Water has had problems due to sheep dip, silage liquors and/or byre waste from farms. Lower down, the city of Dunblane sewage works, although recently extended, has had continual mechanical problems which have resulted in a deterioration of the biological quality of the river below the discharge point. Overall, despite some local problems with sewage works and a water bottling plant, the Allan Water remains of good quality, with a thriving Brown Trout population and strong runs of Salmon and Sea Trout.

The Teith, the largest river in the region, drains a large upland area, including Lochs Katrine and Lubnaig. Overall the water is of excellent quality and the river is a designated salmonid fishery under the appropriate EC directive, as well as being classified as of national importance in terms of nature conservation. Localised problems arise at Callander, where sewage fungus develops below an overloaded sewage works, and at Deanston, where a distillery by-product plant has until recently discharged poor quality effluent.

The Forth, although it has given its name to the whole area, is a much smaller river than the Teith. It rises from two sources, one the Duchray on the eastern slopes of Ben Lomond and the other the Chon which flows through Lochs Chon and Ard. The whole system is dominated by forestry in its upper reaches. This has enhanced the effect of acid precipitation, with the fauna depleted in the upper reaches. The rain falling on central Scotland is often very acidic (mean pH <4.5). The spruce forests effectively collect acid pollutants, which are subsequently washed out, thus accelerating the acidification of the soil. Streams in forested areas therefore become increasingly acidic as the neutralisation capacity of the catchment soils decrease. Within the forested streams Salmon, Trout and mayflies are notably absent. The main River Forth at Aberfoyle is of good quality, and the sewage works in the towns and villages downstream are generally satisfactory.

The Bannockburn and Sauchie burn have been affected by sheep dip, fish farm effluent, and run-off from the M9 motorway. The River Carron upstream of Denny is of good quality, with the Carron Valley reservoir serving the drinking water requirements of much of central Scotland. At Denny, a paper mill discharge adversely affects river quality. Although the effluent is much improved compared to past years, it still clearly affects animal life in the river. Further down the Carron and its tributaries problems arise due to sheep dips, quarry run-off, and urban run-off drainage from Cumbernauld New Town into Bonny Water. Despite these unresolved problems, the quality of the Carron has improved substantially over the past two decades, and by contrast with earlier times, migratory salmonids now occur.

The Avon, like most other rivers has good quality water in its upper reaches. Some problems have recently arisen due to open-cast mine workings. Lower down the dominant influence for many years has been the discharge from Westfield Paper Mill. Following the elimination of a powerful fungicide, pentachlorophenol, from the mill effluent in 1988 there has been a substantial improvement in the biological quality of the river.

The Forth estuary is fed by the clean waters of the Teith, Forth and Allan. Its meandering section between Stirling and Alloa, where sea water and fresh water meet and turbid conditions prevail, is particularly susceptible to organic wastes which are broken down by bacterial action and consequently diminish it's oxygen content. Major improvements to sewage treatment at Stirling and Alloa have alleviated the problem, but low oxygen conditions can still occur during a spell of dry summer weather. Recent findings show a steady improvement in the fauna of the upper estuary, as described earlier.

The Grangemouth area of the estuary receives the waste from the large petro-chemical plants there, as well as the contaminated waters of the Rivers Avon and Carron, the Docks, and waste water from Longannet coal mine and power station. In the immediate vicinity of some of these discharges, a clear effect of the wastes can be seen. As elsewhere in the Forth catchment considerable improvements have been made, with particular reductions in waste from the rivers and a reduction in the amount of mercury discharged by the chemical industry having already been achieved. The amount of oil and other hydrocarbons discharged by the oil refinery is soon set to fall, and by the end of the 1990s the large mudflat areas around Grangemouth should be rehabilitated.

Overall the impression of the water quality of the Forth catchment is that it is good, with some localised and identified problems. Local government and industry have made substantial improvements to the quality of their discharges through sustained effort over several decades, resulting in clear, long term improvements to water quality in the area. Much remains to be done, particularly to deal with the so-called 'accidental spillages', for example of sheep-dip or minor oil waste. In central Scotland, as the structural problems of pollution have been tackled, it has too often not been matched by care being taken by individuals. Often expenditure on waste treatment has been partially negated by the thoughtlessness of others. The preservation of aquatic life depends on the prevention of waste discharge by many sources, and every resident or visitor can play an important part. It is must be stressed that the aquatic habitats of the region are not autonomous. They are an integral part of our landscape and if we affect the catchment we inevitably affect the aquatic wildlife.

(We wish to thank Peter Maitland and Ian Fozzard for their valuable supply of information)

REFERENCES AND FURTHER READING

FORTH RIVER PURIFICATION BOARD. Annual Reports and Annual Summary of Environmental and Discharge conditions. FRPB, Riccarton, Edinburgh.

HARRIMAN, R. and MORRISON, B. 1982. Ecology of streams draining forested and non-forested catchments in an area of central Scotland subject to acid precipitation. *Hydrobiologia*, 88, 251-263.

MAITLAND, P.S. 1981. The Ecology of Scotland's Largest Lochs. Dr W Junk Publishers, The Hague. 297 pp.

MAITLAND, P.S. and SMITH, I.R. 1987. The River Tay: ecological changes from source to estuary. *Proceedings of the Royal Society of Edinburgh*, 92B, 373 - 392.

McLUSKY, D.S. editor 1987 The natural environment of the estuary and firth of Forth. *Proceedings of the Royal Society of Edinburgh*, 93B, 235 -571.

MORRISON, B. 1989. Freshwater life in acid streams and lochs. In: Acidification in Scotland , Edinburgh, Scottish Development Department (pp 82-91)

NEILAND, R., J.PROCTOR and R.SEXTON, 1987. Giant hogweed (*Heracleum mantegazzianum* Somm. & Lev.) by the River Allan and part of the River Forth. *Forth Naturalist and Historian*, 9, 51-56.

TIPPETT, R. et al 1974. A Natural History of Loch Lomond. 112 pp. Reprint L.Lomond Park Authority. 1990.

TIPPETT, R. et al 1993. Symposium on Loch Lomond. *Hydrobiologia*, (in press)

Nature Conservation

C. Crawford, J. Gallacher, J. Evans

INTRODUCTION

Government funded nature conservation began in the 1940s post-war reconstruction period with the passage of the *National Parks and Access to the Countryside Act* in 1949. This provided the legislative framework for the setting up of the Nature Conservancy, whose job was to select, establish and manage National Nature Reserves (NNR), and to identify and designate Sites of Special Scientific Interest (SSSI) throughout Britain. The legislation was subsequently strengthened by the *Wildlife and Countryside Act* 1981. In Scotland, Scottish Natural Heritage (SNH) took on these functions (as well as others inherited from the Countryside Commission for Scotland (CCS)) from April 1992, and under the *Natural Heritage (Scotland) Act* is charged with the responsibility of advising Government on nature and landscape conservation, amenity, access and recreation. The main objective of SNH is to encourage and promote the careful and sustainable use of Scotland's natural resources, and in this respect its *modus operandi* complements the objectives and spirit of the *World Conservation Strategy*. SNH seeks to work in close partnership with other statutory bodies, the voluntary conservation movement and local communities.

Increased Government funding of the statutory nature conservation agencies and the rise in membership of voluntary conservation organisations are partly responses to the losses sustained by our wildlife heritage which have been particularly evident since the 1950s. All main types of habitat have suffered appreciable loss, and for some ecosystems the scale and rate of this has been catastrophic and perhaps irreversible: for example, an estimated 25% loss in central Scotland of ancient semi-natural woodland between 1946 and 1971 caused by underplanting of conifers or conversion to agriculture; a 42% loss of Forth Valley bogs between 1948 and 1978 through afforestation (e.g. west Flanders Moss), peat winning or reclamation for agriculture; and, in the uplands an estimated 30% loss of montane grasslands, heather and blanket bog due to coniferous afforestation, hill land improvement, burning and over-grazing. Our native fauna has undergone losses too, with marked decline of the Otter, Bats, amphibians, reptiles and a range of insects, with even common species such as Curlew and Lapwing showing a population decline due to the loss of suitable habitat.

Central Scotland, covering the districts of Stirling (with a total area of 216,989 ha), Clackmannan (16,099 ha), and Falkirk (29,141 ha) is however, still very rich in nature conservation terms. This richness is reflected in the range, number and extent of existing **SSSIs** (**Table 1**). There are currently 82 such sites in the area representing 6.2 % of the land surface, and a number of proposed SSSIs are still to be designated. Within this area of protected land are some of the best examples in central Scotland, and indeed Britain, of natural or semi-natural vegetation with their distinctive animal communities, large populations of local or rare species, some endangered species and important geological and physiographic features. Outwith the protected sites, the wider countryside also contains much of vital conservation importance.

TABLE 1   **AREA OF SSSIs NOTIFIED WHOLLY OR PARTLY FOR VARIOUS HABITAT TYPES**

HABITAT:	STIRLING AREA (ha)	%	FALKIRK AREA(ha)	%	CLACKMANNAN AREA (ha)	%	TOTALS AREA (ha)	%
WOODLAND	2,318	1.06	61	0.20	178	1.10	2,557	0.97
UPLAND	9,495	4.4	198	0.68	-	-	9,693	3.7
GRASSLAND	164	0.07	6	0.02	282	1.75	452	0.17
RAISED MIRE	1,013	0.46	77	0.26	-	-	1,090	0.41
FEN & OPEN WATER	504	0.23	17	0.05	88	0.54	609	0.23
INTERTIDAL	-	-	1,306	4.5	316	1.96	1,622	0.61
GEOLOGICAL	140	0.06	-	-	20	0.12	160	0.06
TOTAL	13,712	6.31	1,660	5.7	876	5.4	16,183	6.15

Apart from the creation of SSSIs and reserves the success of nature conservation can be measured in a variety of ways. The raising of public awareness by statutory agencies and non-governmental organisations is seen as a success without which the legislative mechanisms, or the resources, for the establishment of reserves are unlikely to have taken place. This has also culminated in a growing opinion which accepts the importance of, and responsibility for, wildlife. Arguably, the most tangible achievement of the nature conservation movement has been the spectacular growth in the membership of voluntary bodies such as The Royal Society for the Protection of Birds (RSPB) (now the largest conservation charity in Europe), the Scottish Wildlife Trust (SWT), the Woodland Trust and the National Trust for Scotland (NTS), all of which may be mobilised into political pressure for the protection and enhancement of our wildlife and wild places.

WILDLIFE RESOURCES

Uplands

The main areas of upland or montane habitat occur to the north and west of central Scotland although further south the Campsie Fells, the Ochil Hills and the Slamannan Plateau are also of interest. Upland areas contain the largest extent of semi-natural wildlife habitat within central Scotland.

The strongly oceanic character of British mountains, as reflected in their soils, vegetation, flora and fauna, is a feature of international importance not duplicated anywhere else in the world (*Nature Conservation Review*, 1977). There are nine large upland SSSIs in the area, covering approximately 19,350 ha, of which six have been identified as being of national importance to nature conservation. Safeguarding these sites, in particular, is regarded as essential to the success of nature conservation in Britain.

The most important upland sites are found within or adjacent to the Breadalbane range (defined as the series of mountains lying between Ben Lui and Ben Lomond in the west to Ben Lawers in the east) along the northern boundary of the region. These are of international importance because they support the largest area of montane vegetation in Britain including rare and restricted species. The most important sites, found on nutrient-rich calcareous schists, include Beinn Dubhchraig, Ben Heasgarnich, Ben Lui, Ben More-Stob Binnein, Meall Ghaordie and Meall na Samhna. A highly important feature of these sites is the conservation of the full altitudinal range of habitats from valley floor to mountain plateaux. The occurrence of this full range within sites outwith statutory protection is very uncommon due to the truncation of habitats by agricultural improvement and/or afforestation.

Flowering plants of the upland zone with a distribution centred around or restricted to the region are of particular importance and sensitive land management

Figure 1   Purple Saxifrage *Saxifraga oppositofolia* Beinn Dubhchraig - local to mountain areas.

is required to protect them. National rarities, with major population centres in the area, include Rock Whitlow Grass *Draba norvegica*, Alpine Woodsia *Woodsia alpina*, Alpine Bartsia *Bartsia alpina* and the two-flowered Rush *Juncus biglumis*.

Further to the south, upland peat and mire habitats are well represented on the Ochils and Campsies and have associated wader populations. Animals or plants of ledge or crag habitat are of particular note. The nationally rare flower Sticky Catchfly *Lychnis viscaria* is found in the Ochils in one of its few British localities. Birds such as Raven and Peregrine are a familiar sight. It is thought that the Campsies may hold the densest population in Britain of the latter. The Bean Goose, found throughout the winter months at its only Scottish locality on the Slamannan Plateau, requires a mix of improved grassland in close juxtaposition to heather covered raised bogs. Unfortunately, much of this habitat has disappeared or is threatened due to a combination of peat winning and opencast mining. Accordingly there is now a serious danger of losing this species from Scotland.

The associated upland breeding bird assemblage in the north and west is particularly important in conservation terms. There are good populations of Golden Eagle (6% of the total GB population), Peregrine (7%), Merlin (2%), Hen Harrier (2%), Red-throated Diver (0.4%), and Black-throated Diver (3%). All these species are listed in Annex 1 of the *EEC Directive on the Conservation of Wild Birds* which requires special measures to be taken to conserve their habitats. The main conservation objective is to ensure that the populations of these species remain viable and distributed across their traditional range.

Afforestation by non-native conifers has been the main land use change by which the upland semi-natural habitats of the area have been altered. A desk study of aerial photographs between the 1970s and 1980s for Stirling District has shown an estimated 20% increase in non-native woodland. Such afforestation has historically concentrated in the uplands due to a combination of low land prices and where competition for agricultural use is least. Planting of conifers in the uplands results in the direct loss, fragmentation or confinement of habitats and/or the displacement or marginalising of the fauna. For example, much open moorland supporting a diversity of birds has been replaced by conifer plantations which support few species of birds.

The location and extent of future afforestation in central Scotland is therefore critical to the viability of certain species such as Merlin and Golden Eagle, as are considerations of landscape, recreation, amenity and access. All these factors should be included in a strategic approach to new afforestation or development in general, and should come under the terms of indicative land use/development strategies for the area in order to provide guidance on the most, and least, preferred options for future land use changes. An *Indicative Forestry Strategy* has been developed as a collaborative effort between the planning authorities, SNH and the forest industry which attempts to divide the region into a number of zones -

preferred - have no major environmental sensitivities and new planting can be actively encouraged
potential - have at least one major sensitivity which might constrain some afforestation schemes
sensitive - have major sensitivities and while planting is not wholly excluded, inappropriate schemes will not proceed.

There is no doubt that this strategic approach to our planned use of natural resources goes some way to help resolve one of the countryside's most controversial issues.

Ecological over-grazing is seen as a major threat to nature conservation of uplands. This results in the conversion of heather moor and species-rich grasslands to species-poor grassland.

Agricultural subsidies encourage high stocking densities resulting in the gradual loss of wildlife in semi-natural habitats. In many instances in the uplands of the area, stocking rates were, or still are, incompatible with the long-term maintenance of wildlife.

Aerial photos of Stirling District indicate a 10% loss of heather moorland between the 1970s and 1980s. This figure mirrors the trend in other parts of upland Britain (e.g. Cumbria has shown a loss of 37% between the 1940s and 1970s) and is accounted for by a combination of over-grazing, afforestation and general poor management such as over-burning. A means of addressing the problem would be to alter the subsidy system and change from a headage to a hectarage payment. Extending the Loch Lomond and Breadalbane ESAs (Environmentally Sensitive Areas) would provide means for increased protection and regeneration of

upland heaths and species-rich grasslands. This would, in turn, maintain and enhance the landscape importance of the area while ensuring the support of rural employment.

Recreational developments, notably hill walking, orienteering, fell running and mountain biking, have in recent years become a factor of some importance in the mountain sections of the area particularly on Ben Lomond, the Trossachs and the Breadalbane Mountains. Increasing recreational pressures create their own kinds of disturbance to habitat and wildlife. Of particular concern is disturbance to breeding bird communities on the open ground of the high plateaux plus the erosion of sensitive vegetation which is slow to recover due to the extreme environmental conditions. Any recreation/access/amenity strategy, along the lines of the aforementioned indicative forestry strategies, should seek to minimize these threats.

Lowland Peatlands

Raised mires are one of the most fragile and specialised habitats in central Scotland. Their high acidity and low nutrient levels limit the plant species to the small number which can survive in these harsh conditions. The most important species are the Sphagnum mosses, the building blocks of a raised mire system. With these, in the wetter areas, grow the Cranberry *Vaccinium oxycoccos*, Sundew *Drosera rotundifolia*, as well as rarer species near the northern limit of their British distribution such as Bog Rosemary *Andromeda polifolia* and White-beaked Sedge *Rhynchospora alba*. On the drier hummocks within the mire the more familiar Ling Heather *Calluna vulgaris* and Cottongrass *Eriophorum vaginatum* are found. Raised mires also support a variety of fungi, invertebrates and reptiles, notably common Lizards *Lacerta vivipara*, and Adders *Vipera vipera* which are now a legally protected species under Schedule 5 of the *Wildlife and Countryside Act*.

Sites in central Scotland cover 1000-1200 ha, mostly relatively small sites in the low lying areas of Stirling, Falkirk and Clackmannan Districts. However one site, Flanders Moss, is the largest remaining remnant of the bog system that formerly covered 5000 ha of the Carse of Stirling. This system, now reduced to isolated fragments, was the most extensive of its type in Great Britain. The Moss is famed for the nationally rare northern mire plant Labrador Tea *Ledum groenlandicum*, and is one of the few lowland sites which support a breeding population of the Mountain Hare *Lepus timidus*. Despite the rarity of this habitat and its associated species part of the site remains threatened by extant planning permission for horticultural peat extraction.

Designation of Flanders Moss and the smaller bogs to the south as SSSIs has been warranted not only by the individual quality of the sites, but also because of their significance in national terms. They amount to almost 10% of the total remaining raised mire in

Britain. Flanders Moss has further significance as a National Nature Reserve, now managed principally to maintain and enhance its conservation interest.

Between 1948 and 1978 there has been a 42% loss of lowland raised mires in The Forth Valley (Nature Conservancy Council, 1984). The principal causes have been agricultural improvement, grazing, afforestation and commercial peat extraction. In Falkirk District, for example, over 500 ha of mire at Gardrum and Letham Mosses have been lost due to commercial peat extraction, while Darnrig Moss, adjacent to Gardrum, has been severely damaged by opencast mining, and other sites have been degraded by drainage and trampling (poaching) by cattle.

The first major clearances of peat from the Carse of Stirling were initiated by Lord Kames with the creation of the 'moss lairds' in 1767. Over the next 30 years 585 ha of raised mire were cleared by hand with the peat being floated off down the Forth. This practice continued until 1865 when it was finally prohibited by an Act of Parliament. Interestingly, this was not due to concern about loss of natural habitat, but because the peat was causing problems to the salmon fishers and oystermen further downstream. Two small mosses on the Forth - Killorn and Shirgarton owe their survival to this Act. Now that peatlands in general, and raised mires in particular, have received greater recognition of their value, some of the threats are being reduced. Commercial peat extraction is still occurring but there is a growing movement towards non peat-based alternatives. This should be encouraged in order to preserve what remains of this exceptionally slow forming habitat. Agricultural grants and forestry grants are unlikely to be given for projects which significantly threaten designated raised mire habitat.

Today a major threat to the remaining mire is its colonisation by birch (Bannister 1973) and pine in particular. This colonization is likely to have occurred as a result of lowering water tables or other changes in the hydrological regime of a site as well as a lack of grazing pressure. Once established, the trees can have a considerable drying effect on the mire surface, thus lowering the water table still further. In addition leaves intercept rainfall and sunshine, further affecting the hydrological regime and increasing shading. In combination these factors will, in time, lead to a change in the vegetation. Ultimately the balance of nutrients and water may be disrupted to such an extent that mire formation may cease. Remedial works to prevent this happening include the construction of dams across internal and external drains to retain water and the removal of trees.

Woodlands

The most important woodlands in conservation terms are those thought to be of ancient origin. This is defined as woodland which has existed from at least Medieval times to the present without having been cleared for pasture, rough grazing, arable or other non-woodland uses. The importance of ancient woods is that the great majority are believed to be primary, that is they are surviving fragments of the original wildwood that developed naturally over much of Britain following the end of the last Ice Age.

Although parts of central Scotland are well wooded, particularly Stirling District which has 32,000 ha or 15% of its total land area under forest, much of this is conifer plantation (e.g. Queen Elizabeth Forest Park) which has often replaced some valuable open ground habitats (see Upland section). However, several native woodlands remain particularly around Aberfoyle at Drumore Wood, Fairy Knowe, Doon Hill and Cuilvona and Craigmore Woods. These sites are wholly or partly owned by Forest Enterprise, and managed by them in consultation with SNH, conservation being given a high priority.

A recent inventory of woodland within central Scotland (Roberts 1986) has shown that only 4,038 hectares, or 3% of the area, remains as ancient woodland habitat, which mirrors the proportion for Britain as a whole. At least half of this critically small remaining area has either been underplanted with, or converted to, non-native conifer plantation, resulting in a 25% loss of this habitat between 1946 and 1971. Notwithstanding this, it encompasses the very extensive native woods on the east side of Loch Lomond, one of the largest complexes of semi-natural woods in Scotland. These are a mix of Sessile Oak, Ash, Alder and Wych Elm. Their 'Atlantic' (cool and damp) nature allows for a rich fern flora including the nationally uncommon Wilson's Filmy *Hymenophyllum wilsonii* and Tunbridge Filmy *H. tunbrigense*. The east Loch Lomondside woods are particularly noted for their large breeding populations of Pied Flycatcher, and like other native woods in the area include good numbers of Wood Warbler and Redstart.

The area also includes the southernmost example of Caledonian pinewood in Great Britain in Glen Falloch on the lower slopes of Ben Chabhair and An Caisteal, south west of Crianlarich. For native pinewoods in general the losses have been even more catastrophic than those for deciduous woodlands. Comparisons of aerial photographs from the 1940s and 1970s has shown that during that period there was a 60% loss of Caledonian pinewood within central Scotland.

Outwith the Loch Lomond area the remainder of the ancient woodland resource is mostly confined to steep or wet ground along river and burn sides such as Dollar Glen in the Ochils, the woods along the Allan Water near Bridge of Allan which contain the region's only known location for Herb Paris *Paris quadrifolia* and the woods along the Carron Valley near Denny where, because of the terrain, the scope for conversion to agricultural land or underplanting with conifers is much reduced. Of the total area of the region (262,229 ha) only 2557 ha or 0.97% has been notified as being of special scientific value for its woodland interest (**Table 1**). Other areas of native woodland lie outside statutory protection.

TABLE 2   MAIN FACTORS AFFECTING CONSERVATION IN WOODLAND SSSIs

	No. of Woodland SSSIs	Poor Structure		Exotic Invasion		Grazing		Lack of Regeneration		Recreation	
		NO.	%	NO.	%	NO.	%	NO.	%	NO.	%
CLACKMANNAN	7	1		4		1		1		1	
FALKIRK	2	1		2		1		0		1	
STIRLING	27	10		11		20		13		15	
TOTAL	36	12	33	17	47	22	61	14	39	17	47

Table 2 summarizes a desk study of the main factors affecting the special features of interest of the SSSI woodlands. This analysis shows that a third of these sites lack good structure which ranges from poor understorey development to an even-aged canopy composition. Lack of regeneration is recorded in some 39% of the sites. Both poor structure and lack of regeneration are particularly related to over-grazing of woodland habitats. These statistics are also likely to reflect the situation in woodlands in the wider countryside.

Both the small area of ancient woodland within the region and the rate of loss (at least until recent times) is attributable to a number of factors. For example, the underplanting and subsequent spread of exotic trees and shrubs within native woodlands has been, and continues to be, one of the major causes of the loss of nature conservation interest in ancient semi-natural woodlands. Figures for SSSI woodlands within the area indicate that nearly 50% of sites have their conservation value compromised by the presence of invasive non-natives such as Sycamore, Beech and Rhododendron. In particular the amenity planting of Rhododendron by large estates in the past has left a legacy of woodland with impoverished ground floras and limited canopy regeneration. It has recently been reported (Soutar 1992) that at least 40 species of non-native plant are increasing in native woods in Scotland.

Many of the upland woodlands within the study area are important for stock feeding, shelter and grazing which today represents the major threat to the few remaining vestiges of wildwood in central Scotland. Over 60% of the woodland SSSIs within the study area suffer from some form of grazing pressure. The main threat posed by stock or deer grazing (recent estimates by the Red Deer Commission show that Scottish deer numbers have doubled since the 1960s to 300,000) is that it prevents, or severely inhibits, the natural regeneration of the wood. This results in the woodland becoming moribund with a steady conversion to woodland pasture and thence to grassland. Where it is evident that the pressure of deer numbers is damaging to the natural heritage value of an area, a properly managed programme of deer culling is one obvious way of reversing this trend. Alternatively, fencing can be erected to exclude domestic stock and/or deer, the costs of which can be financed within land designated as SSSI or Environmentally Sensitive Areas (ESAs). An

Figure 2   Remnant of Caledonian Pinewood in Glen Cononish, Tyndrum - Coille Coire Chuilc SSSI.

excellent example of positive woodland management is seen at the remnant of Caledonian pinewood at Glen Falloch mentioned earlier where two plots, totalling 40 ha, have been fenced off from further stock and deer grazing. There are many other examples, e.g. Glen Cononish **Figure 2,** and SNH will continue to promote this objective.

Nowadays a more balanced approach has been adopted by both the forest authorities and private owners to the extent that inappropriate management will not now be eligible for grant-aid in woods identified as being of ancient origin. Indeed SNH seek to work more closely with other government agencies (particularly the new Forestry Authority and Forest Enterprise), and the private sector, in order to protect and enhance the remaining areas of ancient woodland in central Scotland.

Freshwater and Associated Habitats (see also Aquatic Life chapter)

The abundant and diverse range of freshwater habitats within central Scotland are unique in Britain. Included in this resource are the fast flowing mountain burns, the sluggish lowland rivers, the small lochans and the much larger lochs of the lower ground. Principally the lochs are north of the Highland Boundary Fault and lie in rocky basins: with one exception, the only 'lake' in Scotland, the Lake of Menteith which lies on sedimentary deposits, to the south of the Fault.

Figure 3 Lake of Menteith - a rich open water habitat for aquatic plants, winter geese populations and geological interest.

These waters vary from low nutrient status to highly enriched and most are entirely natural. This variation is reflected by the plant species which they support, both submerged plants and the emergent vegetation which extends back into marshes and fens. Typical of the emergent plants are the floating water-lilies, the rushes, sedges and the taller reed beds. The region's lochs also support several nationally rare plant species including the Least Yellow Water-lily *Nuphar pumila*, Awlwort *Subularia aquatica* and Waterwort *Elatine hexandra*. They are also home to three quarters of the Scottish freshwater fish species, including the increasingly uncommon Arctic Char *Salvelinus alpinus*. In addition, the presence of the other species of game fish is a reflection of the purity and quality of the water within central Scotland lochs. Damsel and Dragonflies can also be found in quantity and in quieter spots Otters *Lutra lutra* breed. In winter the lowlands provide roosting and feeding sites for the Pinkfooted *Anser brachyrhynchus* and Greylag *Anser anser* Geese and in summer they are home to a wide variety of breeding wildfowl and swans.

In national terms the quality of these lochs is high and one third of them are of SSSI standard. The River Teith system, including Lochs Doine, Voil and Lubnaig, is of particular note for its wide variety of habitats. The range of community succession from the mountain source to its confluence with the Forth is unequalled by any other British river. Several of the communities represent the most species-rich examples of their type yet found (detailed in Aquatic Life chapter).

The many smaller ponds and lochans are also an important resource. They provide a suitable habitat for large numbers of Frogs, Toads and occasionally Newts. In addition they should not be underestimated for their

botanical interest, which can be considerable, with species such as the locally rare Greater Spearwort *Ranunculus lingua*, known from only four localities in the region.

There are, however, a variety of potential threats to these habitats. One is pollution, which can be caused by fertiliser run off and waste products from agriculture, forestry and fish farming. In the worst cases it can lead to severe algal blooms. These prevent light penetrating to submerged plants, and by depleting the water of essential oxygen when they decay can be extremely harmful to freshwater ecosystems.

The blocking of watercourses by sediment can be another effect of bad farming and forestry practices, but road construction and urban development can also be responsible. The effects can be so dramatic that aquatic plants are completely covered by a layer of silt. Silt can also lead to a drastic change in the nutrient status of the water body, upsetting the delicate natural balance, and encouraging the proliferation of more aggressive species. Bad forestry practice can also contribute to acidification of water courses if trees are planted in close proximity to burns and rivers.

These threats can be overcome by the adoption of appropriate working practices, for example, buffer strips can be left on farmland and forestry adjacent to watercourses in order to limit phosphate run-off and to help reduce acidification. Forestry drainage ditches can be contoured in order to minimise flash floods and soil loss from steep hillsides.

Increased leisure and recreation, particularly motorised watersports such as power boating, jet and water skiing, could also have dramatic effects with Loch Lomond being under the greatest threat. The wash from boats can lead to increased shore erosion and the loss of emergent vegetation; there may be disturbance to birds and mammals; and the associated pollution by oil and petrol will affect water quality. There is also the threat of increased pollution from development schemes for chalet accommodation and marina facilities which service this demand for leisure.

The most positive way forward to deal with these potential and actual threats is the adoption of a water use strategy. Sites could be divided into those which are capable of absorbing recreational pressure and those which should be managed principally for wildlife. Central Scotland is indeed fortunate that it has a freshwater resource which is large enough to cater for all interests but which may all too easily be compromised by lack of forward planning.

Grasslands

Unimproved, lowland grasslands are a very rare and declining habitat. Species-rich grassland under SSSI designation is critically low, at less than 0.2% of the total central Scotland area, although there are some valuable grassland sites which are not quite of SSSI standard. The main concentration of species-rich, traditionally managed grasslands that have remained unimproved, in the modern agricultural sense, are found along the southern escarpment of the Ochil Hills. Run-off from the basic igneous rocks has led to enrichment of surrounding soils, on which neutral and basic grasslands have developed. Characteristic flora include local rarities such as Burnet Saxifrage *Pimpinella saxifraga*, Crested Hair-grass *Koeleria macrantha*, Quaking Grass *Briza media* and Common Rock-rose *Helianthemum nummularium*. The latter is foodplant for the only known breeding colony in the region of the Northern Brown Argus butterfly *Aricia artaxerxes*.

A range of other flushed grasslands occur throughout the area some of which are habitats for rare and restricted plants such as Dioecious Sedge *Carex dioica*, Marsh Orchid *Dactylorhiza incarnata*, Black Bog-rush *Schoenus nigricans* and Broad-leaved Cottongrass *Eriophorum latifolium*. However, large areas of grassland of conservation interest are rare, and most herb-rich swards are confined to small strips of land along river flood plains, as on some stretches of the Teith and the Carron. Here may still be found a northern hay meadow type flora with Wood Crane's-bill *Geranium sylvaticum*, Globeflower *Trollius europaeus* and the regionally scarce Greater Butterfly-orchid *Platanthera chlorantha*. One of the few SSSIs in Falkirk and Clackmannan Districts notified purely as an example of a herb-rich grassland is Bo'mains Meadow lying just to the south of Bo'ness on the south side of the Forth estuary. An area near the Mugdock Country Park is another example of a herb-rich sward, its most notable feature the number and range of locally rare orchids including Common Twayblade *Listera ovata*, Common Spotted-orchid *Dactylorhiza fuchsii*, and Frog Orchid *Coeloglossum viride*, the latter at one of its few known stations in the central Scotland area.

The main agent of historical change to herb-rich grasslands has been the long period of agricultural intensification most evident since the 1950s. For the few sites left the main threat today is a lack of traditional agricultural management, even total abandonment in some cases, resulting in the loss of grassland by scrub encroachment. One opportunity for stalling or reversing this trend is seen in the wider countryside context of the ESA initiative. Within this scheme farmers are paid to manage the land in a manner sympathetic to nature. Reserves and SSSIs also provide the potential to manage and enhance grasslands and provide grant assistance to help landowners and managers to conserve this much threatened habitat. Local authorities also have a role to play in their management of amenity grasslands in parks and along roadside areas which have a considerable conservation interest which can be improved by the adoption of cutting regimes that allow for the flowering and seeding of the flora.

The Estuary

Estuaries are amongst the most fertile and productive ecosystems, and support an abundant and varied wildlife of high importance for conservation. The populations of invertebrates, fish and birds being of particular significance (see Aquatic Life chapter). British estuaries comprise 28% of the entire estuarine area of the Atlantic and North sea coastal states, more than any other European country (Davidson 1991).

The Forth is one of the most important areas for estuarine wildlife in the UK. A wide range of habitats have developed here, including saltmarsh, intertidal mudflats, reedbeds and brackish lagoons, on which many plants and animals depend. Of particular significance is the outstanding number and variety of migratory and overwintering wildfowl and waders, making it of national and international importance for conservation (Bryant 1987). A high proportion of the estuary within our region is notified as SSSI (See **Table 3**). As of 1989 there were 334 SSSIs associated with estuaries, almost a quarter of all UK SSSIs.

Birds use the estuarine habitats for feeding, roosting and moulting. The moulting flock of Shelduck on the Forth is of particular significance. The intertidal mudflats support huge populations of tiny crustaceans, molluscs and worms and provide crucial low tide feeding grounds for birds. The intertidal zone also functions as a nursery ground for many species of fish, some of which are commercially important. High tide roosting and feeding sites for birds on saltmarshes and surrounding habitats are also vital - for example, the lagoon adjacent to Kinneil Kerse sewage works at Grangemouth (**Figure 4**). Wintering birds of particular conservation importance are Shelduck, Knot, Bar-tailed Godwit, Redshank, Great-crested Grebe, Cormorant, Teal, Dunlin and Curlew (Bryant 1991).

Bird movements and population turnover, especially during migration, mean that a much greater proportion of the international population of each species depends on the estuary than is present at any one time. The birds use a network of sites, and the Forth thus forms a vital link in a chain. In addition to waders and wildfowl it is frequented in winter by various birds of prey and owls. Thanks to long-term studies of bird and invertebrate populations by Stirling University, much invaluable ecological information is available for conservation work and study.

The Inner Forth SSSIs have also been recognised by the UK government as meeting the criteria for designation as a Special Protection Area (SPA) under the terms of the European Community Directive 79/409 *Conservation of Wild Birds* and as a Ramsar Site under the Ramsar Convention. This emphasises the international significance of the estuary and places international obligations for conservation on Government. Apart from SSSIs and international designations, the only other conservation site on the estuary is the Royal Society for Protection of Birds (RSPB) Reserve within the Skinflats SSSI boundary. However, much of the undesignated habitat on the estuary is also of conservation significance, particularly for migrating birds.

TABLE 3   ESTUARINE SSSIs IN CENTRAL SCOTLAND

SITE NAME	AREA (ha)	ESTUARINE HABITATS	MAIN ORNITHOLOGICAL INTEREST
Alloa Inches	316	Intertidal mud, saltmarsh, freshwater fens, reedbeds	Lapwing, Teal, Shelduck, Goldeneye, Cormorant
Blackness Bay (part in West Lothian)	190 (part in West Lothian)	Intertidal mud, rocky shore coastal grassland, saltmarsh	Wigeon, Redshank, Knot, Dunlin, Golden Plover
Kinneil Kerse	764	Inter-tidal mud, saltmarsh, brackish lagoon, reedbeds	Shelduck, Knot, Redshank, Teal, Great Crested Grebe, Bartailed Godwit Curlew
Skinflats	543	Brackish lagoon, inter-tidal mud, saltmarsh, reedbeds	Shelduck, Knot, Redshank, Dunlin, Bartailed Godwit

Over the centuries, agricultural and industrial reclamation has accounted for the loss of almost 50% of the intertidal habitat on the Forth estuary (McLusky 1987). This has been widespread, cumulative and piecemeal and reflects a national picture in Britain where about one third of all estuarine habitat and a half of all saltmarsh has been reclaimed since Roman times (Davidson 1991). In recent years the Forth has become one of the most intensively used sea areas around Scotland and the Grangemouth petrochemical site is one of the largest industrial complexes in Scotland. Thus the remaining habitats on the estuary come under pressure from pollution and effluent discharge; refuse disposal; industrial development; dock, port and harbour operations; coastal protection works; and certain specific proposals such as that for a barrage put forward by Central Regional Council in *Central 2000*. Many of these activities can and do have adverse impacts both individually and cumulatively on estuarine wildlife. Recent threats, successfully averted following public inquiries, have included large scale refuse disposal at Kinneil Kerse SSSI and rubble tipping on saltmarsh at Skinflats. Other estuarine habitats such as brackish lagoons (rare in a Scottish context) may be vulnerable to changes in hydrology and water quality due to changes in drainage patterns and pollution. SSSIs such as those on the Forth estuary do provide a degree of protection against harmful activities proposed by owners and occupiers as well as developments which come under planning control. However, there are limitations in a site based approach to estuarine conservation.

A number of factors contribute to the shortcomings of present mechanisms for conserving estuarine habitats. There is no statutory protection for SSSIs below low water mark, where numerous activities may have adverse effects. Activities such as wildfowling cannot be controlled on the foreshore except under byelaws, which can only be effected following designation of a site as a statutory Nature Reserve. Activities affecting estuaries are controlled by a whole range of domestic and more recently European legislation. A

Figure 4   The intertidal mudflats at Kinneil Kerse; with Grangemouth in the background.

great variety of consent mechanisms therefore operate to control these activities, and controls, safety procedures and emergency plans for oil spills, all have an important part to play, but at the moment no one body can act independently to ensure the conservation or sustainable development of the estuary.

The Forth estuary as a whole is an ecologically functional unit and we should recognise that its survival depends on a complex interaction of researchers, conservationists, decision makers and those that use the estuary. By bringing all interested parties together the concept of Integrated Coastal Zone Planning could be discussed with a view to planning, in a holistic manner, for sustainable use and long term conservation.

The Forth is very important for people, wildlife and industry. Although much wildlife has already been lost or damaged, and many pressures remain, the estuarine ecosystem continues to survive in the meantime, but its future conservation depends on achieving a balance between human economics and wildlife ecology.

Urban Conservation

Until relatively recently nature conservation focused almost exclusively on rural areas in the countryside, but around the mid-seventies the urban wildlife movement came into being in Britain. One publication which sparked off an interest in urban ecology and conservation was *The Endless Village* (Teagle 1979) which described a surprising wealth of habitats and wildlife in the heart of the urban West Midlands. Indeed Teagle found a quality and quantity of wildlife far greater than many equivalent areas of modern farmed countryside. Urban conservation is important because it brings many people into contact with wildlife in their daily lives.

Whilst there are no large cities in this region, Falkirk, Alloa and Stirling and the zone between them contain extensive areas which can be considered as urban and urban fringe/industrial. Cole (1983) divides habitats of urban areas into six broad, overlapping categories -

1. Buildings and streets.
2. Private gardens and allotments.
3. Roadside verges and motorway embankments, canals, rivers, sewage farms, and reservoirs.
4. Recreation grounds, including golf courses, games pitches and urban parks.
5. Areas of encapsulated countryside, reflecting rural habitats caught within the urban environment.
6. Areas of vacant and derelict land awaiting the next cycle of development.

In central Scotland, examples of all these habitats can be found. Buildings and streets in town centres support ruderal weeds such as Rosebay Willowherb *Chamaenerion angustifolium* and opportunist animals such as the House Sparrow, Feral Pigeon and Brown Rat. Private gardens can make a significant contribution to the urban wildlife resource and may support good populations of Tits, Blackbirds, Robins and other familiar birds as well as occasional rarer visitors such as Waxwings.

Linear habitats form important wildlife corridors which may link rural and urban areas. Motorway embankments such as those along the M9 are largely undisturbed areas and support prey populations for hovering Kestrels. The Forth and Clyde and Union Canals near Falkirk support important aquatic ecosystems. The Union Canal contains 44 aquatic macrophytes, of which 50% are uncommon or rare in Scotland, eg Tufted Loosestrife *Lysimachia thyrsiflora* and Flat-stalked Pondweed *Potomageton friesii* (Anderson and Murphy 1987). Man-made urban water bodies can also be rich in aquatic wildlife. A good example is Carron Dams near Stenhousemuir, originally built to supply water for Carron Ironworks, but now supporting abundant wildlife.

Central Scotland contains numerous golf courses, recreation grounds and parks which vary from the horticulturally immaculate with little value for nature conservation to the less intensively managed which may provide a home for a variety of wild plants and animals. Haws Park in Bridge of Allan is an example of the latter type. Golf courses frequently support good wildlife habitats.

Balquhidderock Wood (**Figure 5**) in Bannockburn provides a local example of encapsulated countryside now surrounded by urban development. This ancient wildwood contains areas of wet Alder woodland with abundant Bird Cherry *Prunus padus* and a diverse ground flora including Yellow Pimpernel *Lysimachia nemorum* and Creeping Jenny *L. nummularia*. As well as being of considerable scientific interest, it is highly valued by local people to whom it is known as 'The Bluebell Wood.'

Figure 5   Balquhidderock Wood, Bannockburn.

Areas of vacant and derelict industrial land often develop a surprisingly interesting flora and fauna when left to colonise naturally; eg the old bing at Almond near Falkirk supports a naturally regenerated Birch and Willow woodland with locally rare plants such as Broad-leaved Helleborine *Epipactis helleborine*, and Common Wintergreen *Pyrola minor* (Stewart 1985).

The wildlife resource of urban areas is thus of considerable interest both within its own right and for its potential benefits to local communities.

Urban sites may be subjected to industrial pollution, human access and interference, and pressure from industrial and housing development. This situation has been exacerbated by the failures in the past to fully take account of urban nature conservation in planning and development control. Another less obvious threat is the so-called environmental improvement schemes where, for example, bings already well vegetated with woodland, scrub or grassland, are flattened and planted with amenity grassland of little wildlife value. However in contrast to rural areas, considerable tracts of urban spaces are owned and managed by public bodies rather than private landowners. This creates opportunities for alternative management schemes which may be not only much more sympathetic to wildlife but also cheaper. School grounds are important areas which can benefit from habitat creation projects and many schools in Central Region have been undertaking tree planting, and creating ponds and wild flower meadows, often with grant assistance. Local Nature Reserves (LNRs) can be particularly appropriate in urban areas.

There may also be opportunities to be realised through partnerships with private companies keen to enhance their 'green image', eg the industrial giant ICI's Chemical Division (now called Zeneca) has joined forces with the Scottish Wildlife Trust to create The Jupiter Urban Wildlife Project, a challenging initiative to develop an industrial wasteland of the Grangemouth works into an impressive wildlife site with educational facilities and programmes. This has involved the Scottish Conservation Projects organisation, schools and volunteers from wildlife groups, and aims to become a focal point for urban conservation.

GEOLOGICAL CONSERVATION

Central Scotland has a wide and important range of geological and physiographical features that require conservation as part of our natural heritage and for teaching, training and research purposes. Earth science conservation is part of the statutory responsibility of SNH. Many relevant sites are naturally exposed along river sections as at Ballagan Glen (SWT Reserve), or as landforms in open country, as along the escarpment of the Touch, Gargunnock and Campsie Fells. Others have been artificially exposed in quarries as at Wolf's Hole in Mine Woods (Bridge of Allan), or within old mining areas such as Tyndrum.

The main threat to this heritage of landform and geological exposures comes from their becoming hidden from view, thus preventing, or reducing, the potential for their appreciation, study or scientific interpretation. This may occur by scrub encroachment and by afforestation, particularly in the uplands whereby trees are planted over important landforms or adjacent to geological sections. Likewise, the infill of old quarries has the potential to totally obliterate sites of geological interest as do major engineering works for reservoirs or coastal defence purposes. Other threats include over-use of a site by geologists.

Main places of geological interest are on the Highland Boundary Fault which demarcates the lowland from the upland zone of central Scotland and is particularly evident along the line of islands in the southern basin of Loch Lomond. Periods of glaciation are also a major feature, and the landforms left behind after the retreat of glaciers, e.g drumlins and eskers, are used to determine the extent and timing of such events. One of the best examples of a glacial morraine landscape is to be found between Drymen and Gartness and on the lower northern slopes of Stockie Muir, Strathblane.

In order to ensure the long-term integrity of our geomorphological and geological heritage for future generations SNH seeks to work closely with landowners, quarry operators, wildlife trusts, the forestry industry and the planning authorities to ensure that earth science conservation is taken fully into account particularly where the sites have been designated as SSSI or are important in a more local context.

SUMMARY AND CONCLUSIONS

Central Scotland has a wealth of wildlife, both in unspoilt remote areas and in more urban areas close to towns. However, most types of wildlife habitats, with their characteristic assemblages of plants and animals, have suffered appreciable and irreversible losses over recent decades. There is thus a need for legislative protection to be given to prime wildlife habitats and declining or threatened species. Many of the best remaining habitats in the area are designated as SSSIs - from large sites in the uplands or on the estuary, to smaller ones of woodland, grassland or water bodies in, or near, urban areas. Many of these sites require positive and sensitive management to maintain or enhance the conservation interest.

It is also crucial not to ignore the importance of maintaining the conservation value of the wider countryside. The protection of SSSIs should be seen as a minimum contribution towards successful conservation, not an end in itself. Within the wider context it is taken account of in Local Authority Regional Structure and District Local Plans, Environmental Charters, the production of Indicative Forestry and Nature Conservation Strategies, and in changes to the agriculture and forestry support systems. There is now considerable public support for nature conservation and it is vital that people should have the opportunity to understand and enjoy the natural world. The growing recognition of its importance should not be viewed in isolation but rather as part of a continuum in the maintenance of essential ecological processes and life support systems in order to conserve genetic diversity and to ensure the sustainable utilisation of species and ecosystems. More simply, but no less important, the natural world provides a continuous source of spiritual enrichment and enjoyment for many people and contact with nature is life-enhancing in the profoundest sense.

ACKNOWLEDGEMENTS

The authors are very grateful to Richard Ferguson, John Mitchell and J.B. Pendlebury for comments on an earlier draft. We would also like to thank Carole Gordon for deciphering our writing.

REFERENCES AND FURTHER READING

ANDERSON, K. and MURPHY, K.J. 1987. The Aquatic Vegetation of the Union Canal (Lothian and Central Regions). University of Glasgow report to Nature Conservancy Council, Edinburgh.

BANNISTER, P. 1973. Birch Survey Flanders Moss SSSI. Nature Conservancy Council report, Stirling.

BOOTH, A.B. 1990. Nature Conservation Strategy for Stirling's Urban Areas. Stirling District Council.

BRYANT, D.M. 1987. Wading birds and wildfowl of the estuary and Firth of Forth, Scotland. *Proceedings of the Royal Society of Edinburgh* 93B, 509-520

COLE, L. 1983. Urban Nature Conservation . In: Conservation in Perspective edited by A. Warren and F.B. Goldsmith. Wiley.

DAVIDSON, N.C. 1991. Estuaries, Wildlife and Man. A summary of nature conservation and estuaries in Great Britain. Nature Conservancy Council, Peterborough.

DONALDSON, S. 1992. A Nature Conservation Strategy for Clackmannan. MSc Thesis, University of Stirling.

FORTH RIVER PURIFICATION BOARD, 1989. Trossachs Lochs Policy/Strategy.

GORDON, N.J. 1987. Selection and management of sites of nature conservation importance in the Forth Estuary and Firth, Scotland. *Proceedings of the Royal Society of Edinburgh*, 93B, 545-558

JAMIESON, D. 1990. Towards a Nature Conservation Strategy for Falkirk. MSc thesis, University of Stirling.

McLUSKY, D.S. 1987. Intertidal habitats and benthic macrofauna of the Forth Estuary, Scotland. *Proceedings of the Royal Society of Edinburgh*, 93B, 389-399

NATURE CONSERVANCY COUNCIL. 1984. Nature Conservation in Great Britain. Nature Conservancy Council, Peterborough.

NATURE CONSERVANCY COUNCIL. 1988. Directory of National Nature Reserves in Scotland. Nature Conservancy Council, Edinburgh.

NATURE CONSERVANCY COUNCIL. 1989. Guidelines for Selection of Biological SSSIs. Nature Conservancy Council, Peterborough.

NEWTON, A. and BRYANT, D.M. 1991. Distribution of Feeding Shorebirds at Skinflats, Forth Estuary, January 1991: Implications of barrage proposals. Stirling University report for Nature Conservancy Council.

ROBERTS, A.J. 1986. Inventory of Ancient, Long-established and Semi-natural Woodland (Clackmannan, Falkirk and Stirling Districts). Nature Conservancy Council, Edinburgh.

ROBERTSON, Rev J. 1799. General view of the Agriculture of Perth.

SOUTAR, R.G. 1992. Managing non-native plants in Scottish native woods. In: Aspects of Applied Biology: Vegetation Management in Forestry, Amenity and Conservation Areas.

STEWART, N.F. 1986. Provisional list of vascular plants in Falkirk District. *Forth Naturalist & Historian* 10, 53-79

TEAGLE, W.G. 1978. The Endless Village. Nature Conservancy Council, Peterborough.

APPENDIX 1   ORGANISATIONS ASSOCIATED WITH NATURE CONSERVATION IN CENTRAL SCOTLAND

CENTRAL SCOTLAND WOODLANDS (CSW) - a trust for improving the environment, involved in a wide ranging programme of tree planting, woodland management, and wildlife conservation with public and private support and working local communities. Hillhouseridge, Shottskirk Road, Shotts, ML7 4JS, tel (0501) 22015.

FARMING AND WILDLIFE ADVISORY GROUP (FWAG) - a charitable organisation to promote conservation of wildlife and landscape in the farmed countryside to the fullest extent compatible with modern farming, acts as an advisory service for farmers and landowners. Local adviser FWAG, Alpha Centre, Innovation Park, University of Stirling, FK9 4NE, tel (0786) 50964.

THE FORESTRY AUTHORITY (SCOTLAND) (FA) - arm of the Forestry Commission with a statutory role for promoting the planting and managing of attractive as well as productive woodlands, advice on forest practice, grants, research, and responsible for implementation of regulations. 10 York Place, Perth PH2 9JP, tel (0738) 442830.

FOREST ENTERPRISE (FE) - a self-contained organisation within the Forestry Commission, manages the forest estate owned by the nation, aims to create and maintain attractive and productive woodlands and manage them for public benefits, including active conservation of wildlife. Local office Ballantoan, Aberfoyle, FK8 3UX, tel 041 248 3931.

FORTH RIVER PURIFICATION BOARD (FRPB) - a statutory body to promote and maintain the cleanliness of rivers, inland waters and tidal waters and ensure the quality of water resources. The Whins, Whin Road, Alloa FK10 3SA, tel (0259) 723238.

LOCH LOMOND PARK AUTHORITY (LLPA) - a special partnership formed by Strathclyde and Central Regional Councils with Dumbarton and Stirling District Councils.
  i)   to conserve and enhance the natural beauty and other heritage values of the area;
  ii)   to promote the enjoyment of the area; and
  iii)   to promote the social and economic wellbeing of local communities. Park Authority staff include a ranger service which helps to look after the West Highland Way which runs through the western part of Central Region.
Old Station, Balloch, G38 8LX, tel (0389) 55721.

NATIONAL TRUST FOR SCOTLAND (NTS) - established "to promote the preservation of places of historic and architectural interest or of natural beauty." A charity, owns and manages a number of sites/areas eg Ben Lomond, and these are open to the public. Headquarters 5 Charlotte Square, Edinburgh EH2 4DU tel 031-226-5922.

ROYAL SOCIETY FOR PROTECTION OF BIRDS (RSPB) - principal objective the conservation of wild birds and their habitats; a registered charity with a membership of over 850,000. South and West Scotland Office, Unit 3.1, West of Scotland Science Park, Kelvin Campus, Glasgow G20 OSP, tel 041-945-5224.

SCOTTISH CONSERVATION PROJECTS TRUST (SCP) - the only voluntary body established specifically to involve and train people in practical outdoor conservation work throughout Scotland. Work and management by volunteers for both public and private landowners, urban and rural. Balallan House, 24 Allan Park, Stirling FK8 2QG, tel (0786) 479697.

SCOTTISH NATURAL HERITAGE (SNH) - the independent body established by Parliament in 1992; responsible to and funded by the Secretary of State to secure the conservation and enhancement of Scotland's natural heritage, by advising on policies and promoting projects to improve and support its sustainable utilisation. Beta Centre, Innovation Park, University of Stirling, Stirling FK9 4NF, tel (0786) 450362.

SCOTTISH OFFICE AGRICULTURE AND FISHERIES DEPARTMENT (SOAFD) - the department of the Scottish Office responsible for promoting and developing the agricultural and fishing industries. Government Buildings, 2 St Ninians Road, Stirling FK8 2HR, tel (0786) 473272.

SCOTTISH WILDLIFE TRUST (SWT) - charitable membership organisation whose aim is to conserve Scotland's wildlife and countryside heritage. In addition to campaigning, education and survey projects, it creates and manages nature reserves. Local groups in Stirling, Falkirk and Callander. Cramond House, Cramond Glebe Road, Edinburgh EH4 6NS, tel 031 312 7765.

THE WOODLAND TRUST (SCOTLAND) - a charity and membership organisation, aims to acquire native and broadleaved woodland by purchase and gifts; manage woods as amenities, landscape features and wildlife habitats; and create new woods. Headquarters Autumn Park, Grantham, Lincolnshire NG31 6LL, tel (0476) 74297.

APPENDIX 2   SITE DESIGNATIONS FOR NATURE CONSERVATION IN CENTRAL SCOTLAND

IMPORTANCE	SITE DESIGNATION & EXPLANATION	UK STATUTORY DESIGNATION
International	RAMSAR SITES designated under the Convention on Wetlands of International Importance e.g. Skinflats (nominated but not yet designated)	SSSI
	SPECIAL PROTECTION AREA (SPA) designated under the EC Directive (79/409/EEC)on the Conservation of Wild Birds e.g. Kinneil Kerse (nominated but not yet designated)	SSSI
National	NATIONAL NATURE RESERVE (NNR) declared under Section 19 of the National Parks & Access to the Countryside Act 1949, or Section 28 of the Wildlife & Countryside Act 1981 (as amended) e.g. Flanders Moss/Ben Lui	SSSI
	SITE OF SPECIAL SCIENTIFIC INTEREST notified under Section 28 of the Wildlife & Countryside Act 1981 (as amended) e.g. Dollar Glen	SSSI
Regional/Local	LOCAL NATURE RESERVES (LNR) designated by Local Authorities under Section 21 of the National Parks and Access to the Countryside Act 1949 e.g. Gartmorn Dam	LNR
	NON-STATUTORY NATURE RESERVES established and managed by a variety of public and private bodies e.g. RSPB, Wildlife Trust, Forest Enterprise e.g. Inversnaid RSPB Reserve Loch Ardinning SWT Reserve	
	NON-STATUTORY SITES OF WILDLIFE INTEREST these have different nomenclature and status and may be adopted by Local Authorities for planning purposes. Includes, for example, those identified in the Stirling Urban Nature Conservation Strategy. Many of these may be identified by SWT as Listed Wildlife Sites e.g. Mine Wood, Bridge of Allan	
Wider Countryside	WIDER COUNTRYSIDE FEATURES Include habitats which are of general interest for wildlife - for example, woodlands, uplands, ponds, hedges etc.	

Sites can have multiple designation - e.g. a NNR can also be a RAMSAR and SPA site, a SSSI can also be a LNR or non-statutory reserve.

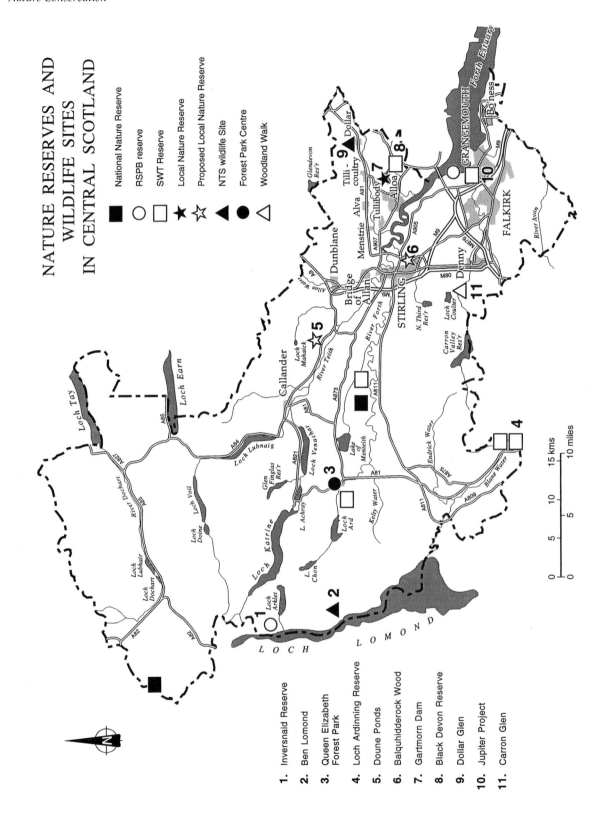

NATURE RESERVES AND
WILDLIFE SITES
IN CENTRAL SCOTLAND

■ National Nature Reserve
○ RSPB reserve
□ SWT Reserve
★ Local Nature Reserve
☆ Proposed Local Nature Reserve
◀ NTS wildlife Site
● Forest Park Centre
△ Woodland Walk

1. Inversnaid Reserve
2. Ben Lomond
3. Queen Elizabeth Forest Park
4. Loch Ardinning Reserve
5. Doune Ponds
6. Balquhidderock Wood
7. Gartmorn Dam
8. Black Devon Reserve
9. Dollar Glen
10. Jupiter Project
11. Carron Glen

On the verso of this page is shown part of the northern area of central Scotland as it was in the 1890s. This is from the One Inch to the Mile Ordnance Survey reprints series by Caledonian Books of Ellon Aberdeen - sheet 39 Stirling

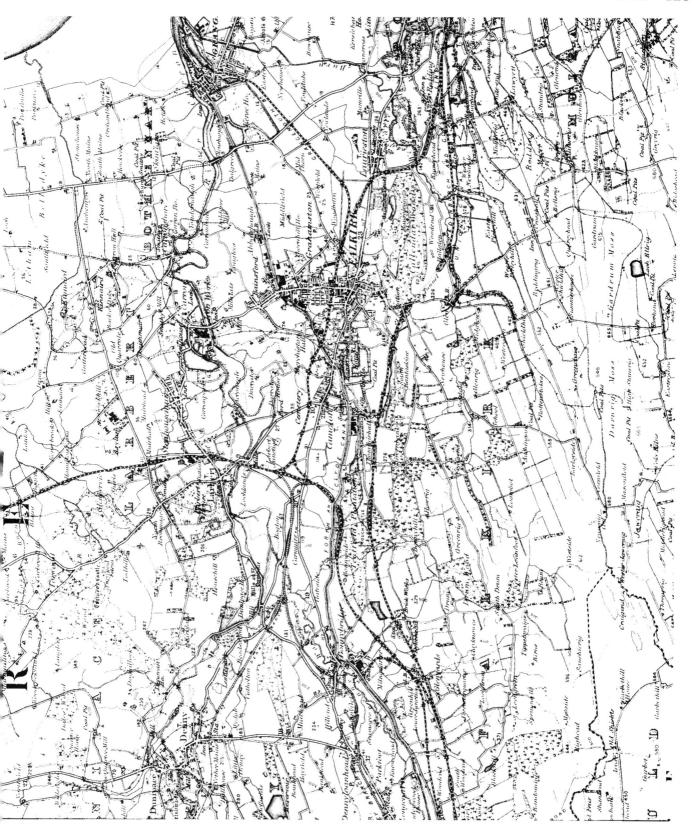

On the verso of this page is shown part of the southern area of central Scotland as it was in the 1890s. This is from the One Inch to the Mile Ordnance Survey reprints series by Caledonian Books of Ellon Aberdeen - sheet 31 Airdrie.

Agriculture

B.J. Elliott

Agriculture Before 1750

Before the age of improvement which began tentatively in the mid 18th century Scottish agriculture was characterised by very low productivity. The yield would often be as low as three-fold, each harvest producing only three times as much food value in the crop as had been contained in the seed sown to produce it. This was the result of a harsh climate and poor quality, unfenced, undrained and weed-choked land, of which only five out of 19 m acres were cultivated in 1707 or the equivalent to five acres per inhabitant. These 5 million acres were of variable quality with the best arable carse lands of about 300,000 acres, including 36,000 in Stirlingshire.

Such was the inefficiency of agriculture that even 5 m acres could not feed the population during the series of cold, wet, sunless summers which began in 1693 and spread to all areas by 1695. By 1700 widespread malnutrition and in places starvation resulted from shortages and soaring food prices. For example, between 1692 and 1698, the price of a quarter of oats, the principal crop, increased from 42p to £1.10. Not until the depth of the crisis were foreign grain imports permitted to relieve the scarcity. Even this was hampered by problems of distribution. By 1706 the price of oats had dropped 32% below the 1692 price but by the following year it was back to the latter level. It then failed to reach £1.00 again until 1762.

There were several reasons why agriculture remained in such a poor condition as late as 1750. First was the system of land tenure of which there were three types in operation. The first, 'steelbow', had been developed in recognition of the poverty of many would-be tenants, unable to stock their land or buy the implements and seed, in which case the landlord would provide everything. This meant that tenants had neither the means nor the motivation to improve their land because any improvements would be absorbed by increased rent, paid in kind. The system of the tacksmen developed mostly in the Highlands in the 17th century to enable landowners, especially absentee ones, to be paid rents in cash instead of in produce. The tacksman in effect sublet the land and became responsible not only for rent collection but also for the general social and economic organisation of the estate. This opened the way for greedy operators to abuse their positions by increasing rents and profits. Moreover neither they nor the landowners, if absentees, had any direct interest in improvements and by 1745 the system was on the way out. Particularly common in central Scotland before the age of improvement, was runrig. Rigs were strips of land of about one quarter of an acre each, separated by butts or balks left unploughed and often wasting 10%

of the land. Normally four joint tenancies were held, with holdings rotating every two or three years over good and bad land. Tenants shared the produce. They had to work as a team to plough because the old Scots plough, four metres in length, required between eight and twelve oxen to pull and up to twelve persons to operate (**Figure 1**). A team could turn about half an acre a day and, by reason both of the unwieldy nature of the whole operation and the need for drainage, worked along a 500 yard banked and crooked [S-shaped] ridge. Each tenant sowed and harvested his own land. It is clear that there would be little motivation to improve land held in this way since any profits would not be individually retained. Furthermore the poor quality of land led in practice to its division into infields and outfields, the inferior Scottish equivalent of the English three-field system. The infield, which was the area nearest to the farm buildings, covered about 20% of the arable land. Divided into small strips it was under constant cultivation using a system of rotation, with oats the principal crop. Oats were sown for two years then the land manured and sown with barley. The outfield, the poorest land, would be partly under oats for four or five years before being rested and manured. The infield and any cropped portions of the outfield were regarded as common grazing in winter. The practice of holding strips gave way in the Lowlands to compact holdings.

A second reason for low productivity was the technical backwardness of agriculture. If the plough

Figure 1 The twelve oxen plough of the 18th century.

was cumbersome, the wooden harrows in use were of little value. Reaping was done by sickle and scythe and hand-flailing was normal relying on the vagaries of the wind to remove the chaff.

The then existing tenancy systems inhibited improvement because of the lack of both capital and motivation. Such was the high cost of agricultural improvements that adequate capital for them was available only when prices rose and surplus profits could be invested. Even a wealthy owner of an estate would be unlikely to spend heavily on improvements whilst prices remained low. The famine in the 1690s retarded the growth of Scotland's population for more than fifty years so that demand, except during bad harvests, was restricted. Any increased sales would have to come from elsewhere, most obviously from England whose markets had been opened by the Treaty of Union in 1707. The low productivity of Scottish cereal crops meant, however, that there was no prospect of their competing with English grain producers in their home markets.

The main agricultural export was beef cattle from the Highlands which, in the early 18th century, were more important than sheep to the local economy. Both sheep and cattle were of low quality; the former were attacked frequently by maggots and, by reason of shortages of fodder, the latter were seriously underfed with annual losses as high as 20%. Rustling was so widespread that, in 1724, the government raised companies of Highland soldiers, the Black Watch, to try to deal with the problem. This heavy reliance on poor livestock was both a reflection of the high level of poverty in much of Scotland and a serious inhibitor to improvement since the profits from it were so limited. About 30,000 head of cattle went south each year, although, thanks to rustlers, not all arrived, and those that did had to be fattened before slaughter. The situation began to improve after 1740 when cattle prices began to rise, from about £18 Scots per head to £60 by the end of the 18th century. The impact was dramatic. Exports of cattle almost trebled whilst sheep, increasingly bred in Scotland after 1750, also joined the export drive south. By 1780 about 150,000 of the latter were being sold annually in this way.

The Age of Improvement, 1750-1875

The principal motivation to improve arable productivity came with the rise of grain prices after 1770, which in turn was the result of the rising populations of both Scotland and England. The price rise continued intermittently for more than a century until the great agricultural depression beginning in the mid-1870s brought an end to this long period of generally increasing prosperity for many landowners and farmers, but not for landless labourers, whose income levels were well below those of industrial workers.

The example of improved farming methods in the 18th century came from England. It was brought

Figure 2 The Moss Water Wheel used in the Blairdrummond peat clearing by Lord Kames, 1768.   (K. Mackay)

north initially by a number of major landowners, very few of whom lived in central Scotland and not all of whom made a financial success of their ventures. Stirlingshire and Clackmannanshire in the late 18th century were characterised by large numbers of smallholders. These people were in the main very poor and lacked the means to improve their lands. The principal prerequisite for improvements was, therefore, the substitution of numbers of smallholdings or jointly held strips into compact enclosed farms.

The enclosure movement in Scotland (Stewart 1991) was assisted by general, rather than particular legislation, beginning with an Act of 1661 and followed by others in 1669, 1685 and two in 1695. The main activity in this field, however, took place only after 1760 and most especially after 1775 because cereal prices began to rise rapidly in the early 1760s and again in the early 1780s. They were very high, though fluctuating, between 1792 and 1815, with peaks, the results of very poor harvests, in 1800 and 1812. The 1812 price of £2.54 per quarter for oats remained unsurpassed until 1917, and was followed by a decline after the Napoleonic Wars.

The result of this great improving activity was that, by 1805 Stirlingshire was almost 70% enclosed. This was particularly the case on the carse of Stirling where runrig was abolished by redistributing the land into compact farms. The land previously wasted by ridges and balks to mark off the holdings was levelled and ploughed. The new fields were enclosed by hedges, or by dykes. In central Scotland the most famous of the great improving landlords was Henry Home, Lord Kames, a judge at the Court Of Session who inherited the estate at Blairdrummond near Stirling. Part of the estate was the Moss of Kincardine, the fertile subsoil of which was covered by more than two metres of peat. At the age of 70, Kames, using labour from the Highlands, began to remove peat by having it cut into small pieces and floated away down the Forth (**Figure 2**). Kames then let out the improved land in lots of eight acres on 38 year leases, twice the normal length to encourage improvements, with the first tenants arriving in 1768. Some 600 acres of the 1800-acre moss were reclaimed for profitable arable farming in this way. This type of heroic reclamation became much less common in the mid and later 19th century because of its high cost.

On an even grander scale were the changes brought about by William Forbes who, in 1783, bought the formerly-forfeited 8,000 acre estate of Callendar at Falkirk for £85,000. With the exception of the Duke of Montrose's lands this was the biggest estate in the county. It stretched 25 km from Slamannanan in the south and east to Denny in the west, lying within four parishes. Forbes enclosed 7000 acres over eight years, evicting the tenants and creating such distress and unrest by his actions that, in 1797, he had to flee from his home. His new fields of three to eight acres were limed at 100 bushels per acre and each was surrounded by white thorn hedges or double drainage ditches a metre deep and 1.5 m wide. He also planted about 200,000 trees for both shelter and ornamentation. He farmed most of the estate himself but also leased some 3000 acres of scrubland, much of it near the new Forth-Clyde canal and required tenants to carry out extensive similar improvements as part of their leases. Forbes also took advantage of the heavy demand for pasture caused by the growing cattle trade through Falkirk. The consequences of this very heavy expenditure on improvements were substantial increases in efficiency and profit. Other improving landlords backed by adequate financial resources were Robert Dunmore at Balfron, Peter Speirs in Fintry and the county's largest landowner, the Duke of Montrose, who planted more than 3 m trees on his less fertile estates in the west.

The area of Stirlingshire in 1800 was 704 sq miles, [1840 sq km or 358,356 Scottish acres, a Scottish acre being about 25% larger than an English one]. Stirlingshire had a wet and windy climate in the west so that the clay soils were often water-logged or covered in mosses or coarse grasses. The annual rainfall was as high as 228 cm near Loch Lomond compared with 82 cms near Falkirk. One result of this was that the seasons tended to be about three weeks later in the west of the county and two weeks later in the east than in East Lothian. Clearly the eastern parts of the county were better suited to arable farming and the upland areas to sheep. The higher moorlands of the west of Stirlingshire, once covered in forests, were also water retentive or loose during dry spells. Between the moors and the carse lay the intermediate land known as the dryfields because it was not subject to the degree of

periodic flooding as was low-lying land. The farms on the moorlands concentrated on sheep-rearing, replacing both the goats which had predominated 50 years previously and, in the process, many small tenants. The Ochil hills, in both Stirling and Clackmannanshire, were also excellent grazing grounds for sheep, whose numbers increased steadily during the early and mid-19th century. The principal sheep breed had been the Highland, a small animal which produced a poor quality wool. In the late 18th century it was increasingly replaced by the Linton or black-faced breed and by Cheviots from Tweedale. These two were much more productive in both wool and mutton. Later it became common to crossbreed both with Leicesters. In 1840 the annual grazing rental for a sheep was £0.30, but each sheep required one and a half acres of rough grazing so very few were kept on the better quality arable farms on the carse. By reason of the low quality of the pasture the farms on the higher ground catering for livestock required more than 20 acres for viability. In total numbers sheep exceeded cattle by a factor of four or five.

The main breed of beef cattle was known also as the Highland, whilst for milk the Ayrshire became increasingly popular. The annual grazing rental for cattle in the late 18th century varied according to the location and quality of the pasture, but was between £2 and £6 per animal. The latter charge was made in the so-called cow parks near Stirling and Falkirk, which covered at least fifty acres in the former. In central Scotland, after 1745, Falkirk became the main beneficiary of the growing trade in livestock, at the expense of Crieff and Doune. The great cattle trysts held on the second Tuesday of August, September and October involved about 60,000 head of cattle by 1790. After two moves the fair settled at Stenhousemuir in 1785 where it remained for more than 100 years. By 1836 Falkirk was handling also 75,000 sheep so that pasture around the town was particularly valuable land. An example of the size and importance of the livestock industry in the late 18th century was found in Clackmannanshire where 7,000 cattle and 2,000 pigs were raised on 850 acres in the vicinity of the huge whisky distilleries at Kilbagie and Kennetpans. The animals were fed on the draff. Heavy increases in duty on whiskey led to the closure of the distilleries. The fate of these herds was not recorded, but it seems certain that only a small percentage of the pigs could have been retained on 800 acres.

Rents for arable land depended on the quality of the soil. The best arable land, on the fertile carses, fetched £2 per acre in the 1790s rising to £5 by 1840. On the carse, farms were much smaller than those on the higher ground and varied between 15 and 100 acres, but most commonly 30-60. However there were even smaller farms, between two and twenty acres, formed following the enclosure of common land, and which became known as pendicles. They were found principally in the parish of Kilsyth [since 1975 no longer in Stirlingshire]. As late as 1854 there were still

326 such smallholdings with a combined acreage of 754 in Stirlingshire, on which 485 head of livestock, mostly cattle, were kept. In Clackmannanshire there were 46 totalling 127 acres, supporting 136 beasts.

The principal development in arable farming in the early 19th century was the widespread cultivation of wheat, although by 1814 only 140,000 of Scotland's 5 m acres (3%) were devoted to this crop. This was made possible by various improvements, particularly draining, liming and manuring. Although farmers used the dung from their own animals there was never enough. However it became possible to buy extra quantities from the cities, some brought by barge along the new Forth-Clyde canal. Arable farms operated a five or six year crop rotation, such as summer fallow, wheat, beans and peas, barley, grass and oats. In the late 18th century turnips were not widely grown outside the stock-rearing areas because of the unsuitability of the clay soils. By the mid-19th century the situation had changed markedly. Clackmannanshire was producing more than 26,000 tons per annum and Stirlingshire in excess of 73,000. Potatoes ,originally a garden crop, began to be grown as a pioneering experiment in Kilsyth in 1728 and on a more commercial scale in 1739. By 1790 some 200 acres there were being sown with potatoes. North of the Campsies potato growing was on a rather smaller, but widespread scale. By the mid-19th century the potato crop for Stirlingshire was more than 10,000 tons. In Clackmannanshire the potato was reportedly a popular crop by the end of the 18th century, but 50 years later the county produced only 800 tons annually.

The increased profits resulting from agricultural improvements were partly spent on new farmhouses and other buildings. By 1800 new two storey brick buildings with slated or tiled roofs were a big improvement on their thatched, wooden, clay and straw-built predecessors which were then kept for storing cattle dung. Farm tenancy leases were normally, but not exclusively, of between 15 and 19 years and mostly of the latter figure. This comparatively lengthy tenure encouraged tenants to embark on potentially profitable improvements. However to protect the landowner from a lazy, careless or unambitious tenant, most leases contained clauses requiring reasonable standards of management to be maintained. In addition while tenants were normally forbidden to sub-let, the lease was passed to the tenants lawful heir if the former died before it expired. A further financial advantage to Scottish tenants was the absence of tithes and, in many cases, poor-rates and other taxes and duties.

Agricultural improvements also included technical advances. The most significant of these was the iron chain or swing plough (**Figure 3**), introduced by James Small in 1767 and cast at the new Carron ironworks near Falkirk. By contrast to the Dutch plough introduced by the Earl of Stair in 1730, and largely ignored by farmers, the new plough was an immediate success. The principal reason for its success was that it could be operated by one person and two

Figure 3 Small's iron/chain plough of 1767 - many cast by Carron Ironworks..

horses, compared with the heavy old Scots plough, which required a dozen oxen. At a ploughing match at Alloa in 1791 all 40 competitors used Small's plough, one of whom was invited to demonstrate his skill to George III at his farm at Windsor. Altruistically Small took out no patents and made his design freely available to farmers. Adaptions to it included some for operating on steep slopes and for ploughing subsoil for drainage by James Smith of Deanston, who also invented the chain harrow. Another for digging drainage ditches was by a Mr McEwan of Stirling.

Until the late 18th century threshing was another highly inefficient operation. A threshing machine invented in 1758, by a Dunblane farmer named Stirling, had worked fairly well for oats but not for wheat or barley. The first successful threshing machine, adopted initially at Kilbagie in Clackmannanshire was invented in 1786 by Andrew Meikle. It was not until it was harnessed to water power by a farmer named Gladstone from Castle Douglas, that threshing became an efficient mechanised operation. By contrast the development of an efficient reaping machine defied all efforts, including those of James Smith in 1815. It was not until 1828 that Patrick Bell built the prototype upon which the commercial models were later designed.

The main technical improvement which took place in Scottish agriculture in the first half of the 19th century was in field drainage. There had been notable attempts to drain unimproved land in the 18th century, in particular by Patrick Barclay at Ury in Kincardineshire in the 1760s. Following the enclosure movement the need to improve drainage became a pressing problem. The answer was found in the installation of underground drains, to deal first with the problem of springs. The usual technique was to dig a trench about 0.75m deep, fill it with stones to a depth of half a metre and lead the water away to the nearest stream. A different and initially difficult problem was surface water which refused to drain away through non-porous subsoil. An attempt to solve this problem by farmers in East Anglia, involving the installation of a series of underground drains at 5m intervals, about 0.75m deep, narrowing towards the bottom and filled with branches, proved satisfactory only for porous soils. The solution for non-porous soils was found by James Smith, of Deanston. Smith put in a series of deep leader drains in the hollows connected to receiving drains and thence to shallower parallel drains on the East Anglian model. Smith went further by adopting the use of Staffordshire drain tiles but, even more importantly, by his invention of a subsoil plough which broke up this impermeable barrier. This followed behind a swing plough, cutting to a further depth of about 0.25m, stirring up the subsoil and removing all but the largest boulders. The results were dramatic. He turned what had been a wet and barren waste into a highly productive farm, attracting visitors from far and wide. The importance which was attached to his achievement can be gauged from the considerable attention devoted to the subject of drainage by the Stirlingshire contributors to the *New Statistical Account*.

The success of drain tiles led to the establishment of tile works in several places in the region, Alloa, Denny, and Throsk, but particularly Falkirk where three works were in operation by the 1840s. Two landowners, one in Killearn and one in Kilsyth, set up their own kilns and were able to produce enough for both their own and their tenants needs. Drainage work of this type, however, was very expensive - from £4 to £7 per acre for basic tile draining and, with the addition of small stones, the cost was even greater. Those landowners who carried out this type of improvement found that greater crop yields and the higher rents chargeable quickly repaid the outlay. In any case the cost was eased for landowners by two Acts of Parliament, in 1840 and 1849, which allowed them to borrow a total of £4 million to carry out this kind of work.

One of the most dramatic drainage initiatives was that carried out between 1790 and 1840 on the Dunmore and Airth estates in south-east Stirlingshire where some 150 and 185 acres respectively, were reclaimed from the banks and mudflats of the Forth. Embankments were built of mud and turf, some faced with stone, and the land was drained and made fertile and productive.

By 1880 Dunmore home farm was considered to be the best in the county, both in the quality of its soil and its buildings, which cost £12,000 or £700,000 in 1990 prices, so it cannot be said to have been typical. As descibed by James Tait in 1884 -

"The steading is exceedingly commodious and contains all the appliances for the health and comfort of the animals. The frontage towards the south-east is about 100 yds; and the measurement from south-east to north-west about 70 yds. For feeding cattle there are 16 boxes, measuring each 12 feet by 11, and three others making 19 altogether. A wide passage, with rails for a waggon, between the rows gives facilities for the easy...distribution of food to the feeding troughs, which are alongside of the open passage on either hand. Beside each feeding trough is a separate trough always full...with clear water..and continuously flowing...always pure. For wintering cattle there are four courts...each to accomodate 15 cattle. Over all is a lofty open roof covered with tiles, which are considered better than slates leaving space for ventilation...The stables are...excellent...lofty roofs and sufficient ventilation... On the north side are sheds for young horses, opening onto a paddock...down to the river. The thrashing machine, driven by steam, is centrally placed, perfect in construction and with ready access to the stack-yard, the cattleboxes and the stable. In...a corner...is a smithy where a blacksmith attends...in the evenings. "

If Dunmore was exceptional, commentators in 1880 agreed that the quality of farm buildings particularly on the rich carselands had never been higher. Cattle courts with tiled roofs and running water were becoming a common feature. The 19-year lease was still in operation but on some estates in Stirlingshire a new nine year lease was being adopted. The restrictive leases of the early part of the century were being replaced, giving tenants more freedom to experiment. In this they were helped by the fact that rents had declined since the mid 19th century, with £3 or more per imperial acre being asked for the best land on the western carse, £1.75 for intermediate land and less than £1 for the poorest quality. On the higher ground the rents were about one third less. In the eastern districts the rents could be 25% or more higher than in the west.

During the third quarter of the 19th century threshing and winnowing machines were seen as essential with about two-thirds of the crop, especially wheat and barley, being prepared by travelling machines. The larger farms had their own threshing machines driven where possible by water power.

Figure 4 Kemp and Nicholson's reaper 1856 (R. Mc Cutcheon)

Otherwise steam power or horses were used, with the former becoming increasingly common in both counties. By contrast steam ploughing, which had been pioneered in Stirlingshire in the 1850s, had been found not to be cost-efficient. The problem was it encouraged some farmers to plough too deeply and to turn up less fertile soils. The ordinary horse-drawn plough was preferred, with grubbers for weeding and iron harrows to break up the clods. By 1880 a wide variety of specialised equipment was available to farmers. This included double-moulded ploughs for drilling and earthing up green crops, patent harrows for turnips, combined hay reapers and mowers, horse rakes for gathering up hay, grain reapers, and potato- and turnip-lifters. Almost all grain crops in both counties were cut with reaping machines (**Figure 4**) but binding machines were not in widespread use. In difficult spots, wheat would still be cut with a sickle, whilst for barley and oats a scythe would be used. Beans were sown with a harrow or drill or even broadcast by hand. They could be harvested with a side self-delivering machine.

In the region reclamation of waste land continued between 1850 and 1875. One notable example of this was on the 5,000 acre Ballikinrain estate, near Killearn, purchased in 1862 by the Orr Ewing family for £55,000. More than 2,000 acres was improved at a cost of £8 per acre for the drainage alone. The land was broken into fields varying from 20 to 100 acres enclosed by stone walls 1.25 m high or by iron fences which cost 17p per metre. Following the installation of the drains at a depth of slightly more than one metre and at five metre intervals, the soil was ploughed and subsoiled using Gray's grubbers. It was then heavily manured and in the first year oats were sown followed by turnips and swedes. After a second crop of oats the land was put to pasture using rye-grass and clover and turned over to sheep at a density of four per acre. It was then kept as pasture for sheep and cattle for 14 years. The whole 17 year process then began again. By 1880 the estate had an annual valuation for rental of £2,395 or £144,000 in 1990 prices. The farm buildings and machinery, including a steam-driven threshing machine, reflected the investment which a very wealthy new proprietor was prepared to make in improvements during the high noon of Victorian farming.

Between 1848 and 1885 farmers in almost every part of the region were helped greatly in their marketing of produce to both Edinburgh and west-central Scotland by the construction of railways. These included the Scottish Central from Larbert through Stirling and Dunblane to Perth [1848], the Stirling and Dunfermline [1850] and the Forth and Clyde Junction [1856], running through the Carse of Stirling, and an extension from Killearn to Kirkintilloch [1867]. The Dunblane to Callander line opened in 1858 and was extended to Crianlarich in 1880. Two years later a branch off the Forth and Clyde line was opened to Aberfoyle. Many lines in the south and east of Stirlingshire served the growing industrial operations; in Clackmannanshire branch lines were laid from Cambus to Alva in 1863; from Alloa to Kinross in stages via Tillycoultry and Dollar, opened throughout in 1871; and the Caledonian line to Alloa from Larbert opened via the swing bridge in 1885.

The enclosing of so much land in the late 18th century meant many people driven off their holdings had either migrated to the industrial towns and coalfields or stayed on the land as hired landless labourers. The latter became one of the lowest-paid groups of workers in Scotland. According to the *Statistical Account of Scotland* [1791-1799], the level of wages varied little according to location. Labourers living closest to industrial centres were only slightly better paid than those in more rural parts with no industrial opportunities. In Buchanan along the banks of Loch Lomond a male farm worker was paid £7-£9 per year whilst women got about half that, though free food worth more than the wages was provided. In Falkirk, the most industrialised part of the county, by contrast, a skilled ploughman could expect about £12 per year plus bed and board and a female equivalent to Buchanan. A farm worker hired by the day received about 5p per day or £15 per annum, if fully employed. Farm wages in different parts of the region in the 1790s were affected by the high demand for labour to carry out improvements, such as hedging and dyking which forced up rural wage rates. Contributors to the *Old Statistical Account* pointed out that wage rates had roughly doubled between 1745 and 1790. By 1840 the rates of pay for agricultural workers had increased a further 30%, although figures in the *New Statistical Account* indicate wide variations of increase for different categories of workers in different parishes.

Apart from the obvious wish to increase their incomes, landowners and tenants were encouraged to introduce the new improvements by the availability of technical information which spread rapidly and uniformly throughout central Scotland and elsewhere, from the late 18th century onward. This was done first through books such as Rev Adam Dickson's two-volume *Treatise on Agriculture* [published in 1762 and 1769], but more importantly through the establishment of agricultural societies. At national level the Highland and Agricultural Society, founded in 1784, promoted ideas, particularly through prize essays and the *Transactions* published annually from 1799, soon followed by the *Farmers Magazine* and other specialised journals. Agricultural shows at various locations were another means of bringing both the means and results of improvements to the attention of the farming community. Within central Scotland agricultural societies were founded at Alloa, Clackmannan, Denny, Falkirk, Gargunnock, and Drymen. Higher education in agricultural science began in 1790 when Britain's first Chair of Agriculture was established at the University of Edinburgh. Proposals for a Chair in veterinary science in Edinburgh were turned down, but in 1816, encouraged by the Highland and Agricultural

Society, William Dick began lectures in this field and the university Veterinary School emerged from this.

Table 1   Agriculture in Stirlingshire in 1855
   - A statistical summary

		Area in imperial acres	Produce in quarters
Total		223,255	
Under	wheat	3,987	107,655
	barley	7,337	234,784
	oats	22,028	726,932
	rye	101	
	beans	4,545	124,994
	vetches	469	
	turnips	5,432	
	potatoes	3,321	
	flax	1,372	
	fallow	1,961	
	rotation grass	34,823	
	permanent pasture	37,323	
	irrigated meadows	1,551	
	sheep walks	72,257	
	waste	10,223	
	woods	13,044	
Livestock			
	horses	4,588	
	milk cows	8,282	
	other cattle	13,387	
	calves	5,598	
	sheep	61,062	
	pigs	3,254	

The Great Agricultural Depression, 1875 - 1914

After 100 years of expansion and relative prosperity, agriculture entered a long period of decline, although not all sectors were equally affected. At this time Britain was operating a system of Free Trade with no restrictions on agricultural imports. Thus when world prices began to decline in the 1870s, British agriculture was particularly vulnerable to competition from cheap imports.

The fall in prices of Scottish products began in 1876 and was fairly continuous until 1895, during which time a quarter of oats fell from £1.44 to 72.5p and from 1895 to 1914 rose above £1.00 only in 1902 and 1912. Wheat prices fell even more heavily due to the greater volume of imports. A Cheviot sheep fetched only £1.40 in the early 1890s compared with £2.25 twenty years previously. Wool prices fell by about half between the 1860s and the 1890s. Cattle prices held up better because of the increased demand for beef and particularly milk.

By the mid-1890s not only had the value of agricultural produce fallen by about half but large tracts of land had ceased to be cultivated. In Scotland the largest reduction proportionately was in barley growing, with almost 30% less acreage by 1914 than in 1875. By comparison the acreage devoted to oats fell by only 10% because of its demand as horse-feed. During the period 1875-1914 the acreage devoted to pasture

increased by 25%. By 1882, as the Depression was beginning to take hold, only 114,543 acres or 38.8% of Stirlingshire was cultivated, of which oats with 20,345 acres was still the dominant crop. Between 1855-1882 there had been a decline in oats production of 9%, in wheat 30% and barley 37%. The importation of Timothy hay from the USA in the 1890s proved a great boon to local farmers as it gave a yield per acre 75% higher than the traditional rye-grass on the higher land. In Clackmannanshire the arable acreage fell from 59% of all farmland in 1854 to 49.5% in 1882 and to 44% by 1914, of which about 20% produced oats. By contrast permanent pasture increased during 1854-1914 from 29 to 40% of the agricultural land of the county.

The number of livestock had continued to rise since 1855, most notably sheep, stimulated in part by the expanding woollen industry. By 1881 the number in the two counties had risen by 70% to over 111,000 of which about 15,000 were found on the Ochils. The blackfaces and Cheviots crossbred with Leicester rams were still the main types. However a few complete flocks of Leicesters were being kept by 1880. Ayrshires still prevailed as the main type of milk cattle, but the importation of some Irish breeds onto farms in Clackmannanshire had begun by 1880. Between 1855 and 1882 the total number of milk cows had increased by 21%, but there was almost no change in the numbers of beef cattle and calves. Pigs declined by 50%.

For those farmers still gaining a living from arable farming, six or even seven crop rotations were normal practice, usually comprising wheat, followed by beans, barley, hay, oats, turnips or summer fallow. The seven crop rotation might involve mashlum (mixed grain) or beans and oats mixed after the oat crop. In more remote areas of Scotland deer forests replaced sheep runs with more than 3.5 m acres devoted to deer in the Highlands by 1912.

The principal cause of the depression was the enormous expansion of cereal crop and beef and mutton production in countries such as Canada, the USA, Russia, Argentina and Australia, combined with improvements in international transport which enabled much of this produce to find its way to the British market, forcing down prices. For example meat imports, costing less than 4p per kg were made possible by the development of refrigeration.

The effect of falling prices was compounded by a worsening of the weather in Britain. Appallingly wet springs and summers devoid of sunshine were reported, most spectacularly in August 1877 when almost 6 cm of rain fell in less than one day. The Hillfoots especially were affected by great cataracts of water pouring off the hills. Two people were drowned in Tillicoultry and some £8000-worth of damage done to the town. This was followed by the Arctic winter of 1878-9 which brought widespread losses of livestock amongst hill-farmers. If all this was not bad enough, there were simultaneous and serious outbreaks of pleuro-pneumonia and foot-and-mouth disease amongst cattle and liver-rot amongst sheep. The summer which followed brought no relief with continuous cold and wet weather until the autumn ruining the cereal crops, whilst the flood of imports prevented any rise in prices. The UK harvest of 1879 was described by *Whitakers Almanac* as "the worst ever recorded".

Scotland survived the Great Depression rather better than England, with a percentage decline of grain acreage only half that of the latter, because the strongest overseas competition came in the wheat markets and Scotland's main crop was oats. By the mid-1890s foreign wheat was supplying 75% of Britain's market, whereas for oats the figure never rose above 20. Potato growing became a profitable alternative to cereals although even here there was a fall in consumption as dietary habits changed. After reaching a peak of more than 189,000 acres in 1881 the acreage devoted to potato growing declined to 152,318 by 1914, though exports of Scottish seed potatoes grew as some compensation. Despite this gloomy overall picture, in the best areas there was no shortage of tenants for vacant farms.

In 1883 there were, according to Tait, 848 owners of land of one acre or more in Stirlingshire, totalling 283,468 acres, at an average valuation of £1.42 per acre, but varying from 25p in Buchanan parish to £7.50 in Logie. Nimmo [1880], however, gives a total of 286,338 acres divided between 926 farmers. Whatever the figure, one man, the Duke of Montrose, owned almost 69,000 acres, with an annual valuation of £16,561. Second in size was the Callendar estate of William Forbes which, because three-quarters of it was in the industrial parishes of Falkirk and Denny, yielded a gross income, including mineral royalties, of £19,811, or £1.2 m in 1990 prices. Other large landowners in the county were the Earl of Zetland, with an estate of an annual value of £10,850, the Earl of Dunmore at £8,133 and the Carron Company at £8890. In Clackmannanshire in 1883 there were 90 individual owners sharing 29,864 acres at an average rental of £2.19 per acre. By contrast the smallholders of the two counties, defined as those with less than one acre each, numbered 3,409 in Stirlingshire and 1,137 in Clackmannanshire. Thus by 1880 only about 4% of the population of the two counties were owners of land, a very considerable decline from the situation in earlier times.

Overall in this period Scottish agriculture saw no dramatic technical revolution comparable to that of 1780-1870. The principal emphasis was on adapting to the problems of world competition and concentrating on quality products rather than trying to undercut the prairie farmers of North America and elsewhere. This applied particularly in cattle-breeding.

The growing concentration on quality products required the development of a more scientific approach to agriculture. The Highland and Agricultural Society was still at the forefront here. In 1848 it employed a chemist to investigate local problems and in 1858 instituted agricultural diplomas. After much prodding it also established two experimental stations and three centres of higher education in Edinburgh, Glasgow and Aberdeen. Between 1899 and 1904, these became the East, West, and North of Scotland Agricultural Colleges, respectively.

Despite the existence of much alternative work and large-scale emigration, particularly in the 1880s, there does not appear to have been a shortage of labour on farms. There are probably three reasons for this. First the high birth rate had continued until the last quarter of the 19th century and beyond amongst farm labourers and coal miners who formed important proportions of the population. Second the development of labour-saving machinery meant that increased productivity could be attained without the need for more labour. Indeed the absolute size of the agricultural workforce fell. By 1891 the number of male and female agricultural workers in Stirlingshire fell to 3,823 and 770 respectively and in Clackmannanshire to 586 and 57, roughly 8% of the total workforce of the two counties. Third, at peak labour times, temporary labour could be recruited from amongst the wives and children of local urban or mine workers. They were paid 8p per day in the summer and 16p at harvest time. Yet another source of casual labour were Irish workers, who had probably immigrated permanently to the region, and were renowned for their ability to put in extremely long hours on their knees thinning turnips by hand and carrying out other equally unpleasant tasks. For this they were paid between 12 and 25p per day plus meals.

The remuneration of Scotland's 213,000 agricultural workers in 1891 varied according to their skills and marital status. Unmarried workers in both counties slept in bothies, were fed in the farm kitchens and received £9-£12 per year. Married ploughmen would be paid between £26 and £32 per year with a free house, garden and coals, and free supplies of oatmeal, milk and potatoes. A foreman ploughman would receive the same perquisites and between £32 and £38 per year, the latter figure converting to about £62 per week gross in 1990 prices. Following the decline in prices between 1876 and 1896, farm workers like most others in Britain benefitted from increasing real wages. After 1896 a steady inflationary drift began to reduce living standards and was largely responsible for the massive wave of industrial strikes in the years before the war.

Scottish Agriculture in the First World War

The long depression reduced considerably Britain's ability to feed itself. Between 1840 and 1914, while the population of Britain rose by 45 %, the number of people fed by home produced food fell by 50 %. By 1914 therefore Britain was able to feed less than 30 % of its population, relying on imports for the remainder. This situation had been caused mainly by the decline of grain crop farming. During the first year of the war, because the submarine had not yet demonstrated its awesome menace to merchant shipping, the government apparently saw no immediate danger in this. Shipping losses due mainly to surface raiders were more than compensated for by prize ships seized by the Royal Navy. By mid-1915 however food supplies were declining as shipping losses mounted and imports fell, especially wheat from Russia, Canada and Australia. Those from the USA rose sharply but overall the decline was more than 750,000 tons or 15 %. Although as a result of a 50 % increase in grain prices, Scottish farmers, mirroring the response of British farmers generally, brought under the plough an extra 33,000 acres, this was still insufficient and the government set up committees to examine the situation. The Scottish Committee, believing that persuasion and rising prices would be sufficient to ensure the necessary production, recommended the establishment of district agricultural committees to oversee land use and the requisitioning of labour and horses. By 1917 local committees had also been set up in every district with wide powers over the allocation of resources (**Figure 5**).

This action by the government between 1915 and 1917 marks a radical change in the history of agriculture in Scotland. Since that time, but particularly since 1939, agriculture has been viewed as a most important national resource to be regulated and supported, by and from Edinburgh, London, and since 1973 Brussels. Henceforth agricultural history in the region must be viewed, not in parochial terms, but as part of these greater entities.

In 1916 imports recovered but were still below 1914 levels. Meanwhile this decline in imports was exacerbated by a poor Scottish harvest in 1915, the product of a cold wet spring, especially in Clackmannanshire. Scottish wheat production fell by more than 25%, both turnips and swedes by 22, oats by 7 and potatoes by a massive 45. Only barley recorded a small increase. Later in 1916, in response to this crisis, powers of compulsion were conferred on the Scottish Board of Agriculture under the *Defence of the Realm Act*.

One increasingly serious problem facing farmers, noted particularly in Stirlingshire in 1916, was a shortage of labour, caused both by the demands of the army and the attraction of higher wages in the munitions factories. Farm workers experienced in handling horses were particularly needed in the horse-drawn army. The task of adjudicating between the army and farmers over individual cases fell to the Scottish Board of Agriculture. In 1917 5,588 Scottish farm workers were given certificates exempting them from conscription. Then in 1917-18 as the casualty lists grew the conscription of skilled men began including 5,500 Scottish farm workers.

To some extent the shortfall in the agricultural labour force was made up by the use of special labour. This included prisoners of war [POWs], though not in significant numbers until the spring of 1918 and reaching 30,000 by the end of the war. British soldiers, many classified as unfit for frontline duty, were also

Figure 5   Ploughing up King's Park in 1917 against public opposition: and it was not successful   (R. McCutcheon)

used in increasing numbers, formed into agricultural companies. In early 1917 18,000 ploughmen, including 1,000 Scots were sent on agricultural leave by the army to help with the spring sowing. This brought the total of soldiers working in British agriculture to more than 36,000. Later in 1917 a further 33,000 were loaned by the army to help with the tillage extension programme, but delays meant that by the end of 1917 only about 48,000 were working on British farms. Unfortunately only a minority of these had the necessary skills, or even the required level of fitness. By March 1918, however, their total number had increased to 63,000 and by November to 79,000.

A women's land army, of 16,000 at its maximum, was established, of whom 1022 were Scottish in 1917. Also tens of thousands of other part-time women workers were employed. Despite all these the UK agricultural labour force declined to 91% of its 1914 level during 1916 and 1917 and was still 4% below in 1918. Without the replacements, however, it would not have been possible to bring into production the 2 m extra acres added to the arable acreage of the UK 1916-1918. Yet another problem, made more difficult as the arable acreage increased, was the shortage of imported and artificial fertilisers. By the end of the war purchasing of fertilisers had been centralised in London to ensure equality of distribution, with 40,000 tons made available to Scotland in 1918-19.

Motorisation, particularly the use of tractors, began partly to compensate for the labour problems. It was promoted by large-scale practical demonstrations in 1915, including one at Stirling where a tillage trial for tractors was held with five entrants, including two American models. The Overtime, designed and built by Scottish Motor Traction, Edinburgh, weighing 2.15 tons and costing £231 was particularly favoured by British farmers who were reported to have purchased 1,500 by early 1917. In the autumn of 1917 the Highland and Agricultural Society organized three major demonstrations of tractors with ploughs at Edinburgh, Glasgow and Perth; 29 models were on display of which 13 were from the USA, 10 from England, four from Canada and two including the Overtime were from Scotland. Only five had caterpillar tracks, 25 were paraffin-fuelled and 18 weighed two tons or more, which the engineer's report, although noting some favourable factors, felt to be too heavy.

On the basis of design, efficiency and price [£150], the Ministry of Munitions, in 1917, opted for 6,000 US Fordson models. These were amongst 9,000 tractors, and more than 10,000 ploughs, 6,500 harrows, 5,000 binders and nearly 400 threshing machines, costing a total of £4.7 m, bought by the Ministry and hired to UK farmers in 1917-18. In Scotland 162 tractors were on hire by the end of 1917 including 20 Overtimes and 106 Canadian-designed Titans and Moguls, though only three of these were working in Stirlingshire and Clackmannanshire. No US imported tractors arrived in Scotland before 1918. By the end of the war Scottish farmers were renting 198 tractors for which they paid £1.25 per acre [about £36 at 1990 prices], 84 grubbers at 62p per acre and 203 binders at 50p per acre which included the tractor and the wages of two men. Thus by 1918 the tractor and its ancillary equipment were widely accepted and eagerly sought after pieces of equipment. One locally-invented piece of equipment was the automatic hay-ricking machine. It was manufactured between 1917 and the early 1930s.

With such human and mechanical help a 21 % increase in the cultivated acreage was achieved by 1918 and a corresponding improvement in crop production after the poor harvest of 1916. Clackmannanshire was one of only half a dozen counties which exceeded its quota increase. Wheat output in Scotland rose by 5% in 1917 and by a further 32% in 1918, but less than 2,000 of Stirlingshire's 115,000 cultivated acres produced wheat and none was grown in the west of the county. In Clackmannanshire the wheat area was only 415 acres. In each county the acreage devoted to oats was eleven times greater. By comparison the neighbouring counties of Perth and Fife, together, grew one-third of Scotland's wheat. Scottish oat production rose by 20% in 1917 and 18% in 1918. The potato crop doubled in 1917 following widespread new plantings and even increased slightly again in 1918. Turnips and swedes increased by 35 % in 1917, but fell by an even larger amount in 1918 as a result of spring frosts and a summer drought. A smaller contribution to the food production effort was also made by Scottish allotment holders whose 44,000 smallholdings totalled 2550 acres by 1918.

Facilitating these increases in output also was government legislation, operating until 1922, which enforced minimum prices for wheat and oats. The guaranteed price for wheat fell from £3 per quarter in 1917 to £2.75 during the following three years and £2.25 in 1920-22. For oats the scale ran from £1.92 down to £1.20. There is little doubt however that the 110 to 200% 1914-18 increase in crop prices was the biggest incentive to increase production. Overall prices doubled during the four years of the war, despite controls on milk, meat and other commodity prices. Financially farmers did well out of the war. Whilst their costs in 1918 were 49% higher than the average for 1909-13, their incomes rose by 240%. Farm workers inevitably did less well. By early 1918 their money wages were less than 60% higher than in 1914. Landowners did even less well as a result of rents rising much more slowly than prices. The result was that investment and maintenance suffered and many owners whose sons and heirs may have died in the war put their estates on the market. The relatively prosperous tenant farmers were happy to buy their holdings, especially in 1919-21.

The increase in arable farming occurred partly at the expense of sheep, whose numbers declined during the war by 150,000 or 2%. Nevertheless, by 1917 there were still 124,000 sheep in Stirlingshire and 15,000 in Clackmannanshire, out of a Scottish total of 6.87 m. Pig farming also declined during the war with a loss of 25,000 animals or 16%. In Stirlingshire and Clackmannanshire the pig figures for 1917 were 2205 and 588 respectively. On the other hand there was virtually no change in the numbers of Scottish cattle, 1.2 m., of which there were 32,000 in Stirlingshire and 3,400 in Clackmannanshire. Of the 25,000 Scottish horses sold to the army each year, 1200 were supplied from Stirlingshire farms and one-tenth that number from Clackmannanshire.

Between the First and Second World Wars

The prosperity which wartime conditions had brought to farming lasted for about two years after the end of hostilities. Apart from potatoes, which, by the spring of 1919 were so plentiful that the government had to intervene to buy the surplus crop, cereal prices remained high throughout 1919 and 1920. In the latter year for example oats reached their highest ever price of £2.84 a quarter, a level not again exceeded until 1948. The situation soon changed as world supply persistently exceeded demand. Cereal and other food imports were increasing so rapidly that by 1922 farm prices were 42% lower than in 1920. British farmers were protected against losses by the 1920 *Agriculture Act* which, subject to annual revision, guaranteed prices at average 1919 levels. Faced with a huge bill for farm support, the government was forced to retreat and it repealed the 1920 Act. The blow was softened slightly by an acreage payment, of which Scottish farmers got £4.4 m. Nevertheless, the Depression of the late 1870s onwards began to be repeated in the 1920s and 1930s.

In 1922 as another long depression in agriculture was beginning, Stirlingshire's farmlands covered 113,193 acres, or 39% of the total area of the county. There were 1,465 holdings in the county representing an average size of 77 acres. The area of farmland under plough was 55,278 acres or 36 % of the total. Of this oats, with 19,169, was still the largest crop. Turnips and swedes covered 3,932 acres and potatoes 3,555 but wheat, only 2,194 acres. Stirlingshire farmers owned more than 114,000 sheep, 30,000 cattle, 5,000 horses and 2,300 pigs, mostly the same breeds as in the 19th century. They employed 3,763 male workers and 657 female in 1921, 4% fewer than in 1891. The Clackmannanshire workforce fell by only thirteen or 2% between 1891 and 1921.

The Depression deepened in 1929 as world prices collapsed due to over-production. In Scotland, farm prices fell by 32% between 1928 and 1933. By the latter a quarter of Scottish oats, at 78p, commanded only 27% of the price it had in 1920. Potato growing and sheep farming were particularly depressed. Between 1928 and 1932 the price of blackface sheep fell by about 60 %. Estate values fell to about one third of their post-war prices and the poorest pasture could be rented annually for only 50p per acre. As in the 1880s much arable land reverted to pasture and the 1.24 m. Scottish acres devoted to oats in 1918 had shrunk to 0.867 m. by 1932.

In Stirlingshire the total area of farmland declined by almost 4,000 acres with some 9,000 acres taken out of arable production. The number of horses continued to decline as mechanisation slowly increased (**Figure 6**). Although cattle declined by more than 5,000, the number of sheep rose by a further 16,000 to 130,000, despite the catastrophic fall in prices.

In Clackmannanshire agricultural land also declined, but by only 350 acres to 15,150. However the decline in land devoted to arable farming fell by almost 2,000 acres. By 1933 only 22% of the county's farmland was devoted to cereal growing, mostly oats, and the number of sheep, 12,450 in 1934, was its lowest for more than a century. The principal new development during this period was in poultry farming and egg production, but was little compensation for general depression. Experience of the war had taught the government the dangers of totally abandoning agriculture to market forces. The acreage payment of £4.4 m to Scottish farmers in 1920 has been noted, and further financial relief was offered to farmers by the progressive removal of rates up to 1929. More assistance was made available to owner-occupiers of farms through the *Agricultural Credits [Scotland] Acts* of 1925 and 1929. *The Wheat Act* of 1932 was of much less value in Scotland than in England and subsidies for cattle given in 1934, incorporated into the *Livestock Industry Act* of 1937, amounted to almost £1 m in 1938. Of the various Marketing Boards established by the Acts of 1931 and 1933 to assist farmers to sell their products, that for milk was the most important, providing Scottish dairy

Figure 6 Four horses plough double furrows to save manpower, but horse power was losing out to the tractor.

(Dunning Historical Society)

farmers with an annual subsidy of more than £113,000 by 1938. Stirlingshire and Clackmannanshire farmers took advantage of this incentive and the number of cattle in the two counties increased by 4,000 and 450 respectively between 1931 and 1939. Arable farmers in Scotland were helped also by the 1937 *Agriculture Act* which provided price guarantees for oats and barley and offered assistance to farmers to improve soil fertility.

Despite these various measures agricultural prices changed only minimally. Throughout the 1930s, except briefly in 1937, they failed to reach 85% of the 1928 levels. The result of this continued depression was that, between 1933 and 1938, a further 3,900 acres of agricultural land in Stirlingshire and 300 in Clackmannanshire were abandoned. The number of sheep in Stirlingshire declined also, from an all time record of 132,137 in 1932 to 126,309 in 1939, whilst by contrast Clackmannanshire reached a record 16,271 head in the latter year.

This depressed state of Scottish agriculture during the inter-war period, particularly the conversion of arable to pasture and increased mechanisation, resulted in a further decline in the labour force. The steam engine driven threshing mills of the 1920s (**Figure 7**) gave way to the combine harvesters of the 30s. Other innovations were retarded by a lack of electricity, supplied to only 11 % of Scotland's farms as late as 1943. Most of those who left farm work between 1921 and 1939 were the youngest and least experienced. The number of male and female farm workers under 21 declined by 21 and 34% respectively. By contrast the

Figure 7   A motley threshing crew, traction engine, with precarious belt drive to the mill, typical of farm to farm harvesting in the 1920s.   (Dunning Historical Society)

number of adult male farm workers fell by only 4%. Although minimum wages for farm workers had been enforced by the 1917 *Corn Production Act* this lasted only three years. Thereafter the wages of Scotland's farmworkers declined. Between 1925 and 1934 the average weekly wage including various allowances, of a married ploughman in Scotland fell from £1.92 to £1.70, and of a shepherd from £1.98 to £1.81. The considerable decline in prices during this period would have helped to cushion this fall. Conditions of employment did improve as a result of the *Agricultural Wages [Regulations] Scotland Act* 1937, whereby minimum wages, hours of work, overtime rates and holidays were all regulated by a Scottish Wages Board. The housing situation of Scottish farm workers was, however, far from satisfactory. As late as 1943 amongst 22,000 farm cottages, more than 8,000 had no piped water, a similar number had water only to a sink, whilst 6,000 had only a wc. Less than 10 % had electricity.

The Second World War

Determined to learn from its mistakes in the First World War, The government moved quickly in the summer of 1939 with the *Emergency Powers [Defence] Act*, which enabled it to make regulations through Orders-in-Council to ensure that agriculture would be organised more efficiently and productively. The regulations included powers to requisition land and take over farms which were being managed inefficiently. Only 73 tenants from amongst 78,000 agricultural holdings in Scotland - of which 32,000 could be

considered full-time farms - were evicted for failing to meet required standards. The Secretary of State also took over 90,000 acres of deer forests for sheep-raising. In 1939 less than 40% of Britain's food was home-produced compared with under 30% in 1914; 66% of concentrated animal feedstuffs were imported. The principal task of British farmers, therefore, became the replacement of imports by greatly increased production of cheap and bulky foodstuffs to save valuable shipping space. On the whole farmers responded well. Grain and flour imports fell from 10 to 4 m tons between 1938 and 1944 and maize from 58 m to 2 m. As in 1914-18 this was achieved largely by a major conversion of pasture to arable land. As the threat of war grew in June 1939 conversion was facilitated by the terms of the *Agricultural Development Act* which provided grants of £2 per acre, increased to £3 in 1943 and £4 in 1944, for ploughing up pasture. The result was that between 1939 and 1945, in Scotland, arable land increased from 2.9 to 3.3 m acres. Most of this extra area was devoted to grain crops.

Between 1939 and 1945 wheat output in Scotland increased 16%, barley by 224, oats by 36, potatoes by 53 and turnips and swedes by 10%. All this was achieved despite some particularly inclement weather, both exceptionally heavy rain and periods of drought, as well as extreme cold and blizzards. The 1945 total of 1.34 m acres producing grain crops was nevertheless 145,000 acres less than in 1918, due mostly to the land requirements of the armed forces, as well as to increased opencast mining.

The price paid for this wartime increase in arable farming was a substantial decline of 513,000 acres of grassland and, despite the addition of more than 200,000 acres of rough grazing, a large decrease in livestock, principally in sheep, from 8 to less than 7 m. Pigs, poultry and horses also declined. Beef cattle, however, increased by 111,000, and dairy cattle by 80,000 to more than 2.28 m by 1945.

These changes were mirrored in Stirlingshire, where in 1945, there were more than 40,000 cattle, 105,000 sheep, 9,280 pigs and more than 3,000 horses. Similarly the area under crops, fallow or temporary grass had risen to almost 61,000 acres. More than 43,000 acres were under permanent grass and almost 143,000 acres were rough grazing. From forced land sales during the depression, the number of agricultural holdings in the county had increased by more than 140 since 1922, exceeding 1,600 in 1945. Their average size had, however, declined, by about 16%, to 64 acres, and these 1600 represented a loss of more than 5,000 acres, presumably to the military.

One serious difficulty restricting increased production was the decline in the agricultural workforce since 1921. This was exacerbated after the outbreak of war as young farmworkers enlisted. By 1946 a total of 6,500 Scottish farmworkers had joined the Armed Forces. It became vitally important therefore, that extra sources of labour be sought - and at a time when the armed forces, the munitions industry and other

Figure 8 The first lease/lend packaged tractor from USA, 1942 - considered the most valuable of many US agricultural equipments received. On display in the Scottish Agricultural Museum, Ingliston, Edinburgh   (L.Corbett)

employers were desperate for additional workers. One solution was the greater employment of women. The Women's Land Army began in Scotland in 1939 with 110 members, reached a peak of 8,250 in 1943 and declined to 7,685 by 1945. Unfortunately the nature of farmwork proved too arduous for about a third of these women who either resigned or were dismissed. Fortunately their numbers were supplemented by an increase in both regular and casual female workers in Scotland which reached a peak of 27,621 and 10,420 respectively in 1943.

School children made notable contributions to the potato and fruit harvests. In the peak years of 1943 and 1944 about 45,000 children helped with their local potato harvests whilst about one third that number came to help from further afield. Other volunteers responded to appeals from the Scottish Department of Agriculture, 9220 persons helping with the 1944 harvest. POWs were an additional form of help and between 1942 and 1945 their numbers increased from 3,000 to 19,000, whilst peripatetic Irish workers also contributed during the war years and afterwards. An indication of the governments's concern to retain skilled farm workers was demonstrated by two Orders issued in the early years of the war. The first in 1940 forbade such workers leaving the industry to work elsewhere and the second in 1941 required farm workers to stay with the same employer until the end of the war. The result of these two measures was that the adult male agricultural workforce in Scotland stabilised at about 75,000, of whom 2,644 were working on Stirlingshire farms in 1945.

In November 1939 another means of expanding the output of grain, a tractor service, administered by the local Agricultural Committees, enabled farmers, particularly those in remote areas who had abandoned arable farming between the wars, to begin a speedy programme of ploughing up. The service expanded until 1942-3, when a total area of more than 300,000 acres was cultivated and almost 120,000 harvested. By the end of 1945 almost 1300 tractors (**Figure 8**), 1675 ploughs and 1058 binders were operated by this service, compared with less than 350 items six years previously. At the same time the number of tractors owned privately by Scottish farmers increased from 6,250 to 19,000 between 1939 and 1944. Government grants, of 50% of the cost, were also made available for approved drainage schemes, with a total of 26,000 acres being so improved in Scotland. In 1942 extra grants, over and above the £2.00 per acre ploughing subsidy were offered to farmers who ploughed up so-called marginal or poor quality land. Some £224,000 was paid in 1944 in respect of 207,000 Scottish acres. A significant contribution was made to vegetable growing by individual men and women who cultivated small allotments and gardens. The number of the former almost quadrupled from 23,000 to 84,000 by 1943 and one estimate of privately grown vegetables in Scotland during the war years was 210,000 tons. Between 1930 and 1945 home produced food expressed in calories, increased by 91%.

In 1939 an experienced ploughman earned £2.00 per week. This was raised at intervals during the war until by 1945 it had reached £3.80, an increase of 90%. Women's wages rose more rapidly, from £1.08 per week in 1939 to £2.35 in 1944. Overall Scottish agricultural wages increased by 111% during the war whilst the official cost of living index rose by only 29% and agricultural prices by 93%. The gap between the last two was plugged by state subsidies of some £37 m per annum.

The Postwar Years, 1945-1990

The end of the war did not mean an immediate end to food shortages. The effects of war damage in Europe, as well as in other parts of the world, had gravely reduced food supplies. For Britain the problem was exacerbated by the end of Lend-Lease from the USA and the consequent need to buy food with scarce dollars. Thus in 1945 there was no rapid change of policy by the incoming Labour government. It remained as vital then as it had been in 1942 to continue growing as much food as possible. Yet as early as 1944 farmers had begun to drift away from grain crops to stockraising. In Scotland 60,000 acres were taken out of wheat production between 1944 and 1945. In response the government extended and increased the ploughing up subsidy and introduced bread rationing in 1946.

Following the appalling winter of 1947, potato rationing had to be introduced, but help was forthcoming through new legislation. In 1946 the *Hill Farming Act* allowed grants of up to 50% to improve upland sheep farms and farmers were quick to take advantage both of this and of the subsidies provided under the 1951 *Livestock Rearing Act*. Even more important was the *1947 Agriculture Act* which guaranteed prices and markets for meat, cereals, potatoes, sugarbeet, milk and eggs. In Scotland it was the Secretary of State's duty to fix these prices, and announce them variously between 18 months and four years ahead to help production planning. It was hoped this measure would so increase production that dollar-earning exports would be made possible. In 1948 the *Agriculture [Scotland] Act* sought to impose high standards of efficiency upon both landlords and tenants in return for security of tenure for the latter, with rights of appeal to the Land Court. Eleven Agricultural Executive Committees were also established as were Advisory Committees. Finally the *Marketing Act 1949* amd the *Wool Marketing Act 1950* provided closer control over the pre-war Boards.

By 1950 4.4 m acres in Scotland were devoted to crops and grass, of which 21% was oats and 6% turnips and swedes. Wheat and barley combined, accounted for only 5%. Grasslands, by contrast, covered almost 60% providing nutrition for 1.75 m cattle and, combined with rough grazing, for 7.5 m sheep. The total output value of Scottish agriculture by mid-century had reached approximately £100 m, of which 95% was produced by 32,000 full-time farms, whose average size was 127 acres. Average rents were only £1.14 per acre, a remarkably low figure considering inflation since 1900.

In Clackmannanshire 75% of its 37,000 acres were used for agriculture in 1950 but only 29% was arable, whilst 40% was permanent grazing and 31% rotated. 4,000 acres were growing cereals, of which 75% were oats. Of the county's 154 holdings 70 were less than 50 acres, 21 between 50 and 100 and 63 more than 100 acres. By 1951 the labour force had declined to 412 male and 41 female workers. The use of the tractor had reduced the number of horses in the county to only 150. By contrast, sheep at more than 16,000 had more than maintained prewar numbers and there were almost 4,400 cattle.

In 1951 in Stirlingshire there were more than 41,000 cattle and 113,300 sheep, but the number of horses had fallen by 1,000 since 1939 to 1,400. By 1960 less than 600 remained, but the number of cattle and sheep continued to rise, to 54,000 and 139,000 respectively. In 1951 53,000 acres of arable land were under the plough, an increase of 9,000 since 1939, of which 24,000 produced grain crops [18,000 oats and 2,000 wheat]. The workforce had increased between 1945 and 1951 to 2,979 males and 287 females, reflecting the urgent need to maintain and increase home-produced supplies.

Agricultural wages had risen, from £3.50 per week for the average male worker in 1946 to £4.50 by the end of 1947. By 1953 the minimum wage for an adult male was £5.40, with higher rates for dairymen; women's rates £2.35 to £3.37 between 1946 and 1947. In addition to native workers, recruitment to Scotland of 5,000 volunteers from refugee camps in Europe had taken place in 1948.

By 1953 food supplies had improved sufficiently for the government to remove many of the controls and regulations imposed since 1939 and modified since the end of the war. Fixed price guarantees were removed and farmers were free to find their own markets, except for milk, potatoes and eggs which were sold through marketing boards. There remained, however, a complex system of price support, known as deficiency payments, which provided the average farmer with two-thirds of his income after the end of rationing in 1954. Overall these interventionist policies had worked well. Food imports declined and nutritional standards rose, with gross agricultural output rising by 17% in Scotland between 1939 and 1951, but if savings on imports are added, this rises to 40%. Prices stabilised and productivity rose more sharply than in almost any other industry, doubling between 1950 and 1980. This was partly due to the rapid decline of regular and casual employment which fell by 60 and 66% respectively - from a total 80,000 to less than 30,000 during these 30 years. By 1990 there were only 28,108 farmworkers in Scotland, - compared with 213,000 a century previously - of whom 20,080 were full-time, 4,918 part-time and 3,110 casual or seasonal. Of these totals 1,032, 686, 211 and 135 respectively were employed in Central Region. Farming had already become very much a family affair by the early 1950s. By 1990 the number of working occupiers, 13,800, exceeded the number of full-time adult male hired workers. In Central Region almost 77% of farms were worked by the occupiers.

Farm rentals had continued to fall behind the general rise in prices since 1945. In the 1960s an acre of good arable land in the region fetched less than £5.00, whilst rough grazing land in the west fetched less than £1.00. Simultaneously wage rates   still lagged behind those in other industries where employment prospects remained good until the late 1970s. Thus few adult male farm workers could hope to earn more than £10.00 weekly in the early 1960s and £23 by 1972. Womens' earnings at the latter date were about £15. By the early 1980s inflation had pushed male earnings to £80. From 1990 the minimum wage for an adult male worker was fixed at £122 per week. Actual earnings were between £30 and £70 higher than this. Women averaged £154 in 1990.

An explanation for both these trends - a declining labour force and increased productivity and relative profitability - can be found in three factors. First the greatly increased application of mechanisation, technology and science to farming.

By the 1960s tractors had become very powerful and versatile machines, some with four-wheel drive and many with hydraulic transmission. The latter facilitated a much more efficient use of power to the diverse types

Figure 9 A modern farm, Manor, Stirling.   (L.Corbett)

of ancillary equipment. Research was being carried out into improved designs of ploughs to enable tractors to advance at higher speeds without either wheelslip or an inefficient action. Another area of development was the improvement of seed drills which simultaneously could plant cereal and root crops and apply artificial fertiliser and pesticides. Machines to make hay concentrated on removing moisture at the harvesting stage, excessive moisture being a major problem with cereal crops also. Experiments in the 1960s included airtight storage and chilling. One contributor to *The Third Statistical Account* for Stirlingshire [1966], defined the new machines as,

"Combine harvesters, power-driven binders and mowers, dung   spreaders and leaders, artificial manure spreaders, pick-up   balers, elevators and draining machines."

He described crop rotation as

"oats followed by potatoes and turnips; it is then sown again with wheat, barley or oats followed by one year`s hay and then one to three years pasture".

Another contributor described a typical carse farm,

"It has from a quarter to a third of its acreage under timothy [hay], the remainder in oats, wheat, mashlum or turnips; practically no potatoes are grown."

A second reason for these improvements was the steady rationalisation of farming units, with a decline of more than 25,000 of all types of holdings, almost one third of the total between 1945 and 1990. This obviously meant a considerable increase in the average size of farms and thus an opportunity to practice economies of scale. Between 1945 and 1990 there was a decline of

almost 5,000 major agricultural holdings in Scotland to 27,166, plus 25,000 small or economically insignificant. Of the former almost 1,000 were in the central region, two-thirds being between 50 and 500 acres.

A third reason was that all these changes were underpinned by support payments, which by the mid-1970s included payments through the European Community Common Agricultural Policy [as well as levies payable to it]. In agricultural subsidies alone, in 1978, Scotland received a net transfer of £24m. Nevertheless Scottish farms were not licences to print money. In 1989-90 the net income per unit varied between £9,350 for a sheep farm in a poorer area to £27,414 for a dairy farm (**Figure 9**).

By 1990 Scotland had the same approximate total area of agricultural land, 19 m acres, that it had had in 1707. Rough grazings of almost 10 m acres, including 331,000 in Central Region have, unsurprisingly, remained the largest single type of agricultural usage. More than 2.5 m acres were producing arable crops. The latter included 1 m of new grasses and 1.566 m of grain, root and other crops. Since the 1960s, as a result of improvements in seeds, fertilisers and machinery, the production of barley has shown the greatest increase, replacing oats as the principal grain crop. By 1990 Scotland was growing more than 830,000 acres of barley, of which more than 23,000 were in Central Region. Oats had declined to 73,000, of which only 3,000 were in Central. Wheat production has also shown dramatic increases in this period and the growing area in Central was more than double that for oats in 1990, whilst for Scotland it was almost four times as much. Another crop to show a dramatic expansion in Scotland has been rape for oilseed with 111,000 acres in 1990, of which 1,600 were in this region. Turnips and potatoes each covered about 66,000 acres, of which 2,060 and 383 respectively were in Central Region.

Thus in the three centuries since the last great Scottish famine, agriculture has undergone the most profound and far - reaching changes. From being the major economic activity in 1700 it now employs directly only about 1% of the working population. Output and productivity, by reason of technical and scientific advances, have increased to levels that the early 18th century farmer could not even have dreamt of. However the problems of differential progress between both areas and types of farming have remained. Whereas for centuries agriculture was very much a local issue, even if markets were sometimes far-flung, it is important to stress again that since 1915 it has become the concern of governments with varying degrees of intensity, and since 1973 of the European Community whose Common Agricultural Policy, by 1990 and again in 1992, was at the heart of a bitter dispute with the USA during attempts to liberalise world trade. Scottish agriculture has come a long way in 300 years.

REFERENCES AND FURTHER READING

AGRICULTURAL STATISTICS [SCOTLAND]. 1855. Report of The Highland and Agricultural Society of Scotland to the Board of Trade, for the Year 1854, London.

BARBIERI, Michael. 1857. Descriptive and Historical Gazetteer of the Counties of Fife, Kinross and Clackmannan.

BEVERIDGE, David. 1888. Between the Ochils and the Forth, Edinburgh.

CARLISLE, Nicholas. 1813. Topographical Dictionary of Scotland, Vol 1, Edinburgh.

CLACKMANNAN COUNTY. 1951. Regional Survey Report, 2 Vols Alloa.

DEVINE T.M. Editor. 1984. Farm Servants and Labour in Lowland Scotland, 1770-1914. Edinburgh.

DONALDSON, Gordon. 1960. Sources for Scottish Agrarian History before the Eighteenth Century. *The Agricultural History Review*, Vol VIII, pp 82-90

DOUGLAS, Charles. 1919. Scottish agriculture during the War, *Transactions of The Highland and Agricultural Society* 5th series, XXXI, pp 1-66

FORSYTH, Robert. 1806. The Beauties of Scotland, volume 3, Edinburgh.

FRANKLIN, T.B. 1952. History of Scottish Farming, Edinburgh.

GRAHAM, Rev Patrick. 1812. General View of the Agriculture of Stirlingshire, Edinburgh.

GRAHAM, Rev Patrick. 1814. General View of the Agriculture of Kinross and Clackmannanshire, Edinburgh.

HOUSTON, George. 1961. Agricultural Statistics Scotland before 1866, *Agricultural History Review*, IX, pp 93-7

MARSHALL, David. 1956. Scottish agriculture during the War, *Transactions of The Highland and Agricultural Society*, 5th series, LVIII, pp6-78

NEW STATISTICAL ACCOUNT OF SCOTLAND. 1845. IX, Dunbarton, Stirling and Clackmannan, Edinburgh.

NIMMO, William. 1880. History of Stirlingshire. Edinburgh.

REGISTRAR-GENERAL FOR SCOTLAND. 1880. Decennial Censuses, 1851.... Edinburgh, various dates.

RENNIE, R. C. and GORDON, T. CROUTHER. Editors. 1966. Third Statistical Account of Scotland, The County of Stirling, The County of Clackmannan, Glasgow.

SCOTTISH OFFICE, DEPARTMENT OF AGRICULTURE. 1991. Economic Report on Scottish Agriculture 1990.

STAMP, L. D. 1946. The Land of Britain, volume 2, Stirlingshire, pp 357-378, Clackmannanshire pp 674-680.

STEWART, L. 1991. The Scottish enclosures .... 1991. *Forth Naturalist and Historian.*

SYMON, J. A. Scottish Farming, Past and Present. 1959. Edinburgh.

TAIT, James. 1883. The agriculture of the counties of Clackmannan and Kinross. *Transactions of The Highland and Agricultural Society of Scotland*, 4th Series, XV, Edinburgh. pp 50-65

TAIT, James. 1884. The agriculture of the county of Stirling. *Transactions of The Highland and Agricultural Society of Scotland*, 4th Series, XV1, Edinburgh. pp 143-179

WANNOP, A.R. 1964. Scottish Agriculture. *Scottish Geographical Magazine*, 80, pp 90-98

WITHRINGTON, Donald J., and GRANT, Ian R. Editors. 1978. The Statistical Account of Scotland, IX, Dunbartonshire, Stirlingshire and   Clackmannanshire, 1790s. Reprint, Wakefield.

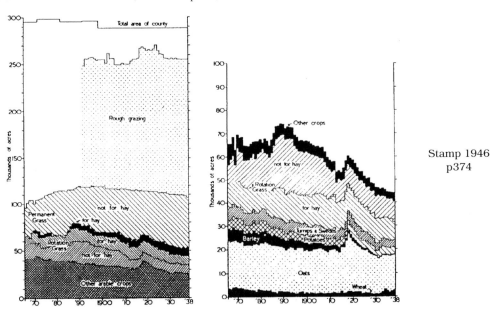

Stamp 1946
p374

Changes in Land Utilisation and in Chief Crops in Stirlingshire, 1866–1938.

Industry and Services

B. J. Elliott

The subject is surveyed in four sections - the three prominent industries, coal, iron and steel, and wool, then services professional and scientific.

COAL

The existence of coal and some of its valuable properties had been known in central Scotland since at least the 13th century. It was not a popular fuel with everyone because of supposed harmful properties, but it was easy to obtain at many open-cast or outcrop workings especially along the coasts. Since the Scottish coalfields ran roughly in a broad band from Ayrshire to Fife, with a detached portion south and east of Edinburgh, a substantial proportion of the coal measures dipped under the river estuaries or into the sea.

One important feature of these coal seams was the presence of embedded iron ore nodules which eventually led to the development of local metallurgical industries. As timber became scarcer, the need for the only available alternative fuel, coal, became pressing. The demands of growing cities such as Glasgow and of the newly established ironworks after 1760 required deeper pits to meet the demand. After 1780 as demand for coal further increased through the expansion of the steam-powered textile industries and later by the French wars, Scottish production rose towards 2 m tons per year. The price of coal at the pithead also began to rise, doubling between 1770 and 1790, by which time it averaged 12.5p per ton and reached 50p for some varieties during the inflationary Napoleonic Wars.

As early as 1760 at least one pit in Clackmannanshire had reached 90 m in depth and by the early 19th century the existence of seams at more than 255 m had been proved, with between nine and eleven workable seams down to 208 m. The thickest seams were about 2.75 m and the thinnest workable at a profit about 0.75, but severe faults along them broke up the field into distinct units. The inevitable result, however, of trying for greater depth was an increase in the number and intensity of technical problems encountered. The first of these, roof falls or wall collapses could be encountered during sinking or digging galleries in the seams. To support the roof vast quantities of coal were left behind as pillars. Digging was made easier, although bringing new dangers, when gunpowder began to be employed. However as the work proceeded away from the mouth of the shaft, the lack of fresh air, compounded by the existence of explosive or poisonous gases, often undetectable, could prove to be rapidly fatal. Fire damp found below 60 m was very explosive; black damp caused asphxiation while white damp (carbon monoxide) was the biggest killer of the three.

Such gas accumulations could lead at times to the abandonment of pits. Deeper pits meant also ever larger accumulations of water, which, while potentially less fatal than gas, required much greater inputs of labour and capital to alleviate or remove. These dangers, combined with the generally arduous, dirty and uncomfortable conditions of work encountered meant that the supply of labour was never abundant.

Another overwhelming factor which deterred potential recruits to the industry was the existence of bondage. Miners, on entering the service of a coalowner were, by an Act of 1601 of the Scottish Parliament, reaffirmed in 1661 and 1701, bound to work for him for the rest of their lives. If the pit was sold the workers were sold with it. The sons of miners were also bound, but as the system of working normally required all the family to work alongside the men in teams, this inheritance was accepted. Criminals and vagrants also could be sentenced, complete with iron collars, to life-long servitude in coalmines.

Thus under the conditions existing around this time, in particular the problems of ventilation, drainage and of labour supply, it was difficult to expand output. The first problem was tackled by the construction of a ventilation shaft with a fire to draw the air upwards causing an inrush of air down the main shaft. Later the invention of Buddles air pump in 1813 was able to circulate 200 cubic metres of air per minute. The Davy lamp from 1815 may have reduced the danger of fires and explosion but there was a serious one every nine days in the 1840s. The drainage problem, which could involve 4 m litres per day, was tackled first by bucket and winch, either man or horse powered, later by an endless chain of buckets, horse or water powered. At Carsebridge colliery in Clackmannanshire, the latter method was used to drain water from 75 m and Gartmorn Dam was constructed to supply the water power **(Figure 1)**. Finally beginning in the early 1760s in Scotland, steam powered beam engines were used.

The conditions attached to labour were so archaic that few Scots sought this work, possibly no more than 3,000 in 1700. Even when servitude was abolished by Acts of 1775 and 1799, the labour shortage continued as miners moved from pit to pit for higher wages whilst employers sought to impose seven and fourteen year contracts on pain of imprisonment. Irish immigrants were one important source of recruitment to substitute for the Scots. Not surprisingly given the above conditions and their physical isolation, miners were widely regarded as a 'race apart.' They enjoyed an unenviable reputation for unsocial behaviour. In Alloa before 1790 each miner had a free house and garden, subsidised flour and free coal, about 0.35 ton per week. They were paid piece rates, which varied with the quality of the seam they

Figure 1 The Great Wheel of the, 6th Earl of Mar, early 1700s; provided waterpower for mines and industries for 150 years. (Alloa Museum)

were working but could be from 7.5 to 25p per ton dug. Many preferred to work by night and the most energetic put in 12 hour shifts. Earnings ranged from 50 to 95p per week. Coal was carried to the surface up ladders - a usual maximum height then of 33 m - by bearers, mostly women related to the hewer. The strongest could manage nine tons per week during which they might walk 10 km, but when the pit became deeper than 33 m it became necessary to raise the coals by

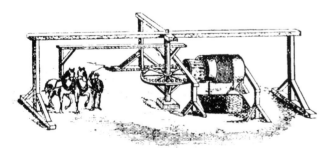

Figure 2 Horse-gin engine for raising coal; superceded the dreadful climbing ladders. (Bannerman, 1886)

mechanical means **(Figure 2)**. However women and children continued to be employed hauling coal to the bottom of the shaft, sometimes yoked to waggons on rails unless pit ponies were used.

In the parish of Clackmannan by the 1790s, three pits were in operation, producing 25,000 tons annually of which 7,000 was taken by the coastwise trade and some of the rest consumed by the newly established [1792] Devon Iron Works. By the 1830s a fourth pit, Gurtary, was in operation. In Alloa the coal industry was long established also, with an annual production of 50,000 tons, greatly so enhanced by the construction in 1766-74 of primitive tramways from the two main pits to the Forth. In Dollar 18 workers were employed in three small pits, but at Tillicoultry the Devon Iron Company had done little to develop production before the end of the century.

In Stirlingshire in the 1790s coal production was centered principally in the parishes of Campsie, where 46 miners dug out about 22,000 tons annually with a total value of £2,750; in Kilsyth where more than 100 pits had been dug since 1670 each employing eight to twelve miners by 1790; in Polmont where the Duke of Hamilton owned several mines and in St Ninians which had three mines, producing about 30,000 tons annually. Thus by 1800 1,000 miners were working in pits along the Forth raising 40,000 tons annually, of which 40% went to ironworks, 13% to distilleries and 6% to glassworks.

By 1854 Scottish coal production had reached about 7.5 m tons. The demand came principally from the rapidly expanding manufacturing industries such as metallurgy and textiles and from the steam-hauled rail network which grew particularly between 1836 and 1856. In addition the growing population in urban areas relied on coal for heat and light (coal gas). The canal network was important in the distibution of coal, as even more so were railways after 1842. This steadily increasing demand had also encouraged the technical innovations necessary to prospect to ever greater depths and to cut and bring up increasing amounts of coal. In the 1840s the centrifugal fan was invented although barely used in Scottish mines for 30 years; also developed was flat, later round, wire rope which enabled 600 tons of coal to be raised every 24 hours. Compressed air was first used for powered coal cutting in a Scottish mine in 1849, with the choice of the circular saw [1843] or the chain machine [1864]. Despite all these developments Scottish coal-getting remained essentially a pick and shovel activity until after the First World War. Electric lighting underground was first installed in a Scottish mine in 1881 and by 1913 more than 300 were wired up. Nevertheless mining remained an extremely dangerous and unhealthy job, with a British miner being killed every six hours and one seriously injured every two hours. Two major disasters took place in Stirlingshire in the late 19th century. In March 1878, 17 men were killed at Barwood no. 2 pit and 13 at Quarter mine in April 1895. In August 1912 22 were killed by an underground fire at Cadder no.15, owned

Figure 3 Miners of Coalsnaughton. (Alloa Museum)

Figure 4 Shotfiring curtain to protect from ricochets. (Alloa Museum)

by Carron Company. Death and injury rates did decline, however, during the 19th and 20th centuries as a result of improved technology and safety practices and regulations (**Figures 3 and 4**). Between 1851 and 1938 there were nine major mine disasters in Scotland in which 432 men were killed, almost half this total at Blantyre in 1877. The most important initiative of the early 1840s although by no means immediately effective, was the passing of the *Mines and Collieries Act* prohibiting the employment underground of all females and males under ten years of age. Further legislation in 1850, 1860, 1862, 1872, 1887, 1896 and 1910 restricted employment of children and improved safety standards, not least through the establishment of H M Inspectorate of Mines in 1850.

The Peak Years

During the 70 years between the first Mines Act and the First World War the Scottish coal industry expanded at a rapid rate, responding to the demands of manufacturing industry, steamships and railways,

domestic users and a buoyant export trade which, including sales to the rest of the UK, accounted for more than 27% of production by 1913. From 7.5 m tons in 1854, production rose to 17 m by the mid-1870s, of which Stirlingshire's 34 mines employing 2,000 men produced almost 1 m tons. One of these, Snab pit at Kinneil, had reached a depth of 365 m, an indication of the improved technology available by then. Scottish production continued to rise, to 30 m in 1898 and finally to an all-time record of 42.4 m in 1913. Considerably more than half of this was produced in the Central coalfield which included Stirlingshire's 3 m tons and one fifth in the Fife and Clackmannanshire fields. The latter's share of 0.4 m tons came almost entirely from the mines of the Alloa Coal Company. Productivity in Scotland also rose sharply during the 19th century, from 214 tons per man-year in 1831 to 392 tons by 1881. The latter figure was the highest of all the UK coalfields. With 353 tons per worker in 1910, Fife and Clackmannan was the most productive part of the Scottish coalfields, by which time the average annual production per mine in Scotland was 87,000 tons. Future prospects looked good with Stirlingshire's coal reserves to a depth of 1,200 m estimated in 1913 at 1.6 bn tons and Clackmannanshire's at 0.9 bn, out of a Scottish total of 21 bn.

The number of coalmines in Scotland also ncreased from 367 in 1854 to 542 in 1913. These new sinkings included Tillicoultry [1876], Cowie [1894], the Lower Polmaise complex at Millhall and Fallin [around 1904] and Brucefield [1905]. Of these 542 mines, 57% employed more than 100 workers, but only 13 [2.5%] employed more than 1,000, the average number of workers per mine being 272. By 1913 138,000 miners were employed, part of the 1 m in the UK. Of these, 11,354, including 7,043 coalface workers, were working in Stirlingshire mines and 1,322 in Clackmannanshire. Women workers had virtually disappeared from the industry with only two female employees in the latter county.

Probably the principal incentive to work in the industry was the high wage rate. In the second half of the century, despite the fall in prices between 1874 and 1896, coalface workers [UK average] doubled their wages from 96p to £1.93 per week and they gained another 12% to £2.16 by 1913. The 1900 figure was 11 % higher than for skilled engineering workers and almost 2.5 times higher than for agricultural workers. Despite their relatively high pay coalminers and their families often lived in very poor company-owned housing, lacking in basic amenities and frequently overcrowded. If they left they became homeless.

Coalmining was both capital and labour-intensive. Heavy capital investment, totalling £200 m for the UK by 1913 [equivalent to £10 bn in 1990], had been necessary to establish the industry at its peak output. Wages represented 70% of colliery running costs. To meet these charges coalowners had to sell into a market where prices often fluctuated considerably. For example prices increased by 2.67 times between 1863 and 1873, but fell back to the 1863 levels by 1886-7. They remained depressed until 1900 but by 1913 they were twice the 1886 levels. By 1913 the average price of a ton of Scottish coal at the pithead was 48p [equivalent to £24 in 1990]. Nevertheless the sustained expansion of sales meant that coalmining was overall a very profitable industry in 1913, producing a total gross profit for its UK owners of about £20 m in 1913. More than one quarter of this profit represented royalty payments to the landowners under whose land the coal was situated.

The First World War and the Depression years

Since 1913 all UK coalfields have declined in size, total production and employment, whilst productivity and safety records generally improved. The First World War disrupted the industry badly. It took away many export markets, whilst tens of thousands of miners joined the Army. During the hostilities the government encouraged maximum production but this proved very difficult; by 1920, despite the inflation of the Scottish workforce to almost 148,000, production had declined to 31.5 m tons, a fall of 26 % since 1913. Despite the increase in the average price of coal to £1.73 per ton in 1920, the industry was making massive losses. Production in Stirlingshire, at 2.38 m was down 23% , whilst Clackmannanshire could achieve only 0.32 m tons in 1920. During the next two decades, as a result of the decline in demand for coal in both the UK and world markets, the industry went through a period of prolonged depression, losing money throughout the 1920s, the basic cause of the long dispute in 1926. Between the Wars total production in Scotland remained around 30 m tons, helped by a quota system after 1930. The old Central or Lanark coalfield continued to decline. By 1938 Stirlingshire's mines raised only 1.33 m tons, a decline of 56% since 1913.

In Clackmannanshire by contrast, production in 1937 at 0.54 m had risen 68% since 1920. This latter statistic reflected the eastward movement of the Scottish industry towards the perceived massive reserves north of the Forth. Despite this latter trend, by 1935 the number of coalmines in Scotland had declined by 178 to 364, a fall of 33% since 1913, whilst the workforce had fallen to less than 82,000 in 1933, a decline of 45% since 1920. The latter trend created very high levels of unemployment especially in small isolated communities which lost their only mine. Furthermore earnings had declined as coal prices fell. From a Scottish average weekly wage of £4.75 in 1920, coalminers earnings dropped to £2.51 in 1933, increasing to £2.80 by 1938.

The result of the decline in the workforce combined with stable production through both quotas and increased mechanisation was a remarkable increase in productivity from 214 tons per man in 1920 to 379 in 1935. This was higher than the UK average, but the price per ton conversely had fallen from £1.73 to 64p over the same period. The depression between the wars did not, however, stop all new initiatives. For example in Clackmannanshire Meta pit opened in 1923 - a boom year- and King O'Muirs in 1938, whilst in Stirlingshire, Plean opened in 1930, following an accident there at the former pit in 1922 in which 12 men were killed. The other major disaster in the county was at Redding no.23 in September 1923 when an inrush of water killed 40 miners. The small Pirnhall mine opened in 1933.

The Second World War, Nationalisation and Decline

The surplus of coal and of coalminers existing before 1939 persuaded the government that there would be no problem in expanding the industry to meet the demands of war. The underlying situation however was poor; young miners were enlisting in the forces; older coal faces were becoming exhausted; the necessary capital investment in the mines was not taking place because of shortages of men, money and engineering capacity; industrial relations remained poisonous and even deteriorated. The labour shortage eventually impelled the government to conscript workers [Bevin boys]. Yet pay increases failed to equal those in other industries and there were several strikes in Scotland between 1940 and 1945 with a total of more than 300,000 working days lost. The result was that, even though 40 more mines were operating than in 1935, including Craigie [1942] and Dollar [1943] in

Table 1 **Stirlingshire coal mines, nationalised 1947**

	No of employees	Annual tonnage
Bannockburn	487	153,000
Barleyside	23	4,000
Carriden	293	48,000
Herbertshire	390	87,000
Kinneil	570	200,000
Manor Powis	420	162,000
Pirnhall	110	37,000
Plean	417	93,000
Policy	150	50,000
Polmaise nos 1 and 2	556	146,000
Polmaise nos 3 and 4	500	176,000
Redding	265	72,000
S. Bantaskine	52	20,000
Drumbeck	451	190,000
Gartshore nos 9 and 11	644	190,000
Gartshore nos 3 and 12	611	140,000
Twechar no.1	365	100,000
TOTALS	6304	1,868,000

Table 2 Clackmannanshire mines nationalised 1947

	No. of Employees	Annual Tonnage
Brucefield	182	67,100
Craigie	155	38,900
Devon	469	244,000
Dollar	71	26,700
King o' Muirs	37	23,100
Melloch/Tillicoultry	124	8,500
Meta	122	46,100
Zetland	78	24,000
TOTALS	1238	479.400

Clackmannanshire, output fell throughout the war. From 30.5 m tons for Scotland in 1939 it declined to 26 in 1942 and 21 in 1945. The election of a Labour government in 1945, committed to nationalisation and investment seemed to promise a brighter future for the UK industry. At the time of nationalisation in 1947 Scottish coal production 22.87 m tons had barely begun to recover from its 1945 trough. There were 275 mines owned by 120 companies, but only 196 were nationalised. The 79 small mines left in private hands were licenced by the National Coal Board [NCB]. £21.87 m was paid in compensation to the former owners of the 196 nationalised mines in Scotland. These included

seventeen in Stirlingshire and eight in Clackmannanshire (**Tables 1 and 2**).

Within the NCB there were five Scottish areas, of which Stirlingshire was in Central West. In 1951 the new Alloa area was formed partly from the latter and partly from Fife and Clackmannan. This increased the number of areas eventually to eight, reflecting the strong optimism in Scotland for an expanded industry of 30 m tons by 1960. This latter target was to be met by a major reconstruction programme, costing £100 m and the largest project ever in the history of Scottish coal. It involved the closure of 144 uneconomic mines, the reconstruction of 39 others, 60 new or reconstructed drift mines and fifteen new sinkings. It was based around a Scottish workforce which by 1951 had fallen to 78,000, a decline of 47% from its 1920 peak. Of these 4,959 lived in Stirlingshire and 1,724 in Clackmannanshire.

The most ambitious part of the reconstruction programme, the new sinkings, involving the working of the very deep limestone measures, would add more than 8 m tons per year to production. One of these new sinkings was at Glenochil which, it was believed, would produce 3.000 tons per day for 50 years. Unfortunately the Clackmannanshire reserves were not carefully checked by geologists nor were local mining engineers consulted! The main local concern was that subsidence would cause flooding of more than 250 ha of agricultural land close to Alva. The geological situation at Glenochil was far worse than could have been imagined in 1948 when the project was first proposed. There were in fact few reserves left after many decades of undocumented extraction by private owners and by 1959 these reserves had been officially reduced from 35 to 15 m tons. In 1962 Glenochil was closed after making heavy losses; the new sinking at Airth was abandoned even before the shaft was sunk!

However other new local projects were underway. In Clackmannanshire Forthbank mine opened in 1950, King o' Muirs no.2 in 1951, Manor Mine in 1954, Harvieston 1955 and Dollar 1956. Closures followed in even greater numbers. Tillycoultry no.1 and Melloch went in 1948, Craigie in 1952, King o' Muirs no.1 and Dollar nos 1 and 2 in 1954, King o' Muirs no.2 in 1957, Forthbank in 1958, Tillycoultry no.2 and Meta in 1959, Devon and Zetland in 1960, Harviestoun in 1961, Brucefield in 1962 and Dollar [new] in 1973. Four private mines also closed at Gartmorn in 1962, Gartenkeir in 1968, Grasmainstoun in 1982 and Devon mine in 1987. In Stirlingshire Barleyside went in 1949, and in 1958-9 Herbertshire, Policy, Redding, South Bantaskine and Polmaise nos 1 and 2 were closed, to be followed in 1962-3 by Pirnhall, Plean and Drumbreck nos 1 and 2. This left only Manor Powis, Bannockburn and Polmaise nos 1 and 2.

The situation was no better in the rest of the Scottish coalfields. By the 1950s Scottish mines were losing large sums of money because costs were higher and productivity lower than in the rest of the UK. The reconstruction programme was well behind schedule and by 1960 the 30 m tons per year target had been abandoned as hydro-electric power and cheap oil imports cut into the supremacy of coal. Nuclear power was being developed and North Sea gas was also imminent. By 1976-7 as the first North Sea oil was coming ashore, only 20 Scottish coal mines were still in operation. By the early 1990s only the Longannet complex on the Clackmannan and Fife border was left mining deep coal in Scotland and even this was said to be threatened. In 1991-2 it produced more than 2.1 m tons with a workforce of 1,352 men, average wage [UK] £350 per week. In addition 4 m tons per annum was being produced at various Scottish open cast sites.

IRON AND STEEL

Central Scotland was the birthplace of the Scottish iron industry through the establishment of the Carron works near Falkirk in 1759. Attempts to found an iron industry in the Highlands at Invergarry in 1727 by taking advantage of the cheap local charcoal were unfortunately offset by a poor quality product and the venture collapsed in less than a decade. A furnace at Bonawe was more successful, remaining in production from 1753 until 1874. The first attempt to use Scottish ores, at Abernethy in 1730, collapsed within ten years.

Carron, founded by William Cadell, Samuel Garbett and Dr John Roebuck, was in a totally different category to these. It was much larger and within two years of its foundation it had a workforce of more than 600. It was designed to use coke as well as charcoal for smelting. The abundance of local ore supplies together with its proximity to the river Forth, a transport facility soon to be supplemented by the Forth and Clyde canal, meant that it was able to plan large-scale production with four blast and four air furnaces, three forges, a boring mill and a rolling mill. It soon became the foremost such establishment in Europe, expanding by 1790 to five blast, three cupola and 16 air furnaces, four boring mills, a claymill for making fire bricks, and a steam engine consuming 16 tons of coal per day. Many of its operations remained water-powered until well into the 19th century and a large dam was built behind the works to ensure a suitable supply. By 1790, the works were employing 1,000 men and using 120 tons of coal daily.

In its early years Carron faced many problems, noteably an inadequate water supply; a shortage of suitable labour especially for the coal pits before 1775; poor transport; and an excess of visitors. The technical side of production also had its difficulties, despite the inspired work of Roebuck. Amongst the most serious was the failure to adopt Henry Cort's puddling process invented in 1784, which facilitated the efficient large-scale conversion of pig-iron into wrought iron. It was to be 50 years before the process was established in Scotland. Technical problems were exacerbated by a lack of skilled and conscientious workers and often

abrasive relationships with those the company did employ.

Carron manufactured a wide variety of products but came to specialize in five categories. These were steam engine components for which demand rose rapidly from the 1780s, cast iron pipes for the supply of water, stoves and grates, and armaments. In 1761 Carron had also begun to manufacture nails, an industry already established at Bannockburn, but this proved unprofitable and was abandoned within a few years. The manufacture of cannon was also initially unsuccessful, principally because of a lack of skilled workers. In 1773 the Board of Ordnance struck the company off its list of suppliers. Despite this the company persisted and by 1778 had produced the carronade, a lighter gun which soon proved its worth to British merchantmen and privateers. A year later the Admiralty began to place large orders and carronades continued in use until the end of the Napoleonic Wars after which they became obsolete. Carron eventually ceased to manufacture ordnance in 1852. By 1842 it had 1,375 employees, including 250 in company-owned mines and on a twelve hour day. It was producing 8,000 tons of pig-iron annually, five times greater than in 1790 and owned a fleet of nine ships, six trading with London and three with Liverpool.

Despite the success of Carron, the iron industry in Scotland remained a relatively minor part of the economy until 1830. By 1800 Scotland had 10 ironworks, producing a total of 23,000 tons. Seven were in the West of Scotland and had been established between 1788 and 1796. In Clackmannanshire, the Devon Ironworks was established in 1792, largely at the instigation of John Roebuck. It was situated 4km northeast of Alloa on the river Devon and designed to use the local coal and iron-ore. By the time it was sold in 1856 its three blast furnaces were producing 6,000 tons of iron annually, largely converted into iron products in its own foundry. It ceased production two years later. In Stirlingshire, a second ironworks had been established at Falkirk in 1819. Its founders led by John Hardy, were former Carron employees, who specialised in ornamental products. By 1840 Falkirk iron works were employing 500 workers; they were taken over by R.W. Kennard in 1849 and during the Crimean War produced 16,000 tons of ordnance including a wide variety of cannon.

Expansion

After 1830 the growth of the shipbuilding industry and railways heralded the onset of a long period of expansion for the iron, and later the steel, industries. For example the Falkirk ironworks began specialising in plates and castings for the construction of bridges, such as the Solway railway viaduct. This increased demand for iron coincided with the development of the blackband seams of ironstone in Lanarkshire and with the invention in 1828 of the highly fuel-economic hot-blast system of blowing furnaces. At the same time the substitution of raw coal for coke in the smelting process reduced even further the costs of production. Scottish iron production rose from 37,400 tons from 27 furnaces in 1830 to 1.2 m tons from 122 blast furnaces in 1870. By the latter date Scotland was producing 25% of UK total of iron. However with the exhaustion of the blackband seams, Scottish ore production fell from 2.2 m tons in the 1870s to less than 600,000 by 1913. Scottish ironmasters had to begin importing ore from Cleveland in north-east England, which, by 1873, was already exceeding Scottish output of pig-iron and at lower prices. By 1913 the amount of imported ores was three times greater than that produced in Scotland.

In Stirlingshire the boom in iron production also accelerated rapidly; between 1854 and 1877 no less than nineteen new works were started. Excluding Carron, with 2,500 workers and Falkirk ironworks with 900, the largest was the Bonnybridge foundry established in 1860 which employed 400, and the smallest, the Bonnybridge Malleable Iron Works, established in 1877, which employed a mere eight. By 1877 the Stirlingshire iron industry employed 6,058, earning from 75p per week to an average £1.42 for blast furnacemen, who were the best paid of any group of industrial workers. By comparison the iron industry in Clackmannanshire remained small; in 1891 its seven foundries employed just 78 men, out of a total Scottish workforce of 68,040. This period of expansion after 1830 saw Carron's profits peak at more than £100,000 in 1872 and was marked by the completion of its new blast furnaces in 1874 (**Figure 5**).

At this point the boom came to an end, due to falling demand and increased competition, particularly from Welsh and Cleveland producers at home and from Germans and Americans abroad. Prices fell sharply. At Carron pig iron production fell from more than 41,000 tons in 1878 to less than 30,000 the following year. Dividend payments fell from more than 25% in the mid-1870s to less than 8% in the early 1890s. In 1887 the company recorded its first half-year loss [£2,000] for more than a century and in in 1891 losses totalled almost £13,000. Partly because of a major reconstruction programme between 1876 and 1880, paid for out of current profits and reserves, Carron was able to weather the depression better than many. Despite this, recovery did not come fully until after 1905 and even this was not continuous. Nevertheless by 1913 Carron enterprises were producing 684,000 tons of coal, 60,000 tons of coke and 150,000 tons of iron ore, the last figure representing 25 per cent of Scottish output. In the years before the First World War, Carron was particularly successful in selling specialised products (**Figure 6**) such as pipes, baths, kitchen stoves and grates, the export sales of which totalled £83,000 in 1913, [equal to £4.15 min 1990]. On the other hand its production of pig-iron, which had reached 90,000 tons in 1907, declined to 62,000 six years later.

The most important change which came about

Figure 5 Carron blast furnaces. (J. Hume)

in the iron and steel industry in the second half of the 19th century was the mass production of steel. This was made possible by the development of the Bessemer converter [1856], the Siemens-Martin open hearth furnace [1867] and the Gilchrist-Thomas basic process after 1878. The last of these enabled Scotland's highly phosphoric ores to be used. Between 1873 and 1913 Scottish steel production rose from 1,200 to 1.4 m tons,

Figure 6 Carron High foundry - from the presentation catalogue to the retiring manager, John Frew in 1899. (Falkirk Museum)

the latter figure being 18% of the UK total. The industry became established in the west of Scotland where it could meet the demands of the booming Clydeside shipbuilding industry. In particular the Steel Company of Scotland, founded in 1872 and based at Cambuslang, became the dominant manufacturer producing more than 1 m tons annually by 1900.

Essentially steel was a replacement for malleable iron and it was the producers of this who moved into steel production. By contrast neither Carron (**Figure 7**) nor any other pig-iron producer in Stirlingshire showed much interest in moving into large-scale steel manufacture. Thus in 1891 only nine men in the county were recorded in the Census as steelmakers and by 1911 this figure had risen to only 83, plus one in Clackmannanshire, although earnings of adult male steelworkers at £1.85 per week [1907], were the highest average for all industries.

War

The First World War had a dynamic effect on the metallurgical and engineering industries of most countries, including Scotland, as armament industries, notably Clydeside warship building, expanded rapidly. The most important change was in increased steel production which overtook pig iron in total tonnage for the first time, with UK steel production rising to 12 m tons. With a 38% increase during the war, Scottish producers were to the forefront of this expansion. By contrast Scottish pig iron declined by more than 26% during the war years. The Carron company, like other engineering manufactures played its part in Britain's war effort. It provided more than £1 m worth of products for government departments and a £1.3 m worth of goods for the Ministry of Munitions. The Falkirk Iron Co. was also involved in large munitions contracts.

As in the case of the coal industry, iron and steel suffered very heavily from the effects of the inter-war depression, particularly from the collapse of shipbuilding in which unemployment reached 76% in 1932. After the initial postwar restocking boom, demand for iron and steel slumped and producers found

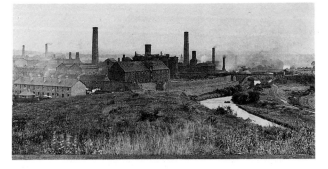

Figure 7   Carron Works - West Carron.   (Falkirk Museum)

themselves with an excess capacity of small, inefficient works with high costs. Not only did Scotland lack integrated steel works, but existing businesses suffered also from wage inflation and initially from expensive raw materials. The collapse of iron ore mining in Scotland from 600,000 tons per year in 1913 to 25,000 in 1929 was particularly devastating. In addition Scotland lacked good coking coal and henceforth had to rely on costlier imports. The inevitable result was rationalisation, cost-cutting innovations, closures and redundancies. Total employment in the Scottish heavy metal trades fell from more than 230,000 in 1907 to 194,000 in 1924. By 1930 employment in the Scottish iron and steel industries had fallen to 35% of its 1913 level. By 1937 only five pig iron producers were left in Scotland and only sixteen furnaces were still in blast, producing around 400,000 tons per annum.

At the onset of the world depression in the late 1920s, Stirlingshire was still an important centre for light castings with about 30 foundries employing 7500 workers and producing, annually about 50,000 tons. Alloa, which remained an important general engineering centre, employed most of the 1,039 workers in this sector of industry in Clackmannanshire in 1931.

The Carron company survived this period quite well. This was because of the growth, especially in the 1930s, of housebuilding, for which so many of Carron's products were manufactured. Thus, even in 1931 Carron was employing more than 4,200 people, 60% more than in 1831, at an average weekly wage of £2.77.

The outbreak of the Second World War meant a greatly increased demand for metallurgical products. The impact was not immediate, but by 1945 employment in the traditional heavy industries in Scotland had increased by 55% since 1939. Pig iron production peaked early at almost 660,000 tons in 1940, an increase of 65% over the 1930s, whilst steel production increased by around 33% to almost 2 m tons a year during the war. Meanwhile unemployment was greatly reduced, helped partly by the opening of new industrial plant in central Scotland. In 1942, for example, part of the Carron works was transformed into a steel works, with electric furnaces which produced millions of manganese steel track links. A new aluminium works was also built in Falkirk. By 1940 the Carron works was already operating a twelve hour day, seven days a week to meet the demands of the armed forces. During the war 92,000 slow combustion stoves, 7,000 double ovens and 21,000 portable boilers were manufactured. Of crucial importance to the war effort were its alloy steel forgings produced for the aircraft industry and, from 1942, the manufacture of sidelights for Royal Naval warships.

Decline

The return of peace with the enormous physical destruction in Germany, France and elsewhere left Britain as the major industrial power in Europe, facing an almost unlimited demand for her manufactured products, both at home and abroad. All sectors of the iron, steel and engineering industries were fully employed meeting this demand. By 1950 almost 360,000 were employed in the metal and engineering trades in Scotland. The output of steel by a workforce of 52,440 men and 4,000 women had risen to an all time record of 2.4 m tons, of which 40% was exported.

Central Scotland shared in this prosperity and Stirlingshire was still an important centre of iron founding, in which 9,491 men and 1,631 women were employed in 1951. In Clackmannanshire while there were only 100 foundry workers, including two women, general engineering had expanded to 1,349 employees, an increase of 30% since 1931. Amongst the goods manufactured there, were electrical products, agricultural machinery and products for the brewing and coal industries. The Falkirk area remained a major producer of both engineering and domestic castings such as pipes, and heating and sanitary appliances. Unfortunately in its heavy reliance on the latter products, many of which were beginning to be made of substitute materials such as plastics and stainless steel, the industry was fostering the seeds of its own decline. The installation of modern kitchens and central heating combined with a loss of orders from the armed forces and the civil service all reduced demand for Falkirk's traditional products. Additionally the local industries appear to have been slow to respond to the changing demands of expanding industries such as automobile manufacturing, which had to buy outwith Scotland. The result was that in the Falkirk area alone more than 3,500 jobs were lost, a decline of 32%, between 1951 and 1964.

A second great decline came with the economic recession of the early 1980s. Large swathes of British industry, especially in the metal trades, were devastated, including the Carron company which went into receivership in 1982. By the early 1990s, at the time of yet another recession, the iron founding industry had shrunk considerably, In the UK only 800 foundries were still in operation. The great majority of these very small with outputs of less than £1 m per annum, and an average return on capital was only 4% per annum. In 1989 about 25% were actually returning a loss. Less than 50 of these foundries were in Scotland, of which thirteen were in Central Region, all in the Falkirk-Larbert-Bonnybridge area. Total employment in the foundry industry in Central Region had declined to 1,250 with 80% of this workforce concentrated in four major plants. Jones and Campbell, producers of high precision castings for the automotive industry had 400 employees. The others were Grahamston Iron, Taylors and Brookes & Co. There were also five medium sized firms four specialising in street and garden furniture, and one, Drysdales of Stenhousemuir, the last non-ferrous foundry left in the region. All these firms continued to make a useful contribution to the local economy, both in terms of the employment they provide and the wealth they produce.

WOOL

Although the cotton industry is synonymous with the industrial revolution in Britain, the major textile industry in central Scotland has long been wool - not surprisingly, given the Scottish climate. In particular, Stirling and Clackmannanshire became and remained, after the Border counties, the second most important part of Scotland for the trade in raw wool and woollen manufactures. By contrast out of 192 cotton factories working in Scotland in 1838, only three were in Stirlingshire. The pre-eminence of the Borders dates back to the 13th century and the establishment of the great abbeys, which reared sheep by the thousand and exported their wool to Flanders, France and Italy. The origin of the wool trade in central Scotland is less clear, except that it is known to pre-date considerably the union of crowns in 1603, certainly by some hundreds of years.

By the early 18th century the region was well established as a centre of manufacture for shalloons, serges, plaidings, blankets and other woollen products. At this stage, however, the efficiency of the industry was reduced by two factors. First the poor quality of the region's traditional Highland sheep made it necessary to import better quality wool, usually from England and Spain. The second factor inhibiting growth and improvements in productivity was the reliance on primitive technology. Before the introduction of water-power in the late 18th century, the woollen industry in the region here was still entirely domestic in structure, spinning and weaving being carried out within the household.

In 1776, there were in Stirling 160 domestic looms, 38 stocking frames and 17 carpet frames, the last figure doubling by the early 1790s, and using largely the wool of the Blackface sheep. The other products were shalloons, serges and Highland plaids, although the last declined after 1760. In the west at Killearn, there were 28 weavers and one renowned dyer and cloth dresser. In Alloa by the 1790s there were twenty employers with a total workforce of 500, using about 150 looms to manufacture light cloths known as camblets. It was not until 1813, with the opening of the Kilncraigs mill, and employing 80 workers, that John Paton brought the textile factory age to the town.

Along the Hillfoots, Alva and Tillicoultry were the principal centres of the industry. The manufacture of Scots blankets and serges had been established in Alva since the 17th century. Despite the high reputation for quality enjoyed by Tillicoultry serges, the industry had begun to decline in the late 18th century. Some Tillicoultry workers moved to Alva, where by 1790 about 67 domestic looms were in operation. Material finished in Alva sold, depending on quality, at between 4p and 9p per yard producing an total annual income for the parish of more than £6,000.

Mills

The decline of Tillicoultry was reversed by the construction of mills, all initially water-powered. The first was Thomas Harrower's mill in Tillicoultry Glen in 1796, followed by the Christie brothers' first wool-spinning mill in 1799, with a second mill a few years later. In 1806-7 two of the three Archibald brothers, who had built Menstrie's first mill in 1800, returned to Tillicoultry to build a third mill in the town. By about 1815 mechanisation, in the form of spinning and carding machines, was being introduced using water power. In 1824 the sons of John Paton opened what was to become the Hillfoots' most famous woollen mill and commenced the manufacture of tartans to add to the staple products of blankets and plaidings. Overall the basic success and lengthy survival of Clackmannanshire's mills was to come from specialising in women's fashions. This success led to the opening of more mills, and there were by 1840 eight in Tillicoultry employing 300 men, 120 women and 140 children. In addition there were an equal number of domestic workers, especially handloom weavers who, despite the rapid increase in the number of power looms after 1850 were not generally superseded until after 1860. As late as 1874 there were still 365 handloom weavers employed in Tillicoultry and Devonside.

The first woollen mill opened in Alva in 1798. More followed and the population of the parish almost doubled to 2,216 between 1821 and 1841, by which date eight mills were in operation. Ninety looms consumed 220,000 kg of wool annually, at a cost of between 11 and 16p per kg. The total workforce in Alva was 565 of whom 149 men, 50 women and 81 children worked in the mills and 89 men, 175 women and 21 children were employed in the domestic industry, which operated 80 handlooms (**Figure 8**). In 1826 following the example of Tillicoultry, tartan shawls were added to Alva's products, followed by cashmeres in 1832. A similar expansion took place in Alloa and, by 1840, following the rebuilding of Patons after a fire, there were six mills operating in the town, four being steam-powered. They employed 190 men, 72 women and 89 children and were converting 220,000 kg of raw wool annually into manufactured "yarns, plaiding, shawls, tartans, druggets, blankets and cloths of various descriptions", with a total annual value of £71,000, about £4 m in 1990 prices.

In 1840 the woollen industry in Stirling was continuing to rely heavily upon domestic workers. Although there were three spinning mills, employing 140 on a 64 hour week, there were also about 650 outworkers with 280 looms producing increasing quantities of tartans and shawls, as the carpet sector declined. In 1831 outputs had been assessed at £90,000 and £23,000 respectively and yarns at £9,000. Apart from carpets, these figures would have increased considerably after that date because the industry was then at the beginning of a period of sustained expansion, due to increased home and overseas demand for what

Figure 8 Handloom weaver at work, Mr Johnston of March Glen Tillicoultry, in the 1920s. (Alloa Museum)

were seen as high quality products.

By 1838, the region had a very large and expanding sector of the Scottish woollen industry, which then employed 5,076 in 112 mills. Of the latter seven were in Stirlingshire and 24 were in Clackmannanshire, the largest number in any Scottish county, although those in Roxburghshire employed more horsepower. By 1850, as a result of further expansion, 45 woollen mills, or 25% of the Scottish total, were in production along the Hillfoots, employing almost 3,700, or about one-third of the Scottish total, mostly on a 64-hour week. By 1856 Scotland's 204 woollen factories, utilising 3,260 horsepower on 800 powerlooms, employed more than 10,000 workers, but this number was dwarfed by the 34,700 cotton workers who had almost 10,000 horsepower harnessed to 21,624 powerlooms in only 152 factories. Clearly cotton was a much larger-scale.

Tillicoultry was a particularly successful woollen centre, with a six-fold increase in population between 1793 and 1861, when it had reached 5,054 persons. Within the parish, in the 1860s, twelve of the twenty buildings identified as 19th century woollen mills by Park [1979], were then operating. All were powered either by water or steam, some by both, although there were more handlooms [340] than power-looms [240] at that time. The 1860s workforce of 2,000 represented more than 40% of Tillicoultry's population. Their main product, manufactured from imported wools had been tartans, until a decline in their popularity in the early 1850s led to a slump. The firm of J.Paton reacted to this

Figure 9 Rockville spinning mill, Stirling about 1900. (Industry in Stirling 1903)

Figure 10 In a Clackmannanshire mill. (Alloa Museum)

by the installation of new machinery, powered by steam, in new buildings to produce tweeds, a trend followed also by the two large mills of the Archibald family. By 1860 Patons had become, one of the largest manufacturing establishments in Scotland, employing a workforce of about 1,000, on a reported average weekly wage of less than 50p. Paton's success was also helped by the receipt of royal patronage. In addition there were nine small handloom weaving establishments in Tillicoultry employing about 180, who made shawls and napkins. By 1861 Alva had nine spinning mills employing 220 and 1,300 others were employed weaving and finishing shawls, plaids and other items, in such places as the towering East Boll [Strude] mill, which had opened in 1847 and was reputed to house 365 looms.

Along the Hillfoots the total number of mills declined between 1850 and 1871 from 45 to 33 as a result of rationalisation, but output and productivity increased greatly due to various technical innovations. The latter trends were demonstrated by the increases in these 20 years; the number of spindles doubled to 143,500; power looms increased from 38 to 715 and workers rose by 500 to 4,123. Despite the overall decline in the number of Hillfoots mills, new ones were constructed. A noteworthy development, in 1862, was the establishment of the firm of Donaldsons in Alva, out of which grew the Donbros Co. Two years later a large, modern mill, called Elmbank, was opened at Menstrie, where in 1833, the Hillfoots' first steam powered machinery had been installed in the only other mill to have been built there in the previous 60 years. In 1888 Beveridge would describe Menstrie as a "thriving manufacturing village". A large new spinning mill also opened in Clackmannan in 1876, at a cost of £1,500, employing workers at between 4p and 15p per day. The

expansion of output continued also in Alloa. By the late 1860s, according to Bremner, the quantity of wool used in the town's six mills had risen to 1.5 m kg annually, with an output valued at £230,000. By 1871, the workforce had increased to 1,000, of whom about half were employed by Patons. At that time there were also four major woollen mills in the Stirling district. Forthvale mill employed 65 workers to spin imported wools. A further 700 were employed at two Bannockburn mills, both confusingly called Wilsons, one of which produced carpets, and the other tweeds, tartans and carpets. The largest mill, Parkvale and Hayford, near Cambusbarron, had 530 power looms and employed 950, producing high quality women's fashions. The organisation of this mill, in putting all operations, spinning, weaving and dyeing under one roof, exemplified the principal trend in the rationalisation of the industry which occurred mostly between 1855 and 1890. Although separate spinning and weaving mills still outnumbered integrated ones in Scotland by 1890, 62% of woollen workers were employed in the latter type.

Depression

Stimulated latterly by the Franco-Prussian War, the industry continued its uneven expansiom until 1872, when UK exports of woollen goods reached a pre-1914 record of £32 m. This was followed by a general economic depression which, for the woollen industry, lasted spasmodically from the mid-1870s until the early 1900s. It was less severe, initially, in certain major sectors of the Scottish industry than elsewhere in the UK. As demonstrated by the success of Patons of Tillicoultry in winning a gold medal at the 1851 Great Exhibition, this was principally because of the excellent reputation for design and quality which Scottish woollen products enjoyed [in particular knitwear and tweeds].

Nevertheless in the 10 years following 1874, the peak year for employment, more than 4,800 jobs, in the Scottish worsted industry, or 47% of the total, were lost permanently. Many of these losses were in the Glasgow and Stirling areas, the latter eventually losing everything except carpet-making. Clackmannanshire was also affected, with Tillicoultry suffering physical damage, from the disastrous flood of August 1877, and then unable to cope with the trough in trade in 1879. There were fewer losses of jobs in the other sectors because of improved sales in the 1880s, which, in 1888 encouraged the Donaldsons to move to Hall Park in Sauchie, where they installed steam-powered machinery, such as Jacquard looms. Recovery culminated in 1889 when exports of woollen goods from the UK reached their highest level for 15 years.

In 1890, following the imposition of a 50% *ad valorem* tariff on imported woollen goods by the USA, the industry entered a further twelve years of recession. Overall during the 1890s the proportion of British woollen exports going to the USA fell from 25 to 9%. France compounded this situation by increasing its tariff in 1892, with the result that unemployment soon became a serious problem amongst woollen workers in both Stirlingshire and Clackmannanshire. The industry began to recover after the turn of the century (**Figure 9**) profiting, in particular, from export-led demand in 1910-1912. At a local level this profitable boom was reflected in the plant extensions and other capital investments, totalling £60,000 or £3 m at 1990 prices, made between 1903-1908, by Patons in Alloa. Profits were increased by low wages which given the preponderance of females workers at an average of less than £1.00 a week, were well below those in the coal and metallurgical industries. The impact of both unstable trading conditions and improvements in technology and productivity is shown by the fall in employment amongst woollen workers in Clackmannanshire, from 4,549 in 1891 to 3,930 in 1911, one third of whom were employed in Paton's Keilersbrae mill in Alloa and of whom more than 60% were female. On the other hand Clackmannan's share of Scotland's woollen workers rose from 11 to 14% between 1891 and 1911. By 1911 the number in Clackmannanshire was second only to the county of Selkirk's 5,736. Overall the industry in Clackmannanshire gave employment to about 50% of all gainfully occupied females and 33% of males. By contrast, between 1891 and 1911 the number of woollen workers in Stirlingshire, fell from 621 women and 448 men to only 117 females and 57 males, a decline of 84%. The industry in the smaller county survived the depression better than its larger neighbour, presumably by meeting more effectively the demands of the market in product, quality and price. Indeed, according to Day, there were still twelve woollen mills in Tillicoultry in 1914, the same as in the 1860s (**Figure 10**).

As with most other British industries, the First World War created full order books for woollen mills, and for a couple of years afterwards as the population restocked its wardrobes. The largest firms, Patons of Alloa, and its namesake in Tillicoultry, were engaged almost entirely on govenment contracts, supplying cloth for uniforms for millions of the armed forces. To meet their contracts, at a time when younger male workers were flocking into the army, the mills had to reemploy retired workers in addition to even more women.

Decline

In 1920, following the collapse of the post-war boom, the wool trade, in company with Scotland's other more traditional industries, suffered severely. Although less dependent than cotton on exports, the loss of many markets resulted in short-time working and unemployment, which exceeded 36% in the UK woollen industry in 1931. In Clackmannanshire the Tillicoultry mills of R.Archibald and Co. closed in 1930. The Oak mill of James Templeton also in Tillicoultry closed early in 1931, following the concentration of manufacturing at the firm's Stirling mill. By this date the latter was, apart from three carpet factories, Stirling's sole surviving woollen manufacturer. Patons of Tillicoultry barely survived, partly by switching some production to more profitable knitwear, a line introduced into the burgh in 1922 by John Hewitt, formerly of Innerleithen. The impact of the depression was partly responsible for the decline in Tillicoultry's population to less than 3,000 by 1931, compared with more than 5,500, seventy years earlier. In Alloa the principal change came in April 1920 with the amalgamation of Patons, then employing 1,700 in three large factories, with the Halifax firm of J. and J. Baldwin and partners, to form Paton and Baldwins, capitalised at £3.2 m and specialising in knitting wools. The various extensions and other improvements to the new combine's Alloa properties, carried out in 1924, 1928, 1931 and 1935 showed this to be a successful enterprise.

Perhaps the most important assistance to the industry came in 1932, with the imposition of a 20% tariff on manufactured imports. This immediately reduced imports of finished woollen cloth by 85% and probably saved a number of mills from closure. By 1937, as Britain had passed the worst of the depression, unemployment in the woollen and worsted industries had declined to 10%. Tillicoultry's employment situation was helped by the arrival of a Jaeger Company subsidiary in September 1939, providing 90 jobs, although it proved a temporary operation.

By 1951, despite the stimulus of wartime and post-war demand, the number of workers in the Scottish woollen industries continued to decline, to less than 20,000 of whom 2,432 lived in Clackmannanshire. According to the Clackmannan Regional Survey [1951], the combined textiles and clothing industries in the county employed more than 4,000 persons or 23% of the total workforce. Paton and Baldwins (**Figure 11**), with 1,970 workers was the largest employer in the county and, as Alloa alone was unable to supply

Figure 11 Paton's mill Kilncraigs, Alloa. (Patons)

sufficient labour, the firm had to bus in 400 each day from Grangemouth, Falkirk and Stirling. By contrast the number of woollen workers in Stirling had fallen as low as 43, most of whom presumably were employed in the solitary spinning mill reported in the burgh of Stirling in the Third Statistical Account.

During the 1950s the local woollen industry entered a long period of contraction accompanied by the loss of almost 1,300 jobs between 1961 and 1971. By the early 1960s Alva had six small factories, employing between 15 and 150 workers each, and manufacturing shawls, scarves, blankets and tweeds. However by 1979 closures on the Hillfoots included all the Menstrie mills and the Strude, Braehead, Brook St, and Greenfield mills in Alva and only four continued to operate. In Tillicoultry Patons survived, but only temporarily. There were still successful manufacturers. On the eve of its amalgamation with J and P Coats of Paisley in 1961, Paton and Baldwins had a workforce of 1,730, earning an average of £13.25 per week for males and £6.55 for women and producing more than 5 m kg of woollen goods annually. In 1956 the firm of Donbros moved from Sauchie to a new factory at Lornshill, employing 750 to operate the latest machinery. In addition Donbros also owned the Forthvale mill at Menstrie, which in 1961, employed 70 women to produce knitware. Donbros was absorbed into the Jaeger Co. in 1976.

By the early 1990s the woollen industry in Central Region had contracted even further. Employment in all sectors of the industry, including clothing manufacture, had declined to about 3,200, of whom the vast majority were skilled and semi-skilled. Since the later 19th century the industry has suffered severe international and intra-national competition and, as a result, has altered radically in size, shape, ownership, organization, technology, products and markets. In particular old businesses have disappeared and new ones have started, many since 1970. Knitwear has gradually increased its dominance and by the early 1990s is the principal product of about half the firms in the textile and clothing industries of the region. UK sales account for most of the annual turnover of this sector, which, in only one-third of firms, exceeded £1 m. Europe is much the most important export market, followed by Japan and the USA. Despite the difficult economic circumstances of the early 1990s, most of the companies active in this sector were optimistic about their future trading prospects.

PROFESSIONAL AND SCIENTIFIC SERVICES

Before the late 19th century only lawyers and medical practitioners were considered to be members of recognised professions in Scotland. This meant they had an exclusive monopoly in the use of their professional knowledge and skills. The mediaeval clergy had had this professional monopoly but following the 16th century Reformation, the power and influence of the Kirk came less from its organisation and monopoly of knowledge than from its ability to use the State to enforce a moral code through legal sanctions and through its control of education and the Poor Law. The decline of the Kirk during the 18th and 19th centuries can be illustrated by the low percentage - about 35 - of Scotland's 5,333 ministers of religion who, in 1901, belonged to the Church of Scotland, slightly less even than to the rival United Free church [UFC].

In addition to the two recognised professions and the clergy there were many persons employed in other professional and scientific services as defined by the Registrar-General for Scotland. Their numbers grew rapidly in the late 19th century and in 1891 more than 111,000 persons were computed to be so employed, with men outnumbering women by more than two to one. Of this total more than 18,000 were employed in national and local government services and about 7,500 were in the armed forces. The remaining 85,000 were in professional occupations. In addition to the clergy, and the medical and legal professions these occupations included teachers, those engaged in literary and scientific careers, engineers and surveyors and those in the Arts, including architects and public entertainers.

Despite the increasing steps towards professionalisation by other groups of workers such as dentists, veterinary surgeons pharmacists, teachers and officers of the armed forces in the late 19th century, the medical and legal professions maintained and even increased their dominance in Scottish society well into the 20th century. This was principally because their services were in demand, whether respectively, to combat the threat of new or existing diseases or to interpret the growing volume of legislation. Their status was also maintained by their relatively small numbers.

In Stirlingshire in 1891, out of a total population of 118,000, there were 1,831 men and 892 women in such professional occupations and in Clackmannanshire 467 men and 243 women out of a population of 33,140. In 1891 Stirlingshire's 74 doctors

Figure 12   Re-enactment of a Victorian primary school class. (Central Region Education, Schools Museum)

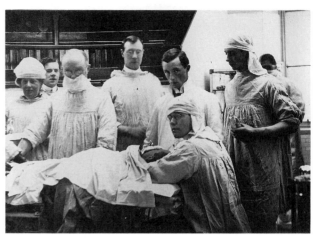

Figure 13   Operating theatre, Stirling Infirmary, 1914. (R. McCutcheon)

and eight dentists were all male and the 93 nurses were all female. There were also eleven male veterinary surgeons. Twenty years later their numbers had increased to 84 medical practitioners, 319 nurses and 29 dentists and their assistants, but veterinary surgeons had declined to seven, reflecting the continued effects of the agricultural depression. The population of Clackmannanshire in 1891 included 21 medical practitioners, eight nurses, two dentists and three veterinary surgeons. By 1911 The number of nurses had increased to 53, and the number of dentists to three and there were also two registered midwives. However the number of medical practitioners was two fewer, and only one veterinary surgeon was still practising.

Between 1891 and 1911 the number of men employed in Stirlingshire's legal profession increased from 182 to 252, most of whom were clerks, whilst in Clackmannanshire, the size of the legal profession increased over the same period from 45 of whom 32 were clerks to 56, including two women clerks. In 1891 the various churches of Stirlingshire had 158 men employees, mostly ministers and priests, and 17 women including one nun, a total which changed little by 1911. In Clackmannanshire over the same period, the number of church employees rose from 46, including three women to 51. At the end of the 19th century the combined number of persons employed in the law, medicine and the church in the region was considerably smaller than the numbers employed by other professional services, much the largest of which was education.

Before 1872 schoolteachers came from a variety of backgrounds, and with no central control over their admission to the profession or their training, only a minority had had a university education. Even by

1891, when compulsory elementary education in Scotland had been on the statute book for nearly two decades, the situation had scarcely changed. In 1891 Stirlingshire (**Figure 12**) had 187 male and 378 female teachers, mostly employed by school boards. In addition 289 male and 285 female pupil-teachers were in training. By 1911, out of a Scottish total of more than 25,000, the number of of teachers in Stirlingshire had risen to 226 men and 583 women. In Clackmannanshire the number of teachers rose from 109 in 1891, mostly women, and 220 pupil teachers, to 209 in 1911, of whom 146 were women. No pupil teachers were recorded in 191.

Other government services in Stirlingshire in 1891 employed 402 males and 55 females, only 156 of whom were civil service officers and clerks. Sixty persons, including one woman, were county and local officials. By 1911 the number of male civil servants had declined to 88 and the number of women to two, out of an overall Scottish total of 3,300. By contrast the number of male local officials had increased to 114 and the number of women to ten, out of a Scottish total of almost 5,500, which reflected the ever increasing growth of State and local statutory duties from the 1870s onwards. In Clackmannanshire national and local government in the county accounted for 86 persons in 1891 and 154 in 1911. Between 1891 and 1911 the size of the Stirlingshire Police Force increased from 104 to 143, or 40%, whilst that of Clackmannanshire rose by only three to 25, out of a Scottish total in 1911 of more than 5,800 officers which included 14 women. Over the 20 year period there was almost no increase in the size of the military in Stirlingshire - about 250 soldiers and twenty commissioned officers - out of a Scottish total, in 1911, of 6,844 men in the Army and 8,529 in the Royal Navy and Marines.

Growth of Professions

During most of the remainder of the 20th century there has been a continued growth in the percentage of workers employed in professional and scientific services as the statutory responsibilities of national and local Governmemt increased. Simultaneously as the number of workers in agriculture, coal-mining and traditional manufacturing industry continued to decline, particularly after 1960, Scotland began moving towards an economy based on hi-tech manufacturing, North Sea oil and gas and financial services. In addition government employment, particularly in the health and education services, has grown considerably.

The Scottish legal profession protected its status in the first half of the 20th century by its exclusivity and masculinity. In 1951 the total of 3,629 solicitors, including 150 women, and 279 judges and advocates, including eleven women, was actually 70 less than in 1901. Of these, 108 solicitors including one woman worked in Stirlingshire and ten in Clackmannanshire including one woman. This lack of expansion in the legal profession could be explained by a limited demand for its services in three areas which were to become the staple work of solicitors in the later post-war period; petty crime, divorce and house conveyancing.

By contrast with the negative growth of the legal profession, the medical and allied professions expanded rapidly (**Figure 13**), boosted by the impact of two World Wars and the establishment of the National Health Service in 1948. By 1951 there were in Scotland almost 6,000 medical practitioners of whom 206 worked in Stirlingshire and Clackmannanshire. More than 1,000 were women, including 36 working in the two counties. Including students, there were almost 29,000 nurses in Scotland, of whom almost 90% were women and girls. Almost 1,600 of these, a figure boosted by the presence of the large psychiatric hospitals at Larbert, worked in Stirlingshire and 108 in Clackmannanshire. In Scotland in 1951 the employment of dental surgeons was being stimulated rapidly by the introduction of free treatment under the NHS and there were 1,500 in practice of whom 90% were men. Of these 35 male dentists and one woman worked in Stirlingshire and five males in Clackmannanshire. More than 6,000 men and women worked in Scotland's auxiliary medical services such as pharmacy, radiography and chiropody. The revival of Scottish agriculture, and the increased ownership of household pets, required the services of 478 veterinary surgeons in 1951, of whom 16 practised in Stirlingshire and two in Clackmannanshire.

Despite the rapid fall in the birth-rate between 1920 and 1933, teaching in Scotland expanded at all levels from nursery classes to universities during the first half of the century. Most notably the introduction of compulsory secondary education by the Education [Scotland] Act of 1945 and the raising of the school leaving age two years later, in addition to a high birthrate in the 1940s, all helped to expand Scottish school rolls to 818,000 primary and secondary pupils by 1951. These pupils were attended by 33,200 teachers of whom two-thirds were women, an overall increase of more than 30% since 1901; 1,235 were working in Stirlingshire's 92 schools and 303 in Clackmannanshire's 19 schools. However, despite more stringent entry requirements and training, teachers in Scotland in 1951 were still a long way from being a fully graduate and trained profession, as medical practitioners had been since the late 19th century. Of 10,900 men teachers employed in 1951, 7,310 were university graduates as were an almost identical number of the 22,300 women teachers.

The traditional Christian churches began to decline in membership after 1900, although this varied considerably in different parts of Scotland and amongst the different denominations. This obviously affected the status of the clergy, a situation which was exacerbated by the assumption by lay persons of some of the roles previously held by the clergy, such as welfare and counselling. However while the population of Scotland rose by 12% between 1901 and 1951, the number of clergy, nuns and other church workers increased by 15% to 6,150. The principal reason for this was the increase of more than 1,000 clergy, monks and nuns of the Roman Catholic Church to 1,817. By contrast the number of Church of Scotland clergy, reunited with the United Free Church in 1929, was, excluding some 78 continuing UFC independents, 116 less than their separate totals fifty years previously.

With the exception of medical and veterinary practitioners, one notable characteristic of professional workers in 19th century Scotland was their lack of formal scientific or engineering training, a fact that has been frequently cited as a cause of economic retardation in Britain. In 1891 in Stirlingshire, whilst there were 32 civil and mining engineers only ONE person was occupied as a professional scientist. Even by 1911 only 446 men and 25 women in Scotland were described as 'persons engaged in scientific pursuits'. Of the engineers and surveyors computed in the Census of the same year, 2,197 men and 16 women appear to have been qualified overwhelmingly for constructional, mining and other environmental activities rather than for the electrical, mechanical or chemical engineering industries.

The increase in highly qualified persons employed in scientific and engineering occupations has been a marked feature of the 20th century Scottish labour market, with the number rising, by 1981, to 7,600 persons including 1,800 women. This group formed the elite of an overall total of more than 86,000 persons who were classified as professional workers in this category. Meanwhile the complexities of financial operations in industry and business created a heavy demand for qualified accountants whose numbers, in 1981, including 810 women, totalled more than 7,000 in Scotland.

The demand for scientific workers developed strongly in Stirlingshire in the 1920s, first with the opening of Scottish Dye's plant at Grangemouth, whose construction was a delayed response to the removal of

Figure 14 Grangemouth refinery, in the 1920s. (BP)

'Paraffin' Young

German dyestuffs from the British market by the First World War. It was further encouraged through the Dyestuffs Act of 1920 which excluded German products from Britain. Within seven years the plant had become part of Imperial Chemical Industries [ICI], and by the early 1930s employed 845 workers, including a dozen graduate chemists. Improved production techniques led to rapidly rising profits but also 300 redundancies by 1936.

In 1942 the dyestuffs division of ICI added the manufacture of pharmaceuticals, although with little profit initially, mainly because of rapidly escalating research costs. Production of anti-malarial drugs was centred at Grangemouth. This new venture helped to expand employment opportunities for science graduates. In 1951 there were 188 graduate chemists, including 11 women and 55 pharmacists, including nine women resident in Stirlingshire and Clackmannanshire. Obviously only a percentage of these would have been employed by ICI Grangemouth and many of the pharmacists would have worked in chemists' shops. Many other graduates in chemistry were employed at Grangemouth's second major development in the 1920s, the refinery of Scottish Oils [BP] (**Figure 14**). This refinery, which opened in 1924 with a capacity of 350,000 tons, was the logical successor to the establishment of oil storage tanks at the docks before the First World War and a trans-Scotland oil pipeline opened shortly before Armistice day in 1918. The refinery stimulated several other oil companies to open storage depots in Grangemouth at various times in the following decades. A larger 90 km long pipeline from Finart terminal on Loch Long was constructed after the Second World War, creating a pumping capacity of more than 3 m tons per year.

In 1951 almost 1,160 workers were employed by the Grangemouth oil industry and a further 3,300 in the chemical industry, mostly in the plants of ICI and those firms whose products stemmed from the petroleum industry. By 1961 following the opening of the new British Hydrocarbon Chemicals plant at Grangemouth, the number of chemical workers employed in the region had risen to more than 5,700. Overall the decline in

employment in the petroleum, chemical and allied industries in Scotland, resulting from improved productivity, was until the early 1980s, cancelled out by the development of the North Sea oilfields so that the number of workers in these industries, in both 1953 and 1978, was almost identical at 29,500. By 1989 employment had declined by a third to 19,500 of whom 5,600 were women and 6,000 worked in pharmaceuticals. In 1992, ICI at Grangemouth employed 1,200 persons, of whom one-third had degrees in science or engineering or other advanced qualifications and one-fifth were employed in the manufacture of pharmaceuticals.

As the site of Scotland's only large-scale petroleum refinery, Grangemouth also grew in importance with the opening, in 1975, of a new pipeline from Cruden Bay, in Grampian Region, where oil from BP's massive Forties field is brought ashore. Refining capacity at Grangemouth expanded from 8.6 m tons in 1980, of which 62% came from the North Sea, to almost

Figure 15 The BP Grangemouth complex in 1993; new cracker in the foreground. (BP)

Figure 16   The University of Stirling,   (Patricia MacDonald)

9 m tons in 1990 of which 88% was from the North Sea. Almost all of Scotland's 2,200 oil processing workers were employed here in 1990 (**Figure 15**). Other than these, direct employment in companies working the North Sea oilfields numbered less than 1,000 in 1980 in Central and Lothian Regions combined, falling to less than 300 in 1990.

Although numbers in the Scottish legal profession had fallen slightly between 1901 and 1951, in the following 40 years there was a very considerable increase to 7,332 qualified solicitors of whom 2,574 were women. Although no separate figures are kept by the Law Society of Scotland on a regional basis, it could be assumed that about 5% of these were practising in Central Region in 1991.

There was also considerable expansion in Scotland's health services. In 1981 there were 6,660 male and 2,310 female medical practitioners, more than 73,000 nurses, mostly women, 1,660 dentists, of whom 20% were women, and 7,270 persons in the auxiliary professions, a total of more than 90,000 employees. By 1990 Forth Valley Health Board employed 482 medical practitioners, 4,294 nurses, 94 dentists and 280 auxiliary medical professionals, such as radiographers and orthoptists.

In 1981 the 41,143 women teachers in Scotland continued to represent about two-thirds of those qualified to work in the primary and secondary education sectors. In 1992 Central Regional Council employed 4,200 teachers and lecturers in primary, secondary and further education and about 3,500 administrative staff in all departments of local government. By contrast with schools, Scottish higher education institutions in 1981 employed more than 9,500 male teachers but only 2,760 women. These figures included persons working at the University of Stirling (**Figure 16**) whose first students arrived in 1967. This foundation led very rapidly to a notable increase in the employment of professional and scientific personnel in the area. By 1971 there were 227 academic and related staff, with high professional qualifications, and a decade later this figure had risen to 416. Despite heavy but differential cutbacks in government funding to UK universities in the early 1980s, in which Stirling suffered disproportionately, by the end of 1991 the number had reached 615. By the 25th anniversary year the numbers of students had also increased, totalling 5,200 in Autumn 1992, of whom 700 were full-time postgraduates; and 800 part-timers, both undergraduate and postgraduate. Approximately 41% of all students were women.

The far-reaching economic and social changes which have taken place in Scotland during the last 100 years can therefore be seen to have altered employment patterns very markedly. In particular employment in primary and most secondary industrial sectors have declined, especially since 1960, to be replaced by a greatly enlarged service sector employing persons with high qualification in such professions as medicine, law, accountancy and education, and many more with much lesser training, and often on a part-time basis, in such areas as catering, retailing and tourism. These changes have brough greatly increased unemployment with approximately the same number of people out of work in Scotland in the early 1990s as in the whole UK in 1955. These changes have thus increasingly emphasised the importance of education and training as a factor in increased employment.

REFERENCES AND FURTHER READING

BALD, Robert. 1808. General View of the Coal Trade of Scotland. Edinburgh.

BREMNER, D. 1869. The Industries of Scotland, their Rise, Progress, and Present Condition. Edinburgh.

BRITISH PETROLEUM COMPANY. 1977. Our Industry Petroleum. London.

CAIRNCROSS, A.K. Editor. 1954. The Scottish Economy. Cambridge.

CAMPBELL, R.H. 1961. The Carron Company. Edinburgh.

CAMPBELL, R.H. 1992. Scotland since 1707. The Rise of an Industrial Society. John Donald. Reprint of the 2nd edition 1985 *plus a chapter for post 1945.*

CARVEL, J.L. 1944. One Hundred Years of Coal. The Alloa Coal Company.

Colliery Yearbook and Coal Trades Directory, 1948. London.

CROWE, P.R. 1929. The Scottish coalfields. *Scottish Geographical Magazine,* XIV, 6

DRON, R.W. 1902. The Coalfields of Scotland.

DUCKHAM, B.F. 1970. A History of the Scottish Coal Industry, volume 1. Newton Abbott.

ELLIOTT, B.J. 1990. The rise and decline of the rail and coal industries of Clackmannanshire. *Forth Naturalist and Historian,* 12, 115-124

EVANS, Eric J. 1972. Tillicoultry, A Centenary History. Tillicoultry.

FORRESTER-PATON, A. 1982. The Romance of Patons Yarn c 1813-1920. Reprint, Clackmannan District Libraries, Alloa.

HALLIDAY, Robert S. 1990. The Disappearing Scottish Colliery. Edinburgh.

JENKINS, David. 1982. The British Woollen Textile Industry, 1770-1914. London.

MOORE, R.A. 1950. Scottish coal. *Scottish Geographical Magazine,* 66, 26-36

NATIONAL COAL BOARD. 1958. A Short History of the Scottish Coal-Mining Industry.

New Statistical Account of Scotland. 1845. Volume IX, Dunbarton, Stirling, and Clackmannan. Edinburgh.

PARK, Brian A. 1979. The Woollen Mill buildings in the Hillfoots. Forth Naturalist and Historian.

PERSONAL COMMUNICATIONS from Stuart Ogg and Peter Freeth, Forth Valley Enterprise, the Law Society of Scotland and Forth Valley Health Board.

READER, W.J. 1970. Imperial Chemical Industries, volume 1. Oxford.

REGISTRAR GENERAL FOR SCOTLAND, Decennial Censuses for Scotland, 1851..., Edinburgh various dates

RENNIE, R.C. and GORDON, Crouther.T, [Editors]. 1966. Third Statistical Account of Scotland, The County of Stirling, The County of Clackmannan. Glasgow.

TURNER, W.H.K. 1964. Wool textile manufacturing in Scotland. *Scottish Geographical Magazine,* 80, 81-89

TURNER, W.H.K. 1985. Burgh, state and the Scottish wool textile industry c 1500-1840. *Scottish Geographical Magazine* 101, 85-90 and 130-138

WARREN, K. 1965. Locational problems of the Scottish iron and steel industry since 1760. *Scottish Geographical Magazine,* 81, 18-37 and pp 87-103

WITHRINGTON, Donald J. and GRANT, Ian R. Editors. 1790s. The Statistical Account of Scotland, volume IX, Dunbartonshire, Stirlingshire and Clackmannanshire. Reprint, Wakefield, 1978

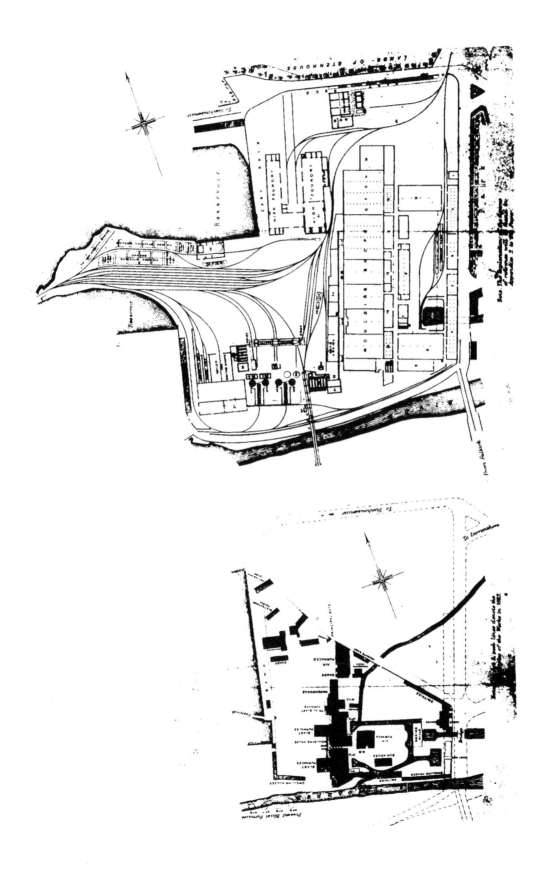

Carron iron works plans - 1750s and 1880s (Cowan Proc. Inst. Civil Engrs., lxxxviii) 1886-7 pt1)

STIRLING Parliamentary Constituency

Dollar Parish

Muchart
Dollar
Tillicoultry
CLACKMANNAN
Alloa
Clackmannan
Airth
Grangemouth
Muiravonside
FALKIRK EAST
Slamannan
Alva
Logie
Dunblane and Lecropt
Sterling
St. Ninians
Larbert
Dunipace
FALKIRK WEST
Falkirk
Kilmadock
Kincardine
Gargunnock
Denny
Kilsyth
Kenmore
Comrie
Callander
STIRLING
Port of Menteith
Kippen
Fintry
Killin
Balquhidder
Aberfoyle
Drymen
Balfron
Killearn
Strathblane
Buchanan

Plan of central Scotland population locations/parishes

Population: Growth, Location and Structure

N. L. Tranter

In the absence of data of the necessary abundance and reliability little of any substance can be said about the history of population change in Scotland and its individual parishes and regions for the period before the middle of the 18th century. Not until 1755, thanks to the initiative of Alexander Webster, the Moderator of the General Assembly of the Church of Scotland, do we have what is now regarded as the first reasonably accurate count of the number of residents in each parish in the country (Kyd 1952). A second, albeit less satisfactory, estimate of the size of parochial populations was not made until the early 1790s, for Sir John Sinclair's *Statistical Account of Scotland*, popularly known as the *Old Statistical Account (OSA)*. But it is only from 1801 that adequately reliable parish by parish population totals, compiled by the civil authorities, become available on a regular decennial basis. Beginning in 1841 and 1851, when methods of collecting demographic data were greatly improved, the range of information contained in the civil censuses increased, to include more detailed and precise data on the age, sex and occupational structures of the population, and new data on, among other items, marital status, household composition and place of birth. For students of the history of changes in the growth, spatial location and structure of population it is fortunate that the improvement which occurred in the quantity and quality of demographic material during the 19th century coincides with the era of greatest change in the economies of both country and region.

If, as is probable, the demographic experience of central Scotland broadly mirrored that of the country as a whole, throughout the 17th and first half of the 18th centuries the population of the region at best grew very little, at worst may even have declined. Sometime around the middle of the 18th century rates of population growth began to increase. Between 1755 and 1981 the population of central Scotland increased more than fourfold, from 64,000 to 278,000. From a modest annual average rate of 0.45% in the second half of the 18th century, itself almost certainly well above that achieved in the preceding hundred years, rates of population growth climbed to an average of 1.18% per annum during the first half of the 19th century at which level they remained more or less unchanged until the outbreak of World War I. Thereafter they fell, to levels roughly similar to those between 1755 and 1801. Rates of population growth were especially low in the decades between the two world wars. After World War II they rose again, though only moderately and rarely to the levels typical of most decades of the 19th century **(Table 1)**.

Table 1 The Growth of Population in Scotland and Central Scotland, Per Cent Per Annum

	Scotland	Central Scotland
1755-1801	**0.60**	**0.45**
1801-11	0.23	1.91
1811-21	1.58	1.22
1821-32	1.30	0.92
1831-41	1.08	1.26
1841-51	1.03	0.57
1801-51	**1.59**	**1.18**
1851-61	0.60	0.35
1861-71	0.97	0.63
1871-81	1.12	1.16
1881-91	0.78	1.02
1891-1901	1.11	1.41
1901-11	0.65	0.96
1851-1911	**1.08**	**1.15**
1911-21	0.25	0.16
1921-31	-0.08	0.14
1931-51	0.52	0.61
1911-51	**0.18**	**0.39**
1951-61	0.16	0.47
1961-71	0.10	0.76
1971-81	-0.09	0.34
1951-81	**0.06**	**0.55**

Except during the period 1951-81, when the growth rate of Scotland's population continued to decline while that of central Scotland once more began to rise, the long-term pattern of population growth in the central region was much the same as that for the country as a whole. In terms of their actual levels, however, rates of population increase in the region were lower than the Scottish average in every decade from the 1750s to the 1860s (except during the 1830s) but higher than the Scottish average in every decade from the 1870s to the 1970s (except between 1911 and 1920). The result was that the region's share of the total population of the country fell from 5.05% in 1755 to a low of 4.23% in 1851 and then began to rise, to 4.34% in 1911, 4.69% in 1951 and 5.37% by 1981, higher than at any time since the middle of the 18th century.

Variations in the size and rate of growth of populations are a product of either variations in rates of natural increase (defined as the difference between the number of births and deaths) or variations in the balance between in- and out-migration. To determine which of these mechanisms has the greater influence on rates of population growth requires the existence of comprehensive and accurate data both on the size of the population and on levels of fertility and mortality. From 1855, when responsibility for the registration of births, deaths and marriages was taken over by the state, this poses no problem. For the period before 1855, when the registration of vital events was the responsibility of the established church, the situation is very different. The problem is that the numbers of births, marriages and, particularly, deaths recorded in the ecclesiastical registers, even where these survive, seriously understate what must have been their true levels. It follows that for the period before the middle of the 19th century, whether we rely on the registers themselves or on the birth and death totals based upon them which are given for many parishes in the Old and New Statistical Accounts, it is impossible to provide wholly satisfactory estimates of levels of fertility and mortality and thus of possible changes in rates of natural increase and in the balance between in- and out-migration.

Despite this, historians of population trends are generally agreed that, before as well as after 1855, the growth of Scotland's population was almost entirely due to a decline in rates of mortality. In contrast to England, where rising fertility was probably the main cause of accelerating rates of population increase in the late 18th and early 19th centuries, the initial phase of Scotland's population 'take-off' appears to have owed nothing to a rise in birth rates. Subsequently, following a period of relative stability during the third quarter of the 19th century, Scottish crude birth rates began a prolonged decline, falling more or less continuously from 35.0 per thousand population in 1871-5 to 27.6 in 1906-10, 17.6 in 1936-40 and 12.7 in 1976-80 **(Table 2)**.

Table 2   Crude Birth Rates (Number of Live Births per Thousand Population), 1861-1981.

	Scotland	Clackmannanshire	Stirlingshire
1861	34.8	36.3	36.9
1871	34.5	33.7	34.9
1881	33.7	33.3	36.3
1891	31.2	31.7	32.1
1901	29.5	25.5	32.9
1911	25.7	23.0	28.3
1921	25.2	24.4	26.9
1931	19.0	17.6	19.7
1941	17.5	17.2	17.8
1951	17.7	20.0	17.8
1961	19.5	20.0	19.2
1971	16.6	18.2	16.9
1981	13.4	14.1	13.3

Even in the hundred years prior to the mid-19th century Scotland is believed to have lost more people through emigration than it gained by immigration, though it is not possible to quantify precisely the extent

of the net loss. In the period between the mid-19th century and 1981 the scale of the net outflow increased **(Table 3)**. In every decade from 1861 to 1981 the number of emigrants substantially exceeded the number of immigrants. During this period a total of 2.3 million inhabitants, over half the nation's excess of births over deaths was lost to net outmigration. The drain was particularly severe during the 1880s, between 1901 and 1931 and in the 1950s and 1960s. In combination with the long-term decline in rates of fertility which began in the later decades of the 19th century, the persistent excess of emigrants over immigrants explains why rates of Scottish population growth were lower between 1851 and 1981 than in the first half of the 19th century and why they declined on trend almost continuously throughout the latter part of the period.

Fortunately, the negative effects of net outmigration and declining fertility on rates of population growth were more than matched by a general, long-term tendency for death rates to fall.

Table 3   Net Emigration (in thousands), 1861-1981

	Scotland	Clackmannanshire	Stirlingshire
1861-71	-118.6	-0.5	-8.1
1871-80	-93.2	-1.8	-1.9
1881-90	-217.8	-0.7	-4.2
1891-1900	-53.4	+0.05	-3.1
1901-10	-254.1	-4.0	-4.6
1911-20	-238.6	-0.2	-14.8
1921-30	-391.9	-2.8	-11.7
1931-50	-220.0	+2.0	-1.1
1951-60	-282.0	+0.5	-7.7
1961-70	-326.5	+1.4	+1.1
1971-80	-144.2	+3.2	

Although many features of Scotland's 17th and early 18th century demographic history remain obscure, there is widespread agreement that its most obvious characteristic, the persistence of abnormally low rates of population increase, was a result of unusually high levels of mortality, themselves a consequence of frequent, calamitous outbreaks of epidemic disease, occasionally, as in the 1690s, associated with severe and widespread food shortages. At some stage in the second half of the 18th century the incidence of epidemics, and thus levels of mortality, started to decrease. The decrease was arrested during the second quarter of the 19th century when a deterioration in environmental conditions associated with the rapid urbanisation of the country's population provoked a temporary resurgence of epidemic disease. Outbreaks of cholera in central Scotland in 1834 and 1837 and a "recent" increase in the incidence of typhus reported in the entry in the *New Statistical Account (NSA)* for the Stirlingshire parish of Drymen provides interesting local illustration of what took place. Throughout the third quarter of the 19th century, though lower than they had been in the 1830s and 1840s, rates of mortality remained roughly stable. From the late 1870s, however, they began a sustained decline, crude death rates falling from 20.6 per thousand population in 1876-80 to 16.1 in 1906-10, 13.5 in 1936-40 and 12.4 in 1976-80 **(Table 4)**.

Table 4 Crude Death Rates (Number of Deaths per Thousand Population), 1861-1981.

	Scotland	Clackmannanshire	Stirlingshire
1861	20.3	18.8	18.3
1871	22.2	20.2	18.8
1881	19.3	16.0	17.6
1891	20.9	17.4	20.3
1901	17.9	15.3	16.9
1911	15.1	14.3	14.4
1921	13.6	12.5	12.9
1931	13.3	14.5	11.4
1941	14.7	13.2	12.1
1951	12.9	11.9	11.8
1961	12.3	10.6	11.2
1971	11.8	10.8	11.0
1981	12.4	11.6	11.4

Except during the 1920s and 1970s, when the excess of emigrants over immigrants exceeded the surplus of births over deaths, the result has been a continual increase in the country's population.

In central Scotland, too, the long period of demographic stagnation in the 17th and first half of the 18th centuries was primarily a result of persistently high levels of mortality caused by frequent outbreaks of epidemic disease, like those of bubonic plague in the mid-1640s, which decimated the populations of Alloa, Dunblane, Falkirk, Glendevon, Stirling and Tillicoultry, and of smallpox and influenza in the 1720s and 1730s, which ravaged the town of Stirling and reduced rates of population increase at Alva to an average of just 0.1% a year. And, as **Tables 2 and 4** show, in the central region, as in Scotland generally, the upturn in rates of population growth which began in the late 18th century and continued without interruption for the next two hundred years was due to falling mortality not rising fertility.

The causes of this long-term decline in mortality have long puzzled students of demographic history. The search for an explanation of that part of it which occurred in the late 18th and early 19th centuries has proved particularly frustrating. Matters have not been helped by the fact that contemporary data on causes of death and how these changed over time are rare and too imprecise or too concerned with symptoms rather than actual cause of death to be of much use. It is, for instance, of little value to learn from the *OSA* that of 437 deaths at Kilsyth between 1785 and 1794 five were described simply as "sudden", 56 were due to "unknown cause", 128 to "old age" and two to "bleeding at the nose".

Local contributors to the *Statistical Accounts* themselves offered two principal explanations. The

first saw it, at least in part, as a consequence of the growing practice of inoculation against smallpox. Smallpox was certainly one of the main causes of high mortality in 18th century Scotland and there can be no doubt that the introduction of inoculation at places like Balquhidder, Buchanan and Kippen, reinforced from the early 19th century by the spread of the more efficacious technique of vaccination, played some part in helping to reduce death rates. On the other hand, as the authors of entries in the *Statistical Accounts* for places as diverse as Baldernock, Bothkennar, Clackmannan, Dollar, Dunblane, Gargunnock, Kilmadock and Tillicoultry pointed out, even at the very end of the 18th century the practice of inoculation was by no means universal and continued to encounter strong opposition, particularly from working class sections of the community. To informed observers of parishes like Baldernock, Clackmannan and Gargunnock, where it was customary for people to continue the dangerous habit of visiting smallpox victims and where sufferers were treated solely with warm milk and whisky and smothered in blankets in front of a blazing fire, it was little wonder that mortality from the disease remained high.

The second contemporary explanation for the late 18th and early 19th century mortality decline in mid Scotland, that it owed much to a decrease in the incidence of ague and other malarial-type fevers brought about by a combination of land drainage and improvements in standards of housing, likewise requires modification. The provision of cleaner, warmer and drier houses noted at Falkirk and Tillicoultry and the drainage of wet, marshy land at Bothkennar, Logie, St.Ninians and Tillicoultry may well have made some contribution to the rise in average life expectancy. But the influence of such factors should not be overstated. Improvements in drainage were restricted in their geographical extent and, in any case, were of potential relevance to only some of the many diseases which together determined the duration of life. Nor, to judge from comments on the cold, damp, dirty and ill-ventilated nature of housing at Baldernock and Slamannan, is there any firm evidence of a general improvement of housing standards in the region.

None of this should be taken to imply that historians of the present day are able to provide us with a more satisfactory explanation of late 18th and early 19th century mortality decline. Currently, it seems, the best that can be said is that it was the result of a variety of influences. Among these probably the most significant were inoculation and vaccination against smallpox, and other less effective innovations in medical practice such as the growth of hospital and dispensary facilities and a greater resort to quarantining those with infectious disease. But modest advances in standards of personal hygiene and, above all, improved levels of nutrition stemming from higher rates of agricultural productivity, the introduction of new crops like the potato and better methods of food distribution also played their part. Perhaps, too, the initial phase of mortality decline owed at least something to a fortuitous reduction in the frequency and severity of epidemic disease viruses themselves, a reduction that occurred independently of the changes made by man to his relationship with the environment. Beyond these broad, inconclusive suggestions regrettably we are not yet able to proceed.

For that part of the decline in mortality which has taken place since the later decades of the 19th century we can be more definite about causes. At the root of the dramatic increase in human life expectation in the last hundred years lies the unprecedented advance in standards of living made possible by the forces of modern economic growth. On the one hand, rising real incomes and improvements in the quantity and quality of the food supply, together with higher standards of personal cleanliness and public health - purer water supplies, improved methods of drainage and sewage disposal and less polluted air - have greatly lessened the risks of falling prey to epidemic disease. On the other, for those who do succumb to life-threatening ailments, advances in medical therapy have considerably enhanced the likelihood of survival. The result has been an extension in the average human life-span unparalleled in its extent and persistence.

In contrast to the experience of the country as a whole, however, the growth of population in central Scotland, at least in the most recent decades, has also been partly due to a tendency for the region to attract more people through immigration than it lost through emigration.

For the period before 1855 the lack of reliable data on numbers of births and deaths makes it difficult to be sure whether the parishes of mid Scotland gained or lost on balance of migration with other areas. From the middle of the 18th century onwards, drawn by increasing opportunities for employment in agriculture and industry, immigrants were being attracted to the region in ever- growing numbers. Down to the middle of the 19th century, however, their numbers were probably exceeded by emigrants leaving the region. Throughout the period between the mid-19th and mid-20th centuries, when levels of in- and out-migration can be estimated with reasonable precision, emigration continued to exceed immigration. Parishes like St. Ninians, which from the later years of the 19th century attracted large numbers of coalminers from Lanarkshire, were not yet typical of the experience of the region as a whole. In the course of the third quarter of the 20th century the relationship between in- and out-migration changed. Beginning in Clackmannanshire in the 1950s and in Stirlingshire in the 1960s the number of immigrants came to exceed the number of emigrants. For the first time since at least the middle of the 18th century central Scotland became a persistent if modest net gainer in the ebb and flow of movement across its borders. The result was that between 1951 and 1981 rates of population growth in the region exceeded those for Scotland as a whole by a margin greater than at any time since the differential in favour of the former had

first become effectively established in the 1870s.

Long-term variations in the extent of immigration into central Scotland are clearly reflected in the changes that have taken place in the percentages of the populations of Clackmannanshire and Stirlingshire born outside the counties. Between 1851 and 1891, when rates of immigration were relatively high, the proportion of residents born outside the counties rose, from 39% to 47.6% in the case of Clackmannanshire and from 32.8% to 38.5% in the case of Stirlingshire. By 1911 the Stirlingshire figure had risen to 39.5% while that for Clackmannanshire had fallen to 36.7%. During the period between the two world wars, when the flow of immigration into Stirlingshire diminished, the share of the non-county born in the total population of the county fell, to 34.4% in 1931 and 35.5% in 1951. It continued to fall throughout the 1950s, to just 28.4% by 1961. By contrast, in the case of Clackmannanshire where the recent trend towards an excess of immigrants over emigrants first became established, the proportion of non-county born began to increase after World War I, to 39.3% in 1931, 46.9% in 1951 and 51.6% in 1961. Were comparable data available for the period between 1961 and 1981, when rates of immigration further increased and Stirlingshire joined Clackmannanshire as a net gainer on balance of migration, it is likely they would show a rise in the share of non-county born residents in both counties.

One of the most striking aspects of the demographic evolution of central Scotland since the middle of the 18th century has been the pronounced variation which has existed in rates of population growth from one part of the region to another **(Table 5)**. Particularly notable is the fact that, with relatively few exceptions, almost throughout the period parishes in the western half of the region have increased their populations considerably less than those in the eastern half. Between 1755 and 1981 the number of inhabitants in western parishes rose from 22,747 to 28,835, an average annual rate of growth of only 0.12%. By comparison, the population of eastern parishes rose from 41,196 to 249,122, at an average of 2.24% a year. The differential in growth rates was especially marked in the 19th century, less obvious in the second half of the 18th century and barely perceptible in the decades following World War I. Disproportionately high rates of increase in the eastern districts were predominantly a characteristic of the period before 1911.

Of the 16 parishes in the west eight declined in population between 1755 and 1801 and in a further three rates of population growth were negligible. Only at Balfron, Campsie and Kincardine-in-Menteith did the number of inhabitants increase substantially in the second half of the 18th century. At Balfron this was chiefly a consequence of the opening of the Endrick printfield and Robert Dunmore's wool and cotton spinning mill in the early 1790s. At Campsie it was largely due to the establishment of extensive printfields in the 1780s, at Kincardine mainly to an influx of immigrant labour from the Highlands in response to

Table 5 Rates of Population Growth, By Parish. Per Cent Per Annum.

West	1755-1801	1801-1851	1851-1911	1911-1951	1951-1981	1755-1981
Aberfoyle	-0.46	-0.55	2.05	-0.03	0.86	0.26
Balfron	2.59	0.33	-0.65	0.55	-0.16	0.35
Buchanan	-1.24	-0.31	0.43	-0.97	0.60	-0.29
Drymen	-0.94	-0.16	-0.24	-0.09	0.46	-0.22
Fintry	0.17	-0.28	-1.10	0.68	1.91	-0.17
Gargunnock	0.00	-0.42	-0.37	0.12	0.78	-0.09
Kincardine	1.71	-0.20	-0.71	-0.15	-0.27	-0.09
Kippen	-0.10	0.20	-0.46	0.16	0.25	-0.06
Port of Menteith	-0.35	-0.19	-0.45	-0.76	0.14	-0.27
Baldernock	0.63	0.01	-0.11	0.03	1.29	0.32
Campsie	2.39	2.76	-0.39	1.29	-0.01	2.10
Killearn	0.19	0.26	0.13	1.09	1.65	0.63
Strathblane	-0.18	0.75	0.02	0.81	2.16	0.80
Balquhidder	-0.30	-0.73	-0.40	0.03	-0.26	-0.27
Callander	0.67	-0.50	0.48	0.19	1.11	0.36
Kilmadock	0.26	0.40	-0.56	-0.39	-0.03	-0.11
Total	**0.15**	**0.27**	**-0.32**	**0.34**	**0.47**	**0.12**
East						
Ardoch	-	-	-	0.23	-0.27	-
Dunblane						
Lecropt	-0.12	-0.10	0.91	-0.21	2.63	0.57
Logie	-0.02	0.59	1.19	1.46	2.24	2.15
Alva	1.79	6.14	1.07	0.11	1.00	6.85
Dollar	0.76	2.54	0.32	-0.36	2.34	1.90
Glendevon	-0.72	-0.28	0.26	-0.15	1.20	-0.06
Muckhart	-0.01	0.55	-0.37	-0.20	0.72	0.05
Tillicoultry	0.47	8.23	-0.01	0.47	0.42	3.21
Airth	-0.44	-0.58	0.25	1.19	-1.09	-0.16
Alloa	-0.23	1.64	1.29	0.74	0.86	1.66
Clackmannan	1.22	1.92	-1.03	0.93	0.63	0.93
Bothkennar	0.19	2.10	-	-	-	-
Denny	1.02	2.68	1.55	0.57	1.85	5.15
Dunipace	-	1.65	0.20	-0.67	3.35	-
Falkirk	2.77	1.72	2.63	0.31	-0.26	4.52
Grangemouth	-	-	-	0.74	1.48	-
Kilsyth	0.58	4.07	1.78	0.21	0.01	3.39
Larbert	2.10	0.54	3.03	0.54	0.75	4.17
Muiravonside	-0.68	2.95	1.93	-0.39	-0.53	0.72
Polmont	2.23	1.43	-	-	-	-
Slamannan	-0.53	1.59	1.80	-0.32	-0.32	0.55
Stirling	0.85	1.72	1.85	0.19	-0.82	1.52
St Ninians	0.12	0.88	0.68	0.54	1.28	1.15
Total	**0.61**	**1.60**	**1.58**	**0.40**	**0.55**	**2.24**

the land drainage programme initiated by Lord Kames in the mid-1760s.

Between 1801 and 1851 the number of western parishes subject to population decline rose to nine, and in a further three cases, Baldernock, Killearn and Kippen, the growth of population was barely noticeable. Only at Balfron, Kilmadock, following the extension to the Deanston cotton mills in the 1820s, and Strathblane, where two bleachfields and a calico-printing works had been instituted, did rates of population growth in the first half of the 19th century struggle marginally above the modest average reached by the western district as a whole. Only at Campsie, under the impact of the development of coal and limestone mining and the opening of new bleaching and print fields and an alum works, were rates of population increase as high as in many eastern parishes.

Between 1951 and 1911 the phenomenon of population decline spread to 11 of the 16 parishes in the western district. At Killearn and Strathblane numbers remained roughly constant while at Buchanan the growth of population was entirely a result of the presence in 1911 of 300 workers temporarily employed on the construction of the Loch Arklet dam. Only at

Callander, boosted by the growth of the tourist industry, did rates of population increase reach reasonable levels, and only at Aberfoyle, again partly due to the rise of tourism following the arrival of the railway in 1881, did they reach levels similar to the highest recorded in parishes of the east.

By comparison, the demographic fortunes of western parishes in the decades between the world wars and after World War II were much healthier. Between 1911 and 1951 the number of parishes losing population fell to six. Elsewhere rates of population growth were always positive, in the cases of Balfron, Campsie, Fintry, Killearn and Strathblane substantially so. In the period 1951-81 the number of parishes in which population declined fell to five and nowhere was the decline as pronounced as it had often been in earlier periods. Generally, for communities in the western half of the region the decades since World War II have been accompanied by significant demographic recovery.

For much of the period between the mid-18th and late 20th centuries the pattern of population growth in parishes in the eastern half of the region has differed markedly from that among those of the western half. Excluding the parish of Dunipace, for which there are no separate data for 1755, and the parishes of Ardoch and Grangemouth, which had still to be formed, eight of 20 eastern parishes experienced a decline in population in the course of the second half of the 18th century, a ratio only slightly lower than that among parishes of the west. In the 19th century, however, the contrast between the demographic evolution of eastern and western districts sharpened dramatically. In the first half of the century only three of 21 eastern parishes decreased in population, and only at Airth, as a result of the closure of the Dunmore colliery, was the decrease other than moderate. At Larbert, Logie, Muckhart and St.Ninians annual rates of population growth between 1801 and 1851 averaged from 0.5% to 1.0%, a level attained in the west only by the parishes of Campsie and Strathblane. At Alloa, where a temporary slump in the distilling industry had led to a decline in population in the later years of the 18th century, Clackmannan, Dunipace, Falkirk, Polmont, Slamannan and Stirling annual rates of population increase averaged between 1 and 2 %. At Bothkennar, Denny, Dollar and Muiravonside they were over 2%: at Kilsyth 4%: at Alva 6%: and at Tillicoultry a staggering 8%.

Significant differences in rates of population growth between the eastern and western halves of the region persisted throughout the second half of the 19th century. During the period 1851-1911 a decline in population occurred in just three of the 19 eastern parishes - at Clackmannan where it was almost entirely due to the transfer of Sauchie to the parish of Alloa, at Tillicoultry where it was in any case negligible, and at Muckhart. In sharp contrast to what happened in the west most parishes in the eastern half of the region continued to increase their populations, albeit usually at a lesser rate than in the first half of the century.

After World War I the demographic contrasts between the eastern and western districts of the region once again narrowed. Of the 21 eastern parishes the number experiencing population decline fell from seven between 1911 and 1951 to six between 1951 and 1981, ratios that were practically identical to those in the west. In the west the frequency of parochial population decline has been lower in the 20th century than it was in the 19th. In the east it has been higher. In western parishes it was not uncommon for rates of population growth to be higher between 1911 and 1951 than at any time during the 18th and 19th centuries. In eastern parishes this was the case only at Logie, where it reflected the advance of residential settlement at Causewayhead and the further development of Bridge of Allan as a tourist and dormitory town, and at Airth which served as a dormitory for Falkirk and Grangemouth. For a majority of parishes in both eastern and western districts of the region rates of population increase were greater between 1951 and 1981 than in the period between the two world wars. Significantly, however, the frequency with which this occurred was lower in the east than the west.

The result of these differences in rates of population growth between eastern and western parishes has been a striking alteration in the geographic distribution of the region's inhabitants **(Table 6)**. The bulk of this alteration in residential location occurred during the 19th century. Around the time of Alexander Webster's census more than a third of the total population lived in the western half of the region. By 1801 the proportion had fallen, but only to just below a third. Fifty years later the share of the western district had declined to less than a quarter and on the eve of the World War I to little more than a tenth. It has remained at that level ever since.

Variations in rates of population growth between the eastern and western halves of the region and between central Scotland and the country as a whole have always owed much more to differences in the balance between in- and out-migration than they have to differences in rates of natural increase. Underlying these differentials in the ability of different regions to attract and retain population were variations in the pace and location of economic growth.

Compared with what was to follow, the pace of economic development in mid Scotland during the second half of the 18th century was modest. By the last decade of the century, it is true, improved methods of arable and livestock farming associated with the so-called Agricultural Revolution had begun to spread to many parts of the region, and as a result the capacity of local agriculture to attract and retain a larger population was already greater than it had been half a century earlier. On the other hand, the extent of agricultural improvement before 1800 should not be exaggerated. As comments in the *OSA* for the parishes of Balfron, Drymen and Killearn make clear, innovations in farming practice had not yet been adopted everywhere, and even where they had they sometimes contributed

Table 6 Geographic Distribution of the Population of Central Scotland, 1755-1981, By Parish. Per Cent of Total.

	1755	1801	1851	1911	1951	1981
Aberfoyle	1.40	0.93	0.42	0.56	0.47	0.51
Balfron	1.18	2.13	1.56	0.56	0.59	0.48
Buchanan	2.66	0.97	0.52	0.38	0.20	0.21
Drymen	4.36	2.09	1.21	0.61	0.51	0.50
Fintry	1.39	1.25	0.67	0.14	0.15	0.20
Gargunnock	1.50	1.24	0.62	0.28	0.26	0.27
Kincardine	1.95	2.88	1.63	0.56	0.45	0.36
Port of Menteith	2.92	2.04	1.16	0.50	0.30	0.27
Baldernock	0.97	1.04	0.66	0.36	0.32	0.38
Campsie	2.19	3.78	5.66	2.57	3.37	2.88
Killearn	1.50	1.35	0.96	0.53	0.65	0.84
Strathblane	1.25	0.96	0.83	0.50	0.57	0.80
Balquhidder	2.49	1.79	0.72	0.32	0.28	0.22
Callander	2.74	2.97	1.41	1.07	1.00	1.14
Kilmadock	4.25	3.96	3.00	1.18	0.86	0.73
West	**35.57**	**31.63**	**22.57**	**10.77**	**10.59**	**10.37**
Ardoch	-	-	-	0.42	0.40	0.31
Dunblane Lecropt	5.17	4.07	2.43	2.22	1.76	2.71
Logie	3.10	2.56	2.09	2.12	2.90	4.16
Alva	0.68	1.02	2.62	2.55	2.30	2.58
Dollar	-0.81	0.90	1.29	0.91	0.67	0.98
Glendevon	0.34	0.19	0.10	0.07	0.06	0.07
Muckhart	0.84	0.70	0.56	0.26	0.21	0.22
Tillicoultry	1.18	1.19	3.84	2.25	2.31	2.24
Airth	3.62	2.42	1.08	0.73	0.94	0.54
Alloa	9.10	6.79	7.77	8.16	9.16	9.91
Clackmannan	2.99	3.86	4.75	1.07	1.27	1.29
Bothkennar	0.83	0.75	0.97	-	-	-
Denny	2.18	2.65	3.89	4.44	4.72	6.31
Dunipace	-	1.23	1.42	0.94	0.59	1.02
Falkirk	6.15	11.51	13.46	20.53	19.95	15.79
Grangemouth	-	-	-	9.42	10.55	13.09
Kilsyth	2.18	2.29	4.38	5.35	5.02	4.33
Larbert	2.92	4.73	3.77	6.28	6.61	6.96
Muiravonside	2.41	1.39	2.17	2.76	2.01	1.46
Polmont	1.71	2.86	3.08	-	-	-
Slamannan	1.89	1.20	1.36	1.66	1.26	0.98
Stirling	6.18	7.12	8.34	10.39	9.67	6.28
St Ninians	10.15	8.92	8.76	6.71	7.06	8.40
East	**64.43**	**68.37**	**77.43**	**89.23**	**89.41**	**89.63**

to population decline rather than growth. In conjunction with the lure of more and better-paid opportunities for employment in nearby urban-industrial areas, the consolidation of farms and displacement of tenants and farm labourers which occurred wherever sheep and livestock farming expanded at the expense of more labour-intensive arable production was rightly regarded by contemporary observers as a significant contributory factor in the decline of population evident at one time or another in the second half of the 18th century at places like Aberfoyle, Buchanan, Drymen, Fintry, Gargunnock, Killearn, Kincardine, Port of Menteith and Strathblane, in the west, and at Airth, Lecropt and Muiravonside, in the east.

Throughout this period developments in the manufacturing, mining and commercial sectors of the region's economy were also too limited in scale to have had more than a moderate impact on rates of population growth and too scattered in location to have markedly altered existing patterns of migration and the spatial distribution of the population. As late as 1800 even places like Callander and Stirling had only just begun to benefit from the opening of the Highlands to tourism. The Forth and Clyde canal, which linked Grangemouth to the Clyde and which in the following century was to have major implications for the region's economic structure, did not become fully operational until 1790. Apart from the establishment of the Carron Ironworks at Larbert in 1760, most of the more important regional innovations in mining and manufacturing did not effectively emerge until the 1780s or 1790s; cotton spinning at Balfron, Fintry and at Deanston in the parish of Kilmadock; calico printing at Campsie and Dunipace; the bleaching and printing of cloth at

Dollar, Killearn and Strathblane; the manufacture of serges and woollen blankets at Alva; the mining of iron ore at Tillicoultry; coal and iron ore mining at Kilsyth and Polmont; coalmining, iron smelting and distilling at Clackmannan. Not until the 19th century were these developments in agricultural and industrial activity sufficiently extensive and sufficiently concentrated in their location to induce radical changes in the pace and geography of population growth in the region.

For parishes which remained predominantly agricultural, most of them situated in the western half of the region, the 19th century was a time of demographic crisis. In a few cases stagnant or declining populations reflected the demise of a once thriving mining or manufacturing enterprise; cotton spinning at Balfron, Fintry and Deanston; cloth printing at Strathblane; and coalmining in the parish of Airth. In the main, however, the decline in population experienced by so many western parishes at one time or another during the 19th century stemmed from the failure of their largely agrarian economies to offer the same opportunities for employment that were becoming increasingly available in rapidly expanding industrial and mining communities nearby. For most western parishes, where agriculture continued to be the principal employer and especially where the trend towards sheep farming and the consolidation of farm holdings was most intense, the ability to attract and retain population steadily declined.

In the eastern half of the region economic circumstances were very different. Here, although agriculture remained an important activity in many parishes, the economy became increasingly industrialised and commercialised, and accordingly found it easier to support ever-larger numbers of people.

In the vicinity of Falkirk and Larbert the industry most responsible for the rapid growth of immigration and population in the century or so leading up to the outbreak of World War I was the iron industry. In turn the requirements of this industry for raw materials helped boost employment opportunities, and thus rates of population growth, in the neighbouring parishes of Bothkennar, Clackmannan, Denny, Dunipace, Kilsyth, Polmont and St.Ninians where there were rich seams of coal or iron ore. Further north economic growth and the increase in population which inevitably accompanied it rested on activities of a different kind. High rates of population growth at Dollar in the first half of the 19th century, for example, were largely due to the establishment of McNab's Academy. At Logie parish they originated chiefly from the emergence of Bridge of Allan first as a summer holiday resort and later as a residential community for the town of Stirling. At Alva, Dunblane and Tillicoultry they rested primarily on the success of the local textile industries and at Alloa on a combination of textiles, brewing, distilling and glass and bottle manufacture. Together, these developments in commercial, industrial and mining enterprise explain why it was that the population of central Scotland in the late 19th and early 20th centuries grew more quickly than that of Scotland as a whole and why most of the growth was concentrated in the eastern half of the region.

In the decades after World War I the pattern of intra-regional population growth that had been established during the 19th century was transformed by the onset of a sustained decline in the prosperity of the coal, iron and textile industries. In western districts, where manufacturing and mining activity was relatively rare and the exodus of people from agricultural communities largely completed by the end of World War I, parochial rates of population growth between 1911 and 1981 were usually higher than they had ever been. Only at Buchanan, Port of Menteith and Kilmadock, in the period 1911-51, were significant reductions in numbers recorded, at Buchanan partly in response to the closure of the Balmaha acid works in 1920 and at Kilmadock as a result of the continued decline of the Deanston cotton mills. Elsewhere the decrease in population was arrested and, particularly after World War II, parish populations once more began to rise. At Campsie the process was greatly assisted by the opening of the Lennox Castle hospital in 1936. At Killearn it owed much to the foundation of a hospital originally intended for wartime casualties from Glasgow, and at Gargunnock to the construction of residential housing for people employed in Stirling. More generally, however, the increase in population which has occurred at places like Aberfoyle, Balfron, Balquhidder, Callander, Drymen and Fintry in the decades since World War II stemmed from a revival of employment opportunities generated by the development of forestry and the further growth of the tourist industry.

In complete contrast to what happened in the west, rates of population increase in parishes in the east of the region during the period 1911-81 were invariably lower than they had been in the 19th and early 20th centuries. Faced by a prolonged decline in the prosperity of its staple industries, the ability of the eastern half of the region to attract and hold people and thus to sustain the high rates of population growth typical of the period before 1914 was greatly reduced.

Even so, both between 1911 and 1951 and 1951 and 1981, rates of population growth in eastern parishes remained higher than those in the west, and higher also than the average for Scotland as a whole.

One reason for this was the fact that the decline of the staple industries was generally less severe in central Scotland than in most other parts of the country. Geared as it was to the production of light rather than heavy castings, the local iron industry was relatively well-placed to take advantage of the national boom in housebuilding which began in the 1930s and re-emerged in the 1950s. For some time after World War II coalmining continued to flourish in the parish of

St.Ninians and at various places on the Clackmannanshire coalfield, where even as older pits closed others remained in operation and new ones - at Clackmannan, Sauchie, Tillicoultry and Tullibody for instance - opened. Situated close to the cities of Edinburgh and Glasgow, to which they were brought ever closer in time by further improvements in road and, at least until the late 1960s, rail transport, and blessed by an attractive natural environment, some communities in the east, like many in the west, have also benefitted from the rise of tourism and the growing demand of urban workers for a desirable residential environment.

The main reason for the maintenance of relatively high rates of population growth in eastern parishes, however, has been the ability of their economies to respond successfully to changes in market conditions by diversifying production away from the staple industries towards a range of industrial goods and commercial services for which demand was increasing more rapidly. At Alloa the economy diversified into the manufacture of agricultural machinery, bricks, general engineering products and knitwear; at Alva into printing, preserves, soft fruits and knitwear; and at Clackmannan into bricks, paper and woollens. In the neighbourhood of Denny and Dunipace the decline of the mining industry was cushioned by the growth of brickmaking, ironfounding and papermaking industries. At Falkirk and Larbert new employment opportunities were generated by the development of bookbinding, coach and caravan, confectionery and enamelling industries and the production of aluminium sheets, chromium plates, paint solvents and special fuels; at Grangemouth by the dyestuffs, oil refining, petrochemical, shipping and shipbuilding industries; in the town of Stirling and its immediate environs by the production of agricultural machinery, leather and rubber goods, textiles and, especially, by the emergence of a wide range of professional and scientific service activities; and at Tillicoultry by the manufacture of coated paper, stationery and knitwear.

Throughout the period between the 1750s and the 1860s the changes which had already started to occur in the economic structure of mid Scotland were too limited in extent to raise regional rates of population growth to the level reached by the country as a whole. From the 1870s, however, rates of population increase in the region have usually exceeded the national average. Driving this transformation in comparative demographic evolution was the emergence of a regional economy which, for all its problems, was more successful than the economies of most other regions of the country. During the late 19th and early 20th centuries, when regional rates of population growth first rose significantly above the national average, the relative economic prosperity of the region rested primarily on the wealth generated by the traditional industries of coal, iron and textiles. In the decades since 1951, when the excess of regional over national rates of population growth was even more pronounced, it has depended on a broader base of economic activity, from forestry and tourism in the west to professional and scientific services and new industries like petrochemicals in the east. This capacity of the region's inhabitants for capitalising effectively on the opportunities afforded by advantages of location and natural resource endowments bodes well for its future ability to attract more people by immigration than it will lose through emigration.

Accompanying the growth of population in central Scotland between 1755 and 1981 were notable alterations in the sex, age and marital composition of the region's inhabitants and in the distribution of residence between urban and rural locations.

Table 7 Males per Hundred Females. 1801-1981

	Clackmannanshire	Stirlingshire	Scotland
1801	87	89	85
1851	97	94	90
1961	94	96	92
1981	95	95	93

The main characteristics of the sex structure of central Scotland's population are summarised in **Table 7 and Appendix 2**. As the latter shows, throughout the period there were always considerable differences in the ratio of males to females from one parish to another and by no means all parishes followed similar trends in the evolution of sex ratios over time. Yet this should not be allowed to obscure the fact that certain aspects of sex structure were common to most parishes. Throughout the period, both for the counties of Clackmannan and Stirling and for the great majority of their constituent parishes, the number of female inhabitants invariably exceeded the number of male, a combined result of lower levels of mortality among the former and higher levels of emigration among the latter. The balance in favour of females, however, was less pronounced at the end of the period than at the beginning, most of the change occurring during the first half of the 19th century. In their levels and trends the sex ratios of the populations of Clackmannanshire and Stirlingshire differed little from those for the whole country.

On the evidence of the limited amount of data on ages contained in the *OSA* around 25% of the resident population of central Scotland at the end of the 18th century was under ten years of age, 44% under 20, 39% between 20 and 50 and 17% over 50, an age structure very similar to that for the country as a whole and probably little different from that of the mid-1750s (Flinn 1977: 257, 263). (**see Tables 8 and 9**)

Table 8 Age Distribution. Central Scotland. Early 1790s, By Parish. Per Cent of Total Population

	< 10	10 - 20	20 - 50	50+
Aberfoyle	22.9	19.6	42.2	15.3
Alloa (10-16, 16-50)	24.6	12.1	48.6	14.8
Alva	27.0	21.6	37.6	13.9
Baldernock	21.9	21.5	39.0	17.6
Bothkennar	22.2			
Callander	29.7	12.4	43.0	14.9
Campsie	35.0			
Clackmannan	25.0	10.2	39.6	16.3
Dollar	23.5	13.3		
Fintry	25.1	20.3	41.1	13.3
Gargunnock	20.1	21.9	39.6	18.3
Kippen	19.3	22.5	39.1	19.1
Muckhart	24.3	22.6	32.9	20.2
Muiravonside	28.4			
Slamannan	26.3	25.5	31.7	16.5
Strathblane	22.6	20.2	39.8	17.4
Tillicoultry	27.9	19.1	35.3	17.7

Except for a slight decline in the proportion of the population aged 50 and over, the age structure of the combined populations of Clackmannanshire and Stirlingshire remained more or less unchanged throughout the first three quarters of the 19th century. Not until the last quarter of the century, largely as a result of falling fertility, did it begin to change. The change has been greatest in the youngest and oldest age-groups. Between 1851 and 1981 the percentage of the population under ten years of age almost halved while that above 50 more than doubled. By contrast, the decline in the share of the population aged between ten and 50 has been modest. Overall, as has been the case for Scotland as a whole, the average age of the population of the central region has risen steadily in the course of the last 100 years or so.

For the 18th and first half of the 19th centuries little information is available on the marital structure of the country's population.

From fragments of data contained in 18th century parish burial registers and in the *OSA* for the early 1790s it is clear that the proportions of women aged 40, 45 or 50 who died never having married varied considerably from one parish to another, the ratios ranging from as low as 2.7% to as high as 39.8%. In the two parishes of central Scotland for which data are extant, Logie (1773-87) and Slamannan (early 1790s), the proportions were 19.9% and 14% respectively, ratios which suggest that, in common with most other areas in the western lowlands and borders, levels of permanent spinsterhood in the central region were higher than in eastern regions of the country (ibid: 280-2). Unfortunately, because of the piecemeal nature of the evidence, we have no way of knowing if the marital composition of the population of Scotland and its different regions altered in the course of this early period, though the fact that the ratio of spinsters aged 50 and over in 1851 was roughly similar to that typical of most of the 18th century parishes for which we have information might be taken to indicate that any change that did occur was relatively small.

For the period beginning around the middle of the 19th century, following the improvements made to methods of census taking in 1841 and 1851, data on regional and chronological variations in marital status become more abundant. **Tables 10 and 11** summarise the unmistakable transformation which occurred between 1851 and 1981, all of it within the period since World War I (ibid: 324-8, 331-4). Two developments are especially noteworthy. First, as a result of the more or less continuous decline in rates of mortality, the percentage of widows and widowers in each age-group in 1981 was distinctly lower than in 1851. Second, for both men and women and in almost all age-groups, the ratio of married to unmarried persons in 1981 was considerably higher than it had been a century or so before. The difference is particularly marked in the ages 20-39 and largely reflects a general trend towards earlier marriage in the decades since World War II.

Table 9 Age Distribution, 1851-1981, Per Cent of Total Population

	Clackmannanshire			Stirlingshire			Scotland		
	1851	1961	1981	1851	1961	1981	1851	1961	1981
0-9	27.4	18.2	14.3	21.8	16.9	13.2	24.6	17.2	13.0
10-19	22.4	17.5	18.4	17.8	16.2	17.4	21.4	15.9	17.3
20-49	39.0	38.7	39.7	49.4	39.8	39.8	39.6	38.7	39.1
50 and over	11.3	25.7	27.6	11.1	27.1	29.6	14.1	28.3	30.6

Apart from a slight overall tendency for the inhabitants of central Scotland to be more prone to marry than those of the country as a whole, neither in 1851 nor in 1981 was there any great difference between the marital structures of the region and the nation.

Throughout the period 1755 to 1981 the central region has remained predominantly an area of small communities. The region has no city nor even a major town, as late as 1971 the two largest urban settlements, Falkirk and Stirling, containing just 37,374 and 32,908 inhabitants respectively.

By 1981 the population of Falkirk had fallen to 36,881 while that of Stirling had risen, though only to 38,842. The most urbanised part of the region runs from Bonnybridge to Grangemouth in the south-east, with less intensive zones of urbanisation around the towns of Alloa and Stirling. Partly because of the ruggedness of its terrain and partly because of the primarily agricultural character of its economy, the western half of the region is largely devoid of urban settlement (Timms 1974: 191, 252-3). Both in 1971 and 1981 over a quarter of the region's inhabitants still resided in continuously built-up areas with populations of less than 10,000.

Table 10 Marital Distribution 1851. Per Cent of Total in each Age-Group

	Clackmannanshire			Stirlingshire			Scotland		
Male	**Unmarried**	**Married**	**Widowed**	**Unmarried**	**Married**	**Widowed**	**Unmarried**	**Married**	**Widowed**
15-19	99.3	0.8	-	99.7	0.3	-	99.6	0.4	0.0
20-29	64.4	35.2	0.4	68.6	30.7	0.7	69.0	30.4	0.6
30-39	21.6	76.0	2.5	24.3	64.4	11.3	27.8	69.5	2.7
40-49	13.0	81.2	5.8	18.5	75.3	6.2	16.9	77.0	6.1
50-59	12.6	74.7	12.6	15.4	73.8	10.8	13.3	76.2	10.6
60-99	10.7	71.5	17.8	14.3	67.2	18.5	11.2	69.8	19.0
70 and over	9.6	53.7	36.7	9.1	47.8	41.2	9.2	54.3	36.5
Female									
15-19	97.9	2.1	0.1	97.4	2.6	0.0	97.9	2.1	0.0
20-9	52.4	46.4	1.2	57.8	40.9	1.3	62.0	36.7	1.3
30-9	21.4	73.1	5.6	25.1	68.6	6.3	28.5	65.2	6.3
40-9	15.9	71.3	12.8	20.2	66.3	13.5	21.7	63.8	14.5
50-9	17.2	55.2	27.6	18.9	55.2	25.9	20.6	53.5	25.9
60-9	16.6	40.9	42.5	19.3	37.1	43.5	20.8	37.7	41.5
70 and over	17.2	17.2	65.6	17.1	18.9	64.1	20.9	18.9	60.2

Table 11 Marital Distribution. 1981. Per Cent of Total in each Age-Group, Divorced are included with married

	Clackmannanshire			Stirlingshire			Scotland		
Male	**Unmarried**	**Married**	**Widowed**	**Unmarried**	**Married**	**Widowed**	**Unmarried**	**Married**	**Widowed**
15-19	97.7	2.3	-	98.5	1.5	0.0	98.4	1.6	0.0
20-9	43.7	56.2	0.1	49.3	50.7	0.1	51.8	48.1	0.1
30-9	9.2	90.6	0.2	12.5	87.2	0.3	14.1	85.6	0.3
40-9	6.0	93.0	1.0	8.3	90.7	1.0	9.7	89.3	1.0
50-9	7.3	89.5	3.3	10.0	86.9	3.2	10.5	86.2	3.3
60-9	7.3	85.2	7.5	11.0	80.6	8.4	10.5	80.7	8.8
70 and over	8.0	67.8	24.2	12.0	63.0	25.1	11.2	63.8	25.0
Female									
15-19	91.9	8.1	-	95.1	4.0	0.0	95.0	5.0	0.0
20-9	26.9	72.9	0.3	33.2	66.5	0.3	36.5	63.2	0.3
30-9	4.5	94.8	0.8	6.7	92.6	0.7	0.8	91.1	0.9
40-9	4.6	91.9	3.5	6.1	90.5	3.5	7.0	89.4	3.6
50-9	6.2	82.8	11.0	9.0	79.9	11.1	10.0	78.1	11.9
60-9	8.4	60.9	30.7	10.8	59.3	30.0	12.5	57.8	29.7
70 and over	17.2	25.5	57.3	16.6	26.3	57.1	18.9	24.9	56.2

A rough indication of the changes which have occurred between 1851 and 1971 in the proportions of the populations of Clackmannanshire and Stirlingshire living in urban settlements is given in **Table 12.**

Table 12 The Percentage of the Populations Resident in Burghs, 1851-1971

	Clackmannanshire	Stirlingshire
1851	43.1	36.0
1861	54.3	41.4
1871	64.0	52.8
1881	63.7	47.7
1891	64.7	49.0
1901	60.6	53.7
1911	66.9	53.2
1921	65.2	52.4
1931	67.6	54.5
1951	60.6	55.4
1961	57.5	56.1
1971	54.0	55.7

In both counties the ratio of burgh residents to total population rose significantly during the third quarter of the 19th century. In Stirlingshire, with only occasional and minor reversals, the ratio has continued to rise ever since, though at a very much slower rate. In the case of Clackmannanshire, however, the further increase in the share of the burgh population between the 1880s and 1930s was barely noticeable and after World War II the ratio of burgh to total population actually declined. Of the four Clackmannanshire burghs only the small burgh of Dollar increased substantially in size between 1951 and 1971. At Alloa and Tillicoultry, by contrast, the number of inhabitants grew by only around 5% and at Alva by less than 2%. In the Stirlingshire burghs of Falkirk, Kilsyth and Stirling, too, the growth of population between 1951 and 1971 was negligible. Much of the difference in trends in the ratio of burgh to total population between the counties of Clackmannanshire and Stirlingshire since World War II is explained by what happened at Bridge of Allan, Denny and Dunipace and, above all, Grangemouth. At Bridge of Allan, boosted by the opening of the University of Stirling and the continued development of the town as a commuter base, the number of inhabitants rose by 36% in the course of the 1950s and 1960s; at Denny and Dunipace, thanks to the growth of the local brickmaking, ironfounding and papermaking industries, by over 45%; and at Grangemouth, where the success of the oil-based industries caused population to grow by over 59%. In neither county, however, have levels of urbanisation ever been more than moderate, a circumstance chiefly explained by a combination of the small-scale nature of much of the region's manufacturing industry and the significant contribution made to the regional economy by agriculture and commercial and service activities.

If detailed comparison of the periods before and after the middle of the 18th century were possible it would undoubtedly reveal that most of the major changes that have taken place in the demographic fabric of central Scotland have occurred in the last two hundred years. Whether assessed in terms of changes in the size and rate of growth of population, rates of fertility, mortality and migration, age, sex and marital structures, the geography of intra-regional settlement or the extent of urbanisation what happened between 1755 and 1981 can only be described as a revolution in the region's demographic character. In its main components the demography of central Scotland around the 1750s would not have been too unfamiliar to earlier generations. That of the 1980s, on the other hand, would have been entirely foreign and wholly unimaginable. At the heart of this transformation in demographic conditions were the forces of modern economic growth and the changes these made possible to the relationship between man and his environment. It is unlikely that the consequences of economic growth for human demography, at least in this region, will ever again be as startling as they have been in the last two hundred years.

REFERENCES AND FURTHER READING

CROUTHER GORDON, T. 1966. The County of Clackmannan. The Third Statistical Account of Scotland. Collins, Glasgow.

FLINN, M. W. Editor. 1977. Scottish Population History from the 17th Century to the 1930s. Cambridge University Press, Cambridge.

FLINN, M. W. 1981. The European Demographic System, 1500-1820. Harvester Press, Brighton.

GRAY, M. 1990. Scots on the Move. Scots Migrants 1750-1914. The Economic and Social History Society of Scotland.

KYD, J. G. 1952. Scottish Population Statistics including Webster's Analysis of Population 1755. Scottish History Society, Edinburgh.

MITCHELL, B. R. with DEANE, P. 1962. Abstract of British Historical Statistics. Cambridge University Press, Cambridge.

MITCHELL, B. R. and JONES, H. G. Second Abstract of British Historical Statistics. Cambridge University Press, Cambridge.

NEW STATISTICAL ACCOUNT OF SCOTLAND. 1845. VIII.Dumbarton, Stirling and Clackmannan. X.Perth. Blackwood, Edinburgh and London.

RENNIE, R. C. 1966. The County of Stirling. The Third Statistical Account of Scotland. Collins, Glasgow.

TAYLOR, D. 1979. The Counties of Perth and Kinross. The Third Statistical Account of Scotland. Culross the Printers, Coupar Angus.

TIMMS, D. W. G. Editor. 1974. The Stirling Region. University of Stirling, Stirling.

TRANTER, N. L. 1985. Population and Society. Contrasts in Population Growth. Longman, London and New York.

WITHERS, C. W. J. 1985. Highland migration to Dundee,Perth and Stirling,1753-1891. *Journal of Historical Geography* 11, 4, 395-418.

WITHRINGTON, D. J. and GRANT, I. R. Editors. 1978. The Statistical Account of Scotland. IX. Dunbartonshire, Stirlingshire and Clackmannanshire. Reprinted by EP Publishing, East Ardsley.

WITHRINGTON, D. J. and GRANT, I. R. Editors. 1976. The Statistical Account of Scotland. XI. South and East Perthshire, Kinross-shire. Reprinted by EP Publishing, East Ardsley.

WRIGLEY, E. A. and SCHOFIELD, R. S. 1981. The Population History of England, 1541-1871. A Reconstruction. Edward Arnold, London.

See also the decennial published Censuses of Scotland 1801-1981 and the annual reports of the Registrar-General of Births, Deaths and Marriages in Scotland 1855-1981.

Appendix 1 The Population of Central Scotland, by Parish, 1755-1981.

	1755	1801	1811	1821	1831	1841	1851	1861
Aberfoyle	895	711	601	730	660	543	514	565
Airth	2,316	1,855	1,703	1,900	1,825	1,498	1,319	1,194
Alloa	5,816	5,214	5,096	5,577	6,377	7,921	9,493	8,867
Alva	436	787	921	1,197	1,300	2,216	3,204	3,282
Ardoch	-	-	-	-	-	-	-	1,418
Baldernock	621	796	806	892	805	792	801	718
Balfron	755	1,634	1,986	2,041	2,057	1,970	1,900	1,517
Balquhidder	1,592	1,377	1,353	1,224	1,949	871	874	746
Bothkennar	529	575	821	895	905	849	1,179	1,722
Buchanan	1,699	748	627	763	787	754	632	705
Callander	1,750	2,281	2,042	2,031	1,909	1,665	1,716	1,676
Campsie	1,399	2,906	3,618	4,927	5,109	6,402	6,918	6,483
Clackmannan	1,913	2,961	3,605	4,056	4,266	5,145	5,802	4,425
Denny	1,392	2,033	2,654	3,364	3,843	4,916	4,754	4,988
Dollar	517	683	743	1,295	1,447	1,562	1,574	1,776
Drymen	2,789	1,607	1,500	1,652	1,690	1,515	1,481	1,619
Dunblane	2,728	2,619	2,733	3,135	3,228	3,361	3,213	2,528
Dunblane/Lecropt	-	-	-	-	-	-	-	-
Dunipace	-	948	1,099	1,168	1,278	1,578	1,472	1,731
Falkirk	3,932	8,838	9,929	11,536	12,743	15,621	16,438	17,026
Fintry	891	958	1,003	1,002	1,051	884	823	685
Gargunnock	956	954	896	862	1,006	803	754	728
Glendevon	220	149	170	139	192	157	128	138
Grangemouth	-	-	-	-	-	-	-	-
Killearn	959	1,039	997	1,126	1,206	1,224	1,176	1,171
Kilmadock	2,730	3,044	3,131	3,150	3,752	4,055	3,659	3,312
Kilsyth	1,395	1,762	3,206	4,260	4,297	5,613	5,346	6,112
Kincardine	1,250	2,212	2,419	2,388	2,455	2,232	1,993	1,778
Kippen	1,799	1,722	1,893	2,029	2,085	1,922	1,892	1,722
Larbert	1,864	3,629	3,842	3,491	4,248	4,404	4,606	4,999
Lecropt	577	508	508	513	443	513	442	538
Logie	1,985	1,967	2,021	2,015	1,945	2,200	2,551	3,483
Muckhart	535	538	540	704	617	706	685	615
Muiravonside	1,539	1,070	1,330	1,678	1,540	2,249	2,647	2,660
Polmont	1,094	2,194	1,827	2,171	3,210	3,584	3,764	4,111
Port of Menteith	1,865	1,569	1,659	1,614	1,664	1,446	1,419	1,375
Slamannan	1,209	923	993	981	1.093	979	1,655	2,916
Stirling	3,951	5,470	6,026	7,314	8,556	9,095	10,180	11,714
St Ninians	6,491	6,849	7,363	8,274	9,552	10,080	9,851	8,946
Strathblane	797	734	795	748	1,030	1,045	1,010	1,388
Tillicoultry	757	916	1,025	1,163	1,472	3,213	4,686	5,054
Total	**63,943**	**76,790**	**83,754**	**94,002**	**102,692**	**115,583**	**122,125**	**126,432**

Ardoch parish was formed in 1855 out of parts of the parishes of Blackford, Dunblane and Muthill.

The parishes of Dunblane and Lecropt were united in 1898.

The parish of Grangemouth was formed in 1900 from a union of parts of the parishes of Bothkennar (the remainder of which was transfered to Falkirk parish), and Falkirk and the parish of Polmont.

No separate figures are available for the population of Dunipace in 1755. Until 1801 Dunipace was returned with Larbert.

1871	1881	1891	1901	1911	1921	1931	1951	1961	1971	1981
432	465	1,023	1,052	1,147	1,169	1,014	1,134	1,316	1,276	1,427
1,396	1,362	1,325	1,360	1,515	1,777	2,226	2,234	1,726	1,585	1,502
9,940	11,638	13,728	16,858	17,130	18,450	18,245	21,874	25,428	28,043	27,547
4,296	5,113	5,360	5,641	5,265	5,120	4,853	5,502	5,314	5,842	7,159
1,316	1,102	959	916	863	985	1,029	944	786	644	867
616	569	553	582	747	763	674	769	740	692	1.066
1,502	1,327	1,203	1,092	1,155	1,190	1,200	1,411	1,393	1,451	1,345
743	627	612	605	664	875	619	671	637	558	618
2,455	3,271	4,134	-	-	-	-	-	-	-	-
591	550	658	487	795	585	438	486	580	588	573
1,870	2,167	2,279	2,171	2,215	2,764	2,423	2,382	2,319	2,230	3,176
6,739	5,873	5,338	5,424	5,304	5,335	5,296	8,039	8,199	8,018	8,016
4,653	4,543	5,072	2,501	2,203	2,373	2,585	3,024	3,030	3,649	3,597
4,993	5,728	6,373	8,268	9,166	9,187	9,488	11,273	13,110	14,822	17,526
2,524	2,500	2,221	2,042	1,874	1,954	1,804	1,604	2,206	2,658	2,730
1,405	1,431	1,512	1,390	1,269	1,214	1,128	1,221	1,152	1,231	1,389
2,765	3,123	3,220	-	-	-	-	-	-	-	-
-	-	-	3,812	4,591	4,654	4,421	4,212	4,248	5,905	7,537
1,733	1,874	1,716	2,050	1,936	1,814	1,786	1,418	2,572	2,505	2,844
18,051	25,143	30,731	36,628	42,423	42,762	45,444	47,664	46,517	45,238	43,886
499	414	357	314	280	381	279	356	286	438	560
675	698	674	633	573	586	570	613	619	745	757
105	147	109	147	148	134	119	139	143	155	189
-	-	-	17,463	19,470	18,708	20,683	25,199	29,112	36,661	36,394
1,111	1,131	1,182	929	1,085	1,054	908	1,556	1,699	1,895	2,328
3,170	3,012	2,837	2,705	2,428	2,363	2,282	2,054	2,004	1,831	2,038
6,313	6,840	7,424	9,840	11,052	10,364	10,047	11,990	11,555	11,574	12,025
1,484	1,351	1,200	1,309	1,150	1,140	1,126	1,080	1,043	929	994
1,568	1,449	1,486	1,456	1,365	1,518	1,356	1,455	1,400	1,368	1,566
5,280	6,346	8,340	11,684	12,984	12,389	13,028	15,788	17,087	18,527	19,348
535	602	613	-	-	-	-	-	-	-	-
4,553	4,696	4,976	4,432	4,373	5,105	4,579	6,921	7,124	9,268	11,574
612	601	542	475	535	599	482	493	487	552	599
2,653	2,713	3,671	5,332	5,706	5,758	5,561	4,813	4,407	4,550	4,049
3,910	3,955	4,949	-	-	-	-	-	-	-	-
1,243	1,175	1,092	1,088	1,035	1,019	940	721	793	762	751
4,164	5,850	6,731	5,286	3,440	3,409	2,959	3,004	3,311	2,798	2,714
12,014	13,480	14,394	18,609	21,461	21,722	22,897	23,105	19,942	19,287	17,456
10,146	10,423	9,347	8,152	13,868	14,812	14,757	16,858	20,873	23,358	23,354
1,235	1,343	1,671	880	1,024	1,275	1,161	1,354	1,466	1,931	2,231
5,118	5,344	5,695	4,987	4,649	4,645	4,461	5,528	5,415	5,357	6,225
134,408	**149,976**	**165,307**	**188,600**	**206,629**	**209,963**	**212,868**	**238,889**	**250,039**	**268,921**	**277,957**

Appendix 2 Males per Hundred Females, By Parish. Central Scotland, 1790s - 1961.

	Early 1790s	1851	1961
Aberfoyle	95	110	94
Airth		97	97
Alloa	92	96	94
Alva		93	91
Ardoch			97
Baldernock		95	98
Balfron		96	93
Balquhidder		112	97
Bothkennar	102	102	
Buchanan		102	101
Callander	91	92	86
Campsie	96	93	93
Clackmannan	91	102	103
Denny		92	100
Dollar		87	94
Drymen		112	97
Dunblane		93	
Dunblane and Lecropt		96	
Dunipace		93	98
Falkirk		98	96
Fintry	101	82	92
Gargunnock	94	99	83
Glendevon		103	86
Grangemouth			103
Killearn		100	86
Kilmadock		80	93
Kilsyth		99	95
Kincardine		96	88
Kippen	91	97	89
Larebrt		98	100
Lecropt		95	
Logie		88	85
Muckhard	83	96	92
Muiravonside		106	106
Polmont		103	
Port of Menteith		113	127
St Ninians		96	98
Slamannan	86	109	98
Stirling		89	90
Strathblane		97	83
Tillicoultry	78	99	91

Parliamentary Politics

I. G. C. Hutchison

The first Reform Act of 1832 greatly widened the extremely narrow Scottish franchise system and initiated the transition to democratic, mass politics: thus the number of electors in Stirling County rose from just under 100 to 1,787. The parliamentary political history of the central Scotland constituencies since 1832 may be said to fall into three broad phases. From 1832 until the First World War, the area was mainly, though not overwhelmingly, Liberal; from the end of that war until the mid-1970s, Labour was by far the most successful party; but since 1974 Labour's pre-eminence has been strongly contested.

Liberal Ascendancy, 1832-1918

Between 1832 and 1918 there were three seats wholly or mainly within the area known as central Scotland. Clackmannanshire was joined with Kinross-shire to form one constituency, but the former had comfortably more voters. The burgh of Stirling was linked with Culross, Dunfermline, Inverkeithing and South Queensferry in the Stirling Burghs constituency. Apart from the towns of Stirling and Falkirk, all the rest of Stirlingshire was contained in the Stirlingshire seat. Falkirk was taken out of the county constituency in 1832 and joined with Airdrie, Hamilton, Lanark and Linlithgow to create the Airdrie district of burghs. Effective power in this seat lay with the Lanarkshire component, and accordingly very little attention has been given to developments in this constituency. In addition, the burghs of Dunblane, Doune and Callander were included in the Perthshire constituency, and so their political history is also largely not treated here.

The first reform act effected its huge transformation by granting the vote to males owning or renting property valued at £10 pa. In practice, this meant a middle class electorate was brought into play: in urban areas this embraced merchants, manufacturers, professional men, shopkeepers and small businessmen; in the countryside, tenant farmers, rural tradesmen and the like.

One object of this exercise was that the Whig government wished to weaken the political power of the Tories by widening the vote to end landlord dominance of small county electorates. In the case of Stirlingshire, this aim was not realised for thirty years, as the Conservatives held the seat continuously from 1835 until 1865. This long Tory grip on the constituency was most unusual in Scotland, where Liberal hegemony even in shire seats was far more common: Clackmannanshire, with no Conservative elected between 1832 and 1918, was more normal. There were various reasons for Stirling's long attachment to the

Conservative cause. One was that the two larger towns, Stirling and Falkirk, were withdrawn from the constituency. This meant that few urban populations of any size were included, and in other seats these formed the core of a Liberal opposition to Tory landlords. Secondly, the large landowners in the county were solidly Conservative, with virtually none inclined to Whiggery. Most shires had some substantial proprietors in the anti-Tory camp, giving a balance to political proceedings. A survey in 1883 identified the main landowners (i.e. those with over 4,000 acres) in Stirlingshire (total area 288,349 acres) as:

Duke of Montrose	68,545 acres
Forbes of Callendar	13,041 acres
Edmonstone of Duntreath	9,778 acres
Graham-Bontine of Gartmore	6,931 acres
Fletcher-Campbell of Bothquan	5,679 acres
Johnstone of Alva	5,340 acres
Seton-Stuart of Touch	4,801 acres
Earl of Zetland	4,656 acres
Earl of Dunmore	4,620 acres

Of these, only Johnstone of Alva and Graham-Bontine were inclined to Liberalism, and even their allegiance was at times questionable. But the overwhelming bulk of the leading proprietors were Tory.

Several consequences arose from this. Firstly, it was possible for landowners to create votes. This was because the old Scottish franchise - which had been based not on physical ownership of land but on ownership of the feudal superiority - had not been abolished in 1832 (Ferguson 1965). So a landowner could divide up his feudal superiorities into £10 units, assign these to political sympathisers, who would then be registered as qualified voters. After the Whigs won the first election held under the new franchise, the Tories set to creating votes with a will in the 1830s and 1840s. Not only was the manufacture of votes carried out on existing estates, but the friends and election agents of William Forbes of Callendar, the Tory MP for the county, set about looking to purchase property suitable for making votes. Great delight was taken in the prospect of buying up a small estate near Campsie previously owned by a Whig, with the aim of breaking it up to produce four new votes.

By the 1841 election the Whig vote had fallen from 995 in 1832 to 895, while the Conservative poll had moved from 465 up to 1,019. How much of this increase was due to fictitious voters cannot be ascertained. The defeated Whig candidate in the 1837 contest, admittedly a less than dispassionate observer, alleged that of the increase of eighty in the Conservative vote since the previous election in 1835, seventy were faggot voters. In the two years 1837-8, a period of intense vote manufacture, the net Conservative gains at the annual registration of voters totalled 105. The Whigs of course were not innocent of using the same device to enhance their electoral prospects, but as we have seen they lacked sufficient property to match their opponents.

There were other means by which the Tory gentry kept control of the seat. Communications were passed on to the tenant farmers on estates indicating which party the laird supported and expressing the hope that his tenants would follow suit. As there was still open voting, it was a brave tenant who risked defying his landlord, who might exact some retribution. It is more likely, however, that the tenantry went with the proprietor not because of naked intimidation but more out of a sense of deference towards the social elite. In addition, landlords frequently withheld permission for the opposition party to canvass personally on their estates. The shopkeeper and tradesman class could also be influenced by the landlords. Many of these small businesses would rely heavily on the custom of the local gentry, and the threat of withdrawal of patronage in retaliation for political deviance could spell financial ruin for a small town trader.

A further strength of the Conservatives was financial. The cost of maintaining the electoral registers and of fighting contested elections was considerable. The bills submitted to Forbes by his election agent for the four years between 1834 and 1837 totalled £10,660. At this time the annual wage of a skilled artisan would not exceed £80. In 1865 Forbes's son was told by the Conservative election agents that a contest would involve spending £6,000 *at least*. To raise the necessary funds, the Conservatives devised a scheme in the later 1830s whereby landowners contributed one per cent of their annual rental income. The Duke of Montrose was stated in 1840 to have an annual rental in the county of £6,000, and Edmondstone of Duntreath £4,000, so there was patently no serious financial difficulties for the party. The Whigs could never hope to keep pace with this level of spending. After the 1841 election showed the conservatives had established a comfortable lead, there was no challenge mounted against them for a quarter of a century.

The other county constituency, Clackmannan/Kinross, was dominated by the Clackmannan element, which contained about 60 per cent of the total electorate. Two large landowners were firmly on the Whig side: Adam of Blair Adam and Abercrombie of Tullibody. The largest proprietor in Clackmannan, the Earl of Mar, was a Conservative but took little part in politics. Unlike Stirlingshire, the urban electorate was proportionately significant and its composition was also different. Alloa and the Hillfoots towns were much more industrial than the small towns in the Stirlingshire seat. This meant there was a solid group of manufacturers and merchants on the electoral register. These were in the main ardent Liberals who formed a solid alliance with the Whig lairds. The Tories were therefore virtually excluded from a share in the representation of the seat. When James Johnstone of Alva offered himself as a candidate in 1851, he was closely questioned by the Liberals of the constituency because he had been identified in the 1830s with the Conservative cause in Stirlingshire. He was forced to disavow any pro-Conservative feelings before standing. So complete was the rout of the Tories in the first two post-reform contests that no Conservative stood between 1835 and 1874.

The Stirling district of burghs was if anything even more intensely Liberal than the Clackmannan/Kinross seat. No Conservative stood in the constituency after 1832 until 1886, and even then the candidate was labelled a Liberal Unionist. But even within this solidly Liberal constituency, great changes were taking place within a decade of the first reform act, and these developments foreshadowed the pattern in the other two central Scotland seats in the latter part of the century. Between 1832 and 1847 the MP for the burghs was Lord Dalmeny, heir to the Earl of Rosebery, who was a significant landowner in the vicinity of the South Queensferry portion of the seat. By 1847, however, the merchants and manufacturers of the two major centres, Dunfermline and Stirling, decided to demonstrate their political power. Dalmeny stood down, and in his stead the Liberals of the burghs chose J.B. Smith, who was the leader of the Anti-Corn Law League. By replacing a member of the landed aristocracy with the champion of the free trade ideology which was the leading doctrine espoused by the urban bourgeoisie, the business community of the constituency made a dramatic symbolic gesture.

But politically correct though the choice of Smith was from the standpoint of economic values, it was hopelessly mistaken when considered in the perspective of the other driving force behind the political activism of the urban middle class of the burghs. Smith was a Unitarian, which in the eyes of strict presbyterians was but one remove from atheism. Stirling and Dunfermline had long been centres of a dissenting presbyterian tradition, and many Voluntaries (i.e. presbyterians outside the established Church of Scotland) were numbered among the electorate. After 1843 the dissenters were joined by the Free Church element, again a substantial presence in these localities. These two churches held a deep grievance against the Church of Scotland, and used their voting power to push Smith aside (he found a seat in England). In his stead, they chose Sir James Anderson, a Stirling-born Lord Provost of Glasgow and a leading light in the newly formed United Presbyterian Church. Anderson thus in his turn became in 1852 the emblem of the values of the post-1832 electorate in towns and cities. As an electoral survey conducted at this point remarked, influence in the Stirling burghs had formerly been held by the Earl of Rosebery, but was now exercised by the manufacturers of Dunfermline and Stirling (Dod 1854).

From the middle 1860s a new phase began,

triggered by several factors. Although the most obvious influence was an expanded electorate, of which more shortly, there were also changing social forces. Thus it is quite remarkable that when after a hiatus of twenty-five years the Liberals in 1865 brought forward a candidate for the Stirlingshire seat, they won. Here the key element was that the old deference of the tenantry towards the lairds was evaporating. Farmers in the 1860s rebelled against what was seen as a greedy attitude of landlords over such matters as the enforcement of the game laws and the law of hypothec, which made the rent due to the landlord a preferential debt, so encouraging landowners to pitch rents at very high levels. This political protest in the elections of 1865 and 1868 against landowner candidates was widespread, and Stirling was no exception. Even although the Conservatives hastened to remedy the breach in relations within rural society, it was obvious that there could be no return to the former position. Moreover, the introduction of the secret ballot in 1872 removed any lingering threats which a landowner could dangle over politically rebellious tenants.

The other cause of the shift in politics was franchise reform. In 1868 the vote was extended to the urban male householder. This altered the electorate numerically: in Stirling town, the number of voters rose from 658 in 1867-8 to 1,746 a year later. Stirlingshire saw its electorate rise by 40 per cent from 1,900 in the 1865 election to 2,751 in the 1868 contest, while the equivalent figures for Clackmannan/Kinross were 1,162 and 1,802, a rise of just under 60 per cent, and mostly concentrated in Clackmannanshire. Not only was the electorate growing, it now comprised a heavy input of working-class voters, shattering the middle-class nature of the franchise established in 1832. In 1884-5 a further reform act widened the householder franchise to include rural dwellers. Clackmannan/Kinross now had over 6,000 voters, and Stirlingshire above 12,000. Here the significance was not just the advent on to the registers of agricultural labourers but also of many miners.

The general tenor of these reforms was to enhance the radical tendency of voters. In the Stirling burghs, a by-election took place early in 1868 under the narrow electorate based on the 1832 act. Here the very moderate Liberal James Ramsay beat the more thorough-going radical Henry Campbell (later Campbell-Bannerman) comfortably by 565 votes to 494. Six months later in a general election fought under the wider household suffrage of the Second Reform Act, Campbell-Bannerman decisively romped ahead of Ramsay by 2,201 to 1,682. In addition the increased size of the electorate meant that the old techniques of individual canvassing and the exercise of personal influence could no longer operate.

Both parties therefore responded in part to the changed context of politics by establishing organisations relevant to the age of mass democracy. The Stirlingshire Conservatives in 1873 set up an association with a formal membership open to all political supporters and a permanent committee structure. This replaced the casual format of gatherings from time to time of the leading Tory proprietors in the county, usually prompted by the bigger landowners. Kinross-shire also set up its association in the same year. The Conservative victory in Stirlingshire in 1874 was ascribed in part to the new democratic association; certainly the Liberals thought so, for in the aftermath of their defeat, a Liberal Association was founded to rival the Tories. The papers of the Stirlingshire Liberal Association for the 1880 election contest still survive. They reveal a very efficient organisation, canvassing voters systematically, tracing voters resident elsewhere and if required issuing railway passes to ensure they came to the poll. This impressive machine won the seat back from the Conservatives.

Another facet of the new political techniques was the founding of party newspapers : the Liberal *Alloa Advertiser* (established in 1850) was matched by the Conservative *Alloa Journal* (1859); the Liberal *Falkirk Herald* (1845) was competing with the Tories' *Falkirk Mail* (1886); in Stirling, the Liberal *Observer* (1836) faced the Conservative *Journal* (1820). The newspapers were used to spread the message of the party to which they were affiliated. Stories favourable to the cause could be 'planted' in a sympathetic organ, as was the case in 1880 when the Liberals used the *Falkirk Herald* to introduce an item claiming that landlords were still trying to influence their tenantry.

The major crisis in late Victorian politics was the Liberal split in 1886 over Irish Home Rule. This proved particularly serious in parts of Scotland, notably in the western lowlands where substantial secessions occurred, and the Gladstonian Liberals lost a number of hitherto safe seats to Liberal Unionists or Conservatives. In this area, the Home Rule Liberals held firm in all three seats, perhaps because, unlike the west of Scotland, there were no strong economic links with Ireland placed at risk by the bill. In addition, the religious aspect may not have been so acute, as there was neither a large Irish Roman Catholic nor a strong Orange presence in the area. It is of course true that several prominent men did quit the Liberals: L. Pullar of Bridge of Allan; Dr A.B. McGrigor, a prominent Glasgow lawyer with a small estate in Stirlingshire; ex-Provost Yellowlees of Stirling. But it may be that the number of these was contained by the presence in the region of one of Gladstone's staunchest lieutenants, Campbell-Bannerman. His correspondence reveals that once he arrived in Stirling and addressed a meeting of the party faithful, he won over many waverers and potential defectors by the force of his argument. He was a very shrewd and sociable politician, and his influence undoubtedly worked to the benefit of his party, but the departure of the more moderate Liberals left the party in a slightly dangerous state. Although middle-class radicals remained loyal, with less internal opposition, they could more easily push their particular hobby-horses, which included disestablishment of the Church of Scotland and temperance. Thus in Clackmannanshire, the Patons dominated the late

Victorian Liberal party. The family was the leading textile manufacturer and the largest employer in Alloa and various members were prominent in the affairs of the United Presbyterian Church and ardent proponents of the cause of temperance. So, when a by-election occurred in 1899, the local Liberals insisted on running a staunch temperance supporter, and rejected the alternative candidate, a member of the whisky distilling family of Dewar. The espousal of what was regarded as slightly cranky issues carried a serious danger. The bulk of the Liberal vote came from working-class men. Workingmen in the region were by and large Liberal voters. There was an old radical tradition in the area - dating back to the Bonnymuir rising of 1820, and including widespread support for the Chartists in the 1840s, particularly in the weaving communities along the Hillfoots. Many workingmen shared the middle class Liberal position on temperance, dislike of the landlord class and commitment to free trade.

But there were, as well as a degree of ideological congruity, traces of potential conflict over economic and social issues. In the constituencies there was a workingmen's Liberal Association, which normally worked closely and loyally with the official Liberal Association. From the late 1880s, however, two connected considerations began to pose problems for the Liberal hegemony. One was the attitude taken by the miners, the other was the emergence of a socialist movement among workingmen. The miners were of cardinal importance not just because they were the biggest occupational group in the two county seats, but also because they were highly organised and well-disciplined. As relations between coalmaster and collier were never very cordial, it was always possible that the miners might feel either that the Liberal leadership locally was too pro-capital or that there was a need for labour to have its voice represented directly in parliament. Indeed, in 1886, the secretary of the Fife and Clackmannan miners' union told a miners' gala in Alloa that it was time for the miners of Scotland to have their own MP. However at no time before 1914 did the Clackmannan miners deviate from backing the Liberal party at elections.

In the general election of 1892 the Stirling miners' leader, R. Chisholm Robertson, stood in that county as the nominee of a sort of embryonic Labour Party. He was an able and energetic organiser, who had been active in forging links with other trade unions and in trying to build up a united labour front (Young 1974, 1980). Robertson polled extremely poorly, receiving 663 (6.3%) from over 10,500 votes cast. The Liberal William Jacks won the day, and no labour candidate came forward again before 1914. But the miners could not be relied on to toe the Liberal line. In the two succeeding contests after 1892 it was agreed on all sides that the miners cast their votes in significant proportions for the Tory, who won in both 1895 and 1900. The Conservative, MacKillop, was a mining engineer, but more importantly, Jacks as MP had refused to support legislation promoting miners' welfare

and had resisted demands for the introduction of an eight-hour day, the great cry of the miners.

Although there was evident discontent with official Liberalism before 1914 this does not seem to have translated into a rampant commitment to socialism. The Independent Labour Party (ILP), the main socialist organisation, had some support in the region, but it was small, patchy and irregular. When the Scottish organiser of the ILP visited Stirling in late 1906 he described them as "the finest collection of cranks I ever struck". Of the 17 individual members, half were Tolstoyans apparently living in a commune just outside Stirling. Alloa, he added, had a grand total of 12 members. While there were branches in various other parts of the region - notably Grangemouth and Falkirk - a disturbing number of these lapsed and presumably became defunct. In the years immediately before 1914, when the socialist movement might have been expected to be gaining because of Liberal disarray, two major branches - Denny and Grangemouth - ceased to function. In 1912, the Stirling and Clackmannan federation of the ILP reported that it had decided to discontinue its annual programme of summer outdoor rallies, as these campaigns had not attracted new members. In the period from its formation in 1900 until the outbreak of war in 1914, the Labour party discussed numerous seats in Scotland where it might put up a candidate. The seats in the central area did not feature in any serious consideration. The Liberals, despite some warning tremors, seemed unshakeable.

Labour Ascendancy: 1918 to the mid 1970s

The end of the First World War marked a major recasting of parliamentary politics in this area. Within the space of half a dozen years the previously dominant Liberal Party was in total and permanent eclipse. At the same time the Labour Party rose from its very low pre-war base to capture the major share of the representation of the three constituencies. Between 1922 and 1970, out of fourteen general election contests, the party lost only one in Clackmannan/East Stirling (1931), two in West Stirlingshire (1924, 1931) and two also in Stirling/Falkirk (1923, 1931).

The rise of Labour was due to several strands which were blended together to make a broad movement designed to represent the interests of the working-class, particularly the organised sections of it. To some extent, there was a socialist element in the equation. The ILP attracted support from those who opposed the First World War either on pacifist grounds, or on the claim that it was a capitalist war. Others were drawn to the ILP because the lessons of war and the social and economic turmoil after it indicated that capitalism was a spent force, with socialism clearly shown to be the only viable alternative system of social and economic organisation. So in the three years after the war, new ILP branches (besides those already existing in places like Falkirk, Stirling and Alloa) formed in the area included: Airth, Cowie, Bonnybridge, Milton of Campsie,

Torrance, Carronshore, Tillicoultry, Alva and Shieldhill. This indicates the spread of the socialist ideal to quite small and fairly remote townships and villages throughout the district. But caution must be applied to assuming that this was some vast tidal wave of spreading socialist support. Several of these branches did not survive: Alva, Tillicoultry, Redding and Bonnybridge lapsed in those three years. In the larger towns, the ILP seems to have had a core of committed members, but not always a very large body of supporters. The main ILP activist in Stirling was Fred Crockart, whose family owned a gunsmith's shop. Despite holding Saturday night meetings in Broad Street, it is not certain what sort of following was built up in the town by the ILP. Crockart tended to be treated as a gadfly rather than a political heavyweight: a typical incident was his refusal to stand for the playing of the national anthem at the end of a Conservative meeting, reducing the rest of the audience to near-apoplexy.

While the ILP had branches in many mining villages, this did not imply that all miners were converted to socialism. The trades unions may have been anxious to return Labour MPs to parliament, but not necessarily for the furtherance of the socialist commonwealth. In fact, there was frequently tension between the ideologically committed ILP types and the unions. When the Stirling anti-war groups tried in 1915 to form a branch of the umbrella body, the Union of Democratic Control, they invited the Trades Council to participate. When it was learned that some Trades Council representatives had attended a preliminary meeting, the delegates of both the railwaymen's and the miners' unions intimated that they would quit the Council if it became involved in the UDC. The war was generally supported by the union movement, several prominent local officials holding public positions during it, among them Hugh Murnin, the Stirling miners' union agent and first Labour MP for the Stirling/Falkirk burghs, who served on the profiteering and recruiting tribunals for the district. Again, it is instructive that Tom Johnston, fighting in West Stirling in 1922, studiously eschewed his reputation as a firebrand Clydeside socialist agitator. Much to the chagrin of his opponents, he took great pains to reject the suggestion that he was a bolshevist.

The reasons for Labour's breakthrough involved more than that a section of the population wished to usher in the socialist millennium. An equal, if not greater, factor was the forging of a wide-based working-class solidarity over the war and immediate post-war years. On the one hand, there was the trade union wing, whose influence had risen during the war and which had also grown numerically in the period. Another major contributor to this sense of unity was the co-operative movement, which in both its retail and socio-political versions, was very strong in the region. Both the Men's and Women's Co-operative Guild organisations were active in various centres, and they were a forum for political education and also provided teams of election workers, all on behalf of Labour. In

1918, indeed, a leading London co-operator ran in Clackmannan/East Stirling on behalf of the Labour movement. By 1922 the Co-operative party was essentially subsumed within the Labour party.

Of equal long-term benefit to the Labour vote was the apparent substantial adhesion to the party of the Roman Catholic vote. The choice of Hugh Murnin to fight the Stirling/Falkirk seat was seen as a very shrewd move in this context. Murnin was a devout Roman Catholic, and it was widely believed that the vote of his co-religionists, numbering about 4,000 by a hostile estimate, went solidly in his favour. Indeed, fear of losing this vote was one of the reasons advocated in 1931 for not dropping Murnin as candidate. In Clackmannan/East Stirling it was also contended by a Liberal source that the Roman Catholic vote was delivered en bloc to Labour. There was of course also a sizeable Roman Catholic congregation in the mining areas of West Stirling. There were two reasons for the Roman Catholic vote to attach itself to Labour. Almost all of the Roman Catholics were of Irish origin, and whereas before 1914 they might well have voted Liberal in the hope of achieving Home Rule for Ireland, after the winning of Irish independence in 1921, these people saw themselves less as Irish nationalists and more as members of the Scottish working class. A second factor was the question of education. After 1918, the Labour party adroitly positioned itself as the sole political party in Scotland prepared to champion the right asserted by the Roman Catholic hierarchy that separate schools be maintained at state expense for the provision of education to adherents of the church.

Labour was thus an amalgam of interests, but this in a way gave it great strength. At the Stirling/Falkirk constituency party meeting to select a candidate for the 1922 election, it was reported that 62 delegates were present, representing over 22,000 members of the affiliated organisations. Moreover, Labour had a ready-made organisational structure through these institutions which were able to pass on the party message and to help manage an election campaign. The Conservative press commented on the efficiency of Labour's machine in the 1922 election in Stirling/Falkirk, contrasting it with the moribund nature of both the Liberal and Tory associations in the seat. Electioneering in mining areas was carried out with the miners' union acting hand-in-hand with the Labour party. Through the Cooperative Women's Guild Labour reached a crucial new electorate very effectively and at little expense.

In addition to these coalescing social processes, there was a spread of issues on which Labour won support in the early 1920s. The first post-war election was held in December 1918, and was conducted largely in a spirit of high patriotic feeling, so that supporters of the government carried the field almost everywhere. By the next election, in 1922, new conditions changed voting intentions. For the miners the decontrol of the coal industry immediately after the war meant the shattering of their ideal of a nationalised industry.

Almost all the interrogation of candidates in the three elections of 1922, 1923 and 1924 in mining communities centred on this topic. While state control of the mines clearly had a socialist aspect to it, for many miners it was not so much a matter of high political doctrine as a belief that better working conditions and higher pay would result from the elimination of private ownership. Railwaymen similarly sought a return to the wartime pattern in their industry, where the private companies were subject to central government direction. For other voters, the unemployment crisis caused by the economic recession of the early 1920s attracted them to Labour, and it is striking how much time was spent by Labour candidates in the 1922 contest hammering away at this issue. Another benefit to Labour in 1922 was that it was the only party to pledge that it would not legislate to overturn a recent court verdict that post-war rent increases were illegal. Also, Labour alone promised to ensure that the excess rents paid before the ruling would be refunded. This position was appealing to the very large number of working class tenants in the private rented sector.

An extra gain for Labour was the fact that from 1918 for the first time there was complete male enfranchisement. Before 1914, large numbers of men had been excluded from the electoral registers, largely for technical reasons. (Mathew, McKibbin, Kay, 1976). The percentage of adult males over 21 in 1911 who had the vote in Stirling burgh was 74% - 3,380 out of a total of 4,550. In Clackmannanshire, in 1911 there was an 82% enfranchisement level - 6,470 out of 7,870 men over 21 years of age. The removal of these disabilities in the fourth reform act of 1918 (which also gave partial enfranchisement to women) undoubtedly contributed to the rise of Labour. Almost all those men without votes were working class, and mainly from the poorer sections. These new voters in 1918 were almost certain to vote Labour, given the sense of class identity which we have seen prevalent in this period. Labour was also greatly helped by the redistribution of seats carried out in 1918. The burgh of Stirling was joined with Falkirk and Grangemouth in one seat. Here the two industrial towns in the east of the county counterbalanced Stirling's more middle-class character, so giving Labour a fair chance. In the West Stirlingshire seat, the rural area to the west of Stirling was overbalanced by the inclusion of mining and factory areas such as Denny, Cowie, Fallin, Bannockburn, Plean and Banknock, so putting Labour in a strong position. East Stirlingshire, with its myriad of mining townships, was yoked with Clackmannanshire, also an area of mining and industry. The Liberal press in the latter county presciently remarked that the effect of the redrawing of boundaries was to make the new seat very difficult for the Liberals to retain.

The collapse of the Liberals was dramatic in the extreme. At the beginning of 1918, they held all the seats in the region. In the election of that year, they retained only one seat (Stirling/Falkirk), which they lost in 1922, regained in 1923 and then lost forever in 1924. In West Stirling, a Liberal stood only once after 1918. In Clackmannan/East Stirling they continued to run candidates (with the exception of 1931) until World War II, but with no success.

Part of the difficulty facing the Liberals was that the great pre-1918 issues which gave the party momentum no longer had saliency or were no longer uniquely Liberal. The religious issue of disestablishment diminished as the union of the presbyterian churches became inevitable in the 1920s. The land question had lost its urgency, as new social questions like housing and unemployment occupied the political forum. Temperance also seemed a less effective solution to social problems than direct state intervention. Moreover, many Labour candidates also advocated temperance - notably Tom Johnston. Even free trade, the ultimate Liberal shibboleth, appeared less sacrosanct in an era of acute foreign competition and economic recession. When in 1929 the Liberal *Alloa Advertiser* urged voters to vote Liberal it emphasised the historic achievement of Liberalism, most of which must have seemed medieval to voters: electoral reform, slave emancipation, Roman Catholic emancipation, repeal of the corn Laws, free trade, free education, national insurance and old age pensions. The Liberals could find no new issues to raise. Moreover, the emergence of class-based politics frightened many Liberals. The West Stirling Tories commented gleefully on the panic felt by Liberals when confronted by the Labour-inclined miners in the seat, a group on whom, claimed the Conservatives, the Liberals had fawned before the war.

Liberals also fell into organisational paralysis during the war. The split between Asquith and Lloyd George left many activists baffled and dismayed, and a good number seem to have withdrawn completely from politics in despair at Liberal disunity. The Liberals in the Stirling burghs in particular had a very bitter struggle during the war which must have damaged morale. The sitting MP, Arthur Ponsonby, virulently opposed the war from the outset. The Liberal executive solidly supported the war effort, and between 1914 and 1917 engaged in a protracted struggle with Ponsonby as he strove to present his case to the rank and file, while the party officials tried to persuade him to stand down. There was much bad feeling and ill-temper on both sides. Ponsonby found succour only among the ILP, and in the 1918 election he stood as independent socialist in Dunfermline. His change of political colours and the whole episode left the Liberal party in Stirling unable to act decisively. The association was not resuscitated until after the 1922 election, by which time Labour had won the Stirling/Falkirk seat, and so established political credibility.

The Liberals also made a series of decisions which in the long term perspective pushed them into an electoral cul-de-sac. In the emotional upsurge at the end of the war, the desire to return pro-government candidates led to a semi-formal pact being struck between Liberals and Conservatives. The deal appears to have involved the two seats of West Stirling and

Stirling/Falkirk. In the county seat, Sir Harry Hope, a Conservative, was backed by both sides, and in the burghs, the sitting Liberal, Murray MacDonald, faced no Conservative. Although a semi-renegade Liberal ran in West Stirling, on the whole the pact held. It was retained in the 1922 election and in the 1923 contest it broadly held despite another Liberal intervention in West Stirling. The turning-point came after the 1923 contest, for the Liberal who won the burghs seat infuriated the Conservatives who had voted for him by giving his vote in parliament to prop up the minority Labour government. In the circumstances the dissolution came too speedily for any Conservative to be put up in the 1924 contest, but in 1929 the burgh Tories picked their own man, and no Liberal stood again until 1974. In West Stirling, no Liberal ran again after 1923 until 1974. In Clackmannan/East Stirling the Liberal presence remained longer.

The fact was that the Liberals found themselves pulled more and more into merging with the Conservatives. The Conservatives were careful not to present themselves as a reactionary or excessively anti-Liberal party. Candidates such as Harry Hope, a progressive Tory, and Commander Fanshawe took care to keep in the electorate's eye their support for social reform. The most explicit instance of the Conservative commitment to liberal policies came in the 1929 contest in the Stirling/Falkirk seat. This was the first time since the war that a Tory was running, and there was no Liberal. Alexander Ratcliffe stood under the label of the 'Protestant and Progressive' candidate. A militant anti-Catholic, Ratcliffe largely based his campaign on claims that the Labour party both nationally and locally was in the pocket of Rome. He also alleged that the local Conservatives were failing to protect the Protestant cause. The Conservatives completely distanced themselves from Ratcliffe and made no concessions to his extreme utterances. Ratcliffe polled nearly 7,000 votes, possibly denying the Conservatives victory. Nevertheless, it is likely that Liberals felt reassured by the moderation of the Conservatives. In the crisis election of 1931, Liberals did not put up candidates in any of the constituencies. Instead prominent Liberals, such as the town clerk of Alloa, turned up on Conservative platforms urging Liberals to vote so as to defeat Labour. The Liberal journal in Alloa saw this contest in apocalyptic terms -to vote Labour would be:

"the very essence of madness .... It is unthinkable, therefore, that any intelligent man or woman elector in this constituency would desire that Great Britain become a second Russia, and to ensure that there is no possible danger of such a calamity taking place, his or her bounden duty is to (vote Conservative)."

In addition to their policy stance, the Conservatives also placed themselves in a strong position vis a vis the Liberals by developing a very effective organisation. From 1922, Conservative associations were set up in all the seats and careful attention was paid to the need to cultivate women voters. Lady Steel-Maitland was made vice -president of the West Stirling association because it was policy to have a woman as either president or vice-president. Women's sections were opened in many places and a judicious mix of political talks and social activities offered. In apparently unpromising localities such as the Baker Street ward in Stirling, branches flourished in the interwar years, and even more surprising, a party hut was constructed in Fallin. Garden fetes, whist drives and dances helped to swell party funds. A youth organisation, the Junior Imperial League, was introduced to recruit the future generation. By contrast the Liberal party could not restart its organisation in any seat after the war, although the Clackmannan association limped along into the 1930s, with the Patons (now named Forrester-Patons) still involved. But effectively elsewhere the Liberal party had become extinct. There was a brief flurry of activity in Stirling just after the second world war, due largely to the arrival there of the prominent Liberal, John M. Bannerman.

After the upheavals of the early to middle 1920s, parliamentary politics in central Scotland settled into a straightforward pattern for half a century of Labour pre-eminence. The only interlude of Conservative success came in 1931. Here, as we have seen, the Conservatives won the whole-hearted backing of Liberals. It is clear that a fair proportion of Labour voters also moved across, but by the following election these returned to Labour. After World War II Labour seemed if anything even more impregnable. The growth of industry in areas like Grangemouth, as local Tories agreed, made Labour even stronger. The great expansion of council housing, normally built by Labour local authorities, proved a long-run vote winner for Labour, both at local and parliamentary level: however, it was only in 1952 that Labour gained control of Stirling County Council, and in 1963 the party became for the first time the largest party on Stirling Burgh Council.

Until the 1959 general election, the movement of votes between Labour and Conservative at each general election had broadly conformed to the national trend obtaining throughout Britain. In 1959 and in the 1960s the central region seats, in common with most of Scotland, deviated from the British trend by moving more and more towards Labour. The reasons for this are obscure, but some pointers are discernible. There is, for instance, little evidence of organisational decay on the Conservative side. The party responded to the great drive initiated by Lord Woolton in the later 1940s to expand membership on a vast scale. The West Stirling Conservatives raised their subscribers from around 1,900 in 1947 to 3,942 three years later, which indicated that about 20% of Conservative voters in the seat were also members. In the Stirling burgh's seat, branches like King's Park claimed remarkably high membership: in 1953 it was said that 798 were enrolled. Growth persisted in many quarters even beyond the electoral downturn in Conservative fortunes of the late 1950s. In 1961, Causewayhead Conservatives reported their highest ever membership.   The Young Conservatives continued to have an active existence for most of the 1960s. There were significant pointers in certain areas however.   While the Riverside, Causewayhead and King's Park wards held their numbers, the East ward Conservatives saw their numbers fall from 412 to 280 between 1959 and 1962. By the later date, the ward party was finding it difficult to keep going.

One reform in the revamping of the Tory party in the late 1940s to which great attention was paid was the drive to break the party's image as a movement dominated by the upper-class by seeking wherever possible to bring forward candidates of less elevated social origins than in the past. These were the changes which brought Edward Heath, Iain MacLeod and Margaret Thatcher into parliament. But in central Scotland there were only slow advances towards the party democratising itself in this way. Even in the middle 1960s the West Stirlingshire party was still presided over by local lairds such as the Steel-Maitlands, and in Clackmannanshire the Earl of Mar remained at the head. The choice of candidates was little better. It seems bizarre to choose for the urban constituency of Stirling & Falkirk in a by-election in 1948 William Forbes of Callendar, the landowner whose ancestors had sat for Stirlingshire in the mid-19th century. Forbes actually remained as candidate for the two subsequent general elections. Simultaneously West Stirling was putting forward Betty Harvie Anderson, the wife of a prominent laird. Thereafter there were signs of candidates being chosen from a less exalted background, with lawyers in particular selected. But these changes seemed only skin-deep, as a discussion in the West Stirling Conservative circles revealed. In 1962 it was reported to the association's annual general meeting that great difficulty was being encountered in finding a suitable candidate. Sir Keith Steel-Maitland said he could not ever recall a time when good candidates were so hard to come by. A lively debate followed, with one member, evidently an unreconstructed relic from the pre-Woolton age remarking that "there were places in the constituency where retired service people might be excellent candidates".   The fact that finding a reasonable candidate was so hard hints at the general malaise affecting the party by then.

After the setback in 1959, a post-mortem was conducted by the Tories in the region. It was agreed that the national campaign jarred badly in the context of conditions in the local constituencies. In particular posters bearing the slogan "You've Never Had It So Good" which were put up all over the district were described by Steel-Maitland as "a blunder", given the rising levels of unemployment prevailing in this part of Scotland.   Another potential problem for the Conservatives was their reluctance to enter local government politics under their party label. Labour had always done so, and it seems pretty evident that by

the 1950s, if not earlier, there was a positive relationship between municipal and parliamentary voting. Conservatives until the 1970s preferred to lurk under the label 'Moderate' or 'Progressive' or 'Independent' which made the party link between the two layers of politics somewhat obscure. This was in part because others could also wear these badges. Sometimes Independents were truly independent, and in the 1940s the Liberal John Bannerman became a county councillor styling himself a Moderate. By contrast the SNP stood under their party label in local contests and this proved an ideal launching pad for their parliamentary campaigns. It is striking that in Stirling burgh the SNP tended to do quite well in wards which had a very sizeable parliamentary Conservative vote such as Riverside. The inexorable electoral decline of the Tories through the 1960s left Labour even more pre-eminent.

Labour's Ascendancy Challenged: from the 1970s

The apparently unassailable position enjoyed by Labour in all three constituencies since 1935 was still apparent in the 1970 general election. In Clackmannan/ East Stirling, Labour's majority in 1970 was 10,551; in West Stirlingshire, 7,419; and in Stirling & Falkirk, 7,230. But this overwhelming dominance was rudely shattered in 1974. In the February general election of that year the SNP won Clackmannan/East Stirling and came a good second in the other two. In the second general election of that same year, held in October, the SNP made further inroads into Labour's pre-eminence. George Reid consolidated his success in Clackmannan/ East Stirling, pushing up his majority from a vulnerable 3,590 to a very comfortable 7,341. In West Stirlingshire, Labour's lead was slashed to a meagre 367, and in the Stirling/Falkirk seat, the SNP came within 1,766 of toppling Labour. The shift was quite remarkable: in the space of four years since the 1970 election, the SNP had raised its share of the poll in the three seats from around 15% to 20% to between just under 40% and over 50%.

Several aspects of this political upheaval attracted attention: the reasons for the fall in Labour's support; the causes of the rise of the SNP; the extent to which this was a watershed in voting behaviour; the reasons for the failure of the Conservatives to benefit from the crisis of Labour.

A number of factors were adduced to explain the decline of Labour. To some degree, the party appeared arrogant and complacent after many years of unquestioned power, particularly with regard to local government, where Labour authorities were seen as petty and dictatorial in matters of housing and education. In some parts of Scotland there was also a whiff of corruption surrounding well-entrenched Labour administrations, and there were rumours that this might apply within the central area. For some, the passing of long-serving MPs may have broken ties of personal affection for the man, rather than support for the party. Arthur Woodburn had represented Clackmannan and East Stirling for 30 years, Malcolm MacPherson sat for Stirling/Falkirk for 23 years. While William Baxter had only sat for West Stirling for a mere 15 years, he had a long record of service on the County Council before moving to Westminster. Moreover, two of the replacement Labour candidates were non-local, and this may have been a factor, In the case of West Stirling, Baxter was removed only after a bitter struggle within the constituency party which almost certainly alienated a good number of traditional Labour voters.

But it seemed to commentators that more profound and perhaps irreversible changes were eroding Labour's position in all three seats. The traditional bases of Labour's strength had been the industrial complexion of the region. Most of these industries were by the 1970s in retreat, as is discussed elsewhere in this book. Coal-mining was but a shadow of its former self as the National Coal Board shut down numerous mines from the late 1960s. Railwaymen, once a vigorous element in Labour politics, were reduced in numbers from the middle 1960s as the contraction in the rail network called for in the Beeching Report of 1963 was implemented. For instance, passenger rail services in Clackmannanshire had disappeared by 1968. The impact of foreign competition forced factory closures and lay-offs of many workers in the textiles sector throughout the 1970s. The foundry and engineering workshops in the Falkirk area also struggled to survive, and cut-backs and redundancies became regular occurrences. The result of these great economic shifts was that Labour could no longer rely on the unwavering support of the mining village or the factory community. The role of the unions as politicising and mobilising agencies on behalf of the Labour party of necessity also diminished in this new context. A further problem was that recruitment of able young trade union activists into the party also tended to dry up as jobs disappeared. A parallel indicator of the withering away of much of the socio-economic milieu which sustained the traditional culture and values of Labour was the crisis in the co-operative movement. In the 1970s the arrival in larger towns of supermarkets and the construction of shopping precincts in places like Falkirk and Stirling - which attracted national retail companies - all acted to weaken the central role of the 'Co-op store', and many branch outlets closed or merged. The social and political side of the co-operative movement also seems to have declined in this period. Labour thus appeared backward-looking and unable to adjust to new social and economic realities: the success of the SNP lay in filling this gap.

The rise of the Nationalist movement in central Scotland was not sudden: there was a history of a pronounced Scottish nationalist presence in the area from the inception of modern nationalist parties in the late 1920s and early 1930s. This may in part be because the remarkable number of important phases in the history of Scotland which are associated with Stirling and its vicinity contributed to an acute sense of Scottish nationality. The annual march by Scottish nationalists through the town to Bannockburn on the anniversary of the battle may have reinforced this sentiment. Again, political nationalism was certainly boosted by the presence of several prominent figures in the area. The Duke of Montrose 's identification with nationalism in the 1930s was seen at the time as a breakthrough for the party, and his influence in the western part of the county was considerable. Indeed, one of the founding fathers of early 20th century Scottish nationalism, R.B. Cunninghame Graham, also had strong local connections through his estate at Gartmore. After World War II, the arrival of the first SNP MP, Dr Robert MacIntyre, to take up a medical post in Stirling certainly stimulated the local party and gave it a high profile.

The SNP tended to maintain electoral activity in the area even when it was not particularly vibrant nationally. In the 1950s, only about half a dozen seats were fought by the party in each general election. But in three of the four general elections of that decade (1950, 1951,1955 and 1959) Stirling/Falkirk was contested. In the following decade all three seats were fought in all three elections (1964, 1966, 1970), the most spectacular result coming in West Stirling in 1966 when Dr MacIntyre beat the Conservative into third place, securing over a quarter of the poll. The party also participated in municipal elections, with some striking successes. In Alva in 1948, Robert Curran became the first SNP provost of a burgh in Scotland. Dr MacIntyre was made provost of Stirling in 1967, serving until 1975.

But the dramatic advance of the party in 1974 seemed to mark a qualitative advance. Much interest attached to the Clackmannan/East Stirling seat, which was won by the SNP and which had perhaps the weakest previous nationalist record of the three seats. Two broad factors seemed to explain the SNP's breakthrough in this seat. Firstly, there were the nature of the candidate and the style of the campaigning used by the party. These marked out the SNP as a modern, sophisticated party, in contrast to the antiquated approach of Labour (Hanby 1976). George Reid was a local man, educated in the county of Clackmannan, with a family involvement in the brewing industry of Alloa. More importantly, he was a journalist and broadcaster, a typical 'modern' occupation. His skills as a communicator were self-evident, but he did not use the older approach of orating to mass audiences: he was more conversational and relaxed. Above all he introduced several American electioneering techniques which he had studied on various trips to the USA. Loud Scottish music blared from his campaign vehicles, making the party's presence noticeable everywhere. He avoided poorly attended public meetings of the party faithful in draughty public halls, preferring walk-abouts in shopping areas and housing estates. When canvassing was undertaken, it was carried out as a mass operation with much attendant publicity. One of the most dramatic devices adopted was that of the motorcade: a vast procession of cars, all covered in the insignia and colours of the SNP, snaked its way across the constituency, creating the impression of a huge volume of support for nationalism. This lively up-to date electioneering approach left Labour gasping and floundering in its wake. By 1979 Labour had adopted virtually holus-bolus these innovations.

But this modern style could only appeal if voters were no longer stuck in traditional modes of behaviour. Here a survey of the constituency carried out just after the 1974 elections seemed to confirm that the SNP had already won the battle for the political future of the constituency (Hanby 1977). This study demonstrated that among the younger voters - those between 18 and 34 - 44% had voted SNP, but only 28% Labour, whereas among those over 55, Labour won 33%, the SNP only 20%. Thus demographic inevitability suggested that Labour would decline steadily. In terms of occupational categories, Labour performed best in the ranks of the semi and unskilled workers, where it got double the SNP share. But these types of occupations were largely associated with the dying industries, so their support was not of long-term benefit. In the expanding lower white-collar and skilled manual worker category, the SNP outperformed Labour, attracting a 25% higher share. Again it seemed significant that among manual workers, the SNP did much better among non-unionised voters, who were normally to be found outside the traditional and decaying heavy industry sectors.

The sense that the political tide was running with the SNP was reinforced in a follow-up study carried out in 1976 on those surveyed two years previously in the Clackmannan/East Stirling seat (Hanby 1977). This found that more people were moving to the SNP, and that there was greater identification with the party. Simultaneous work on the adjacent constituencies indicated that in West Stirling Labour's majority was virtually extinguished, while in Stirling/Falkirk it was badly weakened. To underscore this picture, the SNP scored spectacular victories in the local elections of 1977, seizing control of both Clackmannan and Falkirk district councils. Predictions were accordingly confidently made that a major shift in Scottish politics was occurring and that Central Region was the cock-pit of this process.

The general election of 1979 confounded these hypotheses. Far from the free fall in Labour's support which was anticipated by these earlier studies, it was the onward march of Scottish nationalism which was not only halted but reversed. The Clackmannan/East Stirling seat was regained with relative ease by Labour, and the SNP challenge in the other two seats receded from a dire threat to a containable irritant. The two succeeding general elections of 1983 and 1987 saw a further ebbing in the SNP's fortunes, and their level of support by 1987 had retreated to roughly that of 1970, which had not been an outstanding performance, as it had done less well than in the 1966 contest.

This permitted another analysis of the SNP's achievement to be put forward. So far from being a permanent seismic restructuring of Scottish politics, the 1974 results were the product of transient, negative factors. This view argued that many voted SNP in protest against the two main parties, rather than out of commitment to the cause of Scottish independence. By the 1979 election, Conservatives who had flirted with nationalism in 1974 reverted to their original loyalty. There were two reasons at work here. One was dismay at the support given by the SNP MPs to the minority Labour government between 1974 and 1979. Just as in 1923-4, when the Liberals were in the same position, outraged Conservatives turned away from the Nationalists. Secondly with the advent of Mrs Thatcher as leader, the Conservative party was now clearly ideologically less consensual. Those who felt that the Conservative government of 1970-4 had lost its way and sacrificed its principles, and so had abandoned it, could now return happily to the fold. In the 1979 election there was a heavy swing from SNP to Conservative in all three seats: in Stirling/Falkirk, it was 17.7%, in West Stirlingshire 13.6%, and in Clackmannan/East Stirling, 9.1%.

Labour-inclined voters who had gone over to the nationalists in 1974 felt betrayed by the fact that the downfall of the Callaghan administration in 1979 was primarily caused by the SNP's withdrawal of support. By precipitating a dissolution at a time when Labour's fortunes were at rock bottom, so making possible the election of a very right-wing Conservative government, the withdrawal of SNP support drove these voters back into the Labour camp. An additional disadvantage faced by the SNP in 1979 was a feeling in some quarters that the party was not particularly competent or mature. George Reid was widely admired as an able and hard-working member of parliament, but the district councils administered by the SNP at times appeared to be run by inefficient and inexperienced politicians. Just as a vague sense of disquiet at the calibre of municipal administration may have damaged Labour in the early 1970s, so the SNP perhaps suffered at the end of the decade.

No sooner did it look as if it had repulsed the nationalist onslaught than another blow to Labour's self-esteem was struck. In 1983 a Conservative was returned to parliament from a central constituency, namely Stirling, the first time that had happened since 1931. Despite a determined Labour offensive at the next election in 1987, the seat remained obdurately Tory. This was the first time since the 1900 election for the old Stirlingshire constituency that the Conservative party had succeeded in retaining a seat in the region - and before that, 1859 was the most recent occurrence.

A major ingredient in the Conservative capture of the Stirling constituency was the redistribution of the boundaries, which was the most radical shake-up since 1918. Clackmannan was separated from East Stirlingshire and made a seat in its own right, for the first time since 1832. Falkirk and Grangemouth were detached from Stirling burgh. These two towns, along with East Stirlingshire, plus the more easterly portions

Table 1 Social Characteristics of Stirling Constituency   *Source*: Waller, 1991.

Year	Characteristic	Stirling	Clacks	Falkirk E	Falkirk W
1981	Houses Owner/Occupied	43.3%	27.4%	25.7%	24.0%
1981	Houses Local Authority	44.3%	67.4%	70.0%	71.2%
1981	Employment, Non-Manual	50.0%	38.0%	37.0%	38.0%
1981	Employment, Professional & Higher Managerial etc.	18.0%	13.0%	12.0%	12.0%
1987	Unemployment	9.3%	13.2%	12.6%	12.0%

of West Stirlingshire - including Denny and the mining communities just to the east of Stirling -were divided into two new seats. Falkirk East embraced the easterly part of Falkirk, Grangemouth and Bo'ness (removed from West Lothian). Falkirk West covered the remainder. A fourth seat was allocated by the Boundary Commissioners to the region. This took in the burgh of Stirling and the westerly portion of the former West Stirlingshire constituency, with the addition of Dunblane, Doune and Callander which were uncoupled from West Perthshire/Kinross.

From the viewpoint of the Conservatives, it was the creation of the new Stirling seat that offered the brightest prospect. The other three seats contained the heartland of Labour's vote, and these became predictably safe Labour. But the Stirling constituency now contained the burgh which of the three in the old Stirling/Falkirk seat was regarded on all sides as the least socialist in voting behaviour: in municipal politics it was never a secure Labour stronghold.

The parts of the old West Stirling seat put into the new Stirling constituency were also Conservative inclined, being a mix of agriculture and prosperous Glasgow business and professional commuters. The insertion of the preponderantly middle-class small burghs hitherto in the West Perth/Kinross constituency simply reinforced the general Tory disposition of the seat.

The social characteristics of the Stirling constituency confirmed its atypicality from the rest of the constituencies in the region **(Table 1).** In its socio-economic profile the Stirling constituency was much closer to those semi-urban, semi-rural seats elsewhere in Scotland which were held by the Conservatives, such as Kincardine/Deeside. Perhaps the most telling indicator in the above table is not so much the occupational structure, but the relatively high proportion of owner-occupiers to be found in the Stirling constituency. Recent studies of British voting behaviour have tended to establish the closest correlation with party affiliation to be housing tenure: local authority tenants vote Labour, owner-occupiers Conservative. The link between working-class and Labour or middle-class and Tory is a much less accurate predictor of voting preference.

The Conservative cause was also aided by a number of minor factors. Firstly, the new constituency was one in which there was a pre-existing organisational base for the Tories. They had always been strong in each component part of the seat, whereas these were probably Labour's weakest bases in the region. Certainly Conservative organisation seemed more professional and efficient to outside observers. Secondly, the choice of candidates for each party may have had an effect. Labour chose a controversial figure, the left-wing leader of Stirling District Council, which itself was widely perceived as politically rather to the left of most Scottish Labour local authorities. Such a candidate would not perhaps woo the typical floating voter. The selection of Michael Forsyth as the Conservative candidate for the seat marked an emphatic change from the traditional Tory candidate, for he was neither a laird nor a lawyer, but a self-made businessman. Forsyth probably struck a chord socially and ideologically with the newer social groupings which were growing in this constituency. Whether Forsyth's continued tenure of the Stirling seat marks a new departure in the politics of central Scotland or whether it is merely a temporary blip in the historic pattern of political allegiances remains uncertain.

REFERENCES AND FURTHER READING

1. **Unpublished Manuscripts**
   Adam of Blair Adam MSS, Blair Adam, Kinross-shire
   Campbell-Bannerman MSS, British Library, London
   Joseph Duncan MSS, National Library of Scotland, Edinburgh
   Forbes of Callendar MSS, Scottish Record Office, Edinburgh
   Independent Labour Party MSS, Bristol University, Bristol
   Mathew, McLuckie & Lupton MSS, Central Region Archives, Stirling
   Murray of Polmaise MSS, Central Region Archives, Stirling
   Ponsonby of Shulbrede MSS, Bodleian Library, Oxford
   J.B. Smith MSS, Manchester Public Library

2.   Newspapers

Alloa Advertiser, Alloa Journal, Forward, Falkirk Herald, Falkirk Mail, Stirling Journal, Stirling Observer.

3.   Books and Articles

C. R. DOD, 1854. Electoral Facts from 1832 to 1853 Impartially Stated, London, 1854; reprint, Editor H. J. Hanham, Brighton, 1972.

W. FERGUSON, 1965. 'The Reform Act (Scotland); intention and effect', *Scottish Historical Review* 45, 105-16

V. J. HANBY, 1976. The Renaissance of the Scottish National Party: from Eccentric to Campaigning Crusader, In L. Maisel, Editor, Changing Campaign Techniques. Elections and Values in Contemporary Democracies, Beverley Hill/London, 217-42

V. J. HANBY, 1977.   Current Scottish Nationalism, *Scottish Journal of Sociology* 1, 95-110

I. G. C. HUTCHISON, 1986. A Political History of Scotland, 1832-1924, Edinburgh.

T. JOHNSTON, 1952. Memories, London.

J. MacKILLOP, 1899. Thoughts for the People, Stirling.

H. C. G. MATHEW, R. I. McKIBBIN, J. KAY, 1976. The franchise factor in the rise of the Labour Party, *English Historical Review* 91, 123-52.

J. A. SPENDER, n.d. The Life of Sir Henry Campbell-Bannerman, G.C.B., London.

G. WALKER, 1987. Thomas Johnston, Manchester.

R. WALLER, 1991. Almanac of British Politics, London, 4th edition.

J. WILSON, 1973, CB. A Life of Sir Henry Campbell-Bannerman, London.

J. D. YOUNG, 1974. Working Class and Radical Movements in Scotland and the Revolt from Liberalism, 1866-1900, Ph.D. Thesis, Stirling University.

J. D. YOUNG, 1979. Towards a History of the Labour Movement in Stirlingshire, 1789-1922, *Forth Naturalist and Historian* 4, 111-36

APPENDIX   PARLIAMENTARY ELECTION RESULTS, 1832 - 1987

Key to abbreviations:

C - Conservative; Co C - Coalition Conservative; Comm - Communist; Coop - Cooperative; IDP - Independent Labour Party; Lab - Labour; Lib -Liberal; LibU - Liberal Unionist; Nat Lib - National Liberal; Prot - Protestant & Progressive; SAW - Scottish Anti-War & No Conscription League Council; SDP - Social Democratic Party; SNP - Scottish National Party; SUTCLP - Scottish United Trades Councils & Labour Party

1 : 1832 -1918   A : CLACKMANNANSHIRE and KINROSS-SHIRE

Election	Candidates	Party	Votes				
1832	C. Adam	Lib	527	1880	J.B. Balfour	Lib	Unopp
	R. Bruce	C	196	1885	J.B. Balfour	Lib	Unopp
1835	C. Adam	Lib	447	1886	J.B. Balfour	Lib	3,159
	R. Bruce	C	285		C.C. Bethune	LibU	1,844
1837	Sir C. Adam	Lib	Unopp	1892	J.B. Balfour	Lib	3,541
1841	Hon. G.R. Abercrombie	Lib	Unopp		Dr J.E.T. Aitchison	LibU	1,927
1842	W. Morison	Lib	Unopp	1895	J.B. Balfour	Lib	3,133
1847	W. Morison	Lib	Unopp		G. Younger	C	2,588
1851	J. Johnstone	Lib	328	1899	E. Wason	Lib	3,489
	W.P. Adam	Lib	263		G. Younger	C	2,973
1852	J. Johnstone	Lib	Unopp	1900	E. Wason	Lib	3,284
1857	Viscount Melgund	Lib	Unopp		G. Younger	C	2,933
1859	W.P. Adam	Lib	Unopp	1906	E. Wason	Lib	4,027
1865	W.P. Adam	Lib	Unopp		J.A. Clyde	LibU	2,648
1868	W.P. Adam	Lib	Unopp	1910	E. Wason	Lib	3,971
1874	W.P. Adam	Lib	943	(Jan.)	N.B. Constable	C	2,703
	J.R. Haig	C	468	1910	E. Wason	Lib	Unopp
1880	W.P. Adam	Lib	1,150	(Dec.)			
	J.R. Haig	C	458				

B : STIRLINGSHIRE

Election	Candidates	Party	Votes		Election	Candidates	Party	Votes
1832	Hon. C.E. Fleming	Lib	995		1885	J.C. Bolton	Lib	6,454
	W. Forbes	C	465			M. Shaw-Stewart	C	3,938
1835	W. Forbes	C	779		1886	J.C. Bolton	Lib	5,067
	Hon. C.E. Fleming	Lib	759			E. Noel	LibU	4,360
1837*	W. Forbes	C	859		1892	W. Jacks	Lib	5,296
	Hon. C.E. Fleming	Lib	858			E. Noel	LibU	4,550
1841	W. Forbes	C	1,019			R.C. Robertson	SUTCLP	663
	Sir M. Bruce	Lib	895		1895	J. McKillop	C	5,916
1847	W. Forbes	C	Unopp			W. Jacks	Lib	5,489
1852	W. Forbes	C	Unopp		1900	J. McKillop	C	6,325
1853	P. Blackburn	C	Unopp			Sir G.S. Robertson	Lib	6,023
1857	P. Blackburn	C	Unopp		1906	D.M. Smeaton	Lib	9,475
1859	P. Blackburn	C	Unopp			Marquess of Graham	C	5,806
1865	J.E. Erskine	Lib	726		1910	Dr W.A. Chapple	Lib	10,122
	P. Blackburn	C	692		(Jan.)	R.S. Horne	C	6,417
1868	J.E. Erskine	Lib	Unopp		1910	Dr W.A. Chapple	Lib	9,183
1874	Sir W. Edmondstone	C	1,171		(Dec.)	R.S. Horne	C	6,487
	Sir W.C.C. Bruce	Lib	1,127					
1880	J.C. Bolton	Lib	1,606					
	Sir W. Edmondstone	C	1,246					

*The election of Forbes was declared invalid after scrutiny of the votes. Fleming was duly elected instead of Forbes.

C : STIRLING BURGHS

Election	Candidates	Party	Votes		Election	Candidates	Party	Votes
1832	Lord Dalmeny	Lib	492		1874	H. Campbell-Bannerman	Lib	Unopp
	J. Johnston	Lib	366		1880	H. Campbell-Bannerman	Lib	2,906
1835	Lord Dalmeny	Lib	418			Sir J.R.G. Maitland	C	132
	J. Crawfurd	Lib	345		1885	H. Campbell-Bannerman	Lib	Unopp
1837	Lord Dalmeny	Lib	485		1886	H. Campbell-Bannerman	Lib	2,440
	T. Thompson	Lib	2			J. Pender	LibU	1,471
1841	Lord Dalmeny	Lib	438		1892	H. Campbell-Bannerman	Lib	2,791
	J. Aytoun	Lib	420			W.T. Hughes	LibU	1,695
1847	J.B. Smith	Lib	345		1895	Sir H. Campbell-Bannerman	Lib	2,783
	A.C.R.G. Maitland	Lib	312			S.C. MacCaskie	C	1,656
	A. Alison	Lib	156		1900	Sir H. Campbell-Bannerman	Lib	2,715
1852	Sir J. Anderson	Lib	431			O.T. Duke	LibU	2,085
	J. Miller	Lib	411		1906	Sir H. Campbell-Bannerman	Lib	Unopp
1857	Sir J. Anderson	Lib	Unopp		1908	A.A.W.H. Ponsonby	Lib	3,873
1859	J. Caird	Lib	Unopp			W. Whitelaw	C	2,512
1865	L. Oliphant	Lib	Unopp		1910	A.A.W.H. Ponsonby	Lib	4,471
1868	J. Ramsay	Lib	565		(Jan.)	N.J.K. Cochran-Patrick	C	2,419
	H. Campbell [Bannerman]	Lib	494		1910	A.A.W.H. Ponsonby	Lib	Unopp
1868	H. Campbell-Bannerman	Lib	2,201		(Dec.)			
	J. Ramsay	Lib	1,682					

2 : 1918 - 1979   **A :STIRLING/CLACKMANNANSHIRE,CLACKMANNAN/EASTERN**

Election	Candidate	Party	Votes	% Poll	Election	Candidate	Party	Votes	% Poll
1918	R.G.C. Glyn	Co C	6,771	38.5	1951	A. Woodburn	Lab	25,231	58.7
	H.J. May	Coop	5,753	32.8		Hon. S.D. Loch	C	17,727	41.3
	Dr W.A. Chapple	Lib	5,040	28.7	1955	A. Woodburn	Lab	23,588	58.7
1922	L.M. Weir	Lab	10,312	42.0		R.C. Aitchison	C	16,579	41.3
	C.M. Aitchison	Lib	7,379	30.0	1959	A. Woodburn	Lab	25,004	59.3
	R.G.C. Glyn	C	6,888	28.0		R.C. Aitchison	C	17,132	40.7
1923	L.M. Weir	Lab	10,492	51.1	1964	A. Woodburn	Lab	23,927	57.2
	C.M. Aitchison	Lib	10,043	48.9		A. MacDonald	C	12,815	30.6
1924	L.M. Weir	Lab	13,032	52.6		C.D. Drysdale	SNP	5,106	12.2
	E.J. Donaldson	Lib	11,752	47.4	1966	A. Woodburn	Lab	22,557	55.3
1929	L.M. Weir	Lab	17,677	53.2		A. MacDonald	C	10,037	24.6
	H.P. Mitchell	C	8,778	26.4		C.D. Drysdale	SNP	8,225	20.1
	E.J. Donaldson	Lib	6,760	20.4	1970	R.G. Douglas	Lab	23,729	50.7
1931	J.W. Johnston	C	20,425	59.9		J. Fairlie	C	13,178	28.2
	L.M. Weir	Lab	13,669	40.1		I.C.H. Macdonald	SNP	7,243	15.5
1935	L.M. Weir	Lab	14,881	42.1		R.E. Bell	Lib	2,640	5.6
	J.W. Johnston	C	13,738	39.0	1974	G.N. Reid	SNP	22,269	43.5
	G.G. Honeyman	Lib	5,062	14.4	(Feb)	R.G. Douglas	Lab	18,679	36.4
	D.W. Gibson	ILP	1,573	4.5		A.H. Lester	C	9,994	19.5
1939	A. Woodburn	Lab	15,645	93.7		G. Bolton	Comm	322	0.6
	A. Stewart	SAW	1,060	6.3	1974	G.N. Reid	SNP	25,998	50.7
1945	A. Woodburn	Lab	24,622	62.9	(Oct)	R.G. Douglas	Lab	18,657	36.4
	Sir J.E. Gilmour	C	14,522	37.1		T.N.A. Begg	C	5,369	10.4
1950	A. Woodburn	Lab	22,980	56.5		D.C. Sheilds	Lib	1,268	2.5
	Hon. S.D. Loch	C	13,630	33.5	1979	M.J. O'Neill	Lab	22,780	41.9
	C.H. Johnston	Lib	4,078	10.0		G.N. Reid	SNP	21,796	40.1
						T.N.A. Begg	C	9,778	18.0

B :STIRLING/CLACKMANNANSHIRE, WEST STIRLINGSHIRE

Election	Candidate	Party	Votes	% Poll		Election	Candidate	Party	Votes	% Poll
1918	H. Hope	Co C	6,893	51.9		1959	W. Baxter	Lab	21,008	57.5
	T. Johnston	Lab	3,809	28.7			W.A. Gay	C	15,497	42.5
	R.B.C. Graham	Lib	2,582	19.4		1964	W. Baxter	Lab	21,144	58.8
1922	T. Johnston	Lab	8,919	52.4			J.G.C. Barr	C	14,834	41.2
	Sir H. Hope	C	8,104	47.6		1966	W. Baxter	Lab	17,513	48.6
1923	T. Johnston	Lab	9,242	51.9			Dr R.D. McIntyre	SNP	9,381	26.0
	Sir H. Hope	C	6,182	34.7			J.D.M. Hardie	C	9,148	25.4
	R.I.A. MacInnes	Lib	2,390	13.4		1970	W. Baxter	Lab	18,884	48.9
1924	G.D. Fanshawe	C	10,043	50.7			J. Glen	C	11,465	29.7
	T. Johnston	Lab	9,749	49.3			Dr R.D. McIntyre	SNP	8,279	21.4
1929	T. Johnston	Lab	15,179	56.7		1974	W. Baxter	Lab	17,730	40.8
	G..D. Fanshawe	C	11,589	43.3		(Feb)	J.T. Jones	SNP	12,886	29.7
1931	J.C. Ker	C	14,771	53.3			T.J. Price	C	12,789	29.5
	T. Johnston	Lab	12,952	46.7		1974	D.A. Canavan	Lab	16,698	39.0
1935	T. Johnston	Lab	16,015	55.1		(Oct)	J.T. Jones	SNP	16,331	38.2
	A.P. Duffus	C	13,053	44.9			D.W. Mitchell	C	7,875	18.4
1945	A. Balfour	Lab	16,066	54.4			I.B. MacFarlane	Lib	1,865	4.4
	J.C.L. Anderson	C	13,489	45.6		1979	D.A. Canavan	Lab	22,516	47.7
1950	A. Balfour	Lab	19,930	55.6			A.A. McCurley	C	12,160	25.7
	M. Harvie Anderson	C	15,894	44.4			J.T. Jones	SNP	8,627	18.3
1951	A. Balfour	Lab	20,893	56.0			D.S.P. Cant	Lib	3,905	8.3
	M. Harvie Anderson	C	16,396	44.0						
1955	A. Balfour	Lab	18,935	54.6						
	W.A. Gay	C	15,721	45.4						

C : STIRLING/FALKIRK DISTRICT OF BURGHS

Election	Candidate	Party	Votes	% Poll		Election	Candidate	Party	Votes	% Poll
1918	J.A.M. Macdonald	Lib	9,350	64.3		1955	M. MacPherson	Lab	20,651	48.2
	A. Logan	Lab	5,201	35.7			J.R. McMillan	C	19,345	45.1
1922	H. Murnin	Lab	11,073	53.3			J. Halliday	SNP	2,885	6.7
	J.A.M. Macdonald	Nat Lib	9,717	46.7		1959	M. MacPherson	Lab	22,243	49.6
1923	Sir G. McCrae	Lib	10,721	50.4			R.S. Johnston	C	19,797	43.8
	H. Murnin	Lab	10,565	49.6			J. Halliday	SNP	2,983	6.6
1924	H. Murnin	Lab	13,436	53.9		1964	M. MacPherson	Lab	23,766	52.4
	Sir G. McCrae	Lib	11,512	46.1			J.A. Davidson	C	17,070	37.6
1929	H. Murnin	Lab	15,408	47.4			W.A. Milne	SNP	4,526	10.0
	D. Jamieson	C	10,164	31.3		1966	M. MacPherson	Lab	23,146	52.7
	A. Ratcliffe	Prot	6,902	21.3			I. Docherty	C	13,726	31.2
1931	J.S.C. Reid	C	21,844	63.6			W.A. Milne	SNP	6,322	14.4
	H. Murnin	Lab	12,483	36.4			P.J. McIntosh	Comm	767	1.7
1935	J.C. Westwood	Lab	17,958	51.2		1970	M.MacPherson	Lab	22,984	50.7
	J.S.C. Reid	C	17,087	48.8			D.R. Anderson	C	15,754	34.8
1945	J.C. Westwood	Lab	18,326	56.1			I.M. Murray	SNP	6,571	14.5
	J.F.G. Thomson	C	14,323	43.9		1974	H. Ewing	Lab	21,685	41.9
1948	M. MacPherson	Lab	17,001	49.0		(Feb)	R.D. McIntyre	SNP	17,886	34.5
	W.D.H.C. Forbes	C	14,826	42.8			G.A. Campbell	C	12,228	23.6
	R. Curran	SNP	2,831	8.2		1974	H. Ewing	Lab	22,090	43.2
1950	M. MacPherson	Lab	22,186	49.0		(Oct)	R. D. McIntyre	SNP	20,324	39,8
	W.D.H.C. Forbes	C	20,632	45.5			G. A. Campbell	C	7,186	14.1
	R. Curran	SNP	1,698	3.7			D. Angles	Lib	1,477	2.9
	G. McAlister	Comm	801	1.8		1979	H. Ewing	Lab	29.499	56.5
1951	M. MacPherson	Lab	24,421	52.3			W. Boyles	C	13,881	26.6
	W.D.H.C. Forbes	C	22,313	47.7			J. Donachy	SNP{	8,85	617.9

3 : 1983 - 1987

A : CLACKMANNAN

Election	Candidate	Party	Votes	% Poll	Election	Candidate	Party	Votes	% Poll
1983	M.J. O'Neill	Lab	16,478	45.8	1987	M.J. O'Neill	Lab	20,317	53.7
	J.T. Jones	SNP	6,839	19.0		W.J.A. Macartney	SNP	7,916	20.9
	C. Hardy	C	6,490	18.0		J. Parker	C	5,620	14.9
	H.C. Campbell	SDP	6,205	17.2		A.M. Watters	SDP	3,961	10.5

B : FALKIRK EAST

Election	Candidate	Party	Votes	% Poll	Election	Candidate	Party	Votes	% Poll
1983	H. Ewing	Lab	17,956	47.7	1987	H. Ewing	Lab	21,379	54.2
	D.D.M. Masterson	C	7,895	21.0		K.H. Brooks	C	7,356	18.7
	A.A.I. Wedderburn	SDP	6,967	18.5		R.N.F. Halliday	SNP	6,056	15.4
	J. McGregor	SNP	4,490	11.9		E.G. Dick	SDP	4,624	11.7
	F. McGregor	Comm	344	0.9					

C : FALKIRK WEST

Election	Candidate	Party	Votes	% Poll	Election	Candidate	Party	Votes	% Poll
1987	D.A. Canavan	Lab	20,256	53.2	1987	D. A. Canavan	Lab	20,256	53.2
	D.R.B. Thomas	C	6,704	17.6		D. R. B. Thomas	C	6,704	17.6
	I.R. Goldie	SNP	6,296	16.5		I. R. Goldie	SNP	6,296	16.5
	M.J. Harris	Lib	4,841	12.7		M. J. Harris	Lib	4,841	12.7

D : STIRLING

Election	Candidate	Party	Votes	% Poll	Election	Candidate	Party	Votes	% Poll
1983	M. Forsyth	C	17,039	40.0	1987	M. Forsyth	C	17,191	37.8
	M. Connarty	Lab	11,906	27.9		M. Connarty	Lab	16,643	36.5
	J.R. Finnie	Lib	10,174	27.9		I.B. McFarlane	Lib	6,804	14.9
	W. Houston	SNP	3,488	8.2		I.M. Lawson	SNP	4,897	10.8

Sport and
Physical Recreation

P. Bilsborough and I. Thomson

A range of popular games and contests were widely practised in Lowland Scotland before the advent of modern sports. In central Scotland, as in other parts of the country, these included several ball games, running events, lifting and throwing various implements, animal sports and varieties of fighting (Tranter 1987 21-38). On the whole they were relatively infrequent, loosely organised, often ad hoc affairs whose rules were oral and not particularly elaborate. Events were of only local interest, were rarely published or recorded, had little distinction between the roles of players and spectators and a level of violence which would shock modern observers was tolerated. In contrast, modern sport as it developed in the second half of the nineteenth century and as it remains today, was quite different in both form and character.

Victorian and Edwardian Developments

Beginning around the middle years of the 19th century, levels of participation in sport increased and forms of activity expanded. Participation and spectating rates rose dramatically and the social composition of those involved widened. At the same time, elaborate sets of standardised rules were written down and disseminated, distinctions were made between playing and spectating, a plethora of regional and national events took place, records and reports were assiduously recorded and widely publicised, and relatively low levels of physical violence were tolerated. In this region, as in other parts of the country, a range of agencies such as voluntary sports clubs, schools, local authorities and commercial operators were involved, to a greater or lesser extent, in sport's transformation.

Voluntary clubs were the principal agency for the development of sport but were established in different sports at very different dates: they also experienced markedly different subsequent growth patterns and displayed different survival capacities. **Table 1** provides decade by decade aggregates of the number of sports clubs known to have been established in the period 1831-1900. It illustrates that there was a far from uniform pattern to the growth of organised sport. The first sports to adopt formal club structures to any significant extent were curling and quoiting (**Figures 1 and 2**).

Figure 1 Curling at Polmaise Castle, Cambusbarron. (Smith Art Gallery and Museum)

Figure 2 Quoiting players at Bo'ness. (Falkirk Museum)

Table 1 The number of sports clubs in central Scotland, 1831-1900, by decade. (Tranter 1990 189)

Sport	1831-40	1841-50	1851-60	1861-70	1871-80	1881-90	1891-1900
Angling		1	3	7	13	28	26
Bowling	3	5	15	25	38	42	43
Cricket	3	5	13	74	173	118	86
Curling	25	51	66	87	100	97	87
Cycling					4	12	30
Golf			1	1	2	7	31
Lawn Tennis					3	19	13
Quoiting	21	13	10	21	24	28	46
Rugby					22	16	8
Football					66	506	566

Curling clubs had been established at Doune, Borestone and Bridge of Allan before 1800 but real advances were not made until the 1830s when 25 were formed. By 1881 the number had quadrupled. Similarly, quoiting was reasonably common in the first quarter of the 19th century but became a major sport only in the 1830s when 21 clubs were formed.

Clubs for a second group of sports such as bowling, angling and cricket did not appear in significant numbers until the third quarter of the 19th century. The first angling club was established in Stirling in 1844. In 1855 a second was formed at Alloa and two years later a third was established at Dollar. However, it was in the 1860s, when clubs were formed at Denny and Dunipace (1864), Callendar (1866), Bridge of Allan (1868) and Aberfoyle (1869), that institutional angling first became common. One or two cricket clubs were formed in the second quarter of the century in Stirling and Falkirk but they were short-lived. Most of the growth in organised cricket took place after 1861 and by the mid-1870s there were considerably more clubs playing cricket than any other sport.

Clubs were not formed in a third collection of sports such as rugby, football, cycling, golf and lawn tennis until well into the final quarter of the 19th century. Golf had been played on the Stirling King's Park since the 16th century but it was not until 1857 that the region's first golf club, at Stirling, was instituted and even this lasted less than twelve months. A more successful Stirling Golf Club was launched in 1869 and a second club, the Falkirk Tryst, in 1880. Although by 1890 the number of local clubs had risen to seven, it was only in the last decade of the century that golf firmly established itself as a club sport. The first cycling clubs were started at Falkirk and Stirling in 1879. The following year saw the formation of a club in Alloa and a second in Falkirk, the East Stirlingshire Bicycle Club. In the course of the 1880s their numbers tripled and included Dunblane, Grangemouth, Skinflats, Doune, Callander, Bo'ness, Bannockburn and Bonnybridge.

Folk forms of football which combined both handling and kicking skills survived until the middle of the 19th century in various parts of the region including the Roman Camp at Callander, at Doune by men employed on the Blairdrummond estate, at Deanston cotton mills, on Stirling King's Park by schoolboys and soldiers and on the Westerton estate in Bridge of Allan. Nevertheless, clubs did not begin to emerge until the codification of the separate games of rugby and association football in the 1860s though numbers remained small until the mid-1870s. Of the two sports, rugby was the first to adopt a club structure but most of the 22 clubs established in the 1870s had folded by 1900 leaving a rump of seven. By contrast, interest in playing football soared. Between 1891 and 1900 as many as 566 soccer clubs were known to have existed in the region - almost seven times as many as the next largest cluster in cricket.

The variations in dates at which clubs were formed in different sports were matched by equally marked variations in their subsequent patterns of development. The number of curling clubs continued to rise until 1880 after which it stabilised. The number of angling and bowling clubs displayed similar trends. The enthusiasm for forming new quoiting, cricket, tennis and rugby clubs was not maintained. The early interest in quoiting in the 1830s was not maintained into the 1840s and 1850s but from 1860 enthusiasm slowly increased. New clubs were formed and old ones revived: at Alva in 1871; at Bonnybridge in 1879 which, it was hoped, would stimulate interest in a "once favourite pastime in the village"; in Thornhill in 1885; Balfron in 1894 and Bannockburn in 1898 (Tranter 1990b 46). The decline in the number of cricket clubs after 1880 was never reversed. By contrast, football, cycling and golf clubs were relatively young organisations and they steadily increased in popularity throughout the period.

Patterns of development were also characterised by marked contrasts from sport to sport in the stability of individual clubs. Bowling, angling, curling, cycling and golf clubs led relatively uninterrupted and, for the most part, secure existences, but cricket, quoiting and football clubs were less secure and shorter-lived. Quoiting clubs were typical. Doune Quoits Club was revived in 1864 but in 1877 it had folded. It was formed again in 1883 but lasted less than a year and had to be re-formed in 1885. It had collapsed again by 1888 and was not re-established until 1896. Similarly, football clubs came and went. Doune Vale of Teith Football Club was founded in 1878, broken up in 1886 and was resurrected three times in the 1890s. Both the Cambusbarron Blackwood Rovers and Stirling Excelsior clubs, active in the early 1890s, had to be re-started later in the decade while Bonnybridge Grasshoppers Football Club, founded in 1875, gave way to a Bonnybridge Thistle club in 1886 and was not reformed until 1889.

There are various explanations for the different dates of formation, subsequent growth patterns and survival capacities of sports clubs in the region and among these, variations in consumer tastes, cost and the availability of facilities, appear to be particularly significant. The vagaries of consumer taste adversely affected most sports at one time or another. This was inevitable given the novelty of most codified sports at the time. The local press noted that at Doune in 1883 bowling had superceded quoiting. In 1894 the future of Stirling County Cricket Club was threatened by a growing preference among members for golf and tennis. In 1897 cycling was reported to be robbing tennis of players. However, soccer appears to have afflicted the most widespread damage. In 1895, for example, it was noted that "when football appears it not infrequently claps an instantaneous and effective extinguisher on almost all other forms of sport" (Tranter 1990c 365-87).

The cost of joining a sports club also affected patterns of development. In the final quarter of the 19th century, when the weekly income of a semi-skilled man averaged 20-30s per week, locally an annual subscription of around five shillings seems to have been regarded as the most that a skilled man could be expected to pay. However, clubs in a number of sports charged higher entry fees and annual subscriptions leading to restrictions in their size. At Doune (1883-96), Borestone (1890), Stirling Guildhill (1875-9) and Denny (1866-8), bowling clubs' yearly subscriptions ranged from 5s to 7s 6d. At other bowling clubs, however, they were much higher: 12s 6d at Alloa East End (1894-5), 15s at Bannockburn (1889-90) and 20s at Bridge of Allan Airthrey Spa (1896). Similar patterns existed in angling and cricket. Golf clubs, as a group, were probably the most exclusive: 20s at Stirling (1884) (**Figure 3**), 10s 6d at Stirling Ladies' Club (1897) and between 10s and 12s 6d at Aberfoyle, Bridge of Allan and Dollar in the 1890s.

Although in some sports one or two clubs charged relatively high subscription rates in order to exclude artisans, this was not a typical motive. Wide fee differentials were more a matter of economic necessity. In cricket, the Stirling County Club imposed much higher charges on members than other clubs in the region primarily because it was the representative club of the county, played the leading Scottish teams and was expected to have a superior ground and ancillary facilities. Moreover, bowling greens, golf courses and their attendant accommodation were costly items which required relatively high club fees. In comparison, the

Figure 3   Golf at King's Park about 1880. (Smith Art Gallery and Museum)

costs of operating curling and quoiting clubs were low and membership charges modest.

Curling, bowls and golf clubs had little difficulty in acquiring regular access to the facilities they required. This was not the case for some cricket, cycling and soccer clubs. Although most were sufficiently resourceful to deal with facility problems, some were less successful. At Falkirk in 1865 cricket clubs stopped practising and lost many of their members to bowls because of the loss of the Glebe Park and another field at Gartcows on which cricket had previously been played. Football clubs too faced problems of finding suitable grounds. In 1893 Grangemouth Football Club was evicted from its rented ground because the land was required for cropping. In Falkirk, the loss of Thornbank led to the demise of Stirlingshire Rugby Club in 1895 and Camelon Football Club came close to extinction when its ground was taken over as the site for a new foundry. The club survived but only by leasing a pitch on a weekly basis at a much higher rental. Like Camelon, most clubs relied on the use of private land as support from municipal authorities was lukewarm.

Local authorities were aware of the ever growing demands for facilities, particularly sports pitches and swimming pools, but they offered relatively little help. In part this was due to circumstances beyond their control. Suitably large areas of land for sports pitches were not available for local authorities to purchase or lease, particularly in expanding industrial centres such as Falkirk, Larbert and Stenhousemuir. In the main however, it was largely because the majority of ratepayers, who had little interest in playing sport, did not want their local taxes spent on its provision. At Stirling in 1864 the Town Council refused to add a penny to the rates to provide a new curling and skating pond. Also in Stirling on three occasions between 1887 and 1913 the Town Council balked at providing the capital for public baths for fear of antagonising ratepayers. Prompted partly by the popularity of public baths in Alva, built in 1874 and financed by a local philanthropist James Johnstone, Stirling Town Council carried out a feasibility study in 1887 which included analyses of the operating costs of some existing public baths. Its report on the Dunfermline Carnegie Baths -

> "... is certainly not encouraging as it shows a loss on the year there of £35 22s 2d. Such a state of matters is not very creditable. Are ratepayers prepared to voluntarily tax themselves to cover deficits? Until they signify their willingness at some public meeting or until a plebiscite is taken, it is useless to discuss the matter" (Stirling Town Council March 1887).

Seven years later ratepayers were given the opportunity to vote on the proposal to establish public baths and wash-houses at St Ninian's Well Green. 149 voted in favour but 753 rejected it on the grounds that rate increases would be required if the baths failed to generate sufficient income to cover its capital and operating costs. A third attempt to build baths in 1909 at the Social Institute in Stirling also failed due to similar concerns. Some ratepayers were demanding more facilities and seemed prepared to pay for them but the majority showed no interest and believed that provision was the responsibility of voluntary, private philanthropy.

Not surprisingly, the majority of municipal sports facilities that were built were financed from philanthropic sources. Towns and townships in the region were indebted to the desire of several wealthy men to perpetuate themselves in the memory of the people by donating land and money. At Alva, in 1874, the second public baths and wash-houses built in Scotland were paid for by a donation from James Johnstone. At Alloa in 1898 Thomas Paton gave the Town Council money to build an extensive public baths which included a swimming pool (**Figure 4**), private baths, turkish baths, a gymnasium and billiard room. At Grangemouth in 1880 the Earl of Zetland gave the Town Council eight acres of his estate for a public park. Similarly, at Carronshore in 1887 another local land owner, T. D. Brodie, gifted a public park and recreation ground. In some of these cases additional money to meet running costs or lay out land was met from the rates but in other cases additional monetary gifts or public subscriptions were used.

Municipal authorities laid out parks to provide people with opportunities to participate in activities of an ordered, disciplined, improving and educational nature. Sports pitches were provided in some parks but for the most part parks were regarded as public

Figure 4 Public Baths Alloa 1903.   (Alloa Library)

walking areas in which people could stroll along tree lined paths and drives looking at judicious collections of flora. Local authorities were not prepared to allocate extensive acreages of valuable grass land to games which encouraged the formation of large groups of noisy boisterous youths who destroyed the tranquillity of the parks and caused unsightly bare patches on the grass which gave the areas untidy ragged appearances. At the opening of a public park containing football pitches at Carronshore in 1887 a local minister acknowledged the need for sports pitches but warned his younger sporting parishioners that they should -

> "... never seek to monopolise the park to the exclusion or inconvenience of the greater majority of people who would resort to it for a quiet seat or walk, wherein they found pleasure as sweet as football brought to them" (*Falkirk Herald* 6 November 1887).

Although they may have been exaggerated, the contributions of schools to the development of organised sport in Victorian and Edwardian Scotland were important. In Glasgow, both private and state schools were influential. They aroused interest in sport amongst their pupils and provided the city's clubs with a plethora of knowledgeable participants. By contrast, schools' contributions to the development of organised sport in the region were relatively slight, only a few private making any impact (Tranter 1989 56-7).

Blairlodge near Polmont and Stanley House at Bridge of Allan were two of the region's largest and most established private schools. Both attached considerable importance to games to improve boys' health, manners and morality. On purchasing Blairlodge in 1874, James Cook Gray built a gymnasium and swimming pool, laid out playing fields and established fixtures with other private schools. Similarly, Thomas Braidwood who founded Stanley House School in 1870 purchased 10 acres of fields on which boys played cricket, rugby, athletics and golf. Later a swimming pool and gymnasium were built. Time was allocated in timetables at both schools for attendance at games and staff were expected to be involved in coaching and refereeing. Some members of school teams spent between two and three hours on four or five days each week practising and competing and some members of staff were recruited as much for their sporting ability as for their skill in the classroom. At Blairlodge there was nearly always an international rugby player such as the Rev. E. B. Brutton (Cambridge University and England), R. L. Aston (Blackheath and England), W. Wotherspoon (West of Scotland and Scotland) and the Irish international, H. Lindsay, on the staff. Additional coaches were also frequently hired (*Public School Magazine* 1902 229-30).

Inevitably both schools enjoyed considerable sporting success. The Stanley House cricket team, coached by a procession of ex-English county players like P. Bach (Yorkshire) and B. Hampson (Lancashire), always provided formidable opposition. At Blairlodge, teams remained undefeated in school cricket competitions in 1893, 1894 and 1900 and in school rugby games in seasons 1892-3 and 1893-4. To some extent staff were also involved in local sport. In 1878 W. Somerville, the Stanley House professional played for Stirling Wanderers Cricket Club and in the late 1890s J. C. Baird, a master at the school and former Scottish half-mile champion, was Secretary of the Strathallan Highland Games. By contrast, pupils only played for their school and few joined local clubs on leaving school. Moreover, Blairlodge's influence was short-lived. It was closed in 1910 owing to a diphtheria epidemic.

The region's state schools were even less influential largely because there was no official support for sport. Before 1872 physical education in Scottish elementary schools was for the most part neglected. The *1872 Education (Scotland) Act* made no provision for physical education but the *Code of Regulations* introduced in 1873 allowed attendance of boys at drill under a competent instructor to count as school attendance. The Code of 1875 added the term 'military drill'. The legislation was permissive but the region's school boards instituted drill as part of normal school programmes to teach children habits of sharp obedience, smartness, cleanliness and order. In Stirling, non-commissioned officers of the Argyll and Sutherland Highlanders were paid to drill pupils. Military drill consolidated its position in 1895 when a new Schools' Code made drill or some other form of physical exercise grant earning.

Progressive opinion which saw the need for improvements in pupil health and welfare did not, however, accept drill as the only form of school physical education and by 1910 a wider conception of physical education had been introduced. Drill was replaced by a more scientifically founded course of exercises, swimming programmes introduced and developed and some games taught. However, the number of pupils receiving swimming lessons was relatively small as was the time allocated to games. From 1905 Stirling School Board provided pupils with swimming instruction at Alloa Public Baths but less than 8% of the Board's pupils attended annually. Similarly, Mary McKerchar, instructress of physical training who had been appointed in 1907 by Stirling School Board to introduce Swedish exercises, extended her remit to include games. She taught netball and hockey at Williamfield but only for a total of two hours a week. Patterns of participation in organised sport in the region had long been established by the time local state schools showed much interest.

One of the principal features of sports transformation between 1830-1914 was the development of spectating. However, like the growth of clubs, patterns were far from uniform. Sports which attracted large crowds included horseracing, Highland games events, boat-racing and football. Spectators maintained their interest in some of these throughout the period but not in others.

Annual **boat-racing** regattas were first reported at Grangemouth in 1829 and Kincardine-on-Forth in 1830. After 1850 others were initiated at Alloa (1853), Stirling (1854), Port of Menteith (1857) and Callander (1860). Regattas remained popular in the third quarter of the century but then enthusiasm waned and they largely died out. The Stirling Regatta was held annually for twelve years until 1866 while a regatta started by the Bo'ness Bowling Club in 1883 failed to survive beyond 1890. Boat racing often attracted large crowds. "Some thousands of spectators" attended the second annual Forth Regatta at Dunmore in 1852. The 1856 Stirling Regatta attracted a crowd of 7,000 and in 1858 the Lake of Menteith Regatta drew "an immense number of spectators". A combined regatta and games at Grangemouth drew crowds of 4,000 in 1864, 10,000 in 1865 and 4,000 in 1875. Tragically, however, the sport suffered badly from the inefficient manner in which regattas were often conducted. Stirling's annual regatta was heavily criticised in 1856 and 1859 in the local press for a range of administrative inefficiencies. In 1860 facilities were "almost non-existent" with "not even an old pistol or gunpowder to start the race" (Tranter 1990d 15). Boat-racing also often failed to provide the excitement and variety that spectators desired and consequently found it hard to sustain popularity.

Horseracing attracted enormous numbers of people to watch the aesthetic and athletic powers of thoroughbreds, gamble and generally have a good time: 10,000 watched races at the annual meeting of the Stirlingshire Yeomanry Cavalry at King's Park in 1824, and between three and four thousand in 1830. An estimated 35,000 were reported at the 1830 Stirling Horse Races. Elsewhere there was a similar picture with large attendances at meetings at Bo'ness and Laurieston in the 1830s and 1840s. Nevertheless, public concern over the potentially and at times actually disruptive effects of such large crowds led to its eventual downfall. At the Falkirk races in 1836 there was "much beastly drunkenness and other attendant immoralities", including prostitution. The stimulation of drink, successful gambling and the general holiday atmosphere all too often led to excess. The criminal fraternity also found easy pickings at races. A regular crowd of the underworld travelled the racing circuits. In 1854 the annual Stirling races were described as "a carnival of crime" in which "the number of gamblers, thieves and vagabonds ... comprised a large portion of the entire gathering on the course" (*Stirling Observer*, 19 November 1854). Predictably, it was the last occasion on which races were held in the town.

In contrast to boat-racing and horseracing, Highland games events and football were popular spectator sports throughout the period. **Highland games** were rare for much of the first half of the 19th century. Events were inaugurated at Alva in 1845 (**Figure 5**) and Bridge of Allan in 1849. In the next decade the number increased sevenfold and in the following ten years had doubled again to 28. The number of events remained at between 27 and 30 throughout the rest of the century. Average attendances at the more prestigious Highland games, when not adversely affected by bad weather, lack of publicity or

a nearby counter-attraction, were consistently large: 3,000 at Denny and Tillicoultry, 4,000 at Alloa, 5,000 at Alva and Stirling and 10,000 at Bridge of Allan for the Strathallan Games.

The number of senior **football** clubs of professional status fluctuated sharply. The Stirlingshire Football Association contained seven clubs when it was formed in 1882. In 1884 there were 19 clubs and six years later, at its peak, 24. By 1896 the number had fallen to 15 and in 1899 to 11. Senior football games consistently attracted large crowds. The best supported senior club was East Stirlingshire which had an average attendance of around 1,500. Falkirk and Stirling King's Park were also well-supported with average attendances of 1,000. Other senior clubs such as Stenhousemuir and Dunblane had average crowds of 350-500 and 300-400 respectively.

Although for the most part crowds paid to watch, expectations of profit by clubs and other groups involved in events were never a significant motivator. To the directors and shareholders of the region's senior football clubs for instance, profits were a means to ensuring future playing success and the prestige that came with it rather than an end in themselves (Vamplew 1981 81). Similarly, although most of the region's Highland games events made adequate profits, they were ploughed back into improving the quality of subsequent events or saved to offset losses incurred from a rainy day.

In a relatively short space of time the nature of sport had been transformed in the region. Some popular sporting forms disappeared while others were assimilated into new codes of organised and regularised play. The traditional, relatively small, loosely organised sporting world of the eighteenth and early nineteenth century had given way to a larger structured competitive sports system which went on outside working hours, at regular times, in specially provided places, and according to universal sets of rules.

Between the Wars

Despite persistently high levels of unemployment, strikes, violence and the despair and demoralisation engendered by long-term depression in the country's economy, in this region as in other parts of Scotland, leisure activities thrived during the inter-war period. Dancing, going to the cinema and playing and watching sport were particularly prominent leisure forms in these harsh years of economic slump largely because they brought fun, excitement and a touch of colour to people's lives.

The most popular participatory sports were football, badminton, bowls, angling and golf. Every village, township and town had at least one football club. Even small communities such as Logie, Fintry, Strathblane, Kincardine-in-Menteith and Kilmadock had a team. Badminton was played in halls of one kind or another throughout the region. Social clubs, church organisations, youth clubs and works' recreation

Figure 5 High jump at Alva Highland Games. (Alloa Library)

sections provided the focal points for groups to form clubs. Almost every community also had a bowling club. In Stirling "there are many bowling clubs ... and the greens are crowded throughout the summer" (Rennie 1966 188). Similarly in Balfron, "bowls provokes a great deal of interest and many a happy evening is spent in that pursuit" (ibid 226). However, the most remarkable feature of participation was the widening choice of available sports. Increasing amounts of time, money and mobility provided the backcloth for numerous new sports to emerge and clubs to form. "Falkirk is particularly popular in the range of sporting activities which may be pursued. Accommodation for everyone of them is not always adequate but the range is wide" (ibid 339). In addition to established sports, clubs were formed for gymnastics, skating, hockey, athletics, mountaineering, ski-ing, weight-lifting, carpet bowling, and ice-hockey.

Spectating patterns were also bouyant. Highland games and football sustained their popularity with spectators in the interwar period. At the same time boxing emerged as another popular spectator sport. Amateur boxing was largely in the hands of military personnel and some local clubs while professional contests were arranged by a handful of promoters from Glasgow and Edinburgh. At the end of the twenties and throughout the thirties amateur boxing was particularly popular. The drill halls in Stirling and Alloa and the gymnasium at Stirling Castle were the most common venues and they always seemed to be packed out. For the second round of the Scottish command inter-battalion boxing championships at Stirling Castle in 1939, "the gymnasium was packed to the doors full of ardent fighting fans, and everyone with a most particular interest in the event" (*Stirling Observer* 16 February 1939). Mining villages spawned numerous clubs and the events which they organised were equally popular. There was always "a large following" for contests arranged by the Fallin Physical Culture Club at the Welfare Hall in the village. Wherever contests took place, admission prices were cheap ranging from 3d to 1s and for such sums fight fans could expect to see three 6 round and three 4 round contests between territorials from the Argyll and Sutherland Highlanders and numerous visiting companies and a variety of local boxers from tough mining communities, some of whom out of hunger and the sheer hardness of village life turned to the professional ring to make a few bawbees.

Professional **boxing** was not as common as amateur but it did attract large crowds. There was a 'packed hall' at the Little Theatre, Stirling in March 1938 for a programme arranged by Hunter's Boxing Promotions, Glasgow. Other indoor arenas included Stirling's Albert Hall and Falkirk Town Hall. Forthbank Park, the home of Kings Park Football Club and 'The Recs', Alloa Athletic's stadium, were also used (**Figure 6**). Most of the pros were either local men or from

Figure 6 Lightweight championship of Scotland, Jim Hunter vs Tony Speirs, at the 'Recs' Alloa, 1932. (Alloa Library)

Glasgow, Edinburgh or Dundee. They slugged it out in front of large, rather partisan crowds for relatively small purses ranging from £20-£70.

The buoyant interest in boxing was paralleled by that for Highland games events. Throughout the interwar period games were held at, amongst other places, Dunblane, Doune, Alva, Bridge of Allan, Plean, Cowie, Grangemouth, Bannockburn, Airth, Larbert and Carronshore. Some of these were small, local events while others were of national significance. Two of the largest and nationally popular were the annual Airth and Bridge of Allan (Strathallan) meetings.

Table 2 indicates that the Bridge of Allan meeting attracted consistently large crowds. Similarly, at Airth, attendances of 10,000 were consistently reported. They descended on the small village "by motor boat from Alloa, by bike from neighbouring towns, flocking in from Airth Road Station, disembarking in droves from Penders' Motor Services omnibuses, or simply making

Table 2   Attendances at the Bridge of Allan Games, 1921-39. (*Stirling Observer 1921-39*)

Year	Attendance	Year	Attendance
1921	18-20,000	1931	16,000
1922	16,000	1932	10,000
1923	16-20,000	1933	20,000
1924	20,000	1934	16,000
1925	16,000	1935	15,000
1926	17,000	1936	12,000
1927	14,000	1937	15,000
1928	15,000	1938	"Usual large crowd"
1929	11,000	1939	15,000

the journey on foot" (McGrail 1984 6). Both games were bigger and better than they had ever been. There were all sorts of attractions. At the 79th Strathallan Gathering in 1931, there were: eleven sprint and distance races, including seventeen heats for the 100 yards, four cycle races, six heavy events, eight dancing, three piping, four jumping, three wrestling and two pony trot competitions. There were similar programmes at Airth which also included enormously popular whippet racing and quoiting competitions. Many events attracted competitors from all over the country and increasingly from abroad. In particular, the sprint and distance races were as good as anything seen at Powderhall.

Highland games were not just about athletic and musical competition. Around the field there were shows such as hurdie-gurdies, coconut shies, donkey rides, fortune tellers, steam boats and other garish attractions which, when combined with the smell of fish and chip stalls and the blaring sounds from steam organs, added to the continuing sense of excitement and fun.

Football consolidated its popularity as the region's principal spectator sport between the wars. It was the only sport which could attract thousands of spectators once a fortnight for eight months of the year. Nevertheless, the leading clubs met with mixed fortunes and even the most popular were never as successful as any of the city clubs. Two clubs from the region played in the Scottish Football League prior to 1914, Falkirk in the first division and East Stirlingshire in division two. By the early twenties there were seven clubs playing senior football. They joined the League at the start of the 1921-2 season but in rather strained circumstances. In 1919 the Scottish Football League Management Committee decided not to operate a second division. Some of the spurned clubs, including East Stirlingshire, sought refuge in the Central League, whose main strength lay in the counties of Stirlingshire, Fife and West Lothian and which included, amongst others, Bo'ness, Alloa, Stenhousemuir, King's Park, Falkirk 'A' and Clackmannan. The Central League was not affiliated to the Inter-League Board and was under no obligation to recognise the Scottish Football League's player registration system. Accordingly, the Central League proceeded to recruit where it willed and several prominent players, attracted by relatively high wages, were signed: its games were popular and its clubs in a strong bargaining position. Reconciliation was achieved in 1921-2 and Central League teams were invited en bloc to join a reconstituted second division. As a quid pro quo, the poached players had to return to their own clubs.

The places left by the departed stars were, perforce, filled with less talented players and gates fell. Within a couple of years insolvency hit some clubs which a few seasons earlier had enjoyed prosperity. Clackmannan was the first casualty. The club finished bottom of the second division in 1921-2 and withdrew for a year only to try again when a third division was created in 1923. It played for all of that division's three seasons without distinction and the division's collapse was also the end of Clackmannan's senior career.

Bo'ness also folded: it started very successfully, winning the second division title in 1926-7, but narrowly failed to retain its first division place and thereafter the slide was protracted and irreversible. Its attendances, like most clubs, were badly affected by the General Strike of 1926, but the subsequent protracted resistance of the Miner's Union severely damaged its gates as many of its fans, most of whom were miners, were unable to pay for admission to matches. The club attempted to sustain their loyalty, if visiting clubs agreed, by arranging to admit for nothing half an hour after a match had started men who were on the parish and only received lines for food. Most visiting teams went along with this arrangement but in November 1926 East Stirlingshire objected. The club eventually faltered on the question of guarantee payments to visiting clubs and withdrew from the League in November 1932 (Crampsey 1990 293).

The other clubs retained their membership of the League throughout the period. To survive and flourish they improved their facilities, structures and management. They established youth schemes to aid player recruitment, introduced more scientific training programmes, adopted tougher management regimes and as a result enjoyed some success. Alloa won the second division title in 1921-2, East Stirlingshire in 1931-2 and Falkirk in 1935-6. However, their progress and achievements were always limited by the constant demands of the leading English and Scottish clubs for their best players. Throughout the period local clubs provided a large number of players for the most successful English and Scottish professional sides. "Between the wars English managers regularly headed North to watch the professional and amateur teams of Scotland, just as surely as American boxing promoters turn to the black ghettoes for their manpower" (Walvin 1975 123). Typical of many transferred players was Scottish internationalist James Dougall. Dougall was born in Denny and his first club was Kilsyth Rangers. He moved to Falkirk in 1932 but within two years Preston North End had tempted him south. No English championship side in the interwar period played without a Scot and some had an absolute majority of Scottish players. Football had become not only the provider of hero status but also an aspiration and a way out for talented local players. One of the most talented was Billy Steel, widely regarded as one of the greatest inside-forwards of all time. This "hard little man with bounding vitality, superb footballing brain and a stunning shot" started his career with Dunipace Thistle and Bo'ness Cadora but played his best football with Derby County (Lammington 1987 203-4).

Local senior clubs never attracted attendances to compare with those of clubs in Glasgow, Dundee, Aberdeen and Edinburgh but attendances were nontheless sufficient to allow the game to consolidate its position as a focal point of community interest. In Falkirk in 1928 -

> "the sight of Hope Street, usually a quiet one - on a Saturday afternoon during the football season, more especially since the year 1905, when Falkirk club became one of the first League teams, demonstrates what a hold the game of football has on the young and old of our town and district"
> (Love 1928 16)

The cultural basis of football remained firmly rooted in localism, largely due to the relative immobility of supporters than is normal today. Supporters in the region continued to identify with their local communities through regular support at their local football ground. The local senior football team helped working men flesh out a distinctive sense of place within the wider framework of national competition. By following the progress of their team within the Scottish leagues they were able to assert their membership of their community. It gave them something to belong to and something in common with thousands of other men.

Considerably more sport was played in state schools between 1918-39 than at any time before. In particular, rugby, football, cricket, hockey, athletics and tennis were promoted. Developments took place on two fronts: firstly, in compulsory physical education classes between 9 am and 4 pm, and secondly in voluntary sports clubs after 4pm and on Saturday mornings.

Between the wars physical education started to shake off its associations with drill. In 1919 and 1933 the Scottish Education Department (SED) issued new syllabuses for physical education and on each occasion followed them up with guidance notes suggesting the lines along which the policies of education authorities and practices in schools should be shaped and developed. The new syllabuses and guidance notes attempted to stimulate education authority managers, school medical officers and teachers to adopt much wider views of the scope and purpose of physical education. Teachers were advised to adopt less rigid, more child-centred teaching methods while education authorities were urged to make better provision for physical education, including allocating adequate time, employing specialist teachers, appointing organisers and supplying suitable indoor and outdoor facilities. While the SED documents focussed on physical education's contribution to the physical development of children, they also highlighted its aesthetic, cathartic, and moral purposes. Inevitably, Scandinavian forms of gymnastics lay at the centre of both the 1919 and 1933 syllabuses but games and athletics were also included for the first time. In the primary school simple small-sided games were recommended to provide pupils with elements of fun and enjoyment which were largely missing from classes in gymnastics, and in secondary schools it was suggested that the major team games could be used to develop skill, endurance and a sense of competition.

Education authorities attempted, within available resources, to make suitable provision for physical education. By 1930 the seven secondary schools in Stirlingshire and Clackmannanshire had specialist teachers of physical education who, as well as teaching gymnastics, introduced games, athletics and swimming into schools' curricula. In addition, in 1937, Stirlingshire became the second Scottish county to appoint a specialist organiser. His role included arranging refresher courses for specialist teachers and updating primary school teachers about developments in physical education. There was also a slow but gradual improvement in facilities. Throughout the period most primary schools in Stirlingshire and Clackmannanshire had no indoor facilities - not even a central hall - and field provision for outdoor games was equally poor. By contrast, most intermediate and secondary schools had central halls and newly built schools such as Falkirk Technical and Riverside, Stirling also had a combination of gymnasia, swimming pools and playing fields. Consequently, team games became a significant part of physical education curricula. During the thirties, secondary schools in Clackmannanshire allocated one hour each week to games and similarly in Stirlingshire, specialist teachers were encouraged by the county organiser to develop games in the curriculum.

In addition to compulsory games playing during school hours, pupils were also given opportunities to take part in team games and athletics after school - especially in secondary schools where there was a particular determination to demonstrate that standards were comparable to those in private schools. Leaving Certificate passes were of most value but games were also important. They were a form of cultural capital held to demonstrate comparability. They were also practical instruments for creating and sustaining morale, enthusiasm and goodwill within schools. In 1928 Alexander Third, Stirling High School's Rector, noted -

> "The sporting spirit still remains strongly among us, and is especially notable among the new members upon whom a passionate love of the game has speedily left its mark. Every boy turns up to practices and to matches brimming over the 'pep', and filled with the desire to do his best for the sake of the school" (*Stirling High School Magazine* June 1928 17).

The pattern of extra-curricular sports development at Stirling High was typical of many of the region's secondary schools. In 1921 the school established an athletic union consisting of four clubs: rugby, hockey, cricket and tennis. The union was managed by a committee of teachers and former pupils who arranged fixtures, coached teams and refereed matches. Intra-mural events included house matches in hockey, tennis and cricket, inter-house school sports and staff versus pupils tennis and hockey matches. There was also a well organised structure of friendly inter-school competition. Stirling High School's regular opponents included Alva, Dollar, Alloa and Perth Academies, Queen Victoria School Dunblane, and Falkirk, Dalziel, Balfron, Hillhead, James Gillespie's, Kilsyth and Burghmuir High Schools.

Throughout the inter-war period around 33% of pupils at Stirling High were athletic union members and the individual clubs went from strength to strength as the school roll expanded. In 1929 the rugby club had 75 members playing in three teams. By 1939 there were 134 boys playing in seven teams. In hockey there were 70 girls playing in two teams in 1926 and by 1939 120 playing in four teams. By 1937 the tennis club, begun in the early 1920s with forty members, had 125 members and three representative teams. In each of these sports the number of representative teams could have been even larger but for the limits imposed by a continuing lack of facilities. Throughout the period 1919-39 the school rented Stirling County Cricket Club's ground at Williamfield where there was space for only one rugby and two hockey pitches. In 1939, however, it purchased playing fields at Torbrex and the number of representative teams expanded immediately. Between the wars, the region's state schools played more prominent roles in the developing pattern of organised sport than they had ever done before, though adequate facilities remained problematical.

Parks and bathing facilities continued to be prominent areas of municipal activity between the wars. In 1924 Grangemouth Town Council built an open air swimming pool in Zetland Park. It was 50m long, 15m wide and 1 to 2m deep. On a much larger scale in 1932 Falkirk Town Council built public baths on a slum clearance site in Pleasance. The facility cost £19,000, some of which was raised from a government grant aid initiative aimed at encouraging councils to clear "insanitary areas". The building contained a swimming pool 25m long, 12m wide and 3/4 to over 2m deep, a gallery for 400 spectators, a committee room and a plant room containing the latest filtration equipment (*Falkirk Herald* 28 September 1932).

One of the most striking features of these developments was the relative emphasis on facilities for swimming at the expense of private bathing provision. Although private bathing remained a significant local practice, recreational and competitive swimming saw considerable growth which was not confined to boys and men as were most other sports. Increasing amounts of mixed bathing may have been one major reason for the increase in interest but so too were long overdue improvements in equipment and design. For example, the filtration system at Falkirk Public Baths ensured that clean water was available on a daily basis.

The successful developments in Grangemouth and Falkirk were in stark contrast to those in Stirling.

There, the Town Council was no more successful in building baths between the wars than it had been before 1914 despite a serious attempt in the early twenties. Section 20 of the 1920 Mining Industry Act made provision for the establishment of a fund to improve the social conditions of colliery workers. Money was generated by taking 1d from every ton of Scottish coal mined between July 1920 and December 1925. Local colliery workers' welfare committees were encouraged to draw up capital schemes for which they could receive 80% grant aid. The remaining 20% had to be raised by local collieries. Manor Powis, Polmaise and Millhall developed a scheme with Stirling Town Council to build public baths costing £10,400. However, the development failed when the Council was unable to identify a suitable site at its own cost or offer sufficiently generous users concessions to satisfy the local colliery workers' welfare committee.

Quantitative information about parks and playing fields is patchy and difficult to synthesise. Nevertheless, the interwar years saw local authorities embark on some schemes funded from a combination of philanthropy, rates or grants from the National Playing Fields Association (NPFA) or the National Fitness Council (NFC). During the 1920s Falkirk Town Council opened Dollar Park. The estate, originally known as 'Arnotdale', was bought in 1920 by Robert Dollar and bequeathed to the Town Council, one of several gifts given to the town by this Grahamston man who had made his fortune in Canada. The park was a traditional civic showpiece with clipped lawns, tree shadowed walks, scented gardens, statues and flower beds, but to the disappointment of some rate payers, no provision for sport.

By contrast, another civic showpiece, Zetland Public Park in Grangemouth, was extended in the mid-1920s by 25 acres, almost all of which was given over to sport. It contained six soccer pitches, two rugby pitches, a netball court, six tennis courts, a bowling green, a putting green, a large paddling pond, a pavilion, changing rooms and an open air swimming pool. Provision for sport was further increased in 1943 when the town opened Dalgrain Public Park. As well as the usual lawns, pathways, seats and floral displays, a paddling pool, community hall and football pitch were also provided. Less active forms of recreation clearly remained a priority with local authorities but at the same time they began to acknowledge the need for specially designated sports pitches.

Underlying the municipal provision of sporting and recreational facilities in the region during the decades between the two world wars were a number of objectives: civic pride, a desire to promote physical health, social harmony and good citizenship and, as the prominent siting of a statue of the Prodigal Son in Dollar Park demonstrates, a determination to raise standards of individual and community morality. Great care was taken to ensure that municipal leisure facilities were rationally used. Bye-laws with intricate restrictions, boundary fences, locked gates at night and the monitoring of behaviour by park-keepers were all designed to influence park users. Parks were not 'public' in the widest sense but continued to be supervised places for the public to go to enjoy themselves in a respectable, healthy sober atmosphere -

> "The Dollar Park may justly be regarded as the pride of Falkirk's open spaces. Here, in the heart of an oasis of peace in the desert of industrialism, life moves in a quiet turn, here the town-tired can go to rest, to breath the fresh air and to seek recreation amidst surroundings which are not bounded and circumscribed by drab walls of brick or stone" (*Falkirk Herald* 20 August 1955).

Civic rivalry and prestige was a further motive to provision. At the opening of Grangemouth's open air swimming pool (Figure 7) one councillor emphasised that it "was one of the largest and structurally one of the finest in the country" (*Falkirk Herald* 20 July 1924). Similarly, when Falkirk's public baths were opened, the local newspaper boasted that Falkirk had a "tip-top suite of baths that will be the envy of most towns and cities, and of which Falkirk has reason to be proud" (ibid 28 September 1932).

On the other hand, while councillors publicly indulged in civic boasting, the amount of publicly funded assistance provided for leisure facilities remained limited. Although councils channelled greater amounts of rate money into facilities for sport and recreation during the inter-war years than ever before, the majority of schemes relied primarily on gifts from local philanthropists or grants from national charitable or central government sources. The major provision for sport continued to take place outside the municipal sphere in the dense network of participation in the voluntary sector, increasingly in schools and in the provision for spectating by voluntary groups and commercial operators.

Contemporary Trends

It was not until after the Second World War that central or local government showed any great enthusiasm for investing public funds in sports facilities. Legislation dating back to the mid-19th century permitted local authorities to provide parks, baths, libraries and museums but successive governments saw no need to make this legislation mandatory. All of this changed in a short space of time, mainly through the efforts of national voluntary organisations but also due to political events in Europe. The major protagonists were the NPFA, established in 1925 and the Central Council of Physical Recreation (CCPR), formed in 1935. Both were able to recruit powerful members of the aristocracy and the business world and both enjoyed royal patronage. These two bodies exerted considerable pressure on government to develop policies for sport. They pointed to the need to improve the health and fitness of the population; to ensure that town and country planning took account of the need for open spaces and playing fields; and to provide a supply of trained voluntary leaders.

These arguments might have fallen on deaf ears had the British Medical Association not appointed a Physical Education Committee to report on ways of cultivating the physical development of adults and young people. Its report, published in April 1936, painted an alarming picture of widespread unfitness and a lack of suitably qualified leaders. The government was not inclined to introduce compulsory physical training for any section of the population. It might have chosen to operate through the CCPR which had recruited eighty member organisations within twelve months. However, when the *Physical Training and Recreation Act* was passed in 1937, it created the NFC, a separate Council for Scotland, and area committees in both countries. A budget of £4m for the period 1937-40 (equivalent to £40m today) was approved, mainly to provide sports facilities. Relationships between the NFC and the CCPR were never cordial, although the latter received a grant of £1,000, which increased steadily each year thereafter. The NFC in England and Scotland were wound up at the outbreak of war and it appears that no-one mourned their passing.

The government had signalled its intention of not intervening directly in sport, preferring to operate at arms length through quasi-official bodies funded through the SED. A Scottish branch of the CCPR was formed in 1945 to be replaced in 1953 by an autonomous Scottish Council of Physical Recreation (SCPR). From the outset it received generous funding from the SED. Although central government support for sport

Figure 7 Open air pool Zetland Park, Grangemouth, about 1934. (Falkirk Museum)

increased dramatically after the war, it was insufficient to allow governing bodies to keep pace with world standards. In 1957 the CCPR responded to a pamphlet, *Britain in the World of Sport* (1956), by appointing a committee of enquiry under Sir John Wolfenden. His report appeared in 1960 and recommended that a national Sports Development Council be appointed with an annual budget of £5m (Wolfenden Committee 1960). Although rejected by the Conservative government, the Wilson government created a United Kingdom sports council in 1965 and sports councils for Ireland, Wales and Scotland in 1966. When it was decided that executive sports councils should be created by royal charter in 1972, the SCPR transferred its staff and assets to the incoming Scottish Sports Council (SSC) and wound up its affairs.

The remit of the executive sports councils was extended to include developing the knowledge and practice of sport and physical recreation in the interests of social welfare. From 1972 onwards there has been a growing tendency for sport to be regarded as one of the social services and this was confirmed as official government policy in the 1975 White Paper *Sport and Recreation.* This reaffirmed the idea of recreation as a social right of citizenship but also drew attention to the contribution of sport in reducing delinquency and hooliganism, emphasised the need to alleviate urban deprivation and proposed that sport should be seen as a means of social control in dealing with inner city problems.

The origins of these policies lay in the *Cobham Report* (House of Lords Select Committee Second Report 1973). The timing of the report was important. The sports councils were established in February 1972, three months after Cobham was set up, and legislation for the reorganisation of local government was passed only a few months after Cobham reported. The proceedings of the Select Committee therefore straddled very significant events in British sport and caused the government to consider issues such as the relationship between central and local government in the field of leisure; the shape of recreation departments in local authorities; and who should be the primary funding agents in leisure and recreation. Cobham was emphatic in stating that recreation should be part of the general fabric of the social services and that the new local authorities should be the main executive organisations for providing leisure facilities. The Select Committee recommended that every authority should set up a recreation department under its own chief officer. These and other recommendations confirmed the view that public funds must be made available for investment in leisure, recreation and sport.

In Scotland a working party was appointed to consider the respective responsibilities of the regional and district authorities which were to emerge from the reorganisation of local government (*New Scottish Local Authorities 1973*). The report recommended that district authorities should provide and manage most of the community sports facilities via leisure and recreation departments. The regional authorities should be responsible for long term strategic planning and the provision of sports facilities and services of regional significance. Thus, leisure and recreation was to be a two-tier function and this led almost inevitably to overlapping and a duplication of effort. Since education was to be a single-tier function the regions would continue to own and manage school sports facilities and youth and community centres.

In this region, the new local authorities which came into being in May 1975 adopted different approaches to leisure and recreation. Falkirk District Council established a department of recreation and amenities, and Stirling created the post of superintendent of parks, recreation and burial grounds. Clackmannan began with a baths superintendent. In all three districts, libraries, museums and galleries were managed separately and initially there was no specific commitment to the development of sport. Central Regional Council considered the report of a working party appointed prior to the election of the Council, consisting of officials from education authorities which were amalgamated into the new regional body. In retrospect, the recommendations anticipated structures which would have greatly facilitated sports development but the new regional Education Committee rejected them. They included a proposal to create a post of assistant director of education (recreation and leisure); to establish a section for recreation and leisure, initially within the Education Department; and to set up a regional advisory sports council (Association of Directors of Education in Scotland 1974).

The lack of enthusiasm on the part of local authorities for investing in recreation must be placed in the context of an economic recession, growing unemployment and rapid inflation, fuelled by the quadrupling of oil prices in 1974. A condition of the loan which Britain negotiated with the International Monetary Fund in 1976 was that public spending should be strictly controlled. It was not an opportune time to establish large new leisure services departments.

Starting in May 1973 the four national agencies for tourism, outdoor recreation and sport - the Scottish Tourist Board, the Countryside Commission for Scotland, the Forestry Commission and the SSC - initiated a series of regional planning studies aimed at assisting the regional authorities which were to be elected in 1975 to evolve strategies for these services. It was anticipated that a Strategic Issues Report could be completed before May 1975 and thereafter the authorities themselves would continue the process of gathering data for Situation Reports. A series of regional conferences were held throughout 1974 and 1975 and officials from the education and planning departments of Central Region and the planning departments of the districts began to work together, and published the Situation Report for Central Region

Table 3 Examples of deficits in facility provision. (STARPS 1979)

District	Squash Courts	Outdoor Pitches	Tennis Courts
Falkirk	21	44	38
Stirling	6	57	-
Clackmannan	7	50	11

Strategy for Urban and Countryside Recreation and Tourism (STARPS 1979). Using a supply/demand model it was shown that there were substantial deficits in sports halls, squash courts, tennis courts and playing fields; 45% of all playing fields lacked adequate changing accommodation. Although at first sight there was a surplus of supply for swimming, 14 of the 20 pools were either less than 25 m in length or were school pools, relatively inaccessible to the public for much of the time. The distribution of facilities did not follow any discernible pattern or plan. Most of the playing fields and open spaces were located in Falkirk District whereas the majority of the squash and tennis courts and bowling greens were in Stirling. It was calculated that in order to meet demand, the additional facilities listed in **Table 3** were required.

There was insufficient data to compute the necessary sports hall provision but apart from school and youth and community facilities there was only one major indoor sports centre, at Grangemouth.

A number of issues were identified from this, the first comprehensive survey of sports facilities and activities in Central Region. Firstly, although sports facilities in schools were generally adequate, public access in the evenings, at week-ends and during school holidays was either limited or non-existent. Secondly, even in traditional activities such as football, badminton and swimming there was a dearth of good quality facilities. Thirdly, in the case of sports such as basketball and volleyball prominent in school physical education, the growth of community sports clubs was constrained by the almost total lack of local sports centres, and it was noted that the types of urban recreation activities offered were not relevant to the needs of disadvantaged groups in the community. A prime need was defined as making sport and recreation more relevant to the needs of these groups as a means of reducing social stress. There was also a need to provide for the development of high standards of performance through better coaching. These issues were highlighted in the final version of the STARPS report which was approved by Central Regional Council in May 1981.

The four local authorities responded to the need for sports development in quite different ways. Falkirk District opted to embark on a programme of facility development whereas Stirling District and Central Region proceeded with a rational, systematic approach to activities. Clackmannan District made little or no progress until a department of leisure services was established in 1987. In Falkirk the ruling Scottish National Party was planning a £10m leisure complex when it lost power to the Labour Party in 1980. The new group rescinded the leisure plans and it was not until 1982 that the Director, appointed in 1979, was able to persuade local politicians to proceed with the £2.75m Mariner Centre which was opened in 1985. Between 1982 and 1992, Falkirk District Council installed twenty single pitch changing rooms at public parks and built four small community sports centres at Denny, Polmont, Madison and Carronshore. In due course the authority established management committees for 24 community halls, each of which made limited provision for sport. The Leisure Services Department managed and controlled the two major sports centres, Grangemouth Sports Centre and the Mariner Centre.

When the University received its first intake of students in 1967 there were only modest facilities for sport and recreation. These consisted of playing fields for football, hockey and rugby, a 400 m running track and four outdoor tennis courts. It purchased a large private house for a student and staff club, and added two squash courts and a covered tennis court. The latter was the first air-hall to be used for sport in Scotland, but since it was inflated by an electric fan, it was prone to collapse during power cuts. However, in 1968 the Gannochy Trust agreed to donate £150,000 for the first phase of a sports centre on the playing fields and it was opened in 1970, shortly after the University appointed a director of physical recreation. The Gannochy Pavilion provided a focal point for sports clubs but did not include any facilities for sport. The air-hall accommodated all indoor sports but since it had a concrete surface, it was far from ideal.

The University Grants Committee was reluctant to give approval for the use of its funds for swimming pools due to their steep operating costs. In Stirling's case, they were persuaded by arguments that there would be substantial income from extensive community use including local schools and families, and the possibility that national swimming teams would use the pool for training. A six-lane 25 m pool was duly opened in 1974, attached to the Gannochy Pavilion, and memberships were offered to students, staff and local families and individuals. A contract was signed with the Scottish Amateur Swimming Association (SASA), establishing Stirling as the National Swim Centre, and a separate contract was agreed with Central Regional Council for a schools' swimming scheme. Within twelve months, 450 families and over 1,000 individuals had taken out memberships and SASA had transferred its offices to the University.

Prior to the opening of the pool, the University

Figure 8   Tennis courts, Stirling University, 1978. (Whyler)

received a grant to build three squash courts as part of a government scheme to provide work for the unemployed.   These were reserved exclusively for students and staff, and the two courts attached to the student/staff club were offered to the community. This was a peak period nationally in the popularity of squash and within a year of opening the new courts over 800 memberships had been taken out by students, staff and local people. By 1976 Stirling had not only substantially improved facilities for student sport but had also created the largest programme of community use of any British university. Other schemes followed for children's gymnastics, canoeing on Airthrey Loch, and football and hockey on the floodlit outdoor pitches. The income from these community schemes was ploughed back into facility development and the employment of graduate assistants who provided instruction in a variety of sports.

Three other developments took place in the 1970s. Firstly, the University purchased a large house on the south shore of Loch Rannoch and converted it into an outdoor centre. Secondly, using a grant from the Manpower Services Commission, an area of eighteen acres of the campus was laid out as a par three 9-hole golf course. Designed by local professional John Stark of Crieff Golf Club, it opened for play in spring 1980 and in the first year of operation averaged 600 rounds per week. The third project was the long-awaited sports hall. Approval was given in 1979, it was erected in ten months at a cost of £300,000 and officially opened in November 1980. Since there was no community sports centre in Stirling District, it also attracted a large number of competitions and tournaments organised by local clubs.

The final stage in this process of expansion was the introduction of sports bursaries. Following a visit to Bath University by students and the Director of Physical Recreation to discuss its system of sports scholarships, the University Court approved a scheme for Stirling which permitted bursars to extend their academic courses by up to one year. The first sports bursary was awarded in Spring 1981 to Colin Dalgleish, a young Scottish golfer who was selected that year for the British Walker Cup team versus America (Thomson 1992 57-61).   The scheme attracted considerable publicity through the press, radio and television.

No other major projects were launched during the 1980s, but it had become clear that the tennis courts laid in 1968 were nearing the end of their useful life. The University began to explore sources of external funding and plans for an indoor tennis centre emerged. Eventually a sum of over £1.2m was raised, £500,000 from the Gannochy Trust, £350,000 from the Lawn Tennis Association, £280,000 from the SSC, and £130,000 from the University. The four outdoor courts were resurfaced and a 4-court indoor centre built on to the existing sports hall. A contract was agreed with the Scottish Lawn Tennis Association to designate Stirling as the Gannochy National Tennis Centre (**Figure 8**). Within a space of twenty years, the University had created one of the finest sports complexes in the country and developed an integrated student and community programme.   This was all the more remarkable in that most of the facilities were provided during a most difficult economic period.

In 1976 the SSC initiated a campaign to persuade local authorities to set up district sports councils. It was intended that these bodies, consisting of volunteer representatives of the various sports operating locally, would advise district councils about the needs of sport as perceived by participants. Stirling District Sports Council (SDSC) began modestly in 1976 but by the time that the STARPS report was being prepared it had become a significant policy making organisation. It was serviced initially by a member of the Parks and Recreation Department but in 1980 the new Labour group agreed that SDSC should receive a substantial grant, enabling it to appoint its own sports officer in January 1981. This was the first such appointment in Scotland.   The SDSC has remained an autonomous body enjoying the largest grant of any district sports council in Scotland. From the date of its formation the chairmanship of the policy and development sub-committee has been held by a member of staff from the University. This committee has consistently formulated radical new policies for sports development, many of which have subsequently been adopted by the SSC and other local authorities.

In 1976 the Director of Physical Recreation at the University and the Regional Training Officer for Youth and Community Services produced a plan for a regional sports development scheme, and secured funding of £10,000 from the Manpower Services Commission to appoint a full-time sports development officer. There were three main objectives in this pilot scheme, namely -

    a) to overcome the 'Wolfenden gap' between school and community

    b) to improve and extend community use of school and university facilities

    c) to create a ladder of progression from introductory to excellence level in sport.

Within three years the number of new entrants to sport was sufficient to persuade Central Regional Council to create a 3-year post for a sports development officer. In addition three graduate assistants were appointed who combined their duties as sports-specific co-ordinators with studying for a higher degree. The new Sports Development Scheme (SDS) was accommodated in the University and a complex structure of committees was set up which brought together representatives of the district sports councils from Clackmannan, Falkirk and Stirling, the University and the Central Regional Physical Education Association (Thomson 1983 5-7). In the first year of the new organisation 400 individuals were awarded coaching certificates; 12 secondary schools, 30 primary schools and three youth centres were in use at week-ends and in the evenings for SDS activities; 7000 youngsters and adults were participating in instructional classes, district and regional squads; and a sound working relationship had been established between the four local authorities and the governing bodies of sport. At the end of the 3-year pilot period the SDS was given permanent status and the staff moved from University to Regional offices. The committee structure was dismantled and replaced by a Central Co-ordinating Committee for Sport, a title chosen in preference to a regional advisory sports council.

There were two significant features of the rapid development of SDSC and the SDS. Firstly, this was the only example in Scotland of the adoption by local authorities of a rational, comprehensive and co-ordinated approach to sports development. The original aims of the SDS were achieved and it had been shown that it was possible to implement a strategic approach. Considerable progress had been made in opening up education authority facilities to organised community groups. Groups had been identified which were under-represented in participation statistics and provision had been made for them. A Central Region Sports Association for Disabled People had been established and the SSC had organised an international conference on Sport for Disabled People at the University in 1981. A group of researchers from Edinburgh University had drawn attention to the successful SDSC's Women in Sport scheme (Alexander, Leach and Steward 1984). The authors suggested that the explanation of the success of the scheme, which catered for 400 women in six centres was that the organisers were sensitive to the needs of the participants and listened to what they had to say about what they needed and wanted.

The second feature of this period of progress was the influence of significant individuals. The Director of Physical Recreation at the University wrote most of the policy papers and supervised research projects funded by Central Regional Council and Stirling District Council. The first project consisted of a survey of nineteen sports covering 10,000 participants which led to a completely new system of grant aid to clubs, and demonstrated the need for a Women in Sport Scheme (Reid 1981). The other substantial project extended over a four year period and involved in-depth interviews with 350 young people living in two contiguous areas of Stirling District. (McCusker 1988). The results of this study were influential in SSC's policies for school-aged sport. At the same time, graduate assistants were undertaking research projects dealing with various aspects of sport in Stirling District. No other Scottish university was as involved with local authorities in the development of sport.

Two other individuals played a significant role in this radical approach. Ian Collie, Director of Education for Central Regional Council, gave his whole-hearted support to the SDS and liaised with the Education Committee. Michael Connarty, Labour Group leader of Stirling District Council, and Chairman of the SDSC, ensured that sufficient funds were available. Between 1980 and 1982 the annual grant for the SDSC rose from £2,000 to £35,000 which was then the highest grant of any of the Scottish local sports councils. It was mainly through Connarty's advocacy that the District Council agreed to create a chief officer post of director of leisure services in 1982.

Clearly the decades since 1945 have witnessed a substantial restructuring of sports provision in central Scotland: To some extent, however, the philosophy of the originators of the STARPS Report has been frustrated by then unforeseen economic factors. The creation of regional planning strategies based on a uniform supply - demand model was a major advance, but the economic climate was not favourable for capital investment or for installing the infrastructure for development. Falkirk District Council was the only one of the four local authorities which made real progress in solving the problems of deficit in sports facilities revealed in the STARPS Report, due in large part to the determined efforts of David Mould, Director of Recreation and Amenities. None of the other authorities tackled these problems because sport and leisure were not high on their lists of priorities. Nevertheless, in return for a fairly modest investment in the SDS and SDSC, progress was made in articulating a framework of sports policies which benefited clubs and individuals. As the 1970s drew to a close the government decided that there was evidence of duplication of effort by districts and regions in regard to leisure (Stodart Report 1981). Legislation was passed, the *Local Government and Planning (Scotland) Act* 1982 removed leisure and recreation from the list of functions for the regions, and made district councils solely responsible. This killed off the STARPS concept of regional planning for sport and leisure and recreation.

All four local authorities remained under the control of Labour in the period 1982-92. Politically it was a turbulent time as the government attempted to reduce public expenditure and introduced legislation to curb the powers of local government. The local authorities were committed to improving and extending services while central government was equally determined that these services should be put out to tender. The management of local authority sport and leisure facilities was exposed to compulsory competitive tendering under the terms of the *Local Government Act 1988.*

The main feature of the 1980s with regard to leisure was the gradual and widespread development of integrated leisure services departments encompassing sport and recreation (sports centres, swimming pools, parks and open spaces), libraries, theatres, museums and galleries, and in some cases, tourism. Falkirk District Council was the only local authority in Central Region to produce a comprehensive leisure plan. Generally, local authority leisure services developed unevenly partly due to the absence of any coherent government strategy but also because district councils tended to operate in isolation. In spite of continued economic problems, however, district councils in Central Region have invested heavily in leisure services (**Table 4**). Since the population of the three Districts are quite different, per capita levels of expenditure are perhaps a better indicator of the priority given to leisure and recreation (**Table 5**).

It is evident from the preceding review of expenditures that all three district councils have invested quite heavily in facilities. Clackmannan converted Alloa Baths into a national standard gymnastics centre, took over control of the privately-owned sports centre in Alloa, which had become insolvent, to operate it as a company, and adopted a policy of providing small community sports facilities in each of the centres of population. In also opened a sub-national equestrian centre in May 1992. Falkirk has followed a similar route by opening the Mariner Centre and building small neighbourhood community centres, but it has also developed a system of local management committees. Stirling District Council built a swimming pool in Stirling in 1972, and purchased the Stirling Albion football ground, installing a syntheteic pitch. This was sold in 1992 for housing and office development and a new grass pitch stadium with adjacent all-weather area constructed at Springkerse, aptly named Forthbank. Commercial operators have centres for indoor bowling, snooker and ten-pin bowling. Unfortunately the District never invested in a games hall. The University's sports centre compensates to some extent, but community use has to be balanced with demand from students and staff.

Essentially the three district councils have concentrated their resources on increasing participation and widening access to all sections of the community. Responsibility for organised club sport rests with voluntary organisations who look to the three district sports councils for advice and financial aid. The financial resources of district sports councils are very limited compared to the massive leisure and recreation budgets of district councils. Consequently, apart from a few well-organised clubs there is little evidence of a raising of standards of performance. Possibly local councillors are wary of supporting elitism. However, even SDSC, which enjoys a larger grant than most other such bodies in Scotland can provide only limited assistance to clubs and individuals who aspire to represent their country. Its policy is to spread available funds over a large number of clubs and individuals (**Table 6**). Inevitably this means that each grant is relatively small.

There is an inherent weakness in the structure of sport in the region which is characteristic of sport across the country. This is concerned with the size and organisational strength of the club system. Quite simply, there are too many small clubs which are vulnerable to relatively minor changes such as the departure of a key player or the loss of an industrious official. The survey conducted by SDSC (Reid 1981) showed that 75% of clubs had an average membership of only twenty. Football is a classic case of a sport which has developed around small clubs. There are 150,000 sports clubs in Britain, of which 36,000 are

Table 4   District council expenditures (£1000s) on leisure and recreation, excluding libraries and museums, 1982-92 (1991-2 estimated) (CIPFA Scottish Branch) 1982-92

Year	Clackmannan	Falkirk	Stirling
1982-3	585	3,831	1,825
1983-4	628	3,260	1,816
1984-5	677	3,446	1,702
1985-6	754	3,218	1,563
1986-7	859	3,229	2,130
1987-8	1,371	3,331	2,569
1988-9	1,355	3,504	2,525
1989-90	2,478	5,260	3,748
1990-91	2,882	5,819	4,883
1991-92	2,418	4,418	3,841

Table 5 Per capita expenditures (£s) on leisure and recreation, excluding libraries and museums, 1982-92 (1991-2 estimated) (CIPFA).

Year	Clackmannan £	Falkirk £	Stirling £	Scotland £
1982-3	12.16	26.54	22.65	24.66
1983-4	13.12	22.65	22.46	21.07
1984-5	14.16	23.96	20.97	21.73
1985-6	15.79	22.42	19.26	22.72
1986-7	18.05	22.57	26.24	24.48
1987-8	28.92	23.26	31.55	27.44
1988-9	28.73	24.47	31.12	29.19
1989-90	52.53	36.77	46.18	44.06
1990-91	60.91	40.62	60.02	53.80
1991-92	50.94	30.84	47.21	45.44

football clubs. The vast majority consist of one team and one or two officials. Players progress by moving up from one division to another. There is rarely a conscious process of recruiting and initiating new players and it is not easy for players arriving in an area to enter these tightly knit groups.

Medium size clubs such as bowling, cricket, rugby, squash and tennis can cater both for internal and external competition and coaching. They serve as models for sports development and enjoy the enormous advantage that they normally occupy their own facilities. Swimming is an unusual example of a sport which has managed successfully to develop the same kind of structure, using local authority pools. Medium size clubs are less vulnerable than small clubs to changes in personnel and in some cases are able to employ part-time or full-time coaches. They can provide for different age and ability groups and also for both sexes.

Large clubs are run on the lines of small businesses, often with quite substantial turnovers. Stirling Golf Club with 1,000 members has an annual budget of £275,000. This scale of club is ideally placed to build and manage sports and social facilities, and employ various categories of staff. Apart from golf clubs, only Bridge of Allan Tennis Club and Stirling County Rugby Club come into this category.

There has been no real change in club structures over the past twenty-five years. The whole culture of football militates against change, and indoor sports are vying with each other for limited access to sports halls. Growth has occurred in squash because it has been relatively cheap to build squash courts and also because these are single-purpose facilities. Sports such as basketball, badminton, table tennis and volleyball will not experience the same kind of growth until similar single-purpose halls are provided. Meantime, the same small-club structure will be reproduced and large numbers of youngsters who have been introduced to these activities at school will continue to experience problems in trying to join community clubs. The SSC identified these problems in two major reports published within months of each other in 1988: *Laying the Foundations. Report on School-Aged Sport in Scotland* November 1988 and *Sport 2000 : A Strategic Approach to the Development of Sport in Scotland* March 1989. The first of these reports was produced in response to evidence that school sport had been decimated by the prolonged dispute between the teaching profession and the government in 1985-86 over questions of pay and conditions of service. As in other parts of the country, teachers in Central Region withdrew completely from voluntary extra-curricular activities, including school sport. The number of registered schoolboy footballers fell from 45,000 to 5,000 in the space of one year in Scotland and there were similar reductions in other sports. Inter-school sport (**Figure 9**) has still not recovered and there are as yet few signs that it is likely to do so.

In *Sport 2000* the SSC called for the investment of £360 million in sports facilities up to the year 2000. This included building 44 swimming pools, 210 sports

Table 6 Grants awarded by Stirling District Sports Council, 1987-91. (SDSC)

Year	Number of Grants	Number of Clubs	Number of Individuals	Number of Sports	Total
1987-8	176	60	58	37	£18,000
1988-9	206	46	101	32	£20,000
1989-90	200	58	90	39	£20,000
1990-91	91	50	41	33	£16,000

Figure 9 Five-a-side tournament, Stirling University, 1987. (Whyler)

centres, 150 squash courts, five indoor tennis centres and 1,000 tennis courts. If these targets are met the whole structure of sport in the community will be transformed. It will still be necessary to find ways of replacing the 4m man-hours which teachers were contributing to school-aged sport but the creation of new facilities might encourage local authorities to provide the necessary manpower. Unfortunately *Sport 2000* was published as the country was moving into a recession and government involved in community charge-capping. There is no evidence that the ambitious building programme envisaged in *Sport 2000* will be realised. The community charge has proved difficult to collect and in February 1992 arrears in Scottish local authorities amounted to £0.5billion. Local authorities are feverishly reviewing all services for savings and it is highly unlikely that they will embark on a major capital expenditure programme.

Conclusion

Sport has been a significant element of the way of life in central Scotland since early Victorian times. In the first half of the 19th century it was localised, largely unregulated and essentially ephemeral. As the values of industrial capitalism - achievement, individualism and workforce discipline - permeated sport, it was civilised, codified and subject to the control of governing bodies of sport. The large majority of sporting activities took place outdoors on ground leased from local landowners. Since leases could be terminated at short notice this led to instability.

The evidence in this chapter indicates that football emerged at the turn of the century as by far the most popular sport, but there was a considerable turnover in teams. There was greater continuity in other sporting forms but they tended to operate on a much smaller scale. No sport catered exclusively for women, and this was a reflection of the current definition of the role of women. On other other hand there were no barriers to women spectating at boat-racing, horse racing and Highland games.

Schools in the area were latecomers to organised competitive sport. State schools suffered from a lack of playing fields and indoor facilities but they made some progress during the 1930s by borrowing fields owned by local clubs. The real expansion of inter-school sport occurred in the 1960s when extensive sports facilities were provided in new secondary schools erected to deal with the post-war upsurge in birth-rates.

Comparison of the range of sports involving large numbers of residents of the region during the 1930s and the 1960s supports the notion that there has been an enormous change in patterns of participation. Of all the factors which account for this, the most important were increasing prosperity and widening car ownership. The increase in active participation has been matched by a decline in spectating particularly at professional football matches.

For more than a century local authorities in the region resisted the idea of investing rate-payers money in public facilities for sport. However, between 1960 and 1975 there was a prolonged debate about whether sport could be regarded as a social right of citizenship. The consensus view which emerged was that sport was an essential part of the social services. The new local authorities created in 1975 were charged with responsibility for assessment of need, formulation of policy, and the provision and management of facilities. Within a few years the district councils for Clackmannan, Falkirk and Stirling were spending millions of pounds on leisure and recreation. The opening of the sports facilities at the new University of Stirling to the public, although welcome, was perhaps less significant than the contribution of university staff to the assessment of need and the formulation of sports policies. Nevertheless, the University has demonstrated that it is possible to operate a policy of joint use of facilities for students and community.

In retrospect it seems that the planning and provision of sports facilities has been fragmented. If the new secondary schools built between 1955 and 1970 had been designed for joint use, the task of the new local authorities would have been made easier. Instead, the district councils have had to build separate facilities and to provide grants to sports clubs to extend their facilities. The concept of community development which is being adopted by all four local authorities in Central Region should have been the guiding ideology. The gaps in provision identified in the STARPS Report in 1981 have not yet been filled.

In short, major advances have occurred over the past one hundred and fifty years. Sport has been democratised in that it is now recognised as a social right of citizenship. Although there are still too many small clubs which are vulnerable to change, intervention by local authorities has meant that groups who were previously under-represented in participation are being encouraged to take part in sport. The needs of these groups are being met within a framework of community development in which it is recognised that sport has an important part to play.

REFERENCES AND FURTHER READING

ALEXANDER, D.J., LEACH, J.J., and STEWARD, T.G. 1984. A Study of Policy, Organisation and Provision in Community Education and Leisure and Recreation in Three Scottish Regions. University of Nottingham.

ASSOCIATION OF DIRECTORS OF EDUCATION IN SCOTLAND. 1974. Recreation and Leisure in the Central Region. Central Regional Council, Stirling.

CHARTERED INSTITUTE OF PUBLIC FINANCE ACCOUNTANTS, SCOTTISH BRANCH. 1982-1992. Rating Reviews : Actual Income and Expenditure. CIPFA.

CRAMPSEY, B. 1990. The Scottish Football League : The First Hundred Years. Scottish Football League, Glasgow.

DEPARTMENT OF THE ENVIRONMENT. 1975. Sport and Recreation. Cmnd 6200. HMSO, London.

FALKIRK HERALD. 1887, 1924, '32, '55

HOUSE OF LORDS SELECT COMMITTEE. 1973. Sport and Leisure Second Report. HMSO, London.

LAMMINGTON, D. 1987. A Scottish Soccer Internationalists' Who's Who, 1872-1986. Hutton Press, Beverley.

LOCAL GOVERNMENT AND PLANNING (SCOTLAND) ACT 1982. Cmnd 42.

LOVE, J. 1928. Local Antiquarian Notes and Queries, Volume 4. Falkirk.

MCCUSKER, J. 1988. Youth and sport: a neighbourhood study. Unpublished MSc thesis, University of Stirling.

MCGRAIL, S., HALL, J., DOUGLAS, W., and DETTLAFF, J. 1984. The Story of the Airth Highland Games, 1871-1984. Airth Games Committee.

NEW SCOTTISH LOCAL AUTHORITIES: ORGANISATION AND MANAGEMENT STRUCTURES. Report of a Working Group Appointed by the Scottish Local Authority Associations. 1973. HMSO, Edinburgh.

PHYSICAL EDUCATION ASSOCIATION OF GREAT BRITAIN AND NORTHERN IRELAND. 1956. Britain in the World of Sport. London.

PUBLIC SCHOOL MAGAZINE. 1902. 9, 220-30

RENNIE, R. C. 1966. The County of Stirling. Third Statistical Account of Scotland. Collins, Glasgow.

REID, D. 1981. A Study of Sports Clubs in Stirling. Stirling District Sports Council.

REVISED STRATEGY FOR URBAN RECREATION, COUNTRYSIDE RECREATION AND TOURISM. 1981. Strategy for Central Region. Central Regional Council, Stirling.

SCOTTISH SPORTS COUNCIL. 1988. Laying the Foundations. Report on School-Aged Sport in Scotland. Scottish Sports Council, Edinburgh.

SCOTTISH SPORTS COUNCIL. 1989. Sport 2000 : A Strategic Approach to the Development of Sport in Scotland. Scottish Sports Council Edinburgh.

STARPS. Strategy for Urban Recreation, Countryside Recreation and Tourism. 1979. Summary Situation Report. Central Regional Council, Stirling. (STARPS = Scottish Tourism and Recreation Planning Studies).

STIRLING DISTRICT SPORTS COUNCIL. 1988-92. Annual Reports.

STIRLING HIGH SCHOOL MAGAZINE. June 1928

STIRLING OBSERVER. 1854, 1921-39

STIRLING TOWN COUNCIL. Minutes 4 March 1887.

STODARD REPORT. 1981. Committee of Inquiry into Local Government in Scotland. HMSO, Edinburgh.

THOMSON, I. 1983. A university's involvement with local sports development. British Universities Physical Education Association Occasional Paper.

THOMSON, I. 1992. Giftedness, Excellence and Sport. Research Report No.23. Scottish Sports Council, Edinburgh.

TRANTER, N. 1987. Popular sports and the industrial revolution in Scotland : The evidence of the statistical accounts. *International Journal of the History of Sport* 4, 21-38

TRANTER, N. 1989. Sport and the economy in nineteenth and early twentieth century Scotland : A review of recent literature. *Scottish Historical Review* LXVIII, 53-69

TRANTER, N. 1990a and b. The chronology of organised sport in nineteenth-century Scotland : A Regional Study 1-Patterns, 2-Causes. *International Journal of the History of Sport* 7, 188-203 and 365-387

TRANTER, N. 1990c. Organised sport and the working classes in central Scotland, 1820-1900 : the neglected sport of quoiting. In Holt, R. Editor. Sport and the Working Class in Modern Britain. Manchester University Press, Manchester.

TRANTER, N. 1990d. Rates of participation in club sport in the central lowlands of Scotland, 1820-1900. *Canadian Journal of History of Sport* XX1, 1-19

TRANTER, N. 1992. Quoiting in central Scotland: demise of a traditional sport. *Forth Naturalist and Historian* 15, 99-116

VAMPLEW, W. 1981. Ownership and control in gate-money sport : Scottish football before 1915. *Canadian Journal of History of Sport* XII, 56-83

WALVIN, J. 1975. The People's Game : A Social History of British Football. Allen Lane, London.

WOLFENDEN COMMITTEE. 1960. Sport and the Community. Central Council for Physical Recreation, London.

Index to Central Scotland

Note - references to figures, maps, photos are in italics.

Abbey Craig, 12, 51
Abbotsgrange Formation, 12
Abercrombie, of Tullibody, 178
Aberfoyle, 167
  bats, 78
  conglomerate, 3
  frosts, 22
  Highland Line, 1
  mammals, 79
  marine advance, 12
  population, 166, 168
  quarries, 4, 37
  Quaternary, 14
  railway, 130
  River Forth, 105
  sports, 194
  vegetation, 50
  wildcat, 81
  woodland, 110
Aberfoyle Anticline, 4
Abies alba, 45
Acer pseudoplatanus, 97
Achiearis parthenias, 88
Achillea ptarmica, 48, 50
Acid deposition, 40-1, 105
Adam, of Blairadam, 178
Adders, 109
Afforestation, 107-9, 116
Age distribution, 170
Aggregate, 16
Aglais urticae, 86
Agriculture, land capability, 37-9
Agrostis spp., 47, 51
Airdrie Burghs, 177
Airflow, 19, 23-5
Airth, 9, 94, 129, 145, 166-8, 180, 199-200
Airthrey, 46, 48
Airthrey Castle, 83
Airthrey Loch, 60, 64, 101, 206
Ajuga reptans, 46
Alder, 44-6, 49, 67, 97, 110, 116
Alexandria, 14
Algae, 96, 101
Alisma plantago-aquatica, 97
Allan Water, 34, 39, 49, 73, 79, 81, 84, 94, 97, 105-6, 110
Allium ursinum, 44
Alloa, 9-10, 57, 83, 88
  agriculture, 129-30

aquatic life, 94, 104
  birds, 58
  environment, 106, 115
  fogs, 26
  industry, 142, 15
  politics, 178
  population, 163, 166, 168-9, 171-2
  soils, 35
  sports, 194, 197-8
Alloa Advertiser, 179, 182
Alloa Coal Company, 143
Alloa Inches, 59
Alloa Journal, 179
Alluvial soils, 33-4, 39
Almond, 116
Alnus glutinosa, 44, 97
Alpine-sedge, Black, 53
Althaea hirsuta, 47
Alum works, 165
Aluminium, 148
Alva, 51, 60, 65, 71, 105
  agriculture, 130
  industry, 145, 149-51, 153
  politics, 181
  population, 163, 166, 168-9, 172
  sports, 194, 196, 198-9
Ameletus inopinatus, 102
American Wigeon, 60
Amoeba, 100
Amphibians, 100-1, 107
Amphibolite, 4
An Caisteal, 110
Anderson, Sir James, 178
Andesite, 4
Andreaea rupestris, 52
Andromeda polifolia, 50, 109
Angling, 194
Anguilla anguilla, 104
Anhydrite, 8
Animals, aquatic, 99-105
Anser spp., 112
Anthocharis cardamine, 87
Anthoxanthum odoratum, 47
Anthriscus sylvestris, 47
Anthyllis vulneraria, 51
Aphantopus hyperantus, 88
Apium inundatum, 49
Apodemus sylvaticus, 79
Appin Group, 3
Arabis spp., 52-3
Arable land, 33-5, 39, 125, 127-8, 136, 138
Arbuthnott Group, 6
Arctic Breeding grounds, 59
Arctic Char, 112
Ardoch, 166
Ardtalnaig, 20-21, 23
Argyll Group, 3, 6
Argynnis aglaia, 88
Aricia artaxerxes, 88, 113
Armeria maritima, 51
Arnprior, 14
Arrochar, 4
Arrochymore, 1, 20-21
Arrowgrass, 51
Arvicola terrestris, 79
Asellus, 105
Ash, 44-6, 96, 110
Aspen, 44, 67
Asplenium adiantum-nigrum, 51
Asplenium trichomanes-ramosum, 51

Aster tripolium, 51
Atriplex spp., 51
Auchterarder, 4
Auchtertyre, 3
Auk, Little, 58
Aurochs, 83
Avena strigosa, 44
Avens, Mountain, 53
Avon, River, 15, 79, 94, 105-6
Awlwort, 48, 112
Azolla filiculoides, 48
Badger, *76*, 81
Baillieston Till Formation, 10
Balaenoptera musculus, 83
Baldellia ranunculoides, 48
Baldernock, 163, 165
Balfron, 35, 79, 127, 164-8, 194, 199
Balglass, 51
Ballagan Formation, 8
Ballagan Glen, 116
Ballikinrain, 130
Balloch Formation, 14
Balmaha, 1, 6, 46, 94, 168
Balquhidder, 20, 22, 52, 63, 72, 80, 163, 168
Balquhidderock Wood, *115*, 116
Balrownie association, 36, 39
Balvag, River, 93
Banknock, 182
Bannockburn, 12, 105, 116, 145, 182, 185, 194, 199
Barbush quarry, 72
Barley, 44, 47, 128-31, 133, 136, 138-9
Barleyside, 145
Bartsia alpina, 53, 108
Barwood, mine disaster, 142
Barytes, 3, 16
Bats, 77-8, 107
Batterflats, 20-1, 23
Baxter, William, 185
Beaked-sedge, 50, 109
Bean Goose, *63*, 64, 108
Beans, 128, 130-1
Bedstraws, 47, 50-2
Bee Hawk Moth, 88
Beech, 67, 97, 111
Beech Fern, 45
Beinn Dubhchraig, 77, 108
Beinn Heasgarnich, 3
Bell Heather, 48
Bell, Patrick, 128
Ben Chabhair, 110
Ben Challum, 3
Ben Cleuch, 52, 70-1
Ben Dubhchraig, *69*
Ben Each, 48
Ben Heasgarnich, 108
Ben Lawers, 108
Ben Ledi, 52, 72, 88
Ben Lomond, 1, 52, 72, 82, 86, 88, 108-9
Ben Lui, 3, 52-3, 108
Ben More, 52, 72, 88, 108
Ben Venue, 27, 86
Ben Vorlich, 78, 88
Bent grasses, 47-8, 51-2
Betula spp., 44-5, 89, 97
Bidens spp., 53
Bilberry, 47-8, 52
Binding, 130
Bings, 116

Birch, 44-6, 50, 67, 89, 97, 110
Bird Cherry, 45, 116
Bird counts, 61, 68, 74
Bird's Nest Orchid, 45, *46*
Bird's-foot Trefoil, 47, 86
Birds
  migrating, 113
  nestboxes, 76
  status, 74
Birkhill Fireclay Mine, 15
Birth rates, 162
Bistorts, 48, 52
Black Devon, River, 105
Black Hill, 48
Black Rat, 83
Black Watch, 126
Blackband Ironstone, 146-7
Blackbirds, 66, 73, 115
Blackcaps, 57, 67, 73
Blackcock, *70*
Blackness, 57-8, 83
Bladder-fern, Mountain, 53
Blaeberry, 88
Blairdrummond, 35, 46, 62, 79, 126-7, 194
Blairlodge, 196-7
Blairlogie, 51, 71
Blane Water Formation, 14
Blantyre, mine disaster, 143
Blast-furnaces, *147*
Bleaching, 165, 167
Boar, 83
Boat-racing, 197
Bog Asphodel, 50
Bog Myrtle, 50, 88
Bog Orchid, 53
Bog Rosemary, 50, 109
Bog Rush, 51, 113
Boloria spp., 86, 88
Bo'mains Meadow, 113
Bo'ness, 15, 39, 58, 94, 113, 194
Bonny Water, 105
Bonnybridge, 147, 171, 180, 194
Borestone, 194
Bothkennar, 14, 163, 166, 168
Botrychium lunaria, 53
Boundary changes, 186-7
Bowling, 195, 199
Boxing, *199*
Bracken, 47
Braco, 46, 81, 84
Braes of Balquhidder, 52
Braes of Doune, 62, 72
Bramble, Arctic, 52
Brambling, 66
Brassica rapa, 47
Breadalbane, 1, 3, 108-9
Breccia, 4
Brick-making, 15-16
Bridge of Allan, 8, 45, 48, 62, 73, 79, 88
  climate, 20, 28
  environment, 110, 115-16
  population, 166, 168, 172
  sports, 194, 198-9
Brig o' Turk, 79, 88
Bryophite, 97
British Trust for Ornithology, 57
Briza media, 113
Broch, Fairy Knowe, 44
Brooklime, 49
Broom, 47, 86

Broomhouse Formation, 12
Brothie Burn, 105
Brown earths, 33
Brown forest soils, 34-7
Brucefield, 144-5
Bryum pseudotriquetrum, 50
Bubonic plague, 163
Buchanan, 15, 130, 132, 163, 165, 167-8
Buchlyvie, 44
Bufo bufo, 100
Bugle, 46
Bullfinch, 67
Bulrush, 43
Buntings, 59-60
Bur-marigold, 53
Bur-reed, 48, 97
Burn of Sorrow, 51, 71
Burnet Moth, 89
Burnet Saxifrage, 47, 113
Butterbur, 47
Buttercups, 46-7, 50
Butterfly Orchids, 49, 113
Buttergask Formation, 8
Buzzard, 66, 69, 71-3

Cadder, 10, 142
Cadell, William, 146
Cailness Burn, 79, 81
Caledonian Orogeny, 4
Caledonian pinewood, 110, *111*
Callander, 93
  birds, 62, 72
  bog, 50
  geology, 1, 3, 6, 14
  mammals, 79-81
  moths, 88-9
  population, 166, 168
  railway, 130
  salt-works, 44
  soils, 34
  sports, 194, 197
  tourism, 166-167
  vegetation, 49
  water, 105
Callander association, 36
Callander Craig, 48
Callendar Estate, 127, 132
Calliergon cuspidatum, 50
Callitriche spp., 49, 53, 97
Callophrys rubi, 88
Calluna vulgaris, 47, 78, 109
Caltha palustris, 48, 99
Camberwell Beauty, 87
Cambus, 58-60, 65, 94, 130
Cambusbarron, 12, 151
Cambuskenneth, 58, 94, 103
Campbell-Bannerman, Henry, 179
Campion, Moss, 52
Campsie, 164-8
Campsie Fault, 1
Campsie Fells, 1, 6, 44, 50-1, 60, 69-70,
  78, 82, 108, 116
Canadian Pondweed, 99
Canals, 94, 99, 115, 127, 146, 167
Canary-grass, 49
Capercaillie, 57, 67, 73
Capra hircus, 83
Capreolus capreolus, 82
Caraway, Whorled, 48

Carbeth Loch, 98
Carcinus maenas, 104
Cardamine pratensis, 86-7
Carex spp., 46-53, 113
Carim Lodge, 22-3
Carriden, 57
Carron Company, 143, 146
Carron Dam, 64, 115
Carron Ironworks, 115, 148-9, *159*, 167
Carron Valley, 45, 48, 67, 79, 110
Carron Valley Reservoir, 64, 70, 91-2, 98,
  105
Carron Water, 10, 12, 81, 94, 105-6
Carron Works, *148*
Carronshore, 181, 196, 199, 205
Carse of Stirling, 15, 34-5, 39, 42, 62-4, 67,
  109-10, 130
Carsebreck, 81
Carum verticillatum, 48
Cast iron, 146
Castle Campbell, 71
Castlehill reservoir, 60
Catchfly, Sticky, 51, 108
Cattle, 126-8, 131, 134-6, 138
Causewayhead, 166
Cementstone, 8
Central Coalfield, 143
Cephaloziella stellulifera, 51
Cerastium alpinum, 52
Cereals, Iron Age, 44
Cervus spp., 82
Chaffinch, 66
Chalcopyrite, 3
Chamaenerion angustifolium, 115
Charcoal, 44
Chemical effluents, 106
Chiffchaff, 67
Child labour, 142
Chlorite, 3-4
Cholera, 162
Chon, River, 105
Chrysosplenium alternifolium, 45
Cicuta virosa, 48, 101
Cinclidotus fontinaloides, 49
Cinnabar Moth, 89
Cinquefoil, Spring, 51
Cirsium palustre, 46
Clackmannan, 163, 168-9
  geology, 9-10
Clairinsh Island, 77
Claret Formation, 14, 16
Clayband ironstone, 9
Claytonia sibirica, 49
Cleish Hills, 105
Clethrionomys glareolus, 79
Climate, 19, 43-4
Cloud cover, 21
Cloudberry, 50, 52
Clouded Yellow, 87
Clouds, 25, *31*
Clover, White, 47
Club-rush, 49
Clubmoss, 51
Clupea spp., 104
Coal mining, 16, 141-6, 168
Coals, 8-9
Coastal erosion, 16
Coastal Zone Planning, 114
Coastline changes, 12, *13*, *15*
Cochlearia officinalis, 51

Coeloglossum viride, 51, 113
Coenonympha spp., 86, 88
Coille Coire Chuilc, 46, 111
Coke, 147
Colias crocea, 87
Collared Dove, 73
Colliery waste, 15-16
Combine harvesters, 135
Common Blue Butterfly, 86
Conglomerate, Devonian, 3, 6
Conic Hill, 1, 8, 46, 51
Cononish, 6, 14, *111*
Conservation
   designations, 119
   organisations, 118
Conservatives, 177-9, 182-4, 186-7
Constituencies, 177-8
Continental airstreams, 28
Coot, 57, 60, 62, 64-5
Coppicing, 45, 67
Corby/Boyndie/Dinnet association, 36-7, 39
Cord-grass, 51
Coregonus lavaretus, 102
Cormorant, 57, 60, 62-3, 113
Corn Buntings, *66*, 73
Corncrake, 66, 73
Cornstones, 8
Corophium volutator, 104
Corrie Burn, 102
Corriecharmaig, 4
Corylus avellana, 44, 97
Cotton, 164, 167-8
Cottongrass, 50-3, 88, 109, 113
Cow Parsley, 47
Cowbane, 48, 101
Cowberry, 52
Cowie, 144, 180-2, 199
Crabs, 104
Craig Leith, 71
Craigforth, 104
Craigmore Wood, 110
Craigrie, 145
Cranberry, 50, 109
Crane's-bill, Wood, 52, 113
Crangon crangon, 104
Crangonyx pseudogracilis, 101
Crataegus monogyna, 97
Creag Mhor, 53
Creeping Jenny, 116
Creinch Island, 3
Crenobia alpina, 102
Crepis paludosa, 46
Crianlarich, 14, 130
Cricket, 194-5, 201
Crockart, Fred, 181
Cromlix, 62, 64-5, 98
Cross-leaved Heath, 50
Crossbills, 67, 73
Crowberry, 48, 52
Crows, 57, 66, 69, 71-3
Cuckoos, 72
Cuilvona Wood, 110
Culross, 94
Cultivated land, 46-7
Cultivation, Iron Age, 44
Cumbernauld, 105
Curlew, 58, 66, 70-2, 107, 113
Curling, *193*, 194-6
Cycling, 194

Cynthia cardui, 87
Cystopteris montana, 53
Cytisus scoparius, 47

Dabchick, 57, *64*
Dactylorhiza spp., 48-9, 113
Dalgrain Public Park, 201
Dalmeny, Lord, 178
Dalradian Supergroup, 3-4, 6
Dalveich Meadows, 47
Dama dama, 82
Dams Burn, 105
Damselflies, 112
Daphne hyalina, 101
Darleith association, 34-5
Darnrigg Moss, 44, 110
Darvel association, 35, 39
Daubenton's Bat, 78
Deanston, 105, 165, 167-8, 194
Death rates 162-4
Debris flow, 16
Deer, 82, 111
Deergrass, 50
Deforestation, 44, 47
Denny, 64, 81, 94, 105, 110, 127, 166, 168-9, 172, 182, 194, 198, 205
Depressions, 19, 23, 26, 29
Deschampsia spp., 46-7
Devilla Forest, 82
Devon, River, 10, 15, 39, 65, *71*, 73, 79, 81, 95, 105
Devon Ironworks, 142, 146
Devon mine, 145
Diaptomus gracilis, 101
Dicranella palustris, 52
Dimlington Stade, 10
Diorite, 4
Diphtheria, 197
Dippers, 71, 101
Distilling, 127, 142, 168
Ditching, 128
Ditrichum plumbicola, 52
Divers, 57, 64, 73, 108
Dochart, River, 91, 94, 102
Docks, 43, 48, 97
Dolerite, 4, 9
Dollar, 10, 65, 71, 88, 105, 130, 142, 145, 166-8, 172, 194
Dollar Glen, 110
Dollar Park, 201
Dominant climate, 19
Donaldsons, 151-2
Donbros, 151, 153
Doon Hill, 110
Dotterel, *70*, 71
Dounans Limestone, 3
Doune, 12, 36, 73, 79, 93, 194, 199
Doune Farm Complex, 4
Doune Lodge, 46
Doune Ponds, 48
Downie's Loup Sandstones, 8
Draba spp., 52-3, 108
Dracocephalum parviflorum, 47
Dragonflies, 112
Dragonhead, 47
Drainage, mines, 141
Drilling, 197
Drosera rotundifolia, *49*, 50, 109

Drumbeg Formation, 14
Drumbreck, 145
Drumlins, 12
Drummond Castle, 20-21
Drumore Wood, 110
Dryfields, 127
Drymen, 14, 43, 81, 116, 162, 166-8
Dryopteris spp., 97
Dubh Lochan, 44
Duchray, River, 79, 105
Duckweeds, 99, 101
Duke's Pass, 4
Dumyat, 24, 26, 71
Dunblane, 47, 49, 73, 79, 89, 105, 130, 163, 168, 194, 199
Dunipace, 166-9, 172, 194
Dunlin, 58, 60, 70, 72-3, 113
Dunmore, 60, 94, 104, 129, 166, 197
Dunmore Moss, 45-6, 50
Dunmore, Robert, 127, 164
Dunnocks, 67
Duntanlich, 3
Dutch Elm disease, 45
Dyeing, 151, 156
Dykes, 4, 6

Eagle, Golden, 57, 72, 108-9
Earls Hills, 65
Earl's Seat, 69
Earlsburn, 64
Early-purple Orchid, 52
Earn, River, 12
Earthquakes, 10, 16-17
East Boll mill, 151
Economic development, 166
Eden, River, 12
Edmondstone, of Duntreath, 178
Eel, 104
Effluents, 106
Eider, 58
Elatine spp., 48, 53, 96, 98, 112
Elections, 177, 188-92
Electoral registers, 178
Elk, 83
Elm, 44-5, 67, 87, 110
Elodea canadensis, 98, 102
Emigration, 162, 164
Empetrum nigrum, 48, 52
Enclosures, 126, 130
Endrick, River, 74, 77, 81, 91, 94, 98, 101
Endrick Mouth, 60, 63-5
Endrick Water, 34, 39, 48, 70, 73
Engines, mine, *142*
Environmentally Sensitive Areas, 109, 111, 113
Epidemics, 162-4
Epidote, 3
Epilobium spp., 43, 49-52
Epipactis helleborine, 45, 116
Equisetum palustre, 48
Erebia spp., 88
Erica tetralix, 48
Erinaceus europaeus, 77
Eriophorum spp., 50-1, 88, 109, 113
Errol Beds, 12
Eskers, 12
Euglena, 100
Eurytemora affinis, 104
Faggot voters, 178

Fagus sylvatica, 97
Fairy Flax, 47
Falkirk, 94, 115
  agriculture, 130
  cattle trade, 127
  diseases, 163
  fogs, 26
  frosts, 22
  industries, 129, 148, 169
  plantations, 45
  population, 166, 168, 171-2
  public health, 163
  Quaternary, 12, 14
  rainfall, 26-7
  soils, 35, 39
  sports, 195, 201
Falkirk Herald, 179
Falkirk ironworks, 146-8
Falkirk Mail, 179
Fallin, 60, 94, 144, 182
Famine, 125, 162
Farm sizes, 139
Farm support, 134, 138
Faulting, 16
Felis sylvestris, 81
Felsite, 4
Fens, 48-9, 96
Ferns, 97
Ferrets, 84
Fertilisers, 133
Fescue, Red, 47, 51
Festuca spp., 47, 49
Field drainage, 128, 137, 164
Field Scabious, 86
Fieldfare, 66-7
Filipendula ulmaria, 97
Filmy ferns, 53, 110
Fintry, 79, 81, 166-8, 198
Fintry Hills, 48, 50-1, 82
Fir, Douglas, 45
Fir Clubmoss, *52*
Fireclay, 9, 16
Fish, 102, *103*, 104: fossil, 8
Flanders Moss, 14, 23, 26-7, 34-5, 44, 46, 49-50, 62, 72, 78, 86, 88-9, 93, 107, 109-10
Flatworms, 102
Flies, 100
Flounder, 104
Flushes, 52
Flycatchers, 66-7, 73, 110
Fogs, 26
Fontinalis spp., 49, 97, 99
Food imports, 133
Football, 194-5, 198, 200-1, 208, *210*
Forbes, William, 127, 132, 177-8
Forest Authority, 111
Forest Enterprise, 111
Forest soils, 34-7
Forestmill, 79
Forestry, land capability, 39-40
Forestry Commission, 45
Forget-me-nots, 48-9
Forsyth, Michael, 187
Forth
  bedrock depressions, 10
  carse, 42
  River, 12, 91, 93, 105-6
  agriculture, 39
  birds, 57-75

otters, 81
seals, 83
soils, 34
Forth Area Bird Report, 57
Forth and Clyde railway, 130
Forth Estuary, 91, 93-4, 104, 113-1
  animals, *104*
  birds, 57-60
  effects on temperature, 23
Forth River Purification Board, 105
Forth Valley
  birds, 60-2
  climate, 20
  growing season, 22
  rainfall, 2
  shoreline, 15
Forthbank, 145
Foss, 3
Fossils, 3, 8
Foudland association, 34, 36-7
Foundation conditions, 16
Fox, 79-80
Franchise, 177, 179, 182
Fraxinus excelsior, 44, 97
Free Church, 178
Freshwater habitats, 60, 111-2
Fritillaries, 86, 88
Frog Orchid, 51, 113
Frogbit, 100
Frogs, 100-1, 112
Frosts, 22, 44
Fulmar, 58
Fungi, 109

Gadwall, 65
Gagea lutea, 53
Gales, 24
Galium spp., 46-7, 51
Gannet, 58
Garabal Hill, 4
Garadhban Forest, 79, 81
Garbett, Samuel, 146
Gardrum Moss, 110
Gargunnock, 163, 167-8
Gargunnock Hills, 1, 27, 34-7, 39, 65, 116
  birds, 60, 64, 69
  bog, 50
  climate, 20
  streams, 40-1
  vegetation, 48
Gart, 14
Gartcows, 195
Gartenkeir, 145
Gartmore, 14, 80, 185
Gartmorn, 145
Gartmorn Dam, 60, 64, 105
Gartness, 116
Gas
  in mines, 141
  natural, 16
Geese, 59-60, 62-4, 72, 112
Gentian, Field, 47
Gentianella capestris, 47
Geological map, *2*
Geological sections, *5, 7*
Geology, conservation, 116
Geothermal energy, 16
Geranium sylvaticum, 52, 113
Giffnock association, 34-5, 39

Glacier, 13
Glassmaking, 142, 168
Glasswort, 51
Glaux maritima, 51
Glen Artney, 1, 46
Glen Dochart, 4, 6, 24, 37, 39, 78-9
Glen Falloch, 39, 46, 110-11
Glen Finglas, 92-3
Glen Gyle, 4
Glen Lochay, 3-4
Glen Ogle, 3, 6
Glendevon, 163
Glenochil, 145
Gleys, 33-7
Globeflower, 53, 97, 113
Glyceria maxima, 97, 99
Goats, 82-3, 127
Godwit, Bar-tailed, 58, 113
Gold, 6, 16
Goldcrest, 67
Golden-saxifrage, 45
Goldeneye, 58, 60, 62-5
Goldfinch, 57, 66-7
Golf, 115, 194, *195*, 206, 209
Goodie Burn, 84
Goosander, 58, 60, 63-5
Gorges, 15
Gorse, 47, 86
Grangemouth
  birds, 57-9, 113
  conservation, 116
  effluents, 106
  industries, 93, 114, *156*, 169
  population, 166, 171-2
  port, 94
  Quaternary, 14, 17
  seals, 83
  shrimps, 101
  soils, 34
  sports, 194, 196-7, 199, 201
  temperatures, 23
  thermal effects, 26
  vegetation, 51
  water, 94
Grangemouth Formation, 15
Grangepans, 57
Grasmainstoun, 145
Grasses, 51-2, 99
Grassland, 37, 46-7, 112-116
Gray, James Cook, 197
Grebes, 57, 60, 62-4, 113
Green Beds, 3-4, 6
Green Hairstreak, *87, 88*
Greenfinch, 66
Greenshank, 57-8
Greywackes, 3-4
Ground fogs, 26
Groundwater, 16
Grouse, 70-2, 78
Gualann, 6
Guillemot, 58
Gulls, 60, 66, 72-3
Gurtary, 142
Gymnocephalus cernua, 102
Gypsum, 8

Haar, 26
Habitat loss, 107
Hair-grass, 46-8, 52, 113

Halichoerus grypus, 83
Hamaris tityus, 88
Hamilton, Duke of, 142
Hammarbya paludosa, 53
Handlooms, 150-1
Hardy, John, 146
Hares, 78, 109
Harriers, 60, 66, 72, 108
Harrowing, 126, 128, 130
Harviestoun, 145
Hawfinch, 57, 73
Hawk's-Beard, Marsh, 46, 50
Haws Park, 115
Hawthorn, 97
Hay, 47, 130-1, 134
Hazel, 44-6, 97
Heath, Cross-leaved, 48
Heather, 47-8, 50, 70-1, 78, 109
Hedgehog, 77
Helianthemum spp., 43, 51, 86, 88, 113
Helictotrichon pratense, 52
Helleborine, 45, 116
Hemlock-spruce, Western, 45
Henbane, 47
Heracleum mantegazzianum, 49, 98
Herb Paris, 45, *46*, 110
Herbarium specimens, 43
Herbertshire mine, 145
Herons, 59, *65*, 71
Herring, 104
High Buried Beach, 14
Highland Border Complex, 1, 3
Highland Boundary Fault, 1, 4, 6, 8, 10,
    34, 39, 41, 51, 57, 93, 102, 111, 116
Highland Games, *198*, 199-200
Highland Line, 1
Hill fogs, 26
Hill peat, 36
Hillfoot Hills, *viii*, 24, 131, 149
Hirst coals, 9
Hog-louse, 105
Hogweed, 49, *98*
Holcus lanatus, 50
Home, Henry *see* Kames, Lord
Hordeum vulgare, 44
Horseracing, 197-8
Horses, 135-6, 138
Horsetail, 48
Hospitals, 155
House Martins, 73
Humidity, 25-6
Hummocky moraine, 14
Humus iron soils, 36-7
Huperzia selago, 52
Hydra, 100
Hydrobia ulvae, 104
Hydrocharis morsus-ranae, 100
Hygiene, 163
Hylocomium splendens, 52
Hymenophyllum tunbrigense, 53
Hymenopterum spp., 110
Hyoscyamus niger, 47
Hypnum cupressiforme, 48

Iapetus Ocean, 3
Ice Age, 12, 14, 43
Immature soils, 33
Immigration, 162, 164
Improvements, 128, 130

Inachis io, 87
Inchcailloch Island, 3, 77
Inchcruin Island, 77
Inchfad Island, 77
Inchmurrin Island, 3
Independent Labour Party, 180, 182
Industrial decline, 168, 185
Insects, 100-2, 107
Intrusions, 4, 9
Inversions, thermal, 22
Inversnaid, 4, 67, 80, 82
Iris pseudacorus, 97
Iron Age, cultivation, 44
Iron ore, 141-2, 148, 168
Ironstone, 9

Jackdaws, 66, 69, 71
Jasper, 1
Jays, 69, 73
Jerah, 51
Johnstone, James, 178
Johnston, Tom, 181-2
Juncus spp., 47-8, 50-3, 70-1, 88, 97, 108
Juniperus communis, 46
Jupiter Urban Wildlife Project, 116

Kames, 14
Kames, Lord, 44, 49, 110, 127, 165
Katrine, River, 79
Keir, 46
Keltie Water, 3, 79
Kelvin Valley, 10
Kennetpans, 127
Kestrel, 60, 71, 115
Kettle-holes, 12, 14
Kidston, Robert, 43
Kilbagie, 127-8
Killdeer, 59
Killearn, 79, 129-30, 165-8
Killin, 3, 63, 65, 79, 94, 102
Killorn Moss, 50, 110
Kilmadock, 163, 165, 167-8, 198
Kilncraigs, 149
Kilsyth, 127, 129, 142, 163, 166, 168, 172
Kincardine, 9, 104, 127, 167, 197
Kincardine Bridge, 12, 51, 57-8, 94
Kincardine-in-Menteith, 164, 198
King o' Muirs pit, 144-5
Kingfisher, 57, 73
Kingshouse, 93
Kinlochard, 87
Kinneil, 57-60, 94, 104, 113, 143
Kinneil Kerse, 12, 113, *114*
Kinnesswood Formation, 8
Kinross, 130
Kippen, 62, 81, 163, 165
Kippen association, 34, 36
Kippenrait Glen, 45
Kirkintilloch, 130
Kirkton Glen, 4, 6
Kirkwood Formation, 8
Kittiwake, 58
Knaik, River, 81
Knautia arvensis, 86
Knitwear, 152-3
Knot, 58, 113
Knox Pulpit Formation, 8, 16
Koeleria macrantha, 113

Labour Party, 180-2, 184, 186-7
Labrador-tea, *49*, 50, 109
Lacerta vivipara, 109
Lady's Smock, 86-7
Lake of Menteith, 14, 34, 48, 60, 62, 64,
    93, 95, 98-9, *111-2*
Lambs, 80
Laminated clay, 14
Lamprophyre, 4
Land army, 133, 137
Land capability, 33, 37-40
Land capability distribution, *38*
Land use (planning), 15
Landfill, 16
Landowners, 125, 132, 177-9
Landslips, 16-17, 27
Lanrick Castle, 46
Lapwing, 59-60, 66, 70-1, 73, 107
Larbert, 14, 130, 155, 166-9, 195, 199
Larch, 45, 67
Large Heath Butterfly, 88
Larix spp., 45
Lathyrus pratensis, 47
Lavas, Carboniferous, 8
Law Formation, 15
Lawmuir Formation, 9
Leached soils, 33
Lead, 16, 52
Lecropt, 167
Ledcharrie Burn, 4
Ledum spp., *49*, 50, 109
Lee-waves, 25
Leisure planning, 208
Lemming, 83
Lemna spp., 99, 101
Lend-lease, 137
Lennox Castle Hospital, 168
Leny, River, 46, 93
Leny Limestone, 3
Lepus spp., 78, 109
Letham Moss, 15, 88, 110
Leucojum aestivum, 48
Leven, River, 14, 91
Liberal Party, 178-80, 182-3
Lightfoot, John, 52
Lillies, 97
Lime Craig, quarry, 3
Lime Hill, 51
Limestone Coal Formation, 9, 16
Limestones, 3, 9, 16
Limonium spp., 51
Limosella aquatica, 48
Linnet, 66
Linum catharticum, 47
Linwood Formation, 12
Listera ovata, 113
Little Ringed Plover, 74
Littorella uniflora, 48, 97, 99, 102
Lizards, 109
Loanhead Formation, 12, 16
Lobelia dortmanna, 99
Local Government reorganisation, 204
Local Nature Reserves, 116
Loch Achray, 63-5, 93
Loch Ard, 39, 51, 64, 67, 69, 79, *92*, 93,
    105
Loch Ard Forest, 80, 82, 102
Loch Arklet, 93, 165

Loch Chon, 4, 105
Loch Coulter, 63
Loch Dochart, 63, 78
Loch Doine, 63, 112
Loch Earn, 37, 91
Loch Eck, 102
Loch Ellrig, 64
Loch Essan, 79
Loch Fannyside, 64
Loch Katrine, 4, 48, 50, 65, 79, 91, 93, 105
Loch Laggan, 62
Loch Lomond, 91, 93-4, 101-2
  birds, 60, 73
  climate, 36
  conservation, 116
  ESA, 109
  intrusions, 4
  islands, 3, 77
  land capability, 39
  mammals, 79
  NNR, 81
  Quaternary, 14
  recreation, 112
  soils, 34
  vegetation, 48
  water plants, 98
  woodland, 45, 110
Loch Lomond Dock, *97*
Loch Lomond Stade, 12, 14-15
Loch Long, 4
Loch Lubnaig, 3, 48-9, 63, 93, 105, 112
Loch Macanrie, 62
Loch Mahaick, 62, 65
Loch Oss, 77, 79
Loch Rusky, 62
Loch Tay, 20, 23, 63, 91, 93-4, 104
  agriculture, 37
  soils, 36
  vegetation, 52
Loch Tay Limestone, 4
Loch Turret, 93
Loch Venachar, 63-5, 91, 93
Loch Voil, 48, *63*, 65, 93, 112
Loch Watston, 62, 64-5, 98
Lochan Beinn Chabhair, 79
Lochan Uaine, 79
Lochearnhead, 3, 47, 93
Lochs, 91-2, 112
Logie, 132, 166, 168, 198
Long-eared Bat, 78
Long-tailed Duck, 58, 62
Longannet Mine Complex, 9, 16, 106, 146
Loosestrife, 48-9, 53, 115
Lornshill, 153
Lotus corniculatus, 47, 86
Lower Coal Measures, 9, 16
Lower Limestone Formation, 9
Loxia curvirostra, 67
Lutra lutra, 81, 112
Lycaena phlaeas, 86
Lychnis spp., 48, 51, 100, 108
Lysimachia spp., 46, 48, 115-16
Lythrum salicaria, 49

MacIntyre, Robert, 185
McNab's Academy, 168
Macoma balthica, 104
MacPherson, Malcolm, 185
Madison, 205

Magpie, 57, 66, 69, 73
Mallard, 58, 60, 62-4, 71
Mammoth, 83
Manor Farm, *139*
Manor Mine, 145
Mantola jurtina L., 86
Manx Shearwater, 58
Maps, *121-4*
Marble, 3
Mar, Earl of, 178, 184
Marine sediments, 12
Marital distribution, 171
Maritime airstreams, 28
Marr Bank, 12
Marriage, 170-1
Marsh Orchid, 113
Marsh-bedstraw, 46
Marsh-mallow, Rough, 47
Marsh-marigold, 48, 100
Marsh-orchids, 49
Marshwort, Lesser, 49
Martes martes, 80
Mashlum, 131
Mat-grass, 47
Mayflies, 102, 105
Meadow Brown, 86, *87*
Meadow-rues, 43, 52
Meadows, 113
Meadowsweet, 97
Meall Ghaordie, 108
Meall Mor, 48
Meall na Samhna, 108
Megaptera novaeangliae, 83
Meles meles, 81
Menstrie, 27, 47, 65, 71, 105, 150-1, 153
Menstrie Glen, 45
Menteith Hills, 8, 36, 40, 48, 72
Mentha aquatica, 99
Mergansers, 58, 62-3, 65
Merlin, 60, 71-2, 108-9
Meta pit, 144-5
Metamorphic rocks, 3-4
Mice, 79
Microdiorite, 4
Microtus agrestis, 79
Middle Coal Measures, 9
Midges, 100, 102
Mignonette, 47
Milfoil, 97
Mill effluents, 106
Millhall, 144
Mills, 150, *151*, *153*, 165
Milngavie, 44, 98
Milton of Campsie, 180
Mimulus guttatus, 49, 98
Mine disasters, 142-4
Mine waste, 105-6
Mine Wood, 67
Mineralisation, 3, 6
Mining, 141, *143*, 165, 168-9, 181-2
  lead-zinc, 6
Mining subsidence, 16
Mink, 64-5, 81, 84
Minuartia verna, 51
Mires, 50, 52, 96, 109-10
Moles, 77
Molinia caerulea, 47, 86, 88
Molluscs, 102, 104
Monkey Flower, 49, *98*
Montane vegetation, 52-3

Montrose, Duke of, 127, 132, 178
Moonwort, 52
Moor-grass, Purple, 47-8, 50, 86, 88
Moorhen, 57, 60, 64-5
Moraines, 14, 116
Mortality rates, 162-4, 170
Mosses, 71, 127
Motorcade, 186
Mountain Hare, *78*
Mountain Ringlet, 86, 88
Mouse-ear, Alpine, 52
Muckhart, 89, 166
Mudflats, 57
Mudstones, 9, 16
Mudwort, 48
Mugdock, 44, 93, 113
Muir Dam, 62
Muiravonside, 166-7
Murnin, Hugh, 181
Mus musculus, 79
Muskrat, 84
Mustela spp., 80-1
Myosotis spp., 48-9
Myotis spp., 78, 84
Myrica gale, 50, 88
Myriophyllum alterniflorum, 43, 97, 99, 102
Myrrhis odorata, 47
Myxomatosis, 78

Najas flexilis, 97
Nappes, 4-6
Nardus stricta, 36, 47
Narthecium ossifragum, 50
National Nature Reserves, 50, 81, 107, 110
National Trust for Scotland, 108
Native woodland, 110-11
Natterer's bat, 78
Nature reserves, *110*, *113*, *120*
Neomys fodiens, 77
Neottia nidus-avis, 45, *46*
Nereis diversicolor, 104
Nestboxes, 67, 69, *76*, 80
Nettles, 100
Newspapers, 179
Newts, 100-1, 112
Nickel, 51
Nightjar, 57, 69, 73
Nitella spp., 99
Noctule, 84
Non-native woodland, 108-9
Noncalcareous gleys, 33, 35-6
Northern Brown Argus, 86, 88, 113
Nuphar spp., 97, 112
Nuthatch, 69
Nutrition levels, 163
Nyctalus noctula, 84
Nymphaea alba, 49, 96-7, 99
Nymphalis spp., 87

Oak, 44-6, 67, 88, 97, 110
Oats, 44, 46, 125-6, 128, 130-2, 134-6, 138-9
Ochil Fault, 1, 6, 10, 70
Ochil Hills, *viii*, 1, 6, 108
  agriculture, 37
  birds, 65, 70
  bog, 50
  bracken, 47

buttrflies, 88
grasslands, 113
grazing, 127, 131
land capability, 39
mining, 1
moths, 89
snow, 29
soils, 34-6
streams, 40-1
temperatures, 22
vegetation, 48, 51-2
Ochil Volcanic Formation, 6
Ochlochy Park, *92*
Ochtertyre, 81
Odontoschisma sphagni, 50
Olivine-dolerite, 9
On-shore breezes, 25
Opencast mining, 110, 136
Orache, 51
Orange Tip, *87*
Orange Underwing, 88
Orchis mascula, 52
Organic soils, 33
Orthothecium rufescens, 53
Oryctolagus cuniculus, 78
Osmerus eperianus, 104
Otters, 81, 84, 101, 107, 112
Over-grazing, 109, 111
Owls, 60, 66, 69-70, 73
Oxygen sag, 104
Oxyria digyna, 53
Oystercatcher, 58, 66

Painted Lady, 86-7
Paisley Formation, 12
Parasites, 101
Paris quadrifolia, 45, *46*, 110
Parishes, 161
Parkhead, *19*, 20, 22, 24-5, 27-8
Parks, 115, 201-2
Partridge, 57, 66, 71
Passage Formation, 9, 16
Paton family, 179-80, 183, 196
Paton, John, 149
Patons (Company), 151-2
Peacock Butterfly, 87
Pearl-bordered Fritillary, 86, *88*
Peas, 128
Peat, 15, 33, 35-7, 41
    extraction, 72, 107, 110, 127
    lowland, 109
Peat hags, 50
Peaty gleys, 35-7
Pendreich, 48
Perca fluviatilis, 102
Perch, 102
Peregrine, 60, 70-3, 108
Perla bipunctata, 102
Petasites hybridus, 47
Petrochemicals, 156-7, 169
Phalaris arundinacea, 49, 97
Phalaropes, 59
Pharmaceuticals, 156
Pheasant, 66-7
Phegopteris connectilis, 45
Philonotis fontana, 52
Phleum pratense, 47
Phoca spp., 83
Phocoena phocoena, 83

Phosphates, 112
Phragmites australis, 49
Physical education, 201
Phytoplankton, 101
Picea spp., 45
Pieris spp., 86
Pigeons, 66-7, 115
Pigs, 127, 134-6
Pillwort, 48
Pilularia globulifera, 48
Pimpernel, 46, 116
Pimpinella saxifraga, 47, 113
Pine Marten, 67, *76*, 80, 84
Pines, 44-6, 110
Pintail, 58, 60, 62, 65, 73
Pinus spp., 44-5
Pipistrelle, *77*
Pipistrellus pipistrellus, 77
Pipits, 59-60, 67, 70-2
Pirnhall, 144-5
Pisidium, 102
Planning, 16-17, 109, 112, 114, 117
Plantago spp., 47, 51, 86
Plantains, 47, 51, 86
Plants, aquatic, 95, *103*
Platanthera spp., 49, 113
Platichthys flesus, 104
Plean, 144-5, 182, 199
Plecotus auritus, 78
Pleurozium schreberi, 52
Ploughing, *125*, *128*, 130, *133*, *135*, 137
Plovers, 58-60, 66, 70-3
Pochard, 58, 60, 62-5, 73
Podzols, 33, 35-7, 39
Polecat, 84
Policy Woods, 46
Pollen, 43-4, 47
Pollution, 105, 112, 114-5
Polmaise, 144-5
Polmont, 12, 142, 166, 168, 205
Polygonum spp., 48, 52
Polyommatus icarus, 86
Polytrichum commune, 48, 50
Ponds, 101
Pondweeds, 48-9, 97, 99, 115
Ponsonby, Arthur, 182
Population, 174-6
    distribution, 167
    growth, 161-2, 164-5, 168-9
    structure, 169-72
Population centres, *160*
Populus tremula, 44
Porpoise, 83
Port of Menteith, 167-8, 197
Potamogeton spp., 48-9, 97, 99, 115
Potatoes, 47, 128, 132-4, 136-7, 139
Potentilla spp., 47, 51
Poultry, 135-6
Powan, 102
Power stations, 106
Precipitation, 26-9
Professionals, 153-7
Prunella vulgaris, 50
Prunus padus, 45, 116
Pseudotsuga menziesii, 45
Ptarmigan, 57, 72
Pteridium aquilinum, 47
Public health, 163-4
Puccinella maritima, 51
Purple Hairstreak, 88

Purple Moor Grass, 47, 86, 88
Purple Saxifrage, *108*
Purslane, 49
Pyrite, 3
Pyrola spp., 53, 116

Quaking-grass, 113
Quarries, 3-4, 8, 96, 116
Quarry Coal, 9
Quarter, mine disaster, 142
Quartz-dolerite, 6, 10, 16
Quaternary, 10-15
Quaternary deposits, *11*
Queen Elizabeth Forest Park, 45, 69, 110
Queensferry, 57, 94
Queenslie Marine Band, 9
Quercus spp., 44-5, 88, 97
Quercusia quercus, 88
Quoiting, *193*, 194-5

Rabbit, 78
Rag Worm, 104
Ragged Robin, 48, 100
Railways, 130
Rainfall, 19-20, 26-7, 127
Raised beaches, 12, 34
Raised bogs mire, 49, 109-10
Ramsar Convention, 113, 119
Ramsay, James, 179
Ramsons, 44
Rana temporaria, 100
Ranunculus spp., 46-8, 50, 53, 98, 112
Rape, 139
Raptors, 57
Rationing, 137-8
Rats, 79, 84, 115
Rattle, Yellow, 48
Rattus spp., 79
Ravens, 70-2, 108
Razorbill, 58
Reaping, 126, 128, *129*, 130
Reclaimed land, 16-17
Recreation, 109, 112, 115, 204
Red Admiral, 87
Red Deer, *82*
Redding, 144-5, 181
Redshank, 58, 60, 66, 71, 73, 113
Redstart, 67, 110
Redwings, 66-7
Reed Sweet Grass, 99
Reeds, 49, 97
Regeneration, 111
Reid, George, 184-6
Reindeer, 83
Reptiles, 107, 109
Reseda spp., 47
Rhinanthus minor, 48
Rhinoceros, 10
Rhododendron, 111
Rhynchospora alba, 50, 109
Rhynchostegium riparoides, 49
Ring Ouzel, 72, 73
Ringlet, 88
River catchments, 1
Robertson, R. Chisholm, 180
Robins, 66-7, 73, 115
Rock stability, 16
Rock-cress, Hairy, 52-3

Rockfalls, 16
Rockrose, 43, 51, 86, 88, 113
Rodents, 79
Roe Deer, *82*
Roebuck, John, 146
Rooks, 66, 69, 71
Rorippa spp., 49, 53
Roseberry, Earl of, 178
Roseroot, 53
Rosyth, 12
Rough grazing, 37, 40
Rowan, 44, 46, 67
Rowanhill association, 34-5, 37, 39
Rowardennan, 4
Royal Society for the Protection of Birds,
    108, 113
Rubus spp., 50, 52
Ruddy Duck, 57, 65, 73-4
Ruff, 58
Ruffe, 102
Rugby, 194
Rumbling Bridge, 15
Rumex spp., 43, 48, 86, 97
Runrig, 125-6
Rushes, 47, 50-3, 88, 97, 108
Rustling, 126

SSSIs see Sites......
STARPS, 204
St Ninians, 142, 164, 166, 169
Salicornia sp., 51
Salix spp., 44, 52-3, 97
Salmo spp., 102, 104
Salmon, 104-5
Salt-works, 44
Saltmarsh, 50-1, 57, 114
Saltmarsh-grass, 51
Salvelinus alpinus, 112
Sand and gravel
    extraction, 15
    glaciofluvial, 12, 14
Sand Martins, *72-3*
Sanderling, 58
Sandpipers, 58-9, 70-1
Sandstone, 9, 16
Sandwort, Vernal, 51
Sauchie, 152-3, 166, 169
Sauchie Burn, 105
Sauchie Craig, 87
Sauchs, 45
Saussurea alpina, 53
Saw-wort, Alpine, 53
Saxifraga spp., 45, 52, 108
Scaup, 58, 62
Schist, 3
Schoenoplectus lacustris, 49
Schoenus nigricans, 51, 113
School grounds, 116
Schools, 154-5
    sports in, 196-7, 201, 210
Scientists, 155-6
Sciurus spp., 78-9
Scotch Argus, 86, 88
Scotch Brown Argus, 86, 88
Scoters, 58, 65, 73
Scottish Bird Reports, 74
Scottish Central railway, 130
Scottish Coal Measures, 9
Scottish National Party, 184-6

Scottish Natural Heritage, 53, 82, 107, 110-
    11, 116
Scottish Wildlife Trust, 50, 108, 116
Scurvygrass, 51
Scutellaria galericulata, 49
Sea fog, 26
Sea level changes, 9, 12, 14-16, 34
Sea-lavender, 51
Sea-milkwort, 51
Sea-purslane, 51
Sea-spurrey, 51
Seals, 83
Seatearth, 9
Sedges, 46-50, 52-3, 113
Sedimentary cycles, 8-9
Selaginella selaginoides, 51
Selfheal, 50
Serpentine, vegetation on, 51
Serpentinite, 1, 3-4, 43
Sewage, 105-6, 113
Shag, 58
Sheep, 126-7, 131, 134-6, 138
Sheep farming, 44
Sheep's-fescue, 47-8, 52
Shelduck, *58*, 63-4, 113
Sheriffmuir Formation, 8
Shieldhill, 181
Shirgarton Moss, 50, 110
Shorelines, 12, 14
Shoreweed, 48-9, 97, 99
Shoveler, 58, 60, 62-3, 65
Shrews, 77
Shrimps, 101, 104
Sibbaldia procumbens, 52
Sika Deer, 82, 84
Silene acaulis, 52
Silica sand, 16
Sills, in Dalradian, 4
Siltation, 96, 112
Siltstone, Carboniferous, 9
Silver, 16
Silver-Fir, European, 45
Siskins, 67, 73
Sites of Special Scientific Interest (SSSIs),
    35, 98, 104, 107, 109, 111-114, 117, *120*
Sitka spruce, 40, 67
Six Spot Burnet, 89
Skinflats, 25, 58-60, 96, 104, 113-4, 194
Skuas, 58
Skullcap, 49
Skylarks, 66, 70-1
Slamannan, 39, 64, 108, 127, 163, 166
Slate, 4
Small Copper Butterfly, 86
Small Heath Butterfly, 86
Smallholdings, 127-8, 134
Small, James, 128
Smallpox, 163
Smelt, 104
Smew, 60, 62
Smith, James, 128-9
Smith, J.B., 178
Snab pit, 143
Snails, 104
Sneezewort, 48, 50
Snipe, 59, 66, 70-1
Snow, 28
Snow Buntings, 70-1
Snowflake, 48
Societies, 19, 108, 113, 130

Soft-rush, 48
Soil associations, *32*
Soil groups, 33
Soil permeability, 34
Soil stability, 34
Soil Survey of Scotland, 33-4
Soil temperature, 23
Solanum tuberosum, 47
Solar radiation, 20-1
Sorbus aucuparia, 44
Sorex spp., 77
Sorn association, 35
Sorrels, 43, 53, 86
Sourhope association, 34-6
Southern Highland Group, 3-4, 6
Sparganium spp., 48, 97
Sparrowhawks, 60, 69
Sparrows, 57, 66, 73, 115
Spartina sp., 51
Spearwort, 48, 53, 98, 112
Special Protection Area, 113
Speirs, Peter, 127
Spergularia sp., 51
Sphagnum spp., 50, 52, 99, 101
Sphalerite, 3
Spinning, 150-1, 164, 167-8
Spleenwort
    Black, *51*
    Green, 52
Spoil heaps, 51-2, 116
Sports
    expenditure, 208-9
    as social service, 204
Sports centres, 205, 208
Sports clubs, 193-4, 209
Sports facilities, 205, 208
Sports grounds, 195-6
Spotted-orchid, *48*, 113
Sprat, 104
Springkerse, 208
Springs, 52
Spruce, 40, 45, 67
Squirrels, 79
Stair, Earl of, 128
Stanley House, 196
Star-of-Bethlehem, 53
Starlings, 66, 69, 71-3
Starworts, 97
Steel, 147-8
Steelbow, 125
Stellaria palustris, 53
Stenhousemuir, 64, 115, 127, 195
Stints, 58-9
Stirling, 115
    animals, 104
    birds, 57-60
    climate records, 20-29
    diseases, 163
    fogs, 26
    politics, 177-
    population, 166, 171-2
    River Forth, 106
    salt-works, 44
    saltmarsh, 51
    snow, 28
    soils, 35
    sports, 194-5, 197-8, 201
    temperatures, 21, 23
    tidal limit, 94
    tourism, 167

volcanic rocks, 6
  wind directions, 24
Stirling Association, 34, 39
Stirling Burgh Council, 183
Stirling Burghs, 177-8, 182
Stirling County Council, 183
Stirling and Dunfermline railway, 130
Stirling Infirmary, *154*
Sitrling Natural History Society, 19
Stirling Sill, 16
Stirling University, 205
Stirling, Colonel, 19, 43
Stitchwort, Marsh, 53
Stoat, *80*
Stob a'Choin, 4
Stob Binnein, 52, 72, 108
Stob Garbh, 53
Stock Dove, 66
Stockie Muir, 116
Stocking rates, 109, 127
Stonechat, 71, 73
Stoneflies, 102, 105
Stonehaven Association, 34, 36
Stoneworts, 99
Strathallan, 62, 71, 199-200
Strathblane, 14, 78, 116, 165-8, 198
Strathclyde Group, 8-9
Strathdevon, 70
Strathmore Syncline, 10
Strathyre, 24, 29, 45, 93
Strichen Association, 34, 36-7
Stronachlachar, 4
Sub-Carse Peat, 14-17
Subalpine soils, 37
Subularia aquatica, 48, 112
Sundew, *49*, 50, 109
Sunshine, 20-1
Swallows, 73
Swans, 59-60, *62*, 62-4, 63-4
Swedes, 133-6, 138
Sweet Cicely, 47
Sweet-grass, 97, 100
Swifts, 73
Swimming Baths, *196*, 197, 201-2, 205, 208
Sycamore, 67, 97, 111

Tacksmen, 125
Tall Fescue, 49
Talpa europaea, 77
Tanning industry, 45
Tare, Hairy, 47
Tay, River, 81, 94, 102
Tay catchment, 91, 93
Tay Nappe, 4, 6
Tay valley, 12
Tay-Earn, catchment, 1
Teaching, *154*
Teal, 58, 60, 62-5, 71, 113
Teith, River, 34, 49, 63, 81, 91, 93-4, 97-8, 105-6, 112
Teith Valley, 12, 72
Temperatures
  air, 21-3
  soil, 23
Tennis, *206*
Terns, 58, 60, 73
Terraces, 12
Thalictrum spp., 43, 52

Thistle, Marsh, 46
Thornhill, 62, 194
Thread Rush, 48
Threshing, 128-9, *136*
Thrift, 51
Throsk, 129
Thrushes, 66-7
Thunderstorms, 27
Thyme, 47
Thymus polytrichus, 47
Tile manufacture, 16, 129
Till, 12, 14, 34, 36
Tillicoultry, 71, 105, 130-1, 142, 144-5, 149-52
  diseases, 163
  ILP, 181
  industries, 169
  mining, 168-9
  population, 166, 168, 172
  sports, 198
Timothy, 47, 131
Tits, 67, 73, 115
Toads, 100, 112
Topography, influence on climate, 19-20
Topsoils, 34
Tormentil, 47-8, 50
Torrance, 181
Torrie Farm, 14
Torry Bay, 94
Tortoiseshell Butterflies, 86-7
Touch Hills, 34-5, 37, 39, 46, 60, 116
Touch Muir reservoir, 63
Tourism, 167, 169
Tractors, 134, *137*, 138
Tree planting, 39, 45
Trees, spread of, 44
Trichophorum cespitosum, 50
Trifolium repens, 47
Triglochin maritima, 51
Triticum spp., 44
Triturus spp., 100
Trollius europaeus, 53, 97, 113
Trossachs, 73, 86, 88, 109
Trossachs Hills, 40
Trossachs Lochs, 63, 65, 99
Trout, 40, 102, 105
Tsuga heterophyllya, 45
Tsunami deposit, 17
Tufted Duck, 58, 60, 62-5, 73
Tullibody, 169
Turbidites, 3
Turnips, 47, 130-1, 133-6, 138-9
Turnstone, 58
Twayblade, 113
Twite, 59, 66, 70-3
Tyndrum, 3, 6, 16, 52, 88, 94, 116
Typha latifolia, 43
Typhus, 162
Tyria jacobaeae, 89

Uamh Bheag, 8
Ulex europaeus, 47
Ulmus spp., 44, 87
Undermining, 16
Unitarians, 178
University of Stirling, *157*, 210
Upper Glendevon Reservoir, 65, 71
Upper Limestone Formation, 9, 16
Urban conservation, 115-16

Urbanisation, 171-2
Urtica dioica, 100

Vaccination, 163
Vaccinium spp., 47, 50, 52, 88, 109
Valley fogs, 26
Vanessa atalanta, 87
Vegetation types, 43
Velvet Bent, 47
Vernal Grass, 47
Veronica beccabunga, 49
Vetches, 45, 47, 51-2, 86
Vetchling, Meadow, 47
Vicia spp., 45, 47, 86
Viola palustris, 88
Violet, 88
Vipera vipera, 109
Voles, 79
Vulpes vulpes, 79-80

Waders, 57, *59*
Wages
  agricultural, 132, 134, 136, 138
  miners, 144
Wagtails, 59, 71, 73
Wallace Monument, 26
Warblers, 60, 66-7, 73, 110
Water chemistry, 40
Water features, *90*
Water Fern, 48
Water Mint, 99
Water Plantain, 48, 53, 97
Water pollution, 105
Water Shrews, 77, 84
Water uses, 93
Water Voles, 79, 81, 84
Water Wheel, *126*, *142*
Water-cress, 49
Water-crowfoot, 48
Water-milfoil, 43, 49, 99
Water-starwort, 49, 53
Waterlilies, 49, 97, 99, 112
Waterworts, 48, 53, *98*, 112
Watsonian vice-counties, 43
Waxwings, 115
Weasel, 80
Weather fronts, 19
Weather stations, *18*, 20
Weaving, 149, *150*, 151
Weeds, 47
Westfield Paper Mill, 105
Whales, 83
Wheat, 44, 46, 128-36, 138-9
Wheatears, 70-1
Whigs, 177-8
Whimbrel, 58
Whinchat, 71
Whiskered Bats, 84
White Butterflies, 86
White, Francis Buchanan, 43
Whitethroats, 66-7
Whitlow Grass, 52-3, 108
Whooper Swans, *62*
Wigeon, 58, 60, 62-5
Wild Cattle, 83
Wildcat, 81-2, 84
Wildfowl, 57, 61, 114
Wildfowl and Wetlands Trust, 60

Wildlife Sites, 120
Willow Moss, 97, 99
Willowherbs, 43, 49-52, 115
Willows, 44, 52-3, 67, 97
Windermere Interstade, 12
The Windings, 94
Winds, 24
Winnowing, 129
Wintergreen, 53, 116
Wolf's Hole, 8, 116
Wolves, 44, 83
Women, in mining, 142
Wood Mouse, 79, *80*
Woodburn, Arthur, 185
Woodcock, 69
Woodland, 45-6, 110
Woodland birds, counts, 68
Woodland Trust, 108
Woodmanship, 44
Woodpeckers, 57, 69, 73
Woodsia alpina, 108
Wool industry, 149-53, 164
World Wars
    effects on agriculture, 132-4, 136-7
    effects on industry, 144-5, 148
    effetcs on population, 170
Worms, 102
Wren, 66-7, 71
Wrought iron, 146

Yellow-cress, Creeping, 53
Yellow-sedge, 51
Yellowhammers, 66
Yorkshire-fog, 50

Zetland Public Park, 201, *202*
Zetland, Earl of, 132, 196
Zinc, 16
Zoarces viviparus, 103
Zooplankton, 100, 103
Zygaena filipendulae, 89